CORE TAX ANNUALS
Capital Gains Tax 2006/07

CORE TAX ANNUALS
Capital Gains Tax 2006/07

Andrew Goodall CTA

Toby Harris LLB CTA TEP

and

Iris Wünschmann-Lyall MA (Cantab) TEP

General Editor: Mark McLaughlin CTA (Fellow) ATT TEP

Tottel
publishing

Tottel Publishing Ltd, Maxwelton House, 41–43 Boltro Road, Haywards Heath, West Sussex, RH16 1BJ

© Tottel Publishing Ltd 2006

A CIP Catalogue record for this book is available from the British Library.

ISBN 13   978 1 84592 319 8

ISBN 10   1 84592 319 7

Typeset by Kerrypress Ltd, Luton, Beds

Printed and bound in Great Britain by CPI Antony Rowe, Chippenham, Wiltshire

Preface

Tottel's *Capital Gains Tax Annual 2006/07* is one of six 'core tax annuals', and it has been a privilege for me to be involved in what is a bold and exciting initiative. The book will be useful as a quick reference for tax professionals and will help tax advisers and others to maintain a broad knowledge of the law and practice relating to the taxation of capital gains.

The book focuses on current legislation and the various charging provisions and tax reliefs that are most likely to be met by most readers. I hope you will find that this approach has helped to make the book reasonably digestible given that this can be a dry subject.

I wish to thank the editorial team including Sarah Blair, Heather Saward and Mark McLaughlin (the series General Editor) for their patience and encouragement; Iris Wünschmann-Lyall and Toby Harris for contributing chapters 7, 8 and 12; Juliana Watterston, author of Tottel's *Corporation Tax Annual 2006/07*, for her valuable assistance with chapter 9; and my wife Julia and daughters Jen and Maddie for their constant support throughout the project.

Andrew Goodall CTA

Freelance tax writer and journalist

www.andrewgoodall.co.uk

September 2006

Contents

Preface   v

Table of statutes   xi

Table of statutory instruments   xxi

Table of cases   xxii

List of abbreviations   xxv

Part A: General Principles

Chapter 1: Introduction to capital gains tax   **3**
    Introduction and basis of charge   3
    Background and legislation   3
    Chargeable persons   4
    Exemptions   5
    The capital gains tax calculation   10
    Self-assessment   15

Chapter 2: Disposals   **22**
    Introduction   22
    Assets lost, destroyed or becoming of negligible value   29
    Capital sums derived from assets   31
    Special situations   34

Chapter 3: Computation of gains and losses   **38**
    Introduction   38
    Consideration for the disposal   39
    Allowable expenditure   55
    Losses   61
    Taper relief   65
    Indexation allowance   65
    Spouses and civil partners   70
    Assets held on 31 March 1982   70
    Assets held on 6 April 1965   75
    Double tax relief   76

Chapter 4: Particular assets   **80**
    Shares and securities   80
    Land   85

Contents

Chattels	90
Wasting assets	91
Debts	95
Assets appropriated to or from trading stock	96
Chapter 5: Residence, ordinary residence and domicile	**98**
Basis of the charge to CGT	98
Arriving in or leaving the UK	100
Non-residents doing business in the UK	104
Temporary non-residence	106
Foreign assets of non-UK domiciled taxpayers	110
Apportionment of non-resident company's gains	111
Double tax relief	115
Location of assets	115
Liability to CGT on gains from UK or overseas assets	117
Chapter 6: Partnerships	**118**
Introduction	118
Partnership assets and 'other' assets	119
Fractional share in a partnership asset	119
Disposal of partnership assets	121
Change in fractional share of assets	122
Market value rule	127
Limited liability partnerships	128
Residence, etc	129
Appendix: HMRC Statement of Practice D12	129
Chapter 7: Administration of an estate	**137**
Introduction	137
Capital gains tax in the period to the date of death	137
Capital gains tax in the administration of an estate	138
Legatee or beneficiary	146
Deeds of appointment, variations or disclaimers	147
Sales by legatees	151
Chapter 8: Capital Gains Tax – Settlements	**152**
Introduction	152
Definition of 'settlement' and 'settled property'	153
The creation of a settlement	156
Actual and deemed disposals by trustees	157
Disposal of beneficial interests	162

Sub-fund elections   163
Rates of tax   164
Exemptions and reliefs   166
Settlor-interested settlements   174
Offshore settlements   176
Trusts and vulnerable beneficiaries   178

Chapter 9: Companies   **181**
Introduction and basis of charge   181
Computation   183
Roll-over relief for replacement of business assets   185
Groups of companies   185
Capital losses   191
Relief on disposal of shares   191

Chapter 10: Capital gains tax planning   **199**
Planning and avoidance: recent developments   199
Disclosure of tax avoidance schemes   200
'Ramsay' and anti-avoidance legislation   201
Tax planning   202

Part B: Reliefs

Chapter 11: Taper relief   **213**
Introduction   213
Trustees, personal representatives and legatees   213
Operation of the relief   213
Business assets   216
The rate of taper relief   226
Anti-avoidance rules   230
Special rules   235
Interaction with other CGT reliefs, etc   238

Chapter 12: Main Residence Relief   **240**
What constitutes residence?   240
Periods of residence   247
Lettings relief   252
Two or more residences   252
Residences held by trustees or personal representatives   257
Anti-avoidance   264
Dependent relative relief   267

Contents

Chapter 13: Hold-over relief for gifts   **268**
    Introduction   268
    Gifts of business assets   268
    Gifts on which inheritance tax is chargeable, etc   285
    Valuations   288

Chapter 14: Roll-over relief for business assets   **291**
    Introduction   291
    Conditions   292
    Qualifying activities   294
    Assets   299
    New assets to be used 'on acquisition'   301
    Assets used only partly for business purposes   302
    Operation of the relief   303
    Deemed consideration and deemed disposals   305
    Depreciating assets   306
    Reinvestment: time limits   308
    Claims   310
    Interaction with other reliefs   312

Chapter 15: Incorporation of a business   **314**
    Incorporation relief: conditions   314

Chapter 16: Enterprise Investment Scheme   **327**
    Introduction   327
    CGT disposal relief   327
    CGT deferral relief   332

Chapter 17: Other reliefs   **352**
    Introduction   352
    Venture capital trusts   353
    Loans to traders   357
    Losses on shares in unlisted trading companies   361
    Compulsory purchase roll-over relief   364
    Retirement relief   366
    Reinvestment relief   367

Index   *369*

Table of statutes

[All references are to paragraph number]

Administration Act 1925 .... 8.43
Agriculture Act 1967
  s 27.................................. 1.8
Capital Allowances Act 2001 ...... 3.55
  Pt 2 (ss 11–270)................. 3.55
  s 205–212........................ 3.55
Child Trust Funds Act 2004
  s 13................................. 1.9
Criminal Injuries to Property
  (Compensation) Act
  (Northern Ireland) 1971 ...... 2.13
Diplomatic Privileges Act 1964 ..... 5.6
Finance Act 1965 .... 1.2
Finance Act 1982 .... 1.12
Finance Act 1988 .... 3.68
Finance Act 1991
  s 72(1)............................ 3.52
Finance Act 1993
  Sch 20
  para 9 .... 1.9
Finance Act 1995
  s 90(4)............................ 3.53
Finance Act 1996 .... 11.39
  s 103(1)........................... 3.23
  Sch 15
  para 27 .... 11.39
Finance Act 1998 .... 17.22, 17.23
  Sch 18
  para 55 .... 14.39
Finance Act 1999 .... 12.15
Finance Act 2000 ...... 7.9, 11.9, 11.20,
                        11.24
  Sch 15
  para 5–14 .... 9.26
       15–33 .... 9.27
       36 .... 9.28
       47–58 .... 9.31
       67–72 .... 9.33
       73–79 .... 9.32
       89 .... 9.29

Finance Act 2002 .. 11.10, 11.11, 11.13,
                11.14, 11.16, 14.20
  s 52................................ 7.17
  58................................ 1.10
  Sch 18............................ 1.10
Finance Act 2003 .... 11.22, 11.23
  s 67.............................. 11.18
Finance Act 2004 ...... 1.23, 8.26, 10.2,
                12.32, 17.8, 17.10
  s 107............................. 3.84
  150(5)........................... 8.22
  Sch 22
  para 8 .... 12.34
Finance Act 2005 .... 8.1
  s 23–29............................ 8.42
  30......................... 8.42, 8.45
  31................................ 8.42
  32, 33..................... 8.42, 8.45
  34......................... 8.42, 8.43
  35......................... 8.42, 8.44
  36, 37............................ 8.42
  38......................... 8.42, 8.43
  39......................... 8.42, 8.44
  40–45............................ 8.42
  87................................ 3.80
  Sch 5............................. 3.80
Finance Act 2006 .... 1.21, 7.4, 8.1, 8.2,
                8.7, 8.12, 8.13,
                8.17, 8.21, 8.23,
                8.24, 8.40, 10.16,
                12.35, 13.31
  s 63.............................. 9.24
  69.......................... 9.1, 9.17
  70(4), (6)....................... 9.16
  72.............................. 9.17
  74(3), (4)...................... 5.17
  77(2A)........................... 8.26
  135............................... 9.6
  Sch 12
  para 4 .... 13.31
      7 .... 13.24

Finance Act 2006 – *contd*
Sch 12 – *contd*
  para 8 .... 5.32
    17 .... 4.5
  Sch 14
  para 5 .... 16.3, 16.10
  Sch 15............................. 9.24
  Sch 20............... 12.24, 12.35
  para 32 .... 13.38
Finance (No 2) Act 2005 .... 3.23, 5.16,
                           5.34
  s 64(3)........................... 14.34
Government Annuities
Act 1929 .... 1.8
Income and Corporation Taxes
Act 1988
  s 1A(1B).......................... 1.22
  6.................... 1.1, 1.24, 9.1
  34............................... 4.16
  109A............................ 3.53
  Pt VII Ch III (ss 289–312)..... 16.2
  s 289(1A)...................... 16.14
    (3)........................ 16.14
    (7)........................ 16.15
  289A(6)........................ 16.17
  290............................. 16.10
    (2)......................... 16.3
  291............................ 16.33
  293............................ 16.14
  299............................. 16.6
  300(1A)(a)..................... 16.9
  303(1A)(a)..................... 16.9
  304A............................ 16.8
  305(2).......................... 16.8
  306............................ 16.17
    (2)......................... 16.8
  312(1)................... 16.3, 16.15
    (1A)....................... 16.3
      (a)..... 16.3, 16.32, 16.33
  380...................... 3.52, 17.18
  381............................. 17.18
  393A............................. 9.2
  414............... 5.24, 11.30, 11.34
  415..................... 11.30, 11.34
  416..................... 11.24, 11.32
  417........ 5.24, 5.30, 11.17, 11.32
    (3), (4)................... 16.33
  486(8).......................... 3.70
  503............................. 11.12
  504.............. 4.19, 11.12, 11.22

Income and Corporation Taxes Act
1988 – *contd*
  s 505............................. 1.10
  573............................. 3.57
    (1)–(6)................... 17.20
  574........... 3.57, 16.4, 17.18
    (1)................. 17.16, 17.17
    (2)........................ 17.18
    (3)........................ 17.17
  575............................. 3.57
    (1)........................ 17.17
  576............................. 3.57
    (1A)-(1C)................. 17.17
    (2)........................ 17.17
    (4), (4A), (4B)... 17.17, 17.19
    (5)........................ 17.19
  Pt XIV Ch I (ss 590–612)..... 8.22
  s 615(3).......................... 8.22
  620, 621, 624.................. 8.22
  660G(1), (4).................... 8.31
  686....................... 1.23, 8.18
  703................... 10.4, 15.15
  704–706....................... 10.4
  707................... 10.4, 15.15
  708, 709....................... 10.4
  775, 776................... 3.4, 10.4
  777–780....................... 10.4
  Pt XVIII Ch I (ss 788–791)... 3.82
  s 788............................. 3.81
  790............................. 3.82
    (4)........................ 3.82
    (12)....................... 3.83
  Pt XVIII Ch II
  (ss 792–806) 3.82
  s 797............................. 3.82
  805............................. 3.85
  831(1)..................... 5.2, 9.1
  832...................... 14.2, 17.3
    (1)................... 11.10, 16.5
    (1A), (1B).................. 16.5
  839............................. 9.26
  838............................. 11.10
  841.............................. 3.9
Income Tax (Earnings and
Pensions) Act 2003 .... 12.15
  s 42, 43.......................... 5.7
  303(1).......................... 5.5
Income Tax (Trading and Other
Income) Act 2005 .... 8.32
  s 265............................. 8.36

Income Tax (Trading and Other Income) Act 2005 – *contd*

s 276.............................. 4.16
Pt 3 Ch 6 (ss 322–328)......... 4.19
s 323–326....................... 11.22
620........................ 8.22, 8.32
702............................... 1.8
709, 710........................ 17.3
832.............................. 5.21
833, 834........................ 5.21

Inheritance (Provision for Family and Dependents) Act 1975 .... 12.27

Inheritance Tax Act 1984

Pt V Ch II (ss 115–124B).... 13.25
s 2............................... 13.38
3A, 19, 24, 27, 30, 57A.... 13.38
71(1)........................... 13.40
(4)........................... 13.38
71B(2)......................... 13.38
71E(2)......................... 13.38
72(1)........................... 13.40
78(1)........................... 13.38
160............................. 12.28
161, 178, 190.................... 7.6
Sch 4
para 9, 16, 17 .... 13.38

Interpretation Act 1978

Sch 1.............................. 1.1

Limited Liability Partnerships Act 2000 .... 6.21

Mental Health Act 1983 .... 8.43

Partnership Act 1890 .... 6.1

Taxation of Chargeable Gains Act 1992 .... 1.8, 16.6

s 1............. 1.1, 1.3, 2.1, 3.1, 5.1
1(2).......................... 1.23, 9.1
2.............. 1.3, 5.13, 5.16, 5.19
(1)............................. 5.1
(2)...................... 1.13, 1.19
(3)............................ 1.13
(4)–(8)....................... 1.14
2A......... 1.15, 6.21, 11.3, 11.42
(1)........................... 14.26
(5)............................ 11.3
(6)........................... 11.41
(8)............................ 11.4
3............................... 1.16
(3), (4)...................... 1.17
(5)............................ 1.18

Taxation of Chargeable Gains Act 1992 – *contd*

s 3(5A)-(5C).................... 1.19
(7).......................... 1.20, 7.5
(8)............................ 1.21
3A(1)–(3)....................... 1.30
(4)............................ 1.31
(5)............................ 1.32
4(1)............................ 1.22
(1AA)......................... 1.23
6................................ 1.22
8(1)............................. 9.1
(1A)........................... 1.28
(2)...................... 9.1, 9.17
(2A)......................... 9.17
(3)–(6)........................ 9.1
9(1)............................ 5.2
(2)............................. 5.7
(3), (4)....................... 5.4
10............. 1.4, 3.50, 5.13, 5.18
(1)....... 2.21, 5.13, 5.14, 14.6
(2)........................... 5.13
(4)–(6)....................... 5.13
10A... 1.4, 1.14, 5.16, 5.18, 5.19, 10.4, 11.39
(1)........................... 5.17
(2)........................... 5.18
(3), (4).............. 5.19, 14.5
(5), (6)...................... 5.18
(7)........................... 5.18
(8)................... 5.17, 5.19
(9), (9A)................... 5.17
(9C)......................... 5.19
10B... 2.21, 3.50, 5.15, 5.25, 14.6
11(1)............................ 5.5
(2)–(4)........................ 5.6
12......................... 1.8, 11.40
(1)...................... 5.20, 5.22
(2)........................... 5.21
13... 5.18, 5.23, 5.30, 10.4, 11.35
(1)–(4)....................... 5.24
(5)........................... 5.25
(5A), (5B)................... 5.26
(7)........................... 5.27
(7A).......................... 5.28
(8)................... 5.18, 5.29
(9)........................... 5.31
(10).......................... 5.32
(10A)............... 5.23, 11.35
(10B)......................... 5.25

Taxation of Chargeable Gains Act
1992 – *contd*

s 13(11)........................... 5.24
   (11A)................ 5.24, 11.35
   (12)........................... 5.24
   (13)–(15).................... 5.30
14................................... 5.24
Pt II (ss 15–57)............. 3.1, 3.60
s 15......... 1.6, 2.1, 3.1, 3.4, 11.42
16................................ 1.6, 3.4
   (1)........................... 3.48
   (2).............. 2.10, 3.48, 16.4
   (2A)........................... 3.49
   (3)..................... 3.50, 5.18
   (4)..................... 3.50, 5.22
17.............................. 4.14, 6.21
   (1), (2)................. 3.5, 3.44
18................. 3.45, 6.21, 10.4
   (1), (2)....................... 3.10
   (3)..................... 3.21, 8.6
   (4), (5)....................... 3.21
   (6)–(8)....................... 3.10
19........... 3.11, 3.12, 3.15, 10.4
   (1), (2)....................... 3.11
   (3)........................... 3.11
   (4)........................... 3.11
20................................ 3.11, 10.4
   (3)........................... 3.12
     (a)....................... 3.14
     (b)....................... 3.13
   (5), (6)............... 3.14, 3.15
   (7)–(9)....................... 3.14
21...................... 1.8, 2.22
   (1)..................... 2.2, 4.30
   (2)..................... 2.4, 3.46
22............. 2.8, 2.16, 2.17, 3.29
   (1)........................... 2.12
23(1)–(3)....................... 2.17
   (4)........................... 2.11
     (b)....................... 5.19
   (5)........................... 2.11
     (b)....................... 5.19
   (6), (7)....................... 2.11
24(1), (2)............... 2.10, 17.17
   (3)........................... 2.10
25(1)–(3)................. 2.21, 5.14
   (5), (7)....................... 5.14
26(1), (2)....................... 2.18
27................................... 2.19
28.......... 2.8, 9.21, 9.22, 14.24

Taxation of Chargeable Gains Act
1992 – *contd*

s 28(2)........................... 2.4
29................. 2.6, 10.4, 10.15
30–34........................... 10.4
35(1), (2)....................... 3.69
   (3)........................... 3.70
     (d)........... 3.64, 3.70, 3.73
   (4)........................... 3.70
   (5)–(7)....................... 3.71
36................................... 3.75
37................................... 3.4
   (1)........................... 2.13
   (3)..................... 6.14, 6.21
38................. 2.17, 3.61, 8.20
   (1)........................... 3.37
     (a).... 3.38, 3.39, 3.40, 4.12,
                      15.4
     (b)................... 3.40, 4.13
     (c)........................... 3.41
   (2)..................... 3.39, 3.41
   (3), (4)....................... 3.37
39(1), (2)....................... 3.42
41................................... 3.46
   (1)–(8)....................... 3.55
42.............................. 4.17, 6.21
   (1)........................... 3.46
   (2)..................... 3.46, 4.16
   (3)–(5)....................... 3.46
43................................... 3.47
44.............................. 4.23, 14.31
   (2), (3)....................... 4.28
45................................... 1.8
   (1)........................... 4.22
   (2)–(4)....................... 4.24
46(1), (3)....................... 4.27
   (2)(a)....................... 4.26
     (b)....................... 4.27
47(1), (2)....................... 4.29
48................................... 2.16
   (1)............... 3.22, 3.28, 3.29
   (2), (3)....................... 3.23
49.......................... 3.24, 3.25
50........................... 3.43, 14.30
51................................... 1.8
52................................... 14.10
   (1)........................... 3.37
   (2), (3)................. 3.4, 3.42
   (4)........................... 3.47
53................................... 11.42

**Taxation of Chargeable Gains Act
1992** – *contd*

s 53(1).............................. 3.60
(1A).......................... 3.59
(2)(a)......................... 3.60
(b)......................... 3.61
(2A).......................... 3.60
(3)............................. 3.61
54(1), (1A), (2), (3)........... 3.60
(4)............................. 3.61
55(1)–(4)...................... 3.63
(5), (6)...................... 3.64
(7)–(11)...................... 3.65
56................................ 3.66
(1)............................. 3.62
57................................ 3.61
58..... 2.6, 3.46, 3.70, 3.73, 5.10,
5.19, 6.9, 13.18,
13.21, 15.7
(1)........ 2.7, 3.67, 11.5, 11.28
(2)............................. 3.67
59................................ 6.1, 6.21
(1)(a)......................... 6.1
(2), (3)...................... 6.20
(5), (6)...................... 6.19
59A..................... 6.21, 14.13
(1).................. 6.19, 6.21
(2), (3)............. 6.19, 14.13
(4)........................ 6.19
60......... 1.5, 1.10, 2.20, 8.1, 8.2
(1)....................... 8.3, 8.9
(2)............................. 8.3
62............. 1.8, 2.9, 7.13, 12.28
(2)....................... 7.3, 7.4
(3)............................. 7.5
(5)............................. 7.11
(6)....................... 7.17, 7.18
(7), (8)...................... 7.17
(10)........................... 7.4
64(1)............................ 7.11
(2)....................... 7.11, 7.13
(3)............................ 12.31
68.......................... 8.2, 8.21
68A, 68B, 68C................. 8.2
69....................... 8.2, 13.24
(1)............... 8.7, 8.22, 8.40
(2)–(2B)..................... 8.40
(4).......................... 8.18
70........................... 2.20, 8.5
71..................... 2.20, 7.13, 8.8

**Taxation of Chargeable Gains Act
1992** – *contd*

s 71(1)... 8.6, 8.9, 8.10, 8.11, 8.12,
8.15, 8.16, 8.17,
8.34
(2)............................ 8.19
72 . 2.20, 8.10, 8.12, 12.24, 12.35
(1A)................. 8.13, 12.35
(1B).......... 8.12, 8.13, 12.35
(1C)........................ 12.35
73..... 2.20, 3.70, 5.19, 7.4, 8.10,
8.12
(1)..................... 2.7, 8.12
(a).......................... 2.7
(b).......................... 7.4
(2)............................ 8.12
(2A).......................... 8.12
(a)........................ 8.12
74................................ 7.4
76........................... 1.8, 2.20
(1)..................... 8.14, 8.15
(2)............................ 8.16
76A....................... 2.20, 8.14
76B........................... 2.20
77.. 1.14, 5.8, 7.17, 8.1, 8.2, 8.36,
8.37
(2A)..................... 8.5, 8.25
(3), (4)...................... 8.37
78....................... 5.8, 8.36
79................................ 5.8
80..................... 2.20, 8.41
81(3)........................... 8.6
85................................ 1.8
86.............. 1.14, 5.8, 5.18
87............................. 1.14
89(2).......................... 1.14
Pt IV Ch I (ss 104–125)...... 16.22
s 104................ 4.4, 4.5, 4.7
(1), (3), (6)................. 4.5
(3)..................... 4.1, 6.21
(4)............................ 4.1
105....................... 4.4, 4.7
(1)(a), (b).................... 4.2
(2)............................ 4.2
105A, 105B................... 4.2
106............... 4.4, 4.7, 9.17
106A............................ 4.4
(5)–(7)..................... 4.2
(8)............................ 4.5
(9)............................ 4.2

Taxation of Chargeable Gains Act
1992 – *contd*
s 107.............................. 4.7
108........................ 3.60, 4.7
109.............................. 4.6
110.............................. 4.5
110A............................. 4.5
115................. 1.8, 4.30, 17.11
116(10)................ 5.19, 11.39
(11)......................... 5.19
121.............................. 1.8
125............................. 10.4
126............. 16.7, 16.24, 17.5
127.. 4.4, 9.23, 11.38, 16.7, 16.24,
17.5
128–130......... 16.7, 16.24, 17.5
132........................ 4.1, 17.12
134................... 5.19, 11.39
135.. 3.24, 9.6, 9.23, 16.8, 16.24,
17.6
136........ 3.24, 16.8, 16.24, 17.6
137............................. 10.4
139............................. 3.70
(1)........................... 2.7
140............................. 3.83
140A.................... 3.55, 3.70
140E.................... 3.70, 14.34
142.............................. 4.4
144............................ 11.36
(1)........................... 2.22
(2)........................... 2.23
(4)........................... 2.24
(7)........................... 2.25
150.............................. 1.8
150A............. 1.8, 16.3, 16.11
(1), (2)............. 16.4, 17.3
(3)................. 16.5, 16.9
(4), (5).................... 16.6
(6), (6A), (7)............ 16.7
(8), (8A)-(8D), (9)...... 16.8
150B............................ 16.9
150C........................... 16.10
150D........................... 16.26
151.............................. 1.8
151A........................... 1.8
(2A)...................... 16.4
(3)................. 16.5, 17.8
(4), (5)................... 17.4
(6), (7)................... 17.3
151B(1)........................ 17.4

Taxation of Chargeable Gains Act
1992 – *contd*
s 151B(2)–(4)................... 17.5
(5)......................... 17.6
(6)–(8)................... 17.7
152.. 3.46, 4.19, 6.19, 6.21, 8.33,
9.3, 9.8, 11.43,
14.1, 14.9, 14.10,
14.13, 14.31, 14.36,
14.41, 14.45, 15.19
(1).......... 14.2, 14.22, 14.26
(a)......................... 2.7
(b)...................... 5.19
(3)................. 14.35, 14.41
(4)........................ 14.35
(5)......................... 14.8
(6), (7)................... 14.23
(10)......... 14.2, 14.29, 14.30
(11)...................... 14.23
153.... 3.46, 6.21, 8.33, 9.3, 14.9,
14.10, 14.13, 14.31,
14.36
(1)....................... 14.27
(b)...................... 5.19
153A........................... 14.41
(3)–(5)................... 14.42
154.... 3.46, 6.19, 6.21, 8.33, 9.3,
14.9, 14.10, 14.36
(1)....................... 14.31
(2).. 5.19, 11.39, 14.13, 14.32
(2A)...................... 14.34
(4)......... 5.19, 11.39, 14.33
(5)....................... 14.33
(7)....................... 14.31
155.... 3.46, 6.21, 8.33, 9.3, 14.2,
14.9, 14.10, 14.15,
14.36, 14.41
156.... 3.46, 6.21, 8.33, 9.3, 14.9,
14.10, 14.16, 14.36
156A................... 6.19, 14.13
(1)....................... 14.13
157.... 3.46, 6.21, 8.33, 9.3, 14.9,
14.10, 14.11, 14.36
158.... 3.46, 6.21, 8.33, 9.3, 14.9,
14.10, 14.36
(1)........................ 14.9
(2)................. 14.2, 14.9
159(1)–(3), (5)................ 14.6
159A........................... 6.19
161............................. 9.10

Taxation of Chargeable Gains Act
1992 – *contd*

s 161(2)........................... 4.33
    (3).................... 4.32, 9.10
    (3A), (4)................... 4.32
162... 11.44, 13.35, 13.36, 14.45,
    15.1, 15.6, 15.7,
    15.12, 15.18, 15.19,
    15.20
    (1).... 15.2, 15.8, 15.9, 15.10,
    15.14
    (2)................... 15.3, 15.16
    (3)........................... 15.3
    (b)....................... 5.19
    (4), (5)..................... 15.4
162A................. 11.44, 15.18
    (1)–(8)................... 15.7
163, 164....................... 17.22
164A................. 16.10, 17.23
164B-164N................. 17.23
165..... 2.6, 4.19, 6.19, 8.5, 8.25,
    8.26, 13.1, 13.2,
    13.6, 13.17, 13.19,
.. 13.20, 13.23, 13.24, 13.25, 13.26,
    13.27, 13.34, 13.35,
    13.38, 13.44, 13.45,
    13.46, 15.1, 15.6,
    15.19, 15.20
    (1).......................... 13.3
    (b)................. 8.23, 8.25
    (2).......................... 13.5
    (3).......................... 13.4
    (5).......................... 13.5
    (6).......................... 13.6
    (7).......................... 13.7
    (8)......... 13,14, 13.15, 13.16
    (9)......................... 13.16
    (10), (11)................. 13.17
166............................. 13.19
167............................. 13.23
168............................. 10.4
    (1)......................... 13.20
    (2), (3)................... 13.21
    (4)......................... 13.20
    (5), (6)................... 13.21
    (7)–(9)................... 13.22
    (10)........................ 13.20
169............................. 13.24
169B................... 8.26, 13.27
169C................... 8.26, 13.28

Taxation of Chargeable Gains Act
1992 – *contd*

s 169C(7)...................... 11.39
169D........... 8.26, 13.27, 13.28
169E................... 8.26, 13.30
169F................... 8.26, 13.31
    (5)........................ 13.31
    (6)........................ 13.33
169G................... 8.26, 13.32
170................................. 9.5
171... 3.14, 3.15, 3.46, 3.55, 3.70,
    3.73, 3.83, 9.6,
    9.10, 9.20, 9.21,
    9.23
    (1)........................... 2.7
    (1A)........................ 9.6
    (2)..................... 3.55, 9.6
    (3)........................... 9.6
171A.............................. 9.7
173............................. 9.10
175............................. 9.13
176............................. 9.14
177............................. 9.15
177A............................ 9.16
177B............................ 9.16
179.............................. 9.8
    (3)........................... 9.8
179A, 179B.................... 9.8
184A, 184B, 184G, 184H... 9.17
192A...................... 1.8, 9.20
210.............................. 1.8
215............................. 3.70
217A........................... 3.70
218–221....................... 3.70
222.. 4.18, 12.1, 12.4, 12.6, 12.7,
    12.17, 12.24
    (1)(b)...................... 12.6
    (3)......................... 12.6
    (5)......... 12.18, 12.21, 12.22
    (a)...... 12.3, 12.19, 12.20,
    12.22, 12.24
    (6)........................ 12.18
    (a)...................... 12.23
    (8)........................ 12.14
    (8A)...................... 12.14
    (b)...................... 12.15
    (8B), (8C).............. 12.15
223. 1.8, 4.18, 8.26, 12.14, 12.24,
    12.33
    (1)........................ 12.20

Taxation of Chargeable Gains Act
1992 – *contd*

s 223(2)(a)...................... 12.12
    (3)......................... 12.13
        (a)............. 12.13, 12.20
        (b), (c)................ 12.13
    (4).......... 8.34, 12.17, 12.20
        (b)..................... 12.17
224.................... 4.18, 12.24
    (1).......................... 12.4
    (3).......................... 12.2
225...... 4.18, 8.34, 12.24, 12.25,
                    12.30, 12.32
225A........... 7.11, 12.30, 12.31
    (3)(b)..................... 12.30
    (4)........................ 12.30
226............................ 4.18
    (6)........................ 12.36
226A.. 8.26, 12.32, 12.33, 12.34,
                           12.35
228(7B)........................ 5.17
229........................... 14.31
237............................. 1.8
241...................... 4.19, 14.9
    (3)........... 4.19, 11.22, 14.9
    (4)–(7).................... 4.19
242............................ 2.5
    (2A)....................... 2.5
243............................ 2.5
    (2A)....................... 2.5
244............................ 2.5
247........................... 17.21
    (2)(b)..................... 5.19
    (3)(b)..................... 5.19
248........................... 17.21
249............................ 1.8
250............................ 1.8
251................... 4.30, 17.11
    (6)........................ 11.7
252.................. 4.30, 17.11
    (1).......................... 5.25
253........... 3.56, 4.19, 17.11
    (1), (2).................... 17.12
    (3), (3A)................. 17.13
    (4)............... 17.13, 17.14
    (4A)...................... 17.14
    (5)–(9).................. 17.15
    (12).............. 17.13, 17.14
256..................... 1.10, 7.12
257(2)......................... 3.64

Taxation of Chargeable Gains Act
1992 – *contd*

s 257(2)(a)...................... 2.7
    (3).......................... 3.70
258............................ 1.8
    (4)................... 3.70, 5.19
259(2)......................... 3.64
260.... 6.19, 8.5, 8.12, 8.23, 8.24,
                8.25, 8.26, 12.32,
                12.33, 12.35, 13.1,
                13.4, , 13.20, 13.24,
                13.26, 13.27, 13.34,
                13.37, 13.38, 13.42,
                13.43, 13.44, 13.45,
                                13.46
    (1)........................ 13.38
        (c)..................... 13.45
    (2)........................ 13.38
    (3), (4)................... 13.39
    (5)........................ 13.40
    (7), (8)................... 13.42
    (9)........................ 13.40
    (10)....................... 13.41
261........................... 13.43
262............................ 1.8
    (1)–(3)................... 4.20
    (4)........................ 4.21
    (6)........................ 4.20
263............................ 1.8
263ZA........................ 3.54
264........................... 3.70
267(2)........................ 3.70
268............................ 1.8
269............................ 1.8
271(4)......................... 1.8
272............................ 7.6
    (1), (2).................... 3.6
    (3), (4).................... 3.7
    (5)......................... 3.8
273............................ 3.9
274................. 3.6, 7.6, 12.28
275........................... 5.34
    (1)......................... 5.34
275A-C....................... 5.34
276............................ 1.4
277........................... 3.84
    (1)......................... 3.82
278........................... 3.85
279........................... 11.40
279A.......................... 3.30

Taxation of Chargeable Gains Act
1992 – *contd*
s 279A(1), (2)...................... 3.30
   (3), (4)...................... 3.31
   (5)–(7)...................... 3.32
 279B.............................. 3.33
 279C.............................. 3.34
 279D.............................. 3.30
 280................................ 3.35
 281................................ 13.1
 282........................ 3.67, 13.1
 284A.................. 10.4, 15.12
 284B........................ 15.12
 286...................... 3.16, 11.17
  (2).............................. 3.17
  (3), (3A).................... 3.18
  (4)............. 3.19, 6.18, 6.21
  (5)–(7)........................ 3.20
 288................................ 1.3
  (1)............... 3.9, 5.24, 15.2
  (3)............................ 3.67
 295.............................. 8.23
 Sch 1...................... 1.21, 8.20
 para A1 .... 8.21
  2 .... 1.21
   (6A) 1.32
 Sch A1....................... 4.19, 11.6
 para 1, 2 .... 11.25
  3 .... 11.25, 11.26
  4(1), (2) 11.7
  5 .... 11.22
   (2) 11.23, 11.24
  6 .... 11.20
   (1), (1A) 11.9
   3) 7.9
   (4) 11.17
  6A 11.17
  9 .... 11.27
  10 .... 11.29
  11 .... 11.30
  11A 11.30, 11.38
  12 .... 11.34
  13 .... 11.36
  14 .... 11.37
  15 .... 11.5, 11.28
  16(1) 11.39, 16.25
   (4) 11.40
  21 .... 11.26
  22 .... 11.9, 11.11, 11.12,
       11.16, 11.24

Taxation of Chargeable Gains Act
1992 – *contd*
Sch A1 – *contd*
  (1) 11.13, 11.14, 13.15
  22A 11.10, 13.15
  22B 11.15, 13.15
  23 .... 11.18
 Sch 2.. 3.70, 3.74, 3.77, 3.78, 3.79,
        6.21
 para 4 .... 6.21
  18 .... 6.21
 Sch 3............................ 6.11
 para 1, 2 .... 3.73
  5 .... 3.69
  7–9 .... 3.72
 Sch 4.............. 3.75, 6.11, 14.28
 Sch 4A......................... 8.14
 Sch 4ZA....................... 8.17
 para 4–6 .... 8.17
  20 .... 8.17
 Sch 5............................ 5.8
 para 1A(1)–(7) 16.18
  2(1)–(4) 16.13
  3(1), (3), (4) 16.19
   (5) 16.20
  4(1) 16.21
   (2)–(5) 16.22
   (6), (7) 16.21
  5 .... 16.23
  7(1), (2) 16.24
  8, 9 .... 16.24
  10(1)–(4) 16.27
  11 .... 16.28
  12 .... 16.30
   (2)(a) 16.31
   (4) 16.29
  13(1)–(3), (5)–(11) 16.33
  13A(1)–(5) 16.33
  13B, 13C 16.35
  16 .... 16.19
  19(1) 16.28, 16.32, 16.33
   (1A)-(1D) 16.13
 Sch 5B......................... 11.39
 para 1(1) 16.11
  (2) 16.14
  (3) 16.16
  (4) 16.11
  (5) 16.14
  6 .... 16.17
  13A 16.33

Table of statutes

Taxation of Chargeable Gains Act
1992 – *contd*
Sch 5B – *contd*
    14, 14A, 14AA 16.34
    16 .... 16.36
    17(1)–(6) 16.12
    18 .... 16.12
    19(1) 16.15, 16.33
Sch 5C..................... 11.39, 17.8
para 1 .... 17.8
    3–6 .... 17.10
Sch 5BA..................... 16.26
para 1(1)–(4) 16.26
Sch 6........................... 17.22
Sch 7........................... 13.5
para 1 .... 13.25
    2 .... 13.26
    3 .... 13.26
    4 .... 13.9, 13.10, 13.11
    5 .... 13.9, 13.46
    6 .... 13.10, 13.46
    7 .... 13.11, 13.46
Sch 7A...................... 9.16
Sch 7AA...................... 9.16
Sch 7AC............. 1.8, 4.19, 9.20
para 7–9 .... 9.20
    10 .... 9.20, 9.23
    11–16 .... 9.20
    18 .... 9.21

Taxation of Chargeable Gains Act
1992 – *contd*
Sch 7AC – *contd*
    19 .... 9.22
    20 .... 9.23
Sch 7D........................... 13.5
para 15 .... 11.36
Sch 8........................... 13.5
para 1 .... 4.11
    (4) 4.12, 4.13
    2 .... 4.15
    4 .... 4.17
    5(1) 4.16
    (2) 4.17
    8 .... 4.10
    10(1)(a) 4.10
Sch 12........................... 8.2

Taxes Management Act 1970
s 8............................. 1.27
    (1A)............................ 1.36
12............................. 1.27
12AA(7)........................ 6.1
36............................. 13.34
40(1)............................ 7.2
42............................. 3.49
43............. 3.49, 13.34, 14.38
59A, 59B...................... 1.37

Trustee Act 1925
s 32.............................. 8.11

Table of statutory instruments

[All references are to paragraph number]

Child Trust Funds
Regulations 2004,
SI 2004/1450 .... 1.9

Income Tax (Payments on
Account) Regulations 1996,
SI 1996/1654 .... 1.37

Table of cases

[All references are to paragraph number]

Aberdeen Construction Group Ltd v Inland Revenue Commissioners
[1978] AC 885, [1978] 2 WLR 648, [1978] 1 All ER 962, [1978] STC
127, 1978 SC (HL) 72, 1978 SLT 146, 52 TC 281, [1978] TR 25, 122
SJ 249, HL 3.40
Allison v Murray [1975] 1 WLR 1578, [1975] 3 All ER 561, [1975] STC
524, [1975] TR 157, 119 SJ 712, DC 8.20
American Leaf Blending Co Sdn Bhd v Director General of Inland
Revenue [1979] AC 676, [1978] 3 WLR 985, [1978] 3 All ER 1185,
[1978] STC 561, [1978] TR 243, 122 SJ 641, PC (Mal) 15.8
Balloon Promotions Ltd v Wilson (Inspector of Taxes); Vela-Castro v
Rodin (Inspector of Taxes) [2006] STC (SCD) 167, [2006] STI 623, Sp
Comm 14.19
Caton's Administrators v Couch. *See* Couch (Inspector of Taxes) v
Administrators of the Estate of Caton
Chaney v Watkis (Inspector of Taxes) [1986] STC 89, 58 TC 707, (1986)
83 LSG 205, (1986) 130 SJ 72, Ch D 3.40
CIR v Chubb's Trustee 1972 SLT 81 .... 8.20
Coates (Inspector of Taxes) v Arndale Properties [1984] 1 WLR 1328,
[1985] 1 All ER 15, [1984] STC 637, 59 TC 516, (1985) 82 LSG
201, HL 9.11
Couch (Inspector of Taxes) v Administrators of the Estate of Caton; sub
nom Administrators of the Estate of Caton v Couch (Inspector of
Taxes); Caton's Administrators, Re; Caton's Administrators v Couch
(Inspector of Taxes); Couch (Inspector of Taxes) v Caton's
Administrators [1997] STC 970, 70 TC 10, [1997] BTC 360, (1997)
94(30) LSG 29, (1997) Times, 16 July, CA 8.20
Crowe v Appleby (Inspector of Taxes) [1975] 1 WLR 1539,
[1975] 3 All ER 529, [1975] STC 502, [1975] TR 151, 119 SJ 776, Ch
D 8.4
Daniels v Revenue and Customs Commissioners [2005] STC (SCD) 684,
Sp Comm 11.39, 16.25
Electricity Commission (Balmain Electric Light Co Purchase) Act 1950
[1957] 57 SR (NSW) 100 .... 15.9
Emmerson (Inspector of Taxes) v Computer Time International Ltd (In
Liquidation) [1977] 1 WLR 734, [1977] 2 All ER 545, [1977] STC
170, (1977) 242 EG 963, 50 TC 628, [1977] TR 43, 121 SJ 224, CA 3.42
Fox v Stirk; sub nom Ricketts v City of Cambridge Electoral Registration
Officer; Ricketts v Registration Officer for the City of Cambridge
[1970] 2 QB 463, [1970] 3 WLR 147, [1970] 3 All ER 7, 68 LGR 644,
114 SJ 397, CA 12.1, 12.18

Furniss (Inspector of Taxes) v Dawson [1984] AC 474, [1984] 2 WLR 226,
[1984] 1 All ER 530, [1984] STC 153, 55 TC 324, (1984) 15 ATR 255,
(1985) 82 LSG 2782, (1984) 81 LSG 739, (1984) 134 NLJ 341, (1984)
128 SJ 132, HL 10.4

Goodwin v Curtis (Inspector of Taxes) [1998] STC 475, 70 TC 478,
[1998] BTC 176, (1998) 95(12) LSG 27, (1998) 142 SJLB 91, (1998)
Times, 2 March, CA, affirming [1996] STC 1146, (1996) 140 SJLB
186, (1996) Times, 14 August, Ch D 12.1, 12.3

Gordon v IRC; IRC v Gordon (Cross Appeal) [1991] STC 174, 1991 SC
149, 1991 SLT 730, 1992 SCLR 1, 64 TC 173, [1991] BTC 130, IH 15.9

Griffin (Inspector of Taxes) v Craig-Harvey [1994] STC 54, 66 TC 396,
[1993] STI 1442, [1993] EGCS 200, (1994) 91(4) LSG 46, (1993)
Times, 29 November, Ch D ...., ... 12.18

Gubay v Kington (Inspector of Taxes); sub nom Gubay v Kingston
[1984] 1 WLR 163, [1984] 1 All ER 513, [1984] STC 99, 57 TC 601,
(1984) 81 LSG 900, (1984) 134 NLJ 342, (1984) 128 SJ 100, HL 5.10

Henke and another v HMRC (2006) SpC 550 .... 12.7

Howarth's Executors v IRC [1997] STC (SCD) 162 .... 12.31

Innocent (Inspector of Taxes) v Whaddon Estates [1982] STC 115, 55 TC
476, [1981] TR 379, DC 9.6

IRC v Marine Steam Turbine Co Ltd [1919] 12 TC 174, KB 15.8

IRC v Richards Executors [1971] 1 WLR 571, [1971] 1 All ER 785, 1971
SC (HL) 60, 1971 SLT 107, 21 TC 626, [1971] TR 2, 115 SJ 225, HL 7.8

Jones v Wilcox (Inspector of Taxes) [1996] STI 1349 .... 12.2, 12.3

Jowett (Inspector of Taxes) v O'Neill & Brennan Construction Ltd
[1998] STC 482, 70 TC 566, [1998] BTC 133, (1998) 95(16) LSG 25,
(1998) 142 SJLB 124, (1998) Times, 25 March, Ch D 11.31

Judge and another (personal representatives of Walden, dec'd) v HMRC
(2005) SpC 506 .... 12.25

Kenmir Ltd v Frizzell [1968] 1 WLR 329, [1968] 1 All ER 414, 3 KIR
240, [1968] ITR 159, QBD 15.9

Kidson (Inspector of Taxes) v MacDonald; sub nom Kidson (Inspector of
Taxes) v Mawle's Executors [1974] Ch 339, [1974] 2 WLR 566,
[1974] 1 All ER 849, [1974] STC 54, 49 TC 503, [1973] TR 259, 118
SJ 297, Ch D 8.3

Lang (Inspector of Taxes) v Rice [1984] STC 172, 57 TC 80,
[1983] 5 NIJB, CA 2.13

Lewis v Lady Rook [1992] STC 171 .... 12.6

Longson v Baker (Inspector of Taxes) [2001] STC 6, 73 TC 415, [2001]
BTC 356, [2001] STI 44, (2001) 98(3) LSG 43, (2000) Times,
5 December, Ch D 12.6

Lynch v Edmondson (Inspector of Taxes) [1998] STI 968 .... 12.2

Lyon (Inspector of Taxes) v Pettigrew [1985] STC 369, 58 TC 452, (1985)
82 LSG 1643, Ch D 2.8

Marren (Inspector of Taxes) v Ingles [1980] 1 WLR 983, [1980] 3 All ER
95, [1980] STC 500, 54 TC 76, [1980] TR 335, 124 SJ 562, HL 3.29

Marshall (Inspector of Taxes) v Kerr [1995] 1 AC 148, [1994] 3 WLR 299,
[1994] 3 All ER 106, [1994] STC 638, 67 TC 81, (1994) 91(30) LSG
32, (1994) 138 SJLB 155, (1994) Times, 5 July, HL 7.17

Milton v Chivers [1996] STC (SCD) 36 .... 14.22

Moore v Thompson (Inspector of Taxes) [1986] STC 170, 60 TC 15,
 (1986) 83 LSG 1559, Ch D 12.1
Oram v Johnson [1980] 1 WLR 558, [1980] 2 All ER 1, [1980] STC 222,
 53 TC 319, [1980] TR 5, 124 SJ 188, Ch D 3.40
O'Sullivan v Philip (Inspector of Taxes); sub nom O'Sullivan v IRC
 [2005] EWHC 2130, [2005] STC 1712, [2005] BTC 544, [2005] STI
 1681, (2005) Times, 13 October, Ch D 11.4
Prosser v IRC [2001] RVR 170, [2002] WTLR 259, Lands Tr 12.29
R v Inland Revenue Commissioners, ex p Fulford-Dobson [1987] QB 978,
 [1987] 3 WLR 277, [1987] STC 344, 60 TC 168, QBD 5.8, 5.10
Randall v Plumb [1975] 1 WLR 633, [1975] 1 All ER 734, [1975] STC
 191, 50 TC 392, [1974] TR 371, (1975) 119 SJ 188, (1974) Times,
 10 December, Ch D 3.25
Regina v HM Inspector of Taxes, Reading ex p Fulford-Dobson. *See* R v
 Inland Revenue Commissioners, ex p Fulford-Dobson
Revenue and Customs Commissioners v Salaried Persons Postal
 Loans Ltd. *See* Salaried Persons Postal Loans Ltd v Revenue and
 Customs Commissioners
Salaried Persons Postal Loans Ltd v Revenue and Customs
 Commissioners; sub nom Revenue and Customs Commissioners v
 Salaried Persons Postal Loans Ltd, [2006] EWHC 763, [2006] STI
 1269, (2006) Times, 20 April, Ch D 11.31
Sansom v Peay (Inspector of Taxes) [1976] 1 WLR 1073, [1976] 3 All ER
 375, [1976] STC 494, 52 TC 1, [1976] TR 205, 120 SJ 571, Ch D 12.25,
 12.26
Steibelt (Inspector of Taxes) v Paling [1999] STC 594, 71 TC 376, [1999]
 BTC 184, (1999) 96(20) LSG 40, (1999) 143 SJLB 140, (1999) Times,
 19 May, Ch D 14.22
Stephenson (Inspector of Taxes) v Barclays Bank Trust Co Ltd
 [1975] 1 WLR 882, [1975] 1 All ER 625, [1975] STC 151, 50 TC 374,
 [1974] TR 343, (1974) 119 SJ 169, Ch D 8.9
Tod v Mudd [1986] 60 TC 237, Ch D 14.12
Varty (Inspector of Taxes) v Lynes [1976] 1 WLR 1091, [1976] 3 All ER
 447, [1976] STC 508, 51 TC 419, [1976] TR 209, 120 SJ 525, Ch D 12.8
WT Ramsay Ltd v IRC; Eilbeck (Inspector of Taxes) v Rawling [1982] AC
 300, [1981] 2 WLR 449, [1981] 1 All ER 865, [1981] STC 174, 54 TC
 101, [1982] TR 123, (1981) 11 ATR 752, 125 SJ 220, HL 10.4
Wardhaugh (Inspector of Taxes) v Penrith Rugby Union Football Club
 [2002] EWHC 918, [2002] STC 776, 74 TC 499, [2002] BTC 237,
 [2002] STI 785, (2002) 99(24) LSG 36, (2002) 146 SJLB 135, [2002]
 NPC 68, (2002) Times, 29 May, Ch D 14.30
Watton (Inspector of Taxes) v Tippett; sub nom Tippett v Watton (Inspector
 of Taxes), [1997] STC 893, 69 TC 491, [1997] BTC 338, (1997) Times,
 27 June, CA 14.21
Williams v Evans (Inspector of Taxes); Jones v Evans; Roberts v Evans
 [1982] 1 WLR 972, [1982] STC 498, 59 TC 509, 126 SJ 346, Ch D 14.17
Zim Properties Ltd v Procter (Inspector of Taxes); sub nom Procter
 (Inspector of Taxes) v Zim Properties [1985] STC 90, 58 TC 371,
 (1985) 82 LSG 124, (1985) 129 SJ 68, 129 SJ 323, Ch D 2.15

List of Abbreviations

AIM	alternative investment market
BES	business expansion scheme
CA	Court of Appeal
CGT	capital gains tax
CTF	child trust fund
EIS	Enterprise Investment Scheme
ESC	Extra-statutory Concession
FA	Finance Act
HMRC	Her Majesty's Revenue and Customs
ICTA 1988	Income and Corporation Taxes Act 1988
IHT	inheritance tax
IHTA 1984	Inheritance Tax Act 1984
IHTM	Inheritance Tax Manual
IRC	Inland Revenue Commissioners
ITEPA 2003	Income Tax (Earnings and Pensions) Act 2003
ITTOIA 2005	Income Tax (Trading and Other Income) Act 2005
LLP	limited liability partnership
reg	regulation
s	section
Sch	Schedule
SCO	Special Compliance Office
SI	Statutory Instrument
SP	HMRC Statement of Practice
TCGA 1992	Taxation of Chargeable Gains Act 1992
TMA 1970	Taxes Management Act 1970
VCT	venture capital trust

Part A

General Principles

Chapter 1

Introduction to capital gains tax

INTRODUCTION AND BASIS OF CHARGE

1.1   Capital gains tax (CGT) is charged on capital gains, defined as chargeable gains accruing to a person on the disposal of an asset (*Taxation of Chargeable Gains Act 1992 (TCGA 1992), s 1*). Spouses and civil partners are chargeable separately but where the members of a couple are living together transfers of assets between them are deemed to take place for a consideration that gives rise to no gain and no loss. There is no CGT on death, and the deceased's assets are deemed to be inherited at their market value.

A 'person' may be an individual, a trustee or personal representative, or a company. However, companies are excluded from CGT and are chargeable to corporation tax on their chargeable gains instead (*Interpretations Act 1978, Sch 1; ICTA 1988, s 6*).

In very broad terms, the chargeable gain arising on the disposal of an asset is the excess of the disposal value over the acquisition value. **Chapters 1** to **6** focus on rules as they apply to individuals only. There are special rules for personal representatives of a deceased person (see **Chapter 7**) and trustees of a settled property (see **Chapter 8**). The chargeable gains accruing to a company for an accounting period are included in the company's total profits for the accounting period and are chargeable to corporation tax (see **Chapter 9**).

BACKGROUND AND LEGISLATION

1.2   CGT was introduced in 1965, at the same time as corporation tax. Previously, short-term gains on disposal of capital assets were chargeable but were taxed as income. The charge under Case VII of Schedule D was not introduced until 1962 and its scope was limited. HMRC's Capital Gains Manual at CG 10220 discusses the rationale for a broader tax on capital gains. It says that the introduction of the tax 'gave official recognition to a concept of taxable capacity based not only on income but on gains from the realisation of capital assets'. It adds that proponents of CGT argued that capital receipts, particularly those from short-term transactions, 'added to a person's spending or saving power in just the same way as did income'. On this basis, the tax could be justified 'on grounds of equity alone'.

The CGT legislation contained in the *Finance Act 1965* and subsequent acts was consolidated in 1979 and 1992. The *Taxation of Chargeable Gains Act 1992*, as amended by subsequent Finance Acts, now contains the main provisions concerning taxation of chargeable gains.

CHARGEABLE PERSONS

1.3 'Accruing' means realised or deemed to be realised, rather than accumulated over a period. A person is chargeable to CGT in respect of chargeable gains accruing to him in a year of assessment, ie a 'tax year' ending on 5 April:

- during any part of which he is 'resident' in the United Kingdom; or

- during which he is 'ordinarily resident' in the UK (*TCGA 1992, ss 1, 2, 288*).

Anti-avoidance rules provide for a person to be chargeable to CGT on gains accruing to others in certain circumstances. For example, the gains of a non-resident trust or company may be attributed to a UK-resident individual. Residence and related matters are discussed in detail in **Chapter 5**.

Territorial limits

1.4 The UK comprises Great Britain and Northern Ireland. It includes the UK's territorial seas but excludes the Isle of Man and the Channel Islands. A person who is a 'temporary non-resident' may also be chargeable. A non-resident person carrying on a business in the UK through a branch or agency (or through a permanent establishment, in the case of a company) is chargeable to CGT (or corporation tax) on gains arising from assets in the UK that are used for the purposes of the business (*TCGA 1992, ss 10, 10A, 276*).

CGT is not limited to gains on disposal of UK assets. However, an individual who is not domiciled in any part of the UK is chargeable on gains arising on non-UK assets only if, and to the extent that, the gains are remitted to the UK. See **Chapter 5** regarding residence, etc and the location of assets.

Beneficial ownership

1.5 The beneficial owner of the asset disposed of is normally the chargeable person in relation to the disposal. There is no disposal where an asset is transferred between a beneficial owner and a nominee for him (*TCGA 1992, s 60*).

EXEMPTIONS

1.6   Every gain accruing on the disposal of an asset is a chargeable gain, unless otherwise expressly provided. Losses are computed, as a general rule, in the same way as gains. A loss accruing on a disposal is generally not an allowable loss if a gain accruing on the same disposal would not be a chargeable gain. The exemptions provided in the CGT legislation or elsewhere are summarised below. There are also various reliefs, examined in Part B, which either provide a reduction in the CGT liability or defer it until a later date (*TCGA 1992, ss 15, 16*).

Exempt assets or gains

1.7   The main exemptions applied to particular assets or gains by virtue of *TCGA 1992* are set out in Table 1.1, in the order in which they appear in the legislation. Exemptions provided elsewhere are set out in Table 1.2. See also the special rules relating to particular assets examined in **Chapter 4** and the reliefs discussed in Part B.

Exemptions provided by *TCGA 1992*

1.8   **Table 1.1**

Exempt assets or gains	TCGA 1992
Foreign assets: CGT is not charged on gains accruing to individuals who are resident or ordinarily resident but not domiciled in the UK from the disposal of assets situated outside the UK. Where amounts are remitted to the UK in respect of such gains, however, CGT is charged on the amounts received in the UK.	s 12
Sterling is not an asset for CGT purposes (but currency other than sterling is an asset).	s 21
Wasting assets: No chargeable gain accrues on a disposal of tangible movable property that is a wasting asset as defined, subject to certain exceptions.	s 45
Winnings from betting, lotteries or games with prizes are not chargeable gains.	s 51
Compensation or damages for any wrong or injury suffered by an individual in his person or in his profession or vocation are not chargeable gains.	s 51
Death: The assets of which a deceased person was competent to dispose are deemed not to be disposed of by him on his death (see **Chapter 7**).	s 62

5

Exempt assets or gains	**TCGA 1992**
Interests in settled property: No chargeable gain accrues on the disposal of an interest in a settlement by the original beneficiary or by any other person except one who bought the interest, subject to exceptions (see **Chapter 8**).	ss 76, 85
Gilt-edged securities and qualifying corporate bonds: A gain accruing on a disposal of such assets, or of any option or contract to acquire or dispose of them, is not a chargeable gain.	s 115
Savings certificates and certain government securities are not chargeable assets, so that no chargeable gain accrues on a disposal.	s 121
Business expansion scheme (BES) shares: A gain accruing to an individual on disposal of shares issued after 18 March 1986 for which tax relief was given under the BES and has not been withdrawn is not a chargeable gain. Special rules apply to losses on disposal of such shares (see **Chapter 4**).	s 150
Enterprise investment scheme (EIS) shares: Gains accruing on the disposal after the end of the 'relevant period' of shares for which income tax relief under the EIS regime has been given (and not withdrawn) are not chargeable gains. Partial CGT exemption is available where income tax relief was restricted. Special rules apply to losses on disposal of such shares (see **Chapter 4**).	s 150A
Individual Savings Accounts and Personal Equity Plan investments: No tax is chargeable on either the investor or the account manager in respect of gains arising on ISAs or PEPs provided certain conditions are met.	s 151
Venture capital trusts: A gain accruing to an individual on a 'qualifying disposal' of ordinary shares in a venture capital trust is, subject to certain conditions, not a chargeable gain. Special rules apply to losses on disposal of such shares (see **Chapter 4**).	s 151A
Companies – substantial shareholdings in trading companies: A gain on a disposal of a 'substantial shareholding' (broadly, an interest of at least 10%) that has been held for at least 12 months is not a chargeable gain provided various conditions are met (see **Chapter 9**).	s 192A, Sch 7AC
Life insurance and deferred annuities: A gain accruing on a disposal of (or of an interest in) rights conferred by a policy of insurance or contract for a deferred annuity is not a chargeable gain unless the policy, etc (or the interest in it) has been acquired for actual (not deemed) consideration.	s 210

Exempt assets or gains   **TCGA 1992**

Private residences: No part of a gain on the disposal of a   s 223
dwelling house meeting certain conditions is a chargeable
gain, so long as the house has been the individual's only or
main residence throughout the period of ownership, or
throughout that period except for all or part of the last 36
months (see **Chapter 12**).

Annuities, etc: No chargeable gain accrues on the disposal   s 237
of a right to (i) an annuity or lump sum payable out of a
superannuation fund; (ii) an annuity, other than a deferred
annuity, granted by a life insurance company; (iii) an
annuity granted (or deemed to be granted) under the
Government Annuities Act 1929; or (iv) annual payments,
due under a covenant, which are not secured on any
property.

Agricultural grants, etc: A sum receivable under the   s 249
Agriculture Act 1967, s 27 in return for relinquishing
occupation of an uncommercial agricultural unit is not
treated as part of the consideration on the disposal of any
asset.

Woodlands: Any part of the consideration for a disposal of   s 250
woodland in the UK that is attributable to trees (including
saleable underwood) growing on the land is excluded from
the CGT computation together with the related costs. Where
the occupier of woodlands manages them on a commercial
basis with a view to the realisation of profits, consideration
for the disposal of trees standing or felled or cut on the
woodlands is excluded from the computation. Any capital
sum received under an insurance policy relating to the
destruction of (or damage to) trees or saleable underwood
by fire or other hazard is also excluded.

Debts: Where a person (A) incurs a debt to another person   ss 251, 252
(B), no chargeable gain accrues to the original creditor (B)
on a disposal of the debt, except in the case of (i) a debt on
a security, and (ii) money held in a foreign currency bank
account that does not represent currency acquired for
personal expenditure outside the UK.

Works of art, etc: A gain is not a chargeable gain if it   s 258
accrues on the disposal of assets such as works of art,
historical building, etc to which a conditional exemption
from inheritance tax applies.

7

Exempt assets or gains	TCGA 1992
Chattels: A gain accruing on a disposal of tangible movable property is not a chargeable gain if the amount or value of the consideration for the disposal is not more than £6,000 (see **Chapter 4**).	s 262
Motor cars: A mechanically-propelled road vehicle is not a chargeable asset (so that no chargeable gain or allowable loss can accrue on a disposal) if it is constructed or adapted for the carriage of passengers. A vehicle of a type not commonly used as a private vehicle and unsuitable to be so used, however, is a chargeable asset.	s 263
Decorations for valour or gallant conduct: A gain accruing on the disposal of a decoration awarded for valour or gallant conduct is not a chargeable gain unless the taxpayer acquired it for a consideration in money or money's worth.	s 268
Foreign currency for personal expenditure: A gain accruing on the disposal by an individual of currency acquired for his own or his family's or his dependants' personal expenditure outside the UK is not a chargeable gain.	s 269
SAYE savings schemes: Interest on certified SAYE savings arrangements within *ITTOIA 2005, s 702* is disregarded for all purposes of CGT.	s 271(4)

Other exemptions

1.9   Table 1.2

Exempt assets or gains	Source
Cashbacks: These are lump sums received by a customer as an inducement for entering into a transaction for the purchase of goods, investments or services and received as a direct consequence of entering into the transaction (eg a mortgage). HMRC consider that a cashback does not derive from a chargeable asset for CGT purposes so that no chargeable gain arises. This practice does not extend to a cash payment by a building society to members, etc on a take-over by, or conversion to, a bank; or a payment by other mutual organisations such as insurance companies or friendly societies on demutualisation.	SP 4/97, para 35

Exempt assets or gains   **Source**

Child Trust Funds: Assets held by a named child as account   *Child Trust*
investments are regarded as held by him in a separate capacity   *Funds*
from that in which he holds similar assets outside the CTF. The   *Act 2004,*
child will be treated as selling the account investments and   *s 13;*
reacquiring them in his personal capacity at their market value   *SI 2004/*
on attaining the age of 18. Losses accruing on account invest-   *1450*
ments are disregarded for CGT purposes.

Compensation paid by foreign governments: By   ESC D50
concession, and subject to conditions, certain capital sums
paid as compensation by a foreign government for the
confiscation or expropriation of property outside the UK are
not treated as giving rise to a chargeable gain.

Lloyd's underwriters' special reserve funds: Profits and   *FA 1993,*
losses arising from disposal of assets forming part of a   *Sch 20,*
special reserve fund are excluded from CGT.   *para 9*

Exempt persons

1.10   The main exemptions likely to be met in practice are set out in Table 1.3. Others include full or partial exemptions for the Crown, local authorities, health service bodies, friendly societies, certain museums, housing associations, self-build societies, pension schemes, trades unions, scientific research associations, certain central banks and diplomats.

Table 1.3

Exempt person(s)   **Source**

Nominees and bare trustees: Where assets are held by a   *TCGA 1992,*
person (A) as nominee or bare trustee for another person   *s 60*
(B), the property is treated as vested in B and acts of the
nominee or bare trustee are treated as acts of B, so that there
is no occasion of charge where the bare trustee, for example,
passes assets to B.

Charities: A gain is not a chargeable gain if it accrues to a   *TCGA 1992,*
charity and is applicable and applied for charitable purposes   *s 256*
(subject to restrictions found in *ICTA 1988, s 505*).

Community amateur sports clubs: A gain accruing to a   *FA 2002,*
registered club is not a chargeable gain if the whole of it is   *s 58, Sch 18*
applied for qualifying purposes and the club makes a claim.

9

THE CAPITAL GAINS TAX CALCULATION

1.11   Individuals, trustees and personal representatives pay CGT at the rate applying in the relevant year of assessment. **Chapter 3** deals with the detailed computation of chargeable gains.

Indexation allowance and rebasing

1.12   'Paper gains' attributable to inflation were taxed prior to 1982 without any compensation for the fact that the taxpayer's purchasing power had been reduced. An indexation allowance to be used in arriving at the chargeable gain was introduced by the *Finance Act 1982* and designed to ensure that CGT was charged on 'real gains' only. For individuals, indexation allowance is not available in respect of assets acquired or enhancement expenditure incurred after 31 March 1998, and the allowance was 'frozen' at its April 1998 value for later disposals. It continues to be available to companies. The allowance is examined in detail in **Chapter 3**.

Where an asset acquired before 1 April 1982 is disposed of after 5 April 1988, as a general rule the market value of the asset at 31 March 1982 is used instead of the actual cost in the computation of the gain, including the calculation of the indexation allowance. Rebasing is also examined in **Chapter 3**.

Prior to the introduction of the March 1982 rebasing rules, special rules applied to eliminate from charge any part of a capital gain that had accrued prior to 6 April 1965 when CGT was introduced. These rules, discussed in **Chapter 3**, will still be relevant in a relatively small number of cases where the 1982 rebasing is not applied.

The amount chargeable

1.13   Once the gains have been computed as set out in **Chapter 3**, several adjustments may be required before the taxpayer can ascertain the taxable amount and then apply the appropriate rates of CGT.

CGT is charged on the total amount of chargeable gains accruing in the year of assessment, after deducting:

●   any allowable losses accruing to the taxpayer in that year of assessment; and

●   any allowable losses accruing to him in a previous year of assessment (not earlier than 1965/66) that have not already been allowed as a deduction from chargeable gains.

An allowable loss cannot be carried back to an earlier year of assessment, except where the loss has been sustained by an individual in the year of assessment in which he died (see **Chapter 7**). Relief cannot be given twice for the same loss under *TCGA 1992* and is not available for a capital loss that has been, or may be, relieved under the income tax legislation (*TCGA 1992, s 2(2), (3)*).

Gains accruing to others

1.14 This general rule is modified where gains have accrued to others but are attributed to the taxpayer, as settlor or beneficiary of a trust, under any of the following provisions (read, where appropriate, along with the rules in *TCGA 1992, s 10A* relating to temporary non-residents):

(a) *TCGA 1992, s 77* – charge on settlor with interest in settlement;

(b) *TCGA 1992, s 86* – attribution of gains to settlor with an interest in a non-resident or dual resident settlement;

(c) *TCGA 1992, s 87* – attribution of gains to a beneficiary; and

(d) *TCGA 1992, s 89(2)* – migrant settlements, etc.

The effect of these special rules, examined further in **Chapter 8**, is that the taxpayer's own capital losses cannot be set against such gains (*TCGA 1992, s 2(4)–(8)*).

Taper relief

1.15 Taper relief is available to individuals where, for a year of assessment, chargeable gains exceed any allowable losses and those gains include gains that are eligible for taper relief. The effect of the relief is that only a percentage of the gain, instead of the full amount, is chargeable (*TCGA 1992, s 2A*). Taper relief is examined in detail in **Chapter 12**.

Annual exemption

1.16 Every individual is entitled to an annual exemption, the effect of which is to provide that a slice of the 'taxable amount' (see below) for a year of assessment is not chargeable to CGT. Any unused part of the annual exemption is lost – it cannot be carried forward to the following year. Spouses and civil partners are entitled to their own annual exemption, which is not transferable. The amount of the annual exemption is as set out in Table 1.4 (*TCGA 1992, s 3*).

Table 1.4

Year of assessment	Individuals, certain trustees (see **1.21**) and personal representatives	Other trustees
2006/07	£8,800	£4,400
2005/06	£8,500	£4,250
2004/05	£8,200	£4,100

11

Indexation of the annual exemption

1.17   The annual exemption is increased each year in line with changes in the retail prices index, unless Parliament decides otherwise. For this purpose the RPI for the month of September preceding the year of assessment is compared to the RPI for the previous September. The new annual exemption is specified each year in a Treasury order (*TCGA 1992, s 3(3), (4)*).

The 'taxable amount'

1.18   The taxable amount is usually the amount of chargeable gains accruing to the taxpayer for a year of assessment after deduction of losses and taper relief. In some cases, gains accruing to others but chargeable on the taxpayer under anti-avoidance rules will be added at this stage in arriving at the taxable amount (see **1.14**) (*TCGA 1992, s 3(5)*).

Losses and the annual exemption

1.19   Allowable losses must be set against chargeable gains arising in the same year of assessment, even if this means reducing the taxable amount below the annual exemption. In other words, the set-off of current year losses cannot be restricted in order to utilise the exemption and preserve some of those losses for future use. However, allowable capital losses carried forward from an earlier year (or carried back from the year of the taxpayer's death) need not be deducted where the 'adjusted net gains' (see below) of the current year of assessment are covered by the annual exemption (*TCGA 1992, ss 2(2), 3(5A)*).

If the taxpayer's adjusted net gains exceed the annual exemption, then the amount set off in respect of losses carried forward (or back) is restricted to the excess. For this purpose the 'adjusted net gains' are, in most cases:

- the chargeable gains accruing to him for the year, before deduction of losses and taper relief, less

- allowable losses arising in the current year (*TCGA 1992, s 3(5B), (5C)*).

However, where gains have accrued to others but are attributed to the taxpayer as beneficiary of a settlement under the rules mentioned in (c) or (d) of **1.14**, then the smaller of the following amounts is added in arriving at the adjusted net gains:

- the amount of gains so attributed to him; and

- the amount of the annual exemption (*TCGA 1992, s 3(5C)*).

Personal representatives

1.20 The CGT treatment of personal representatives is considered in **Chapter 7**. Personal representatives of a deceased individual are entitled to the same annual exempt amount as an individual for:

- the year of assessment in which the individual died; and

- the next two following years of assessment (*TCGA 1992, s 3(7)*).

Trustees

1.21 The CGT treatment of trustees is considered in **Chapter 8**. Two sets of rules, set out in *TCGA 1992, Sch 1* but modified by the *Finance Act 2006*, fix the annual exemption. Broadly, trustees generally are entitled to an annual exemption equal to one-half of the exemption available to an individual, but trustees of settled property held for people with disabilities and others are entitled to the full annual exemption (*TCGA 1992, s 3(8); Sch 1, para 2*).

Rates of tax

Individuals

1.22 The rates of tax payable by an individual on any gains remaining after deducting the annual exemption are computed by:

- treating the gains as though they were the top slice of the individual's income (after allowing for deductions against income); and

- applying the relevant income tax rates to those gains.

However, the 20% 'lower rate' of income tax applicable to savings income (also known as the 'savings rate') is applied, instead of the basic rate of 22%, to gains falling within the basic rate band on this basis. To summarise:

- gains that fall within the starting rate band, when treated as the top slice of income, are taxed at 10%;

- gains that fall within the basic rate band when so treated are taxed at 20%; and

- gains falling into the higher rate band when so treated are taxed at 40%.

The starting rate and basic rate limits are set out in Table 1.5. Any part of the income tax personal allowance that is not used against income cannot be set against capital gains (*TCGA 1992, ss 4(1), 6; ICTA 1988 s 1A(1B)*).

Table 1.5

Year	Starting rate limit	Basic rate limit
2006/07	£2,150	£33,300
2005/06	£2,090	£32,400

Adjustments may be required to the calculation of the taxpayer's income, for the purpose of determining the appropriate rates of CGT, where:

- that income includes a gain on a life insurance contract, etc; or

- a deduction is available for (i) a 'deficiency' in relation to such a contract, or (ii) a reduction in the residuary income of an estate where inheritance tax has been charged on accrued income.

Example 1.1

Helen is under 65 years old and has employment income of £22,000 for 2006/07. She realises chargeable gains of £33,000 (after deduction of allowable losses and taper relief) in the same year. Her taxable income after deduction of the personal allowance of £5,035 is £16,965.

	£	£
Chargeable gains	33,000	
Annual exemption	(8,800)	
Taxable	24,200	
Taxable income	16,965	
Starting rate band	(2,150)	
Basic rate band used	14,815	
Unused basic rate band (33,300 – 14,815)	18,485	
CGT at lower rate 20% on	18,485	3,697
CGT at higher rate 40% on	5,715	2,286
Taxable	24,200	
Total CGT		5,983

Trustees and personal representatives

1.23   The rate of CGT is the same as the 'rate applicable to trusts' under *ICTA 1988, s 686* where the gains accrue to either the trustees of a settlement or the personal representatives of a deceased person. This rate was increased to 40% in *FA 2004* (*TCGA 1992, s 4(1AA)*).

Companies

1.24   Companies do not pay CGT. They are chargeable to corporation tax on their chargeable gains instead (see **Chapter 9**) (*TCGA 1992, s 1(2)*; *ICTA 1988, s 6*).

SELF-ASSESSMENT

1.25   The self-assessment system has applied to individuals, trustees and personal representatives, broadly, since 1996/97. An individual's tax return must include a self-assessment of income tax and CGT liabilities. The taxpayer is required to pay the tax on or before the due date, based on that self-assessment.

Self-assessment and related matters, including compliance with the regime for disclosure of tax avoidance schemes, are examined in detail in Tottel's Income Tax 2006/07, Chapter 2. This chapter focuses on the fundamental aspects of self-assessment relating to capital gains. HMRC provide general guidance on a range of topics at http://www.hmrc.gov.uk/individuals/ and an introduction to CGT in leaflet CGT 1. They have also published the following internal guidance manuals relating to self-assessment:

- Enquiry manual.
- Self Assessment Guides.
- Self Assessment Manual.

Tax returns

1.26   Taxpayers may file their return online via the HMRC website. Alternatively, return SA 100 may be downloaded, or requested from the local tax office or via an online order form. The basic tax return comprising ten pages includes a series of questions on page two. The capital gains supplementary pages are required if the taxpayer answers 'yes' to any part of question eight in 'Step 1' of the tax return. Page seven of the Tax Return Guide sets out in greater detail the circumstances in which the capital gains pages should be completed.

HMRC provide notes to the capital gains pages, including examples and a worksheet for 'simple' disposals, and the helpsheets on various topics as set out in Table 1.6. These are available from the HMRC orderline on 0845 9000 404 or via the HMRC website:

Table 1.6

IR 261	Foreign tax credit relief: capital gains
IR 276	Incorporation relief
IR 277	Trusts with settlor interest and trusts for the vulnerable: taper and losses
IR 278	Temporary non-residents and capital gains tax
IR 280	Taper relief
IR 281	Rebasing – assets held at 31 March 1982
IR 282	Death, personal representatives and legatees
IR 283	Private residence relief
IR 284	Shares and capital gains tax
IR 285	Share reorganisations, company take-overs and capital gains tax
IR 286	Negligible value claims and income tax losses on disposals of shares you have subscribed for in qualifying trading companies
IR 287	Employee share and security schemes and capital gains tax
IR 288	Partnerships and capital gains tax
IR 290	Business asset roll-over relief
IR 292	Land and leases, the valuation of land and capital gains tax
IR 293	Chattels and capital gains tax
IR 294	Trusts and capital gains tax
IR 295	Relief for gifts and similar transactions
IR 296	Debts and capital gains tax
IR 297	Enterprise investment scheme and capital gains tax
IR 298	Venture capital trusts and capital gains tax
IR 299	Non-resident trusts and capital gains tax
IR 301	Calculation of the increase in tax charge on capital gains from non-resident, dual resident and immigrating trusts

Notice to deliver a return

1.27   An officer of Revenue and Customs may give notice to the taxpayer requiring him to make and deliver a return to enable the officer to establish the amount of any income tax or CGT liability. The notice may request such accounts, statements and documents, relating to information contained in the return, as may reasonably be required (*TMA 1970, ss 8, 12*).

Information required to sent with the return

1.28   The notice may require different information, accounts and statements for different periods or different sources of income. While there is no statutory authority for HMRC to require a taxpayer to provide a list of investments or other assets held at a particular date, HMRC guidance indicates that they may possibly ask for such a list if they are aware that one exists. The return includes a declaration by the person making it to the effect that the return is, to the best of his knowledge, correct and complete (*TCGA 1992, s 8(1A)*).

Reporting limits

1.29   A return of capital gains is required only if certain reporting limits, set out below in relation to individuals, personal representatives and trustees respectively, are exceeded. This is subject, however, to two important exceptions. The capital gains pages should be completed if there are allowable losses or the taxpayer wishes to make a claim or election for the year.

Individuals

1.30   Where the taxpayer's chargeable gains accruing in a year of assessment do not exceed the amount of the annual exemption (£8,800 for 2006/07, £8,500 for 2005/06) and the aggregate amount or value of the consideration for all 'chargeable disposals' (see below) that he made in the year does not exceed four times that annual exemption (ie £35,200 for 2006/07, £34,000 for 2005/06), then a statement to that effect is sufficient to comply with the request for information contained in such a notice. In practice, HMRC appear to regard this requirement as satisfied where a taxpayer who has not made a detailed return of gains did not actually make such a statement in the basic return. HMRC guidance merely says: 'These conditions are reflected in the notes to the Self-Assessment return which explain when the CGT supplementary pages must be completed'.

For this purpose, the amount of chargeable gains accruing in the year is taken to be:

- the amount after reduction for any taper relief due, in a case where no deduction is to be made for allowable losses; and

- the amount before any deduction for allowable losses and before reduction for any taper relief, where a deduction for allowable losses is to be made.

'Chargeable disposals' for the purpose of these reporting limits exclude both disposals on which any gain accruing is not a chargeable gain and 'no gain/no loss' disposals between spouses or civil partners (*TCGA 1992, s 3A(1), (2), (3)*).

Personal representatives

1.31 The above reporting limits are applied to personal representatives for the year of assessment in which the individual concerned died and for the next two years of assessment (*TCGA 1992, s 3A(4)*).

Trustees

1.32 The above rule applies also to trustees of a settlement but the reporting limits are calculated by reference to the reduced annual exemption available to the trustees where appropriate (see **1.16** and **Chapter 8**) (*TCGA 1992, s 3A(5); Sch 1, para 2(6A)*).

Estimates

1.33 A taxpayer who has used estimated figures to calculate gains or losses should:

- tick the relevant box in column B of page CG 1 or CG 2 of the capital gains pages; and

- identify and give reasons for the estimates, either in page CG 1 or in pages CG 4 to CG 6 as appropriate.

Valuations

1.34 Similarly the use of any valuation, where, for example, the allowable expenditure is based on the 31 March 1982 value or there was a transaction with a connected person, should be indicated by ticking the relevant box B. HMRC may check the valuation and in the absence of any agreement the valuation may be referred to the independent General or Special Commissioners.

The taxpayer may ask HMRC before submitting the tax return to carry out a 'post-transaction valuation check', using the form CG 34 available at http://www.hmrc.gov.uk/pdfs/cg34.pdf. Use of this procedure does not change the filing date for the return. HMRC guidance says:

'If we agree your valuations we will not challenge your use of them in your tax return unless there are any important facts affecting them that you have not told us about. Agreement to your valuations does not necessarily mean that we agree the gain or loss. We will not consider the other figures you have used until you make your tax return.

'If we cannot agree your valuations we will suggest alternatives. We use specialist valuers to value some assets, mainly shares, land, goodwill and works of art. You will also be able to discuss your valuations with our valuers. You must file your tax return by the filing date printed on it even if we have not been able to agree your valuations or suggest alternatives. Your return must also tell us about any valuations that we have checked but been unable to agree.'

The taxpayer should indicate in the relevant capital gains pages any transactions that are, or have been, the subject of a valuation check.

Alternatively, it may be appropriate to request a post-transaction ruling on the application of tax law to a transaction. HMRC's code of practice COP 10, 'Information and Advice', sets out the ways in which HMRC will give information or advice to taxpayers. The stated aim is to help taxpayers understand their rights and obligations. HMRC's internal guidance draws a distinction between explaining how HMRC consider tax law should be applied and advising taxpayers how to arrange their personal affairs. Further details are set out in COP 10, available at http://www.hmrc.gov.uk/pdfs/cop10.htm.

Provisional figures

1.35   HMRC advise taxpayers not to delay filing a tax return just because some of the required information is not available. Provisional figures should be provided and identified in the return (by ticking box 23.2 and saying in box 23.9 which figures are provisional). HMRC say that it would help if the taxpayer could say why final figures could not be given and give some indication of when they will be provided.

HMRC's tax return guide warns that a taxpayer who negligently submits a provisional figure that is 'either inaccurate or unnecessary' may be liable to a penalty. A taxpayer who uses provisional figures must have taken 'all reasonable steps' to get the final figures, and must ensure that they are submitted as soon as they are available.

The guide adds: 'You could be charged a penalty if you did not have a good reason for using a provisional figure or you did not take sufficient care to calculate the provisional figure in a reasonable amount. We would not regard pressure of work either on you or your tax advisor, or the complexity of your tax affairs, as reasons for using a provisional figure'.

Filing date

1.36 The return must be delivered to HMRC by the filing date, which is normally 31 January following the end of the relevant year of assessment, ie 31 January 2007 for the year ended 5 April 2006. Where a notice to deliver a return is given after 31 October following the year, the filing date is three months after the date of the notice. However, there is an incentive for taxpayers filing a paper return to do so by 30 September following the end of the year because in that event HMRC undertake to calculate the tax liability. Electronic filing provides users with a tax calculation (*TMA 1970, s 8(1A)*).

Payment of tax

1.37 Broadly speaking, CGT for a year of assessment is payable by 31 January following the end of the year of assessment for which the liability arose. However, a system of interim and final payments means that the position will be more complicated than this appears to be in many cases. The taxpayer is required to make two interim payments (or 'payments on account') of income tax on 31 January during the year of assessment and 31 July following the end of the year of assessment if:

- he is assessed to income tax for the previous year ('assessed' for this purpose includes assessed by the taxpayer in a self-assessment) and the amount assessed exceeds any income tax deducted at source under PAYE or otherwise; and

- the excess is at least £500 and at least 20% of the amount assessed.

The payments on account, calculated as shown above, may be reduced on a claim if the taxpayer believes that his liability will be satisfied by tax deducted at source, or that it will be less than calculated. Class 4 National Insurance contributions are treated as income tax for this purpose. No payments on account are required in respect of CGT.

The taxpayer is required to make a final payment, normally on or before 31 January following the end of the year of assessment, if his total liability to income tax and CGT exceeds the sum of any payments on account and any tax deducted at source. A repayment will be due if the sum of payments on account and any tax deducted at source exceeds the total liability for the year (*TMA 1970, ss 59A, 59B*; *SI 1996/1654*).

Chapter 2

Disposals

INTRODUCTION

2.1 Every gain accruing on the disposal of an asset is a chargeable gain, unless otherwise expressly provided – see the exemptions listed in **1.6–1.10** (*Taxation of Chargeable Gains Act 1992* (*TCGA 1992*), *ss 1, 15*).

Meaning of 'asset'

2.2 All forms of property, wherever they are situated, are assets for CGT purposes. Assets include options, debts, incorporeal property, and currency other than sterling. Property that has been created by the person disposing of it, or has otherwise come to be owned without being acquired, is also an asset (*TCGA 1992, s 21(1)*).

Meaning of 'disposal'

2.3 *TCGA 1992* does not define 'disposal'. HMRC guidance indicates that the word takes its ordinary meaning and that a disposal is 'an occasion when you sell an asset or give it away'. It would include a sale, gift or exchange of an asset, but it would not include a transfer of property by way of security, or the disposal of a liability. HMRC may contend that a series of transactions is so closely linked that, as a matter of legal construction, the transactions should be regarded as a single disposal (CG 10242, CG 12700). The legislation deems certain transactions to be disposals, and it is provided that a 'disposal' includes a part disposal (see **2.4**).

Part disposals

2.4 Any 'part disposal' of an asset is a disposal for CGT purposes. A part disposal occurs where a person makes a disposal and any description of property derived from the asset remains undisposed of. There is also a part disposal of an asset where the disposal itself creates an interest in, or a right over, the asset (eg where a lease is granted by the person holding the freehold interest in land) as well as in the case where the interest or right existed before the disposal (*TCGA 1992, s 21(2)*). Where there is a part disposal, any allowable costs of acquisition and improvement which cannot be wholly attributed to either the part retained or the part disposed of are apportioned by reference to the following formula (*TCGA 1992, s 28(2)*; see also **Chapter 3**):

$$\frac{A}{A+B}$$

Where:

A   is the proceeds received (actual or deemed); and

B   is the market value of the part retained.

Example 2.1—Part disposal

Robert buys a piece of land in April 1986 for £182,000. He subsequently sells half of it to Lesley in May 2006 for £150,000. The remainder of the land, because of its better position, is estimated to be then worth £200,000. The land is a non-business asset for taper relief purposes.

Robert's capital gain is computed as follows:

A = £150,000

B = £200,000

The cost attributable to the part disposed of is:

$$\frac{150,000}{(150,000 + 200,000)} \text{ x } £182,000 = £78,000$$

	£	£
Proceeds of land sold to Lesley		150,000
Less: Cost allocated to part disposed of	78,000	
Indexation allowance £78,000 x 0.665		
(April 1986 to April 1998)	51,870	
		129,870
Gain before taper relief		20,130
Taper relief at 35% (8 years + 1 bonus year)		7,046
Net gain after taper relief		13,084
Less annual exemption		8,800
Robert's chargeable gain for 2006/07		£4,284

The cost allocated to the remaining land, when that is disposed of, will be:

	£
Original cost of all the land	182,000
Less: Cost of part disposal	78,000
Cost of remaining land	£104,000

'Small disposal' proceeds

2.5   Where a capital sum is received for an asset which is not lost or destroyed (see below), the receipt is not treated as a disposal if certain conditions are satisfied (for example, where the proceeds are small compared with the value of an asset). The capital sum is instead deducted from the allowable expenditure on a subsequent disposal.

In practice, 'small' for these purposes means the higher of the following (RI 164):

- 5% of the value of the asset; or

- £3,000.

There are special rules for part disposals of land. Where certain conditions are satisfied, the taxpayer may claim that the part disposal of land does not constitute a disposal for capital gains tax purposes. The disposal proceeds are instead deducted from the cost of the land when calculating a gain on its subsequent disposal. The qualifying conditions are as follows (*TCGA 1992, s 242*):

1   The proceeds on the part disposal of land is:

- not more than 20% of the land's market value; and

- not more than £20,000; or

2   the land is subject to compulsory purchase by an authority and the proceeds received are small (*TCGA 1992, s 243*). The definition of 'small' is:

- not more than 5% of the market value of the entire land; or

- £3,000 or less (irrespective of whether the 5% test is satisfied).

Whilst these limits will stand, the taxpayer can also argue that larger amounts should also be considered as 'small' for a particular case, or that smaller receipts should be treated as a full disposal. In both of the above cases, a claim must be made within one year of 31 January following the tax year in which the transfer is made, or for corporation tax purposes within two years following the accounting period of transfer (*TCGA 1992, ss 242(2A), 243(2A)*).

Example 2.2—Part disposal of land

Cuniliffe owns farmland which cost £134,000 in May 1987. In February 1995, a small plot of land is exchanged with an adjoining landowner for another piece of land. The value placed on the transaction is £18,000. Cuniliffe makes a claim for this transaction not to be treated as a disposal for capital gains tax purposes.

The value of the remaining estate excluding the new piece of land is estimated at £250,000. In May 2006, Cuniliffe sells the whole estate for £300,000.

	£	£
Small land swap in February 1995		
Allowable cost of original land		134,000
Less: Disposal proceeds		18,000
Adjusted allowable cost		£116,000
Allowable cost of additional land		£18,000
Disposal in May 2004		
Disposal proceeds		300,000
Allowable cost:		
Original land	116,000	
Additional land	18,000	134,000
Unindexed gain		166,000
Indexation allowance (to April 1998)		
Original land (£134,000 x 0.596)	79,864	
Additional land (£18,000 x 0.107)	1,926	
	81,790	
Receipt set-off £18,000 x 0.107	1,926	79,864
Chargeable gain 2006/07 (subject to taper relief)		£86,136

2.6 *Disposals*

If Cuniliffe had not claimed that the small disposal should be ignored for capital gains tax purposes the capital gain in 1995 would be:

Disposal in February 1995	£
Disposal proceeds	18,000
Allowable cost:	
$\dfrac{18,000}{18,000 + 250,000}$ x £134,000 =	9,000
Unindexed gain	9,000
Indexation allowance (£9,000 x 0.442)	3,978
Chargeable gain 1994/95	£5,022

The above rules for small part disposals of land do not apply if the allowable expenditure is less than the part disposal proceeds. However, the taxpayer may elect that the costs are deducted from the part disposal proceeds, with none of the expenditure being an allowable deduction on subsequent part disposals. In other words, the gain is treated as in the same way as a disposal of the whole asset. A claim must be made within one year of 31 January following the tax year of the part disposal, or for corporation tax purposes within two years following the accounting period of transfer (*TCGA 1992, s 244*).

Deemed disposals

2.6   The legislation treats assets as having been disposed of in certain circumstances, including the following:

(a)   *Capital sums derived from assets.* A deemed disposal for capital gains tax purposes can arise where a capital sum is derived from an asset, even where the person who pays the capital sum does not acquire the asset (subject to the small disposal exception). The time of disposal in this context is when the capital sum is received (see **2.12**).

(b)   *Negligible value.* Where the value of an asset has become negligible, the owner may claim to be treated as having sold and immediately reacquired it at market value, in order to realise an allowable loss (see **2.10**).

(c)   *Death.* The assets of a deceased individual's estate are deemed to be acquired by the personal representatives at market value on death but are not deemed to be disposed of by the deceased (see **2.9**).

(d)   *Trusts.* Trustees are deemed to dispose of and immediately reacquire assets at market value in certain circumstances, eg where a person becomes absolutely entitled to assets as against the trustees, or if the trustees cease to be resident in the UK (see **2.20**).

(e) *Other deemed disposals*. See also **2.21** for deemed disposals which can arise when chargeable assets are transferred abroad. In addition, anti-avoidance rules ('value shifting') deem a disposal (or a part disposal) of land or shares to take place if certain conditions are satisfied (*s 29*). However, where those provisions apply, there is a corresponding acquisition by the person or persons who receive the value. In addition, deemed disposals between spouses or civil partners are exempt as for disposals of other assets (*s 58*), and relief may be available under other capital gains tax provisions if the relevant conditions are satisfied (eg relief for gifts of business assets within *s 165*). The value shifting rules are broadly designed to prevent value passing from one holding or interest into another without there being any disposal for capital gains purposes. For further commentary, see **Chapter 10**.

No gain, no loss disposals

2.7   Certain disposals are effectively treated as giving rise to neither a gain nor a loss. Examples of no gain/no loss disposals generally include the following:

- disposals between husband and wife (*TCGA 1992, s 58(1)*);

- disposals within the same 75% group of companies (*s 171)(1)*);

- disposals of business assets where a claim is made to roll over the gain against a replacement asset (*s 152(1)(a)*);

- transfers on a company reconstruction (*s 139(1)*);

- on the termination of pre-22 March 2006 (and certain other) interests in possession in settled property by reason of the death of the person so entitled, if the property reverts to the settlor (*s 73(1)(a)*); and

- gifts to charities (*s 257(2)(a)*).

The deemed disposal consideration (and the transferee's acquisition cost) is an amount equal to the original cost plus indexation allowance (if applicable).

Time of disposal

2.8   The general rule is that where an asset is disposed of and acquired under a contract the time of the disposal and acquisition is the time when that contract is made. It is not the time of the conveyance or transfer of the asset (if different). In the case of a conditional contract, the time of disposal and acquisition is the time when the condition is satisfied. This applies in particular to a contract that is conditional on the exercise of an option (*TCGA 1992, s 28*).

There is no statutory definition of what a 'conditional' contract is, and the meaning of the term varies according to context. However, for capital gains tax purposes, a contract is only conditional if:

- the condition has to be satisfied before the contract is performed; and

- it is not something that one of the parties has covenanted to bring about.

A condition which must be satisfied before the contract becomes legally binding is termed a 'condition precedent'. Such a condition must be distinguished from a 'condition subsequent', which is broadly a condition that is not fundamental to the immediate performance of the contract. In such cases, the contract continues to be legally binding. The Capital Gains Manual (at CG 14273) gives an example of a conditional contract, based on the comments of Walton J in *Lyon v Pettigrew* [1985] 58 TC 452:

> 'It would, for example, be possible for a hotelier to make a booking with a tour operator conditionally upon the next Olympic Games being held in London. Then, until it had been decided that the next Olympic Games were going to be held in London, there would be no effective contract: the whole contract would be conditional, the whole liabilities and duties between the parties would only arise when the condition was fulfilled.'

Where a disposal is deemed to arise on the receipt of a capital sum derived from an asset and is listed in (a) to (d) at **2.12**, then the time of disposal is the time when the capital sum is received (*TCGA 1992, s 22*). The general rule for gifts of assets (eg gifts into a trust) is that the date of disposal is the date on which beneficial ownership passes. However, general law principles will determine whether that transfer is effective (eg contracts in respect of land must be evidenced in writing).

Death

2.9   The assets which the deceased was competent to dispose of are deemed not to be disposed of, whether or not they are the subject of a will. The deceased's personal representatives are deemed to acquire the assets at their market value at the date of death.

A disposal by way of *donatio mortis causa* is a lifetime gift that will take effect only if the donor dies. When the donor dies he is not competent to dispose of the relevant assets, so the above rule cannot apply and there is a disposal at the time of death. However, it is provided separately that no chargeable gain accrues on a disposal by way of *donatio mortis causa* (*TCGA 1992, s 62*). See also **Chapter 7**.

ASSETS LOST, DESTROYED OR BECOMING OF NEGLIGIBLE VALUE

2.10   As a general rule, there is a disposal of an asset on the occasion of the entire loss, destruction, dissipation or extinction of the asset. This applies whether or not a capital sum is received by way of compensation or otherwise. If a gain arising on the disposal would have been a chargeable gain, any loss arising will be an allowable loss (*TCGA 1992, ss 16(2), 24(1)*).

The owner of an asset which has become of negligible value cannot claim relief for a capital loss under the normal rules because he has not disposed of the asset. However, the taxpayer may claim to be treated as having sold and immediately reacquired the asset, either at the time of the claim or at some earlier time (see below). The deemed consideration for both the deemed disposal and the deemed reacquisition is the value specified in the claim. The legislation does not define 'negligible' but HMRC regard it as meaning 'next to nothing' (*TCGA 1992, s 24(2)*; CG 13124).

The claim may specify an earlier time for the deemed disposal if the taxpayer owned the asset at that time and it had become of negligible value at that time. The earlier time must not be more than two years before the beginning of the year of assessment in which the claim is made. In the case of a company chargeable to corporation tax, the earlier time must fall within the earliest accounting period ending not more than two years before the date of the claim.

For these purposes a building may be regarded as an asset separate from the land on which it stands. The taxpayer is treated as if he had sold and immediately reacquired the site at its market value (*TCGA 1992, s 24(3)*).

HMRC operate a post-transaction valuation service for capital gains. This service involves the taxpayer completing an application for a post-transaction valuation check (form CG 34). The form may be used for an asset that is the subject of a negligible value claim. Form CG 34 cannot precede the negligible value claim for an asset. However, HMRC will treat the post-transaction valuation check as having been made after the negligible value claim if form CG 34 is submitted at the same time as the claim (CG 13130).

Asset lost or destroyed: replacement asset acquired

2.11   If the asset is lost or destroyed, a capital sum received in compensation for the loss or destruction, or under an insurance policy against the risk of such loss or destruction, gives rise to a disposal as described in **2.12**. However, a form of roll-over relief is available where the taxpayer applies the capital sum in acquiring a replacement asset within one year of receiving that sum, or within a longer period allowed by HMRC. The taxpayer is treated as if:

(a)   the consideration for the disposal of the old asset was reduced to an amount giving rise to no gain and no loss on the disposal; and

(b)   the consideration for the acquisition of the new asset was reduced by the excess of (i) the capital sum received and any residual or scrap value over (ii) the reduced consideration in (a).

Partial relief is available where only part of the capital sum is reinvested in this way. Where the assets concerned are buildings, and the old building is destroyed or irreparably damaged, then for these purposes the old building is treated as lost or destroyed and each building is regarded as an asset separate from the land on which it is stands (or stood) (*TCGA 1992, s 23(4)–(7)*).

Example 2.3—Treatment of compensation

Arthur bought a Hockney painting for £50,000 in February 1991. It was destroyed by fire in October 2006 and Arthur receives £90,000 compensation later in that month. Arthur buys a Hirst painting to replace the Hockney in April 2007 for £100,000. Arthur makes a claim that the disposal of the Hockney painting should be treated as at no gain/no loss and the allowable expenditure on the Hirst painting should be reduced by the amount of excess capital received.

The indexation factor for the period from February 1991 to April 1998 is 0.242.

	£
Cost of destroyed asset	50,000
Indexation allowance (£50,000 x 0.242)	12,100
Deemed consideration	£62,100
Compensation received	90,000
Deemed consideration	62,100
Excess (ie the gain otherwise accruing)	£27,900
Consideration for acquisition of new painting	100,000
Excess as above	27,900
Reduced allowable expenditure on new asset	£72,100

If Arthur only spends £80,000 on the replacement Hirst painting, he can make a claim to reduce the capital gain arising to the amount of compensation not applied.

	£	£
Gain on disposal (as above)		27,900
Compensation monies received	90,000	
Compensation monies expended	80,000	
Excess (being less than the gain of £27,900)	£10,000	
Chargeable gain (as reduced)		10,000
Less taper relief (35%)		3,500
Net chargeable gain 2005/06		£6,500
The chargeable gain is reduced by: (£27,900 – £10,000)		£17,900
The allowable expenditure on the new asset is:		
Actual expenditure on new Hirst painting		80,000
Amount by which chargeable gain is reduced		17,900
Total allowable expenditure		£62,100

CAPITAL SUMS DERIVED FROM ASSETS

2.12   There is a disposal of assets by their owner where a capital sum (which may include 'money's worth', see below) is derived from assets, whether or not the person paying the capital sum acquires an asset. This general rule is applied in particular to the following receipts:

(a)   compensation for damage or injury to assets, or for the loss, destruction or dissipation of assets or for any depreciation (or risk of depreciation) of an asset;

(b)   capital sums received under an insurance policy against risk of damage or injury to (or loss or depreciation of) assets;

(c)   capital sums received in return for forfeiture or surrender of rights (or for refraining from exercising rights); and

(d)   capital sums received as consideration for use or exploitation of assets.

Receipts within (a) would include physical damage to an asset, infringement of copyright and 'injurious affection' of land; (c) would include the release of another person from a contract or restrictive covenant; and (d) would include a lump sum paid to a farmer in return for the granting of easements (*TCGA 1992, s 22(1)*; CG 12942–12945).

31

Capital or revenue?

2.13   Any sum received that is chargeable as income is excluded from CGT. In *Lang v Rice* [1984] 57 TC 80, CA (NI) the taxpayer carried on business in two rented bars in Belfast. They were both destroyed by bombs and neither business was restarted. He claimed compensation from the Northern Ireland Office (NIO) under the *Criminal Injuries to Property (Compensation) Act (Northern Ireland) 1971*. Although the claim referred to 'loss of profit, ie goodwill, 1.5 years' purchase of net profit', in making the payment the NIO specified a sum as 'in respect of the temporary loss of profit for … the length of time allowed for the … business to resume normal trading'. The Inspector of Taxes raised an assessment to CGT on the basis that these were capital sums in respect of compensation for loss of goodwill. The Court of Appeal in Northern Ireland held that there was no reason not to accept at face value the revenue nature of the sums paid, as stated by the NIO.

This case and others relevant to the treatment of compensation receipts as income are discussed in HMRC's Business Income Manual at BIM 40101–40140 (*TCGA 1992, s 37(1)*; CG 12951).

Money's worth

2.14   HMRC regard this phrase (see **2.12**) as taking its ordinary meaning, ie 'anything which … can be recognised as equivalent to, or can be converted to, money'. They will ask (a) whether it can be turned into money, and (b) whether its value can be expressed in money terms (CG 12952–12954).

Capital sum derived from rights

2.15   Compensation may be derived from rights such as statutory rights, contractual rights or rights to take action for compensation or damages, rather than directly from the asset itself.

The decision in *Zim Properties Ltd v Proctor* (1984, 58 TC 371, Ch D) established the general principle that the right to take court action for compensation or damages is an asset for capital gains tax purposes, the disposal of which (eg by negotiated settlement) could result in a capital gain. In that case, a company brought an action against its solicitors alleging that the solicitors had drawn a contract for the sale of land negligently. A compromise agreement was subsequently reached, resulting in a payment to the company by the solicitor's insurers. The Court held that the capital sum was derived from an asset, ie not the land but Zim's right to take action against the solicitors for compensation or damages. The receipt of that capital sum for disposing of the right was therefore taxable.

HMRC subsequently introduced an Extra-Statutory Concession (ESC D33) to remove some of the unintended consequences of this decision. The effect of ESC D33 is broadly that, although the receipt of damages and compensation payments can strictly give rise to a CGT liability, by concession the damages will be treated as derived from the underlying asset if there is one. Hence the receipt will be taxable if the underlying asset is taxable, or exempt if the underlying asset is exempt. Alternatively, the damages will be treated as exempt if there is no underlying asset.

Time of disposal

2.16   In the four cases (a) to (d) in **2.12**, the time of the disposal is the time when the capital sum is received. In other cases of deemed disposals within *TCGA 1992, s 22*, the time of disposal is determined as in **2.8** if the capital sum is received under the terms of a contract for the disposal of an asset. Where there is no such contract, HMRC regard the date on which the sum is received as the time of disposal (CG 12941).

The full disposal proceeds must be brought into account at the time of disposal (ie without any discount for postponement of the right to receive any part of it, and without regard to a risk of any part of it being irrecoverable, or to the right to receive any part of the consideration being contingent (*s 48*). However, there is effectively an entitlement to a form of 'bad debt relief' if a claim is made on the basis that any part of the consideration brought into account has subsequently become permanently irrecoverable (CG 14930–14933).

Capital sum applied in restoring the asset

2.17   Special rules apply where the whole or a part of the capital sum received is used to restore the asset. In any of the following circumstances, the receipt of a capital sum within (a) to (d) above is not treated as a disposal. Instead, the consideration that would have been taken into account on that deemed disposal is deducted from the allowable expenditure on a later disposal of the asset (*TCGA 1992 s 23(1)*), where:

(i)   the whole of the capital sum is applied in restoring the asset;

(ii)   all but a part of the capital sum is applied in this way, and that part is not reasonably required for the purpose and is small compared to the capital sum received; or

(iii) the amount of the capital sum is small in relation to the value of the asset.

The allowable expenditure is fixed by reference to *TCGA 1992, s 38* (see **Chapter 3**). These rules are modified in relation to wasting assets.

Where there is no such allowable expenditure, or the consideration for the deemed disposal is greater than the allowable expenditure, then (ii) and (iii) above do not apply. This means that the deduction from allowable expenditure on a later disposal applies only if the whole of the capital sum is applied in restoring the asset.

Where there is allowable expenditure the taxpayer may elect for the amount of the consideration for the disposal to be reduced by the amount of the allowable expenditure. This would result in none of that expenditure being deducted in computing the gain accruing on a future disposal (*TCGA 1992, s 23(2)*).

In a case where the taxpayer makes no such election and applies in restoring the asset a part of a capital sum within (a) or (b) above that has been derived from an asset that is not lost or destroyed, then he may make a claim for that part of the capital sum not to be treated as consideration for the disposal as provided by *TCGA 1992, s 22*. Instead, the capital sum is deducted from any allowable expenditure deducted in computing a gain on a future disposal of the asset (*TCGA 1992, s 23(3)*).

SPECIAL SITUATIONS

Mortgages and charges

2.18 The following transfers are not treated as involving any acquisition or disposal of an asset:

- the conveyance or transfer of an asset (or of an interest or right in or over the asset) by way of security; and

- the transfer of a subsisting interest or right by way of security in or over an asset (including a retransfer on redemption of the security).

A lender enforcing the security and selling the mortgaged property is treated as acting as nominee for the borrower (*TCGA 1992, s 26(1), (2)*).

Hire-purchase transactions

2.19 Under a hire-purchase transaction a person obtains the use of an asset for a period, and at the end of that period the property in the asset will (or may) pass to him. The hire-purchase transaction is treated as the entire disposal of the asset to that person at the beginning of the hire period. An adjustment will be required if the hire period ends without ownership passing to him (*TCGA 1992, s 27*).

Settlements

2.20   A transfer into a settlement is a disposal of the property that becomes settled property, even if that transferor is a trustee of the settlement or has some interest as a beneficiary (*TCGA 1992, s 70*). See **Chapter 8** regarding this and other rules relating to settled property, including:

- person becoming absolutely entitled to settled property (*TCGA 1992, s 71*);

- termination of life interest on death of the person entitled (*TCGA 1992, s 72*);

- death of life tenant: exclusion of chargeable gain (*TCGA 1992, s 73*);

- disposal of interests in settled property (*TCGA 1992, ss 76, 76A, 76B*);

- trustees ceasing to be resident in UK (*TCGA 1992, s 80*).

Nominees or bare trustees may hold assets for beneficiaries who are absolutely entitled to those assets (or would be entitled but for being an infant or a disabled person). For capital gains tax purposes, disposals by nominees or bare trustees are treated as having been made by the beneficiary for whom they act (*s 60*).

Deemed disposal by non-resident

2.21   There is a deemed disposal and reacquisition of assets at their market value where 'chargeable assets' (see below) that have been used in a business carried on through a UK branch or agency (or a permanent establishment in the case of a company) are transferred abroad, unless the transfer occurs on the occasion of the cessation of the business (*TCGA 1992, s 25(1), (2)*).

Assets are 'chargeable assets' for this purpose if a chargeable gain on their disposal would be chargeable under *TCGA 1992, s 10(1)* or *s 10B* (non-residents with a UK branch, agency or permanent establishment). For further details, and the situation where the business ceases or is transferred, see **Chapter 5**.

Options and deposits

2.22   It is made clear in *TCGA 1992, s 21* that options are assets. In addition, it is provided that the grant of an option is the disposal of an asset (ie the option itself) even in the case where the option is abandoned. In many cases the grant will be treated as part of a larger transaction (see below). The basic rules relating to the grant, exercise and abandonment of options are set out below (*TCGA 1992, s 144(1)*). See also **Chapter 4**.

Exercise of an option

2.23   If an option is exercised, the grant of the option and the transaction taking place on its exercise are treated as a single transaction. Where the option binds the grantor (A) to sell, the consideration for the grant is added to the sale consideration in A's CGT computation. Where the option binds the grantor (A) to buy, then the consideration received by A for that option is deducted from the cost of A's acquisition (*TCGA 1992, s 144(2)*).

Where the person (B) who is entitled to exercise an option does so, there is no disposal by him. The acquisition of the option and the transaction taking place on its exercise are treated as a single transaction. Where the option binds the grantor (A) to sell, the cost of acquiring the option forms part of B's allowable expenditure on acquisition of the asset. Where the option binds the grantor (A) to buy, the cost of the option is treated as a cost incidental to B's disposal to A (*TCGA 1992, s 144(2)*).

Abandonment of an option

2.24   The abandonment of any of the following options is a disposal of the option:

- a quoted option (as defined) to subscribe for shares in a company;
- a traded option or financial option (as defined); or
- an option to acquire assets exercisable by a person intending to use them, if acquired, for the purpose of a trade that he carries on.

The abandonment of any other option by the person entitled to exercise it is not a disposal of an asset by him (*TCGA 1992, s 144(4)*).

Forfeited deposits

2.25   Where a deposit of purchase money for a prospective purchase is forfeited because the transaction is abandoned, there is no disposal by the prospective purchaser and no capital loss can arise. The prospective seller, however, is treated as disposing of an option (*TCGA 1992, s 144(7)*).

Chapter 3

Computation of gains and losses

INTRODUCTION

3.1   The general rules governing the computation of gains and losses accruing on the disposal of assets are set out *TCGA 1992, Pt II*. Every gain is a chargeable gain except where provided otherwise – see **1.6** (*Taxation of Chargeable Gains Act 1992* (*TCGA 1992*), *ss 1, 15*). This chapter summarises the general rules for computing chargeable gains and losses, and **Chapter 4** deals with special rules applying to particular assets.

An indexation allowance, designed to compensate for the effect of inflation, is available to companies in computing chargeable gains for corporation tax purposes. The allowance is also available, in respect of inflation up to April 1998 only, in computing chargeable gains for CGT purposes accruing to individuals, trustees and personal representatives (see **3.59**).

Example 3.1

Colin bought a holiday cottage in April 1993 for £40,000 and sold it in June 2006 for £160,000. Indexation allowance (see **3.59**) at 0.156 is due for the five years from April 1993 to April 1998. Taper relief (see **3.58**) is due at 35% for a non-business asset held for nine years (being eight complete years of ownership after 5 April 1998 plus a bonus year as the asset was acquired before 17 March 1998). Colin has a capital loss brought forward of £5,000 and makes no other disposals in 2006/07. His chargeable gain for 2006/07 is £70,694:

	£	£
Proceeds		160,000
Cost	40,000	
Indexation allowance £40,000 x 0.156	6,240	
		(46,240)
Indexed gain		113,760
Loss brought forward		(5,000)

Net chargeable gains before taper relief	108,760
Taper relief: £108,760 x 35%	(38,066)
Chargeable gain after taper relief	70,694

Interaction with VAT

3.2   The cost for CGT purposes of the acquisition of an asset, and any enhancement expenditure, excludes any VAT where the VAT represents deductible input tax. In any other case the cost for CGT purposes includes the VAT suffered.

If the taxpayer charges VAT on the proceeds of disposal of a chargeable asset, the consideration for the disposal (see **3.3**) excludes the VAT. The treatment of any VAT suffered on expenses relating to the disposal follows the treatment of acquisition and enhancement costs.

CONSIDERATION FOR THE DISPOSAL

3.3   The first step in the computation is to determine the consideration for the disposal. The consideration may be receivable some time after the date of the disposal, but the full amount must be brought into account without any discount for postponement of the right to receive it or the risk that not all of the consideration may be recovered (see **3.22**).

Consideration includes money or money's worth and any assumption by the purchaser of a liability of the person making the disposal. See also the items listed in **3.4** as receipts that can be taken into account for CGT regardless of the exclusion for sums chargeable as income. Consideration also includes the value of any asset received in exchange for the asset disposed of, and the capitalised value of:

- the right to receive income or payments in the nature of income;
- relief from liability, eg to repay a loan;
- the benefit of loans on non-commercial terms; and
- the benefit of rights to obtain goods or services on favourable terms.

Sums chargeable as income

3.4   Sums that are chargeable to tax as income, or taken into account in computing income or profits or gains or losses for income tax purposes, are excluded from CGT. This rule does not preclude the following receipts being taken into account for CGT:

- receipts giving rise to balancing charges or certain other adjustments to income tax capital allowances;

- the capitalised value of a rentcharge, or ground annual, or feu duty; and

- the capitalised value of a right of any other description to income, or to payments in the nature of income over a period, or to a series of such payments (*TCGA 1992, s 37*).

A profit on the disposal of trading stock is included in trading profits and charged to income tax. HMRC consider that the disposal of an asset not normally regarded as trading stock may mark the end of 'an adventure in the nature of trade', in which case any profit is chargeable to income tax. However, see **4.31** regarding assets appropriated to or from trading stock.

An income tax liability may arise under anti-avoidance rules on the disposal of land, including buildings, or an interest in land, or assets such as shares which derive their value from land; or on the sale by an individual of income derived from personal activities. In such a case the gain is not charged to CGT. See also **2.13** regarding the question whether compensation received is chargeable to income tax (*TCGA 1992, ss 15, 16, 775, 776*; CG 10260, CG 14340, CG 14342).

Sums are regarded for this purpose as chargeable to (or taken into account for) income tax purposes as mentioned above if they would be so chargeable (or taken into account) but for the fact that the profits or gains concerned are not chargeable to income tax or that losses are not allowable. Income or profits taxable by deduction at source are treated as chargeable to income tax for this purpose (*TCGA 1992, s 52(2), (3)*).

Market value rule for disposals

3.5   The market value (see below) of an asset is substituted for the actual consideration for the disposal where the taxpayer disposes of the asset:

(a) otherwise than by way of a bargain made at arm's length (see below), and in particular where he disposes of it (i) by way of gift, or (ii) on a transfer into a settlement by the settlor, or (iii) by way of distribution from a company in respect of shares in the company; or

(b) wholly or partly for a consideration that cannot be valued; or

(c) in connection with his own or another's loss of office or employment or diminution of emoluments; or

(d) otherwise in consideration for (or in recognition of) his or another person's services or past services in an office or employment, or any other service rendered to another person (*TCGA 1992, s 17(1)*).

The market value may be substituted even if there is no corresponding acquisition, eg when a debt is repaid. HMRC regard a bargain as made 'at arm's length' if it is a normal commercial transaction in which all of the parties involved try to obtain the best deal for themselves in their particular circumstances. They accept that both a 'bad bargain' and one that is made when one party to the transaction has better information than another party can be bargains made at arm's length. HMRC provide the following examples at CG 14541:

- Mr A may wish to sell his property quickly so that he can go and live in Malta. Mr B knows that Mr A wants to sell his property quickly so he offers him a low price for a quick sale. No-one else makes an offer. Mr A accepts the price Mr B has offered. This may not have been the best possible price which Mr A could have achieved if he had left the property on the market for longer but he was still trying to achieve the best deal possible for himself. It was a bargain made at arm's length.

- Mrs S sells a picture from her attic to Mr T for £500. Mr T, who is an art dealer, knows that the picture is worth £5,000. There has been a bargain with both people trying to get the best deal for themselves. Again, this is a bargain made at arm's length even if the price paid is not the 'market value' of the asset.

A disposal is treated as made otherwise than by way of a bargain made at arm's length – so that the market value rule above applies – if the person acquiring the asset is 'connected' with the person making the disposal (see **3.10**).

Ascertaining market value

3.6   It is the taxpayer's responsibility to make a valuation if one is required, by virtue of his obligation to provide a return of chargeable gains, but HMRC may assist a taxpayer who does not have a professional advisor in preparing a computation (CG 16230).

The general rule is that the 'market value' of an asset is the price that it might reasonably be expected to fetch on a sale in the open market. No reduction is made to take account of the possible impact of all of the assets concerned (eg a holding of shares) being placed on the market at once.

Where the value of an asset has been ascertained for inheritance tax purposes, that valuation fixes its market value for CGT as at the date of death. HMRC consider that a value has been ascertained only if their Capital Taxes Office has used a valuation to arrive at the final inheritance tax liability, and the amount of that liability was dependent on that valuation (*TCGA 1992, ss 272(1), (2), 274*; CG 32220–32230).

Quoted shares and securities

3.7   The market value of shares or securities quoted on the Stock Exchange Daily Official List is generally taken to be the lower of the figures found in (a) and (b) below, or the figure found in (a) where there were no recorded bargains on the relevant date:

(a)   the 'quarter-up value', ie the lower of the two prices quoted on the relevant date plus a quarter of the difference between them;

(b)   the midpoint between the highest and lowest prices at which bargains were recorded for that date, ignoring bargains at special prices.

This measure of market value does not apply where 'special circumstances' have affected the quoted prices. If the London Stock Exchange is closed on the relevant date, the above exercise is to be done for both the latest previous date and the earliest subsequent date on which it is open. The lower of the two measures found in this way is taken to be the market value (*TCGA 1992, s 272(3), (4)*).

Unit trust holdings

3.8   Where the buying and selling prices of units in unit trusts are published regularly, the market value is the lower published price (ie the price that the managers will pay to someone wishing to sell units). If no prices were published on the relevant date, the lower of the latest prices published before the disposal is taken (*TCGA 1992, s 272(5)*).

Unquoted shares and securities

3.9   The market value of shares and securities that are not quoted on a 'recognised stock exchange' (see below) when their value is to be fixed is the price that the shares, etc might reasonably be expected to fetch on a sale in the open market. For this purpose it is to be assumed that, in such an open market, any prospective buyer would have available all the information that a prudent prospective buyer might reasonably require if he were proposing to buy it from a willing vendor by private treaty and at arm's length (*TCGA 1992, s 273*).

The shares valuation division of HMRC Capital Taxes is responsible for checking and negotiating the valuation of unquoted shares and certain other assets including the goodwill of a business. The district valuer at the Valuation Office Agency deals with the valuation of land and buildings in the UK.

A 'recognised stock exchange' means the Stock Exchange and any such stock exchange outside the UK that is designated by HMRC as a recognised stock exchange for the purpose of *ICTA 1988, s 841 (TCGA 1992, s 288(1))*. HMRC has published a list of such exchanges at www.hmrc.gov.uk/fid/rse.htm.

Disposals to connected persons

3.10   A disposal is treated as made otherwise than by way of a bargain made at arm's length – so that the market value rule in **3.5** applies – if the person acquiring the asset is 'connected' (see **3.16**) with the person making the disposal.

See **3.67** regarding the special rules for transactions between spouses and civil partners and **3.11** regarding assets disposed of in a series of transactions.

There must be both a disposal and a corresponding acquisition for this rule to apply. It cannot apply, for example, to an issue of shares by a company, or the purchase by a company of its own shares (*TCGA 1992, s 18(1), (2)*; CG 14570).

The market value of the asset, to be used in place of the actual consideration, is adjusted where the asset is subject to a right or restriction such as a restrictive covenant (*TCGA 1992, s 18(6)–(8)*).

Assets disposed of in a series of transactions

3.11   If assets are disposed of in a series of transactions to one or more connected persons, anti-avoidance rules may operate to increase the deemed consideration for one or more of the disposals. The rules are designed to prevent an advantage being gained where the total value placed on a number of separate gifts of shares to relatives, for example, would be less than the value that would apply to a single gift of all of the shares (*TCGA ss 19, 20*).

The rules apply where:

- a person disposes of assets, to a person (or persons) connected with him, by means of a series of linked transactions, ie two or more 'material transactions' that are linked; and

- the 'original market value' of the assets disposed of by any of those transactions is less than the 'appropriate portion' of the 'aggregate market value' of the assets disposed of by all the transactions – all of these terms are defined below.

43

In these circumstances the consideration for the disposal effected by any linked transaction is deemed to be equal to the appropriate portion of the aggregate market value. However, this rule does not affect the operation of the no gain/no loss rule for transfers between spouses or civil partners (see **3.67**) (*TCGA 1992, s 19(1), (2)*).

A 'material transaction' is a transaction by way of gift or otherwise, and two or more material transactions are linked if they occur within a period of six years ending on the date of the last transaction (*TCGA 1992, s 19(3)*).

This rule applies when a series of linked transactions is created by a second material transaction and it applies again, with any necessary adjustments being made, when an existing series is extended by a further material transaction. An adjustment may be required if an earlier transaction ceases to form part of the series because of the six-year rule (*TCGA 1992, s 19(4)*).

Original market value

3.12   The original market value is determined as follows where there is a series of linked transactions:

(a)   if the transaction is the most recent in the series of transactions, the 'original market value' of the assets disposed of is the market value that would be deemed to be the consideration in the absence of *TCGA 1992, s 19*; and

(b)   for any other transaction in the series, the original market value of the assets disposed of is the value which, prior to the transaction in (a), was (or would have been) deemed to be the consideration for that transaction, whether as a result of *TCGA 1992, s 19* applying or under any other provision (*TCGA 1992, s 20(3)*).

Appropriate portion

3.13   The 'appropriate portion' of the aggregate market value (see below) of the assets disposed of by all the transactions in a series is the portion of that value that it is reasonable to apportion to the assets actually disposed of by the particular transaction (*TCGA 1992, s 20(4)(b)*).

Aggregate market value

3.14   The aggregate market value of the assets disposed of by all the transactions in a series of linked transactions is the market value that would have been attributed to all of those assets if, considering all of them together, they had been disposed of by one disposal occurring at the time of the transaction (*TCGA 1992, s 20(4)(a)*).

When the assets are considered 'together' they are considered as a group, holding or collection of assets each of which retains its separate identity. However, they are also considered as brought together to form a single asset (or number of assets) distinct from the assets comprised in the individual transactions, where this would give a higher market value (*TCGA 1992, s 20(5)*).

Some of the assets disposed of in a series of linked transactions may have been acquired after the time of the first transaction. In such a case the aggregate market value is apportioned to each transaction without regard to assets acquired after the time of that transaction, unless the assets were acquired by means of a no gain/no loss transfer within *TCGA 1992, s 171*.

The number of assets taken into account is limited to the maximum number held by the taxpayer at any time in the period covered by the series, ie beginning immediately before the first of the transactions and ending immediately before the last. This is modified where a company disposed of any assets on a no gain/no loss transfer to a company in the same group before the time of the first transaction in the series. In that event the maximum number of assets taken into account is determined as if that transfer had occurred after the first transaction in the series (*TCGA 1992, s 20(6), (7)*).

If the assets disposed of are securities – including any assets of a nature to be dealt in without identifying the particular assets disposed of or acquired – they are identified with assets acquired on an earlier date (rather than with assets acquired on a later date) on the occasion of each disposal (*TCGA 1992, s 20(8), (9)*).

Example 3.2

Richard owned 10,000 shares in an unquoted company. He made the following gifts to his son. The aggregate market value of 6,000 shares at the date of each gift is shown in the third column of the table:

Transferred in	Number of shares	Value of 6,000 shares	Portion of market value
October 2004	2,000	£12,000	£4,000
October 2006	4,000	£36,000	£24,000
Total	6,000		

The appropriate portion of the aggregate market value is computed thus:

October 2004: 2,000 / 6,000 x £12,000 = £4,000

45

3.15   *Computation of gains and losses*

October 2006: 4,000 / 6,000 x £36,000 = £24,000

If the company is Richard's personal company he may be able to claim hold-over relief (see **Chapter 13**).

Groups of companies

3.15   A transfer of assets between members of a group of companies is not a material transaction if it is a 'no gain/no loss' transfer by virtue of *TCGA 1992, s 171* (*TCGA 1992, s 19(5)*).

An anti-avoidance rule is designed to prevent a group circumventing *TCGA 1992, s 19* by having one company transfer assets to other group companies under the no gain/no loss rule in *TCGA 1992, s 171* and then arranging for the assets to be transferred to connected persons outside the group (*TCGA 1992, s 19(6)*; CG 14702).

Connected persons

3.16   The rules for determining whether one person is connected with another (so that those persons are 'connected with one another') are set out in *TCGA 1992, s 286* and summarised below.

Individuals

3.17   A person is connected with an individual if that person is:

- the individual's spouse or civil partner;
- a relative of the individual;
- the spouse or civil partner of a relative of the individual;
- a relative of the individual's spouse or civil partner; or
- the spouse or civil partner of a relative of the individual's spouse or civil partner.

A 'relative' for this purpose is a brother, sister, ancestor or lineal descendant. The term excludes, for example, uncles, aunts, nephews and nieces (*TCGA 1992, s 286(2)*).

HMRC's Capital Gains Manual provides a diagram showing all of the people who are connected with an individual. It points out that death, divorce or the dissolution of a civil partnership can lead to persons other than the former spouse or civil partner ceasing to be connected with an individual (CG 14583).

Trustees

3.18   The trustee of a settlement is connected with:

● any individual who is a settlor in relation to the settlement;

● any person connected with such an individual; and

● any body corporate that is connected (see below) with that settlement.

A body corporate is connected with a settlement if it is a close company (or would be a close company if it were UK resident) and its participators include the trustees of the settlement; or it is controlled by such a company. Any connection between the trustee and the settlement other than in his capacity as trustee is ignored (*TCGA, s 286(3), (3A)*).

Business partners

3.19   A person is connected with:

● any person with whom he is in partnership; and

● the spouse or civil partner or a relative of any individual with whom he is in partnership.

However, this rule does not apply in relation to acquisitions or disposals of partnership assets pursuant to bona fide commercial arrangements (*TCGA 1992, s 286(4)*). Partnerships are examined further in **Chapter 6**.

Companies

3.20   A company is connected with another company:

● if the same person has control of both, or (i) a person has control of one and (ii) persons connected with him (or he and persons connected with him) have control of the other company; or

● if a group of two or more persons has control of each company, and the groups either consist of the same persons or could be regarded as consisting of the same persons by treating (in one or more cases) a member of either group as replaced by a person connected with him.

A company is connected with another person if (i) that person has control of it, or (ii) that person and persons connected with him together have control of it.

In addition, any two or more persons acting together to secure or exercise control of a company are treated as (i) connected with one another in relation to that company, and (ii) connected with any person acting on the directions of any of them to secure or exercise control of the company. HMRC consider that it is not sufficient for the persons to have control of the company – they have to 'act in some way' to control it – but exercising control could include refraining from voting in a particular way. Directors who are connected with each other under this rule are 'connected persons' only in relation to their transactions with the company. The question whether they are connected in relation to transactions between themselves is a separate issue (*TCGA 1992, s 286(5), (6), (7)*; CG 14622–14623).

Losses

3.21   A loss accruing on the disposal of an asset by the taxpayer (A) to a connected person (B) is not deductible from chargeable gains generally, under the normal rules for allowable losses (see **3.48**). It is deductible only from a chargeable gain accruing to A on another disposal to B at a time when A and B are connected. HMRC guidance refers to such losses as 'clogged losses' (*TCGA 1992, s 18(3)*; CG 14561).

This restriction is waived for a gift in settlement if the gift – and the income from it – is wholly or primarily applicable for educational, cultural or recreational purposes, so long as the persons benefiting are confined to members of an association and most of them are not connected persons. The restriction does not affect the transfer of trustees' unused losses to a beneficiary on the occasion of the beneficiary becoming absolutely entitled to the settled property (*TCGA 1992, s 18(4)*; CG 37207).

If A's first disposal to B in the above scenario is the grant of an option to enter into a sale or other transaction, and the option holder (B) disposes of the option, any loss accruing to B on the disposal of the option is allowable only if the disposal is made at arm's length to a person who is not connected with B (*TCGA 1992, s 18(5)*).

Delayed or irrecoverable consideration

3.22   The consideration for a disposal is taken into account:

- without any discount for postponement of the right to receive any part of it; and

- in the first instance, without regard to either (i) a risk of any part of the consideration being irrecoverable, or (ii) the right to receive any part of it being contingent.

An adjustment is made, by way of discharge or repayment of tax or otherwise, if any part of the consideration taken into account in this way proves later to be irrecoverable (*TCGA 1992, s 48(1)*; CG 14933).

Exception in respect of loan relationships

3.23   Changes to the 'manufactured interest' regime (enacted in *Finance (No 2) Act 2005*) included a consequential change to the above rule for companies. It no longer applies with effect from 20 July 2005 to consideration consisting of rights under a 'creditor relationship' where a company becomes a party to such a relationship as a result of the disposal. In such a case, the amount to be taken into account is the 'fair value' of the creditor relationship. 'Creditor relationship' and 'fair value' both take their meaning from *Finance Act 1996 (FA 1996), s 103(1)* (*TCGA 1992, s 48(2), (3)*).

Contingent liabilities

3.24   When an asset (typically, a holding of shares in a company) is sold, the vendor may provide warranties or representations to compensate the purchaser if, for example, the asset does not meet certain requirements or there are tax liabilities in addition to those disclosed to the purchaser at the time of the disposal. The liability is contingent on there being a breach of the warranty, etc. It is specifically provided that no allowance is made to the vendor in the first instance, when the gain is computed, for:

(a)   any liability, remaining with or assumed by the person (B) assigning a lease, that is contingent on the assignee's (C's) default in respect of liabilities assumed by C either at the time of the assignment or subsequently – eg where the original lessee B may remain liable to account to his immediate lessor (A) in the event of a breach of covenant by C;

(b)   any contingent liability of the person making the disposal in respect of a covenant for quiet enjoyment or other obligation as vendor of land (or of any estate or interest in land) or as a lessor;

(c)   any contingent liability in respect of a warranty or representation made on a disposal (by way of sale or lease) of any property other than land.

If such a contingent liability is enforced, the payment made is deducted from the consideration for the disposal and an adjustment to the vendor's tax liability is made by discharge or repayment of tax, or by means of an increased loss available to be carried forward. If the contingent liability ultimately paid exceeds the consideration received on the disposal, the consideration is reduced to nil and no relief is available to the vendor for the excess. In practice, HMRC accept that this treatment may be extended to a payment made under an indemnity (as opposed to a warranty or representation) given by the vendor to the purchaser (*TCGA 1992, s 49*; ESC D33, para 13; CG 14805, CG 14807).

By concession, where the disposal is a sale of shares in exchange for an issue of shares or debentures other than qualifying corporate bonds and the new asset is treated as acquired at the same time as the old asset, HMRC allow the vendor to treat his payment as consideration given for the new shares or debentures. The purpose of the concession, which applies only to cases within (c) above, is to provide relief for the payment where there is no disposal of the old asset because of the way in which the rules concerning share reorganisations in *TCGA 1992 ss 135* and *136* operate (ESC D52; CG 14818–14822).

Disposals outside the terms of *TCGA 1992, s 49*

3.25   Where the disposal is made subject to a contingent liability to which (a) to (c) in **3.24** above do not apply, the consideration for the disposal is reduced by the value of the contingent liability and there is no adjustment if and when the liability is enforced. This was established in *Randall v Plumb* [1975] 50 TC 392, Ch D.

The purchaser

3.26   So far as the purchaser is concerned, his receipt under the terms of the warranty, etc represents a capital sum derived from an asset (see **2.12**). HMRC guidance indicates that in practice the purchaser's acquisition cost may be reduced by the amount received, but any excess over that cost will be taxable (CG 14808).

Deferred or contingent consideration

3.27   As indicated in **3.22**, the consideration for a disposal must be brought into account without any discount for postponement of the right to receive it. The first step to consider, in the event that part of the consideration is to be deferred, is whether the amounts to be received by the vendor in the future are 'ascertainable'.

Ascertainable deferred consideration

3.28   The full amount of any deferred consideration the amount of which can be ascertained is treated as part of the consideration for the disposal, without any discount for postponement of payment (*TCGA 1992, s 48(1)*). However, the

CGT may be paid in instalments where the consideration is payable over a period exceeding 18 months (beginning not earlier than the time of the disposal) (see **3.35**).

The amount of any deferred consideration is ascertainable if it is either known at the time of disposal or capable of being calculated by reference to information known and events that have occurred by that time. HMRC provide the following examples of ascertainable deferred consideration:

- The agreement for the disposal provides for a consideration of £300,000, of which £100,000 is payable on completion and £200,000 will be payable in four annual instalments of £50,000.

- The agreement for the disposal of a business provides for a consideration of £100,000 and a sum equal to half of the taxable profits of the business for the year ended on the date of disposal payable nine months after the date of the contract (CG 14882).

Payments that are ascertainable but are contingent, ie they depend on the occurrence of some future event, are treated in the same way as ascertainable amounts that are not contingent (*TCGA 1992, s 48(1)*). Terms stipulating a ceiling on the amount of deferred consideration do not make the amount of that consideration ascertainable (CG 14883, CG 14889).

Unascertainable deferred consideration

3.29 Where the amount of deferred consideration cannot be ascertained, the value of the right to receive that consideration is treated as part of the consideration for the disposal, as established in *Marren v Ingles* [1980] 54 TC 76, HL. The House of Lords held that the right to the deferred consideration was a chose in action and that when the deferred consideration was received there was a disposal of an asset, namely the chose in action, within *TCGA 1992, s 22* (capital sums derived from assets, see **2.12**).

The amount of any deferred consideration is unascertainable if the events or circumstances fixing that amount do not occur or exist at the time of the disposal. HMRC provide the following examples of unascertainable deferred consideration:

- The agreement for the sale of shares in a company provides for an initial payment of £100,000 plus three further payments equal to the excess of the company's profits over £300,000 in each of the three years following the date of the contract.

- The agreement for the sale of land provides for a consideration of a capital sum payable in three annual instalments to be calculated by reference to the tonnage of landfill dumped on that site in the three years after the date of the contract (CG 14888).

Each receipt of consideration gives rise to a disposal, or part disposal, of the right to future consideration. The value of the right acquired at the time of the original disposal is taken to be the acquisition value for the purpose of the CGT computation, and in the case of any part disposal it is necessary to value the right to the remaining future consideration (following the rules for part disposals described in **3.46**).

If any part of the unascertainable deferred consideration becomes 'irrecoverable', no relief is available under *TCGA 1992, s 48(1)* (see **3.22**) because, instead of receiving quantifiable consideration at the time of the disposal, the vendor in this situation received a right which was valued at that time in computing the gain on that disposal. However, a loss may arise on the disposal of the right (see **3.30**).

Election to carry back loss on disposal of right

3.30   A loss may accrue on the disposal of the right to unascertainable deferred consideration (see **3.29**), where the value of the right – which forms the acquisition value in the CGT computation – exceeds the consideration ultimately received. Where such a loss accrues after 9 April 2003, the taxpayer may elect to carry it back for set-off against the gain accruing on the disposal of the asset in return for which the right was received. This option is only available to taxpayers within the charge to CGT; it is not available to companies subject to corporation tax (*TCGA 1992, s 279A*).

The form of the election, which is irrevocable, is set out in *TCGA 1992, s 279D*. In many cases the effect of an election will be reasonably straightforward, but several complications can arise and detailed guidance is provided in HMRC's Capital Gains Manual at CG 15082–15122. The election is available if:

(a)   the right was acquired wholly or partly by the taxpayer as the whole or part of the consideration for a disposal (the 'original disposal') by him of another asset (the 'original asset');

(b)   the year of the original disposal was earlier than the year of disposal of the right;

(c)   when the taxpayer acquired the right there was no corresponding disposal of it; and

(d)   the right is a right to unascertainable consideration (*TCGA 1992, s 279A(2)*).

Where the taxpayer disposes of the right and an allowable loss accrues (under the normal rules) on that disposal, and the disposal takes place in a year of assessment in which the taxpayer is within the charge to CGT (the 'year of loss'), then – subject to the two conditions mentioned below – he may elect for the loss to be treated as accruing in the year of the earlier disposal (*TCGA 1992, s 279A(1)*).

Condition 1

3.31   The first condition is that a chargeable gain accrued to the taxpayer (or would have accrued to him but for a claim to deferral relief under either the enterprise investment scheme or the venture capital trust scheme) on any one or more of the following events:

- the original disposal;
- an earlier disposal of the original asset by the taxpayer in the year of the original disposal;
- a later disposal of the original asset by the taxpayer in a year earlier than the year of disposal of the right to future consideration.

This condition is modified where the right was acquired in consideration for more than one disposal (*TCGA 1992, s 279A(3), (4)*).

Condition 2

3.32   The second condition is that a chargeable gain accrued to the taxpayer as described in either (a) or (b) below in the 'eligible year' (ie a year of assessment earlier than the 'year of loss' but not earlier than 1992/93), and a 'relevant amount' remains on which CGT is chargeable for that year:

(a)   a chargeable gain meeting condition 1 above; or

(b)   a chargeable gain that would have met condition 1 if it had not been deferred under the reliefs for investment in the enterprise investment scheme or the venture capital trust scheme, where that gain was treated as accruing at a later time by virtue of a chargeable event – such a gain is called, for this purpose, a 'revived gain'.

There is a 'relevant amount' remaining for a year of assessment if there remains (ignoring the effect of the election) an amount on which the taxpayer is chargeable to CGT after taking account of any previous elections made by the taxpayer and after excluding certain trust gains assessed on the taxpayer (against which losses cannot be set) (*TCGA 1992, s 279A(5), (6), (7)*).

Definitions, etc

3.33   Various definitions and further conditions are set out in *TCGA 1992, s 279B*. A key condition is that a right is a right to unascertainable consideration if, and only if:

- it is a right to consideration the amount or value of which is unascertainable at the time when the right is conferred; and

- that amount or value is unascertainable at that time because it is referable, wholly or partly, to matters which are uncertain at that time because they have not yet occurred.

Effect of election

3.34 The effect of the election is set out in *TCGA 1992, s 279C*. Broadly, the rules are designed to ensure that any losses already set against gains accruing in the earlier year are not disturbed.

Payment of CGT in instalments

3.35 The general rules for payment of CGT are set out in **1.37**. However, CGT may be paid in instalments if all or part of the consideration taken into account in the computation of the gain is payable by instalments over a period longer than 18 months and beginning not earlier than the time of the disposal. If the taxpayer opts for payment by instalments, HMRC may allow payment of CGT over a period of up to eight years, ending not later than the time when the last of the instalments of consideration is payable. The taxpayer does not need to demonstrate hardship in order to pay CGT in instalments – this requirement was removed following the introduction of self-assessment (*TCGA 1992, s 280*).

Due dates for payment

3.36 HMRC normally expect the vendor to pay instalments of CGT equal to 50% of each instalment of consideration due (without any deduction for incidental costs of disposal) until the total CGT liability has been paid.

- Where instalments of consideration fall due on or before the normal due date for the payment of the tax, the corresponding instalments of tax are payable on that normal due date.

- The instalments of tax relating to later instalments of consideration will be payable at the time when the vendor is contractually entitled to receive that consideration, but HMRC are likely to seek to agree a schedule whereby the instalments of tax are paid at intervals of at least six months (CG 14912).

ALLOWABLE EXPENDITURE

3.37   Three categories of expenditure are allowable as a deduction from the consideration in computing a chargeable gain or loss. These are:

- the costs of acquiring (or providing) the asset, including certain incidental costs (see **3.39**);

- the costs of enhancing the asset's value, and any costs of establishing, preserving or defending title to it (see **3.40**); and

- certain incidental costs of disposal (see **3.41**).

No payment of interest may be deducted. Any deemed disposal and reacquisition of an asset cannot give rise to a deduction for assumed incidental costs. No deduction is allowed more than once in the computation of a gain (*TCGA 1992, ss 38(1), (3), (4), 52(1)*).

Expenditure that is, or would be, allowable in computing trading income chargeable to income tax is not allowable (see **3.42**). Special rules apply to 'wasting assets' (see **4.22**).

Costs of acquisition

Consideration for the acquisition

3.38   This is the amount or value of the consideration, in money or money's worth, given by the taxpayer – or on his behalf – wholly and exclusively for the acquisition of the asset. If he did not acquire the asset – for example, where goodwill or copyright is created by the taxpayer himself – the allowable expenditure is any expenditure wholly and exclusively incurred by him in providing the asset (*TCGA 1992, s 38(1)(a)*).

Incidental costs of acquisition

3.39   These are the incidental costs to the taxpayer of the acquisition, as specified below:

(a)   expenditure wholly and exclusively incurred by him for the purposes of the acquisition, being (i) the costs (including stamp duties) of the transfer or conveyance of the asset, and (ii) any fees, commission or remuneration paid for professional services of a surveyor, valuer, auctioneer, accountant, agent or legal advisor; and

(b)   the costs of advertising to find a seller (*TCGA 1992, s 38(1)(a), (2)*).

No deduction is allowed for expenditure by the purchaser in transporting a chattel from the point of acquisition (CG 15260).

Costs of enhancement, etc

3.40   These are the amounts of:

(a)   expenditure wholly and exclusively incurred on the asset, by the taxpayer or on his behalf, for the purpose of enhancing its value, so long as the asset's state or nature at the time of the disposal reflects that expenditure (see below); and

(b)   expenditure wholly and exclusively incurred by the taxpayer in establishing, preserving or defending his title to, or to a right over, the asset (*TCGA 1992, s 38(1)(b)*).

With regard to (a) above, Lord Emslie observed in *Aberdeen Construction Group Ltd v CIR* [1978] 52 TC 281, HL that what the provision was looking for, as the result of relevant expenditure, was 'an identifiable change for the better in the state or nature of the asset'. This change must be a change distinct from the enhancement of value, he added. HMRC regard the time of the disposal for this purpose as the date of completion and not the date of the contract (CG 15185).

TCGA 1992, s 38(1)(b) does not refer (in the way that *TCGA 1992, s 38(1)(a)* refers) to consideration in money or money's worth, but the High Court held in *Chaney v Watkis* [1986] 58 TC 707, Ch D that money's worth given (in the form of an agreement to provide a tenant with rent-free accommodation) for the purpose of enhancing the value of an asset was allowable as a deduction.

However, HMRC may seek to challenge a deduction for money's worth where the recipient is connected with the taxpayer or there are other grounds for suspecting that enhancing the asset's value may not have been the only purpose of the transaction. *Oram v Johnson* [1980] 53 TC 319, Ch D established that 'expenditure' means money, or money's worth, in the sense of something which diminishes the total assets of the person making the expenditure. It does not, therefore, include the value of an individual's own skill and labour.

Incidental costs of disposal

3.41   These are the incidental costs to the taxpayer of the disposal, as specified below:

(a) expenditure wholly and exclusively incurred by him for the purposes of the disposal, being (i) the costs (including stamp duties) of the transfer or conveyance of the asset, and (ii) any fees, commission or remuneration paid for professional services of a surveyor, valuer, auctioneer, accountant, agent or legal adviser;

(b) the costs of advertising to find a buyer; and

(c) costs reasonably incurred in making any valuation or apportionment required in computing the gain, including establishing market value where required for the purposes of *TCGA 1992* (*TCGA 1992, s 38(1)(c), (2)*).

The cost of the transfer or conveyance of a chattel would include the vendor's costs of transporting it to the point of sale (CG 15260). The costs mentioned in (c) include costs incurred for the purposes of rendering a tax return or for the purposes of a post-transaction valuation check (see **1.34**) in advance of submission of the return, but they exclude costs of resolving valuation disputes with HMRC (CG 15261).

Expenditure allowable in computing income

3.42 No deduction is available, in computing chargeable gains, for any of the following expenditure, irrespective of how the benefit of the deductions mentioned is (or would be) obtained:

(a) expenditure allowable as a deduction in computing the profits or losses of a trade, profession or vocation for income tax purposes;

(b) expenditure allowable as a deduction in computing any other income or profits or gains or losses for income tax purposes; or

(c) expenditure that would be allowable as a deduction in computing any losses but for an insufficiency of income or profits or gains (*TCGA 1992, s 39(1)*).

Expenditure that would have been deductible in computing the profits or losses of a trade, had the asset disposed of been a fixed asset used for that trade, is not deductible in computing a chargeable gain (*TCGA 1992, s 39(2)*).

Example 3.3

Mrs Gold inherited two cottages in 1980. In 1985 she converted the properties into one house and she let the house until March 2007, when it was sold. She incurred the following expenses which are treated as deductions from the rental income (for income tax purposes) or from the proceeds of the sale (for CGT purposes) as shown:

Expenditure	Income Tax	CGT
	£	£
Market value at 31 March 1982		1,000
Legal costs to establish the property boundary		2,500
Planning permission to convert cottages to one		200
Conversion costs		20,000
Drawing up tenancy agreements	500	
Commission to letting agent	1,500	
Decoration of interior		2,000
Replacement of front door	400	
Double glazed windows (an improvement)		5,000
New carpets and curtains (sold with property)		3,000
Estate agents fees and commission		2,400
Replacement of hot water system (a repair)	1,400	

In *Emmerson v Computer Time International Ltd* (*in liquidation*) [1977] 50 TC 628, CA, a payment of arrears of rent, made in order to obtain the landlord's consent to an assignment of a lease, was held to be rent paid in respect of a fixed asset of the trade and was not deductible in computing the chargeable gain.

Sums are regarded for this purpose as chargeable to (or taken into account for) income tax if they would be so chargeable (or taken into account) but for the fact that the profits or gains concerned are not chargeable to income tax or that losses are not allowable. Income or profits taxable by deduction at source are treated as chargeable to income tax (*TCGA 1992, s 52(2), (3)*).

These rules do not deny a deduction for expenditure qualifying for capital allowances, but any capital loss arising may be restricted by reference to such allowances (see **3.55**).

Expenditure reimbursed out of public funds

3.43   Any expenditure met (or to be met) directly or indirectly by the Crown or UK or other government, public or local authority is to be excluded from the computation of a gain (*TCGA 1992, s 50*). If, on a disposal of the asset, the taxpayer is required to repay all or part of a grant out of the proceeds of sale, or can demonstrate that there has been a corresponding reduction in the amount of a later grant, then by concession HMRC allow the consideration received on the disposal to be reduced by the amount of the repayment (ESC D53).

Market value rule for acquisitions

3.44   The market value of an asset (determined as set out in **3.6**) is substituted for the actual consideration given for the acquisition where the taxpayer acquires the asset:

(a)   otherwise than by way of a bargain made at arm's length (see **3.5**), and in particular where he acquires it (i) by way of gift, or (ii) on a transfer into a settlement by a settlor, or (iii) by way of distribution from a company in respect of shares in the company;

(b)   wholly or partly for a consideration that cannot be valued;

(c)   in connection with his own or another's loss of office or employment or diminution of emoluments; or

(d)   otherwise in consideration for (or in recognition of) his or another person's services or past services in an office or employment, or any other service rendered to another person (*TCGA 1992, s 17(1)*).

However, market value is not substituted on an acquisition if there is no corresponding disposal of the asset and:

• there is no consideration in money or money's worth; or

• the amount or value of the consideration is less than the asset's market value (*TCGA 1992, s 17(2)*).

Where a company issues its own shares, there is no disposal corresponding to the shareholder's acquisition. The above exception applies only if no consideration is given or the consideration is less than market value. The market value is substituted, therefore, if the consideration given is higher than the market value. The effect of this rule is that the lower of the actual consideration and market value is taken in a case where there is an acquisition but no corresponding disposal (CG 14551, CG 14553).

Acquisitions from connected persons

3.45   The acquisition is treated as made otherwise than by way of a bargain made at arm's length – so that the market value rule in **3.44** applies – if the person acquiring the asset is 'connected' with the person making the disposal. See **3.16** as to whether persons are connected with one another; **3.21** regarding restrictions on the use of losses accruing on transactions between connected persons; and **3.67** regarding the special rules for transactions between spouses and civil partners (*TCGA 1992, s 18*).

Part disposals

3.46   A part disposal occurs where a person makes a disposal and any description of property derived from the asset remains undisposed of. There is also a part disposal of an asset where the disposal itself creates an interest in, or a right over, the asset (eg where a lease is granted by the person holding the freehold interest in land) as well as in the case where the interest or right existed before the disposal (*TCGA 1992, s 21(2)*).

If the taxpayer disposes of an interest or right in or over an asset, or makes any disposal of an asset which leaves any description of property derived from that asset undisposed of, the allowable expenditure attributable to the asset is apportioned. The apportionment is made for the purpose of computing the chargeable gain on (i) the part disposal, and (ii) any future disposal of the part retained (*TCGA 1992, s 42(1)*).

The fraction of the allowable expenditure that is to be deducted in computing the gain on the part disposal is:

$$\frac{A}{A + B}$$

where A is the amount or value of the consideration for the disposal (see **3.3**) and B is the market value of the property retained. The remaining allowable expenditure is then attributed to the part retained. However, if on the facts any of the allowable expenditure is wholly attributable either to the part of the disposed of or to the part retained, that amount is allocated accordingly instead of being apportioned (*TCGA 1992, s 42(2), (4)*). Special rules apply to part disposals of land (see **4.9**).

This apportionment is made before applying any restriction of capital losses by reference to capital allowances (provided by *TCGA 1992, s 41*). On a subsequent disposal of the part of the asset retained, the capital allowances or renewals allowances to be taken into account (in the event that a loss accrues on that disposal) include such allowances relating to expenditure both before and after the part disposal, but in order to avoid double counting they exclude any allowances that were applied in restricting the capital loss on the part disposal (*TCGA 1992, s 42(3)*).

This apportionment (and all similar apportionments of expenditure provided for elsewhere) is also made before – and without regard to – any of the following rules in *TCGA 1992*:

- transfers between spouses and civil partners – *s 58*;
- transfers within a group of companies – *s 171*;
- roll-over relief on replacement of business assets – *ss 152* to *158*;

- any other rule providing for neither a gain nor a loss to accrue on the disposal (*TCGA 1992, s 42(5)*).

Assets derived from other assets

3.47   The value of an asset may be derived from another asset in the same ownership where:

- assets have been merged or divided or have changed their nature; or

- rights or interests in or over assets have been created or extinguished.

In such a case it is necessary to apportion the allowable expenditure incurred on the 'old' asset and then apply the appropriate proportions to the old asset (if it is retained) and the new asset. The apportionment is to be made on a 'just and reasonable' basis (*TCGA 1992, ss 43, 52(4)*).

LOSSES

3.48   Losses accruing on disposal of assets are, as a general rule, computed in the same way as gains. Where it is provided that a gain accruing is a chargeable gain it generally follows that a loss accruing is allowable. Similarly, if a gain accruing on a disposal would not be chargeable, any loss is not allowable (*TCGA 1992, s 16(1), (2)*). Special rules apply to chattels and wasting assets (see **Chapter 4**).

Claims

3.49   A loss must be 'claimed' before it can be set against gains. It is not an allowable loss unless the taxpayer gives a notice to HMRC for the year in which the loss accrued. The notice, which must quantify the amount of the loss, is treated as a claim within *Taxes Management Act 1970* (*TMA 1970*), *ss 42* and *43* (*TCGA 1992, s 16(2A)*).

This means that the notice must be given no more than five years after 31 January following the year of assessment to which it relates. For example, a loss accruing in 2005/06 must be notified by 31 January 2012. However, if the taxpayer is required to complete the capital gains pages (see the reporting limits in **1.29**) he will need to include the allowable losses in those pages. In any event, a taxpayer who has accrued losses but is within the reporting limits should consider completing the capital gains pages in order to notify the losses.

Non-residents, etc

3.50   If the taxpayer is not resident or ordinarily resident in the UK at all during any part of the year of assessment, a loss accruing to him in that year is not an allowable loss. There is an exception where a gain accruing on the relevant disposal would be chargeable on the non-resident taxpayer under *TCGA 1992, s 10* or *10B* (non-residents with a UK branch, agency or permanent establishment) (*TCGA 1992, s 16(3)*).

CGT is not charged on gains accruing to individuals who are resident or ordinarily resident but not domiciled in the UK from the disposal of assets situated outside the UK, unless those gains are remitted to the UK. At the same time, losses accruing on the disposal of assets situated outside the UK to such individuals are not allowable losses (*TCGA 1992, s 16(4)*). See **Chapter 5** regarding residence, etc.

Loss accruing on disposal to connected person

3.51   Special rules apply to losses incurred on a disposal to a connected person (see **3.21** above).

Trading losses set against chargeable gains

3.52   Where the taxpayer makes a claim under *Income and Corporation Taxes Act 1988* (*ICTA 1988*), *s 380* to set trading losses against income for income tax purposes, he may also make a claim for an amount – the 'relevant amount' – to be treated as an allowable loss for CGT purposes (*FA 1991, s 72(1)*).

The relevant amount for the year of assessment to which the claim relates is the part of the trading loss that cannot be set off against his income for the year and has not already been relieved for any other year under *ICTA 1988, s 380* or *FA 1991, s 72(1)* or otherwise. However, if the relevant amount exceeds the 'maximum amount' (see below), the excess is not treated as a capital loss.

The 'maximum amount' is the amount on which the taxpayer would be chargeable to CGT disregarding both taper relief (see **Chapter 12**) and the annual exemption (see **1.16**). It is calculated without regard to any event, occurring after the relevant amount has been determined, which would otherwise reduce the maximum amount.

In the absence of this limitation a claim to CGT roll-over relief on the replacement of business assets, for example, could reduce the maximum amount so that part of the trading loss could no longer be treated as a capital loss. Instead, the maximum amount is unchanged and the effect of the roll-over relief claim is to create unrelieved losses available to carry forward and set against future chargeable gains.

Post-cessation expenditure

3.53   Where the taxpayer claims relief for post-cessation expenditure under *ICTA 1998, s 109A* he may specify that any amount of that expenditure that cannot be set off against his income is to be treated for CGT purposes as an allowable loss. This relief is not available to companies within the charge to corporation tax (*FA 1995, s 90(4)*).

Former employees: employment-related liabilities

3.54   Where income tax relief is available for liabilities related to a former employment and the deduction exceeds the taxpayer's total income, the excess relief may be treated as an allowable loss accruing to the former employee (*TCGA 1992, s 263ZA*).

Restriction by reference to capital allowances

3.55   Although expenditure allowable as a deduction in computing trading profits, etc is not deductible in computing chargeable gains (see **3.42**) there is no general exclusion of expenditure for which a 'capital allowance' or 'renewals allowance' (defined below) is made. However, if a loss accrues on the disposal it may be restricted by reference to those allowances. The restriction is applied by excluding from the sums allowable as a deduction in the CGT computation any expenditure to the extent that a capital allowance or renewals allowance has been – or may be – made for that expenditure. This rule can have the effect of reducing the capital loss to nil but it cannot turn that loss into a gain (*TCGA 1992, s 41(1), (2), (4), (5)*).

A 'capital allowance' is any allowance under the *Capital Allowances Act 2001* (*CAA 2001*) or certain provisions relating to expenditure on sea walls and cemeteries. A 'renewals allowance' is a deduction, allowed by concession in computing trading income, for the cost of a replacement asset for the purposes of the trade. For the purpose of this restriction, the renewals allowance given on the acquisition of the replacement asset is regarded as an allowance for expenditure incurred on the old asset (*TCGA 1992, s 41(3)*; CG 15404).

63

The capital allowances to be taken into account include any balancing allowance available on the disposal. Any balancing charge arising by reason of the disposal or any earlier event is deducted from the allowances to be taken into account (*TCGA 1992, s 41(6)*).

If the taxpayer acquired the asset on a transfer treated for capital allowances purposes as made at its written-down value, this restriction takes account of capital allowances made to the transferor (and the previous transferor in relation to any earlier transfers) as well as the taxpayer (*TCGA 1992, s 41(3)*; CG 15411).

Similarly, capital allowances made to the previous owner (or owners) of the asset may be taken into account where the taxpayer acquired the asset on a transfer to which either of the following provisions applied:

- *TCGA 1992, s 140A* – transfer of a UK trade between EU member states; or

- *TCGA 1992, s 171*, ignoring for this purpose the exceptions in *s 171(2)* – transfers within a group of companies (*TCGA 1992, s 41(8)*).

On a disposal of plant or machinery that has attracted allowances under *CAA 2001, Pt 2* without restriction for either non-qualifying use or partial depreciation subsidies (*CAA 2001, ss 205–212*), the allowances taken into account for the purpose of this restriction are taken to be the difference between the capital expenditure incurred (or treated as incurred) on providing the asset and the asset's disposal value for capital allowances purposes (*TCGA 1992, s 41(7)*).

Loans to traders

3.56   Relief is available where the taxpayer lends money to a person carrying on a business; that money is used wholly for the purposes of the borrower's business; and the loan becomes irrecoverable or the taxpayer makes a payment under a guarantee of the loan – see **17.11** (*TCGA 1992, s 253*).

Losses incurred on shares in trading companies

3.57   A capital loss arising on the disposal, by the original subscriber, of unlisted shares in a trading company may be available for set-off against income for income tax or corporation tax purposes – see **17.16** (*ICTA 1988, ss 573–576*).

TAPER RELIEF

3.58   Taper relief is available to individuals, trustees and personal representatives where, for a year of assessment, accrued chargeable gains exceed any allowable losses and those gains include gains that are eligible for taper relief. A chargeable gain is eligible for taper relief if it is a gain on the disposal of a business asset with a qualifying holding period of at least one year; or a non-business asset with a qualifying holding period of at least three years. Taper relief is examined in detail in **Chapter 11**.

INDEXATION ALLOWANCE

3.59   The indexation allowance was introduced in 1982 in order to eliminate 'paper gains' attributable to inflation. Combined with the rebasing of CGT by reference to March 1982 values (see **3.69**) with effect from April 1988, indexation provided 'inflation-proofing' of gains.

The allowance was frozen with effect from April 1998 (see Table 3.1) for individuals, trustees and personal representatives, who may continue to claim indexation allowance but only in respect of inflation up to April 1998. The allowance may be obtained in addition to taper relief (see **Chapter 11**) where appropriate. Companies chargeable to corporation tax continue to be eligible for indexation allowance and cannot claim taper relief (*TCGA 1992, s 53(1A)*).

Table 3.1

Indexation factors for disposals made by individuals in or after April 1998

	1982	1983	1984	1985	1986	1987	1988	1989	1990	1991	1992	1993	1994	1995	1996	1997	1998
January	–	0.968	0.872	0.783	0.689	0.626	0.574	0.465	0.361	0.249	0.199	0.179	0.151	0.114	0.083	0.053	0.019
February	–	0.960	0.865	0.769	0.683	0.620	0.568	0.454	0.353	0.242	0.193	0.171	0.144	0.107	0.078	0.049	0.014
March	1.047	0.956	0.859	0.752	0.681	0.616	0.562	0.448	0.339	0.237	0.189	0.167	0.141	0.102	0.073	0.046	0.011
April	1.006	0.929	0.834	0.716	0.665	0.597	0.537	0.423	0.300	0.222	0.171	0.156	0.128	0.091	0.066	0.040	–
May	0.992	0.921	0.828	0.708	0.662	0.596	0.531	0.414	0.288	0.218	0.167	0.152	0.124	0.087	0.063	0.036	–
June	0.987	0.917	0.823	0.704	0.663	0.596	0.525	0.409	0.283	0.213	0.167	0.153	0.124	0.085	0.063	0.032	–
July	0.986	0.906	0.825	0.707	0.667	0.597	0.524	0.408	0.282	0.215	0.171	0.156	0.129	0.091	0.067	0.032	–
August	0.985	0.898	0.808	0.703	0.662	0.593	0.507	0.404	0.269	0.213	0.171	0.151	0.124	0.085	0.062	0.026	–
September	0.987	0.889	0.804	0.704	0.654	0.588	0.500	0.395	0.258	0.208	0.166	0.146	0.121	0.080	0.057	0.021	–
October	0.977	0.883	0.793	0.701	0.652	0.580	0.485	0.384	0.248	0.204	0.162	0.147	0.120	0.085	0.057	0.019	–
November	0.967	0.876	0.788	0.695	0.638	0.573	0.478	0.372	0.251	0.199	0.164	0.148	0.119	0.085	0.057	0.019	–
December	0.971	0.871	0.789	0.693	0.632	0.574	0.474	0.369	0.252	0.198	0.168	0.146	0.114	0.079	0.053	0.016	–

Calculation of indexation allowance

3.60   If an 'unindexed gain' accrues on a disposal of an asset, an indexation allowance is allowed against it. No allowance is available where a loss has accrued. The allowance is set against the unindexed gain and the result is the 'gain' for the purpose of *TCGA 1992* (also known as the 'indexed gain').

Where the indexation allowance is equal to or greater than the unindexed gain, the result is that neither a gain nor a loss accrues. The 'unindexed gain' is the gain computed as required by *TCGA 1992, Pt II* (as described in this chapter) (*TCGA 1992, s 53(1), (2)(a), (2A)*).

The indexation allowance is the aggregate of the 'indexed rise' in each item of 'relevant allowable expenditure' (see below) excluding – except for corporation tax purposes – any such expenditure incurred on or after 1 April 1998. The 'indexed rise' for each item of expenditure is found by multiplying the amount of the expenditure by the figure (the 'indexation factor') given by the formula:

$$\frac{(RD-RI)}{RI}$$

where:

- RD is the retail prices index for the 'relevant month'; and
- RI is the retail prices index for the later of March 1982 or the month in which the expenditure was incurred.

The indexation factor is expressed as a decimal and rounded to the nearest third decimal place, but HMRC may accept computations prepared using computer software where this rounding adjustment is not made, so long as computations are prepared on a consistent basis that favours neither HMRC nor the taxpayer (CG 17275). HMRC publish indexation factors at www.hmrc.gov.uk/rates/cgt.htm and announce the retail prices index on a monthly basis together with indexation factors for disposals in each month.

There is no indexed rise if RD is equal to or less than RI. The 'relevant month' for CGT purposes (ie in non-corporation tax cases) is April 1998. For corporation tax purposes the relevant month is the month in which the disposal occurs.

There is no indexed rise where expenditure concerned relates to acquisition of 'relevant securities', as defined in *TCGA 1992, s 108*, and the securities are disposed of within ten days of the expenditure being incurred (*TCGA 1992, 54(1), (1A), (2), (3)*). Other aspects of indexation allowance are also modified in relation to disposals of shares, securities and options (see **Chapter 4**).

Relevant allowable expenditure

3.61   'Relevant allowable expenditure' above means any sum allowed as a deduction by *TCGA 1992, s 38* in computing the unindexed gain, adjusted as necessary for any provision increasing, reducing, writing down or excluding such expenditure. It includes, therefore, incidental costs of disposal as well as incidental costs of acquisition and enhancement expenditure. Any foreign tax charged on a gain is not regarded as relevant allowable expenditure. Costs of acquisition are taken to have been incurred when the asset was acquired or provided, and costs of enhancement are taken to have been incurred when the expenditure became due and payable (*TCGA 1992, ss 53(2)(b), (3), 54(4), 57*).

Part disposals

3.62   The apportionment of allowable expenditure on the part disposal of an asset (see **3.46**) takes place before the calculation of indexation allowance. This means there is no indexed rise to be computed for the part of the relevant allowable expenditure that is apportioned to the part retained (*TCGA 1992, s 56(1)*).

Assets held on 31 March 1982

3.63   The effect of inflation prior to 31 March 1992 is eliminated by a provision requiring that where the person making the disposal held the asset on that date he is deemed for indexation allowance purposes to have sold and immediately reacquired it on that date at its then market value.

This rule applies in every case where the taxpayer has made a rebasing election (see **3.71**). However, neither this rule nor the rebasing rule (see **3.69**) applies if there is no rebasing election and the effect of these rules would be to reduce the indexation allowance otherwise available (*TCGA 1992, s 55(1), (2)*).

The following provisions are modified where there is a deemed disposal and reacquisition at 31 March 1992 under this rule:

- restriction of losses by reference to capital allowances (see **3.55**);
- disposal of wasting assets qualifying for capital allowances (see **4.24**); and
- assets derived from other assets (see **3.47**) (*TCGA 1992, s 55(3), (4)*).

Assets acquired on a no gain/no loss transfer

3.64   If the person making the disposal acquired the asset after 31 March 1982, and the disposal by which he acquired the asset – and any previous disposal of the asset after that date – was a no gain/no loss disposal (see below), then:

- in computing the indexation allowance on the disposal he is treated as having held the asset on 31 March 1982 so that the allowance may be based on the market value at that date, but

- in computing the gain or loss accruing on his disposal, any indexation allowance taken into account in fixing the consideration that he is deemed to have given for the asset is deducted from that consideration (*TCGA 1992, s 55(5), (6)*).

For this purpose a no gain/no loss disposal is one on which neither a gain nor a loss accrues by virtue of:

- any of the provisions listed in the *TCGA 1992, s 35(3)(d)* (rebasing, see **3.69**); or

- the rules relating to gifts to charities and housing associations in *TCGA 1992, s 257(2)* and *259(2)* respectively (*TCGA 1992, s 55(5)*).

Acquisition on a no gain/no loss transfer before 30 November 1993

3.65   As already indicated, the indexation allowance can neither create nor increase a loss – it can only reduce the unindexed gain to nil. This was not the case before 30 November 1993. Special rules apply where the person making a disposal on or after that date acquired the asset on a no gain/no loss transfer before that date. Broadly, their effect is that a measure of indexation allowance that accrued on the no gain/no loss transfer – called the 'rolled-up indexation' – may create or increase a loss on the subsequent disposal.

For this purpose it is necessary to compute the gain under the normal rules and compute the amount of the rolled up indexation. No adjustment is required if indexation allowance included in the computation exceeds the rolled-up indexation. If it is less than the rolled-up indexation, the full amount of the rolled-up indexation is allowed in computing the chargeable gain or allowable loss (*TCGA 1992, s 55(7)–(11)*; CG 17764).

Assets disposed of on a no gain/no loss transfer

3.66   Where the indexation allowance is available and the disposal treated as a disposal on which neither a gain nor a loss accrues (other than by virtue of certain rules concerning the operation of March 1982 rebasing and the amount of the indexation allowance itself), then the consideration for the disposal is taken to be the amount that would give rise to an unindexed gain equal to the indexation allowance available on the disposal. The effect of this rule is that after deducting the indexation allowance there is no chargeable gain and no allowable loss. An adjustment to the deemed consideration may be required in some cases, to prevent a loss accruing on a subsequent disposal by the transferee (*TCGA 1992, s 56*).

SPOUSES AND CIVIL PARTNERS

3.67   Transfers of assets between spouses living together are treated as 'no gain/no loss' transfers. This treatment is extended with effect from 5 December 2005 to transfers between civil partners.

If an individual is living with his spouse or civil partner in a year of assessment and during that year one of them disposes of an asset to the other, both the transferor and transferee are treated as if the asset was transferred for a consideration that would give rise to neither a gain nor a loss in the hands of the transferor (*TCGA 1992, s 58(1)*).

Individuals who are married to each other, or are civil partners of each other, are treated as living together unless they are either:

● separated under an order of a court of competent jurisdiction, or by deed of separation; or

● in fact separated in such circumstances that the separation is likely to be permanent (*TCGA 1992, s 288(3)* applying *ICTA 1988, s 282*).

The no gain/no loss rule described above applies regardless of the rules substituting market value for transfers between connected persons (see **3.10**) and appropriations to and from trading stock (see **4.31**) and regardless of any other rule fixing the amount of the consideration deemed to be given on the disposal or acquisition of an asset.

However, it does not apply if:

● the asset formed part of the taxpayer's trading stock until the disposal;

● the asset is acquired, by a person carrying on a trade, as trading stock; or

● the disposal is by way of *donatio mortis causa* (see **2.9**) (*TCGA 1992, s 58(2)*).

ASSETS HELD ON 31 MARCH 1982

3.68   The rebasing of CGT introduced in the *Finance Act 1988* means that, broadly speaking, CGT is now charged only on gains that have accrued since

31 March 1982. This measure, combined with the indexation allowance given to recognise inflation since 1982, resulted in full 'inflation-proofing' of gains. However, the position is now more complex for taxpayers other than companies) following the withdrawal of indexation allowance from 1998. The allowance was replaced by taper relief, which is more generous for gains on disposal of business assets than for those on disposal of non-business assets. The benefit of taper relief may bear little resemblance to the amount of a gain that is attributable to inflation (see **Chapter 11**).

Rebasing to 31 March 1982

3.69   The general rule is that where the taxpayer held an asset at 31 March 1982 and makes a disposal of it after 5 April 1988, the gain or loss accruing is calculated on the assumption that he sold the asset on that date, and immediately reacquired it at its market value on that date. The effect is to substitute the 31 March 1982 value for the actual cost of the asset and any enhancement expenditure incurred prior to that date. If the value of the asset being disposed of is derived from another asset held on 31 March 1982 rebasing may apply by reference to the original asset's value on that date (*TCGA 1992, s 35(1), (2), Sch 3, para 5*).

Exceptions to the rebasing rule

3.70   The general rebasing rule does not apply in any of the following cases, unless a rebasing election (see below) is made (*TCGA 1992, s 35(3)*):

(a)   where the effect of rebasing is to increase a gain arising under the normal rules, or to turn a loss arising under the normal rules into a gain;

(b)   where the effect of rebasing is to increase a loss arising under the normal rules, or to turn a gain arising under the normal rules into a loss;

(c)   where neither a gain nor a loss would accrue in the absence of rebasing, either on the facts or because of the rules for assets held on 6 April 1965 found in *TCGA 1992, Sch 2*;

(d)   where neither a gain nor a loss would accrue on the disposal by virtue of any of the provisions listed in *TCGA 1992, s 35(3)(d)*. Many of those provisions are no longer relevant. The ones that remain relevant relate to the following disposals (statutory references being to *TCGA 1992* unless otherwise stated):

- disposals between spouses and civil partners – *s 58*;

- deemed disposals where settled property reverts to the settlor on the death of a life tenant – *s 73*;

- transfers of assets on company reconstructions – *s 139*;

- transfers of UK trades by non-resident companies in exchange for securities – *s 140A*;

- transfers of assets as part of a merger forming a European Company or SE – *s 140E*;

- transfers within a group of companies – *s 171*;

- disposals on amalgamations of building societies – *s 215*;

- transfers of assets from a building society to a company – *s 216*;

- transfers of assets on incorporation of a registered friendly society – *s 217A*;

- certain disposals by housing associations – *ss 218–220*;

- certain transfers of assets to a harbour authority – *s 221*;

- deemed disposals where a charity becomes absolutely entitled to settled property – *s 257(3)*;

- gifts of heritage property – *s 258(4)*;

- transfers of land between local constituency associations of political parties on reorganisation of constituencies – *s 264*;

- disposals relating to the sharing of transmission facilities between national broadcasting companies – *s 267(2)*;

- transfers on the amalgamation of industrial and provident societies – *ICTA 1988, s 486(8)*.

A disposal is treated as giving rise to neither a gain nor a loss in a case where:

- the effect of the rebasing rule would be to turn a gain into a loss, or to turn a loss into a gain, but

- that rule has been disapplied by one of the exceptions listed above (*TCGA 1992, s 35(4)*).

Rebasing election

3.71 The taxpayer may elect that the rebasing rule will apply to any disposal he makes of assets that he held at both 31 March 1982 and 5 April 1988, whether or not the disposal is within the list of exceptions at **3.70**. The election, once made, is irrevocable and applies to all such disposals, including those made before the time of the election. An election made by a person in one capacity does not cover disposals that he makes in any other capacity (eg as trustee of a settlement) (*TCGA 1992, s 35(5), (7)*).

The election is to be made at any time before 6 April 1990 or during the period beginning on the day of the 'first relevant disposal' (see below) and ending:

(a)   for individuals and trustees, with the first anniversary of the 31 January following the year of assessment in which that disposal takes place;

(b)   for companies, two years after the end of the accounting period in which that disposal takes place; and

(c)   in either case, at such later time as HMRC may allow (*TCGA 1992, s 35(6)*).

The 'first relevant disposal' is the first disposal to which the 31 March 1982 rebasing rules apply. HMRC take the view that strictly the disposal of any asset, whether chargeable or not, can be the first relevant disposal, but in exercising their discretion in (c) above to extend the time limit they will disregard certain disposals. These are set out in HMRC statement of practice SP 4/92 and include:

●   disposals on which a gain would not be a chargeable gain by virtue of a particular statutory provision, eg the exemption for private motor cars;

●   disposals that do not give rise to a chargeable gain in practice, eg a withdrawal from a building society account, the disposal of a dwelling house where the gain is wholly covered by private residence relief, or a no gain/no loss transfer between spouses; and

●   certain disposals that could not be covered by a rebasing election (see 'excluded disposals' below).

Excluded disposals

3.72   Certain disposals cannot be covered by any rebasing election. These include disposals of (or disposals of an interest in) plant or machinery, or an asset used in a trade of working mineral deposits, where in either case capital allowances were available. These disposals are also excluded if (i) the person making the disposal acquired the asset on a no gain/no loss transfer, and (ii) capital allowances were available to either the last person to acquire the asset other than on such a transfer or to any person who subsequently acquired the asset on such a transfer (*TCGA 1992, Sch 3, para 7*).

As a general rule, a rebasing election to cover assets held by a group of companies on 31 March 1992 may be made only by the group's principal member (*TCGA 1992, Sch 3, paras 8, 9*).

Assets acquired on a no gain/no loss transfer

3.73   Where the taxpayer makes a disposal after 5 April 1988 of an asset that he acquired after 31 March 1982 by virtue of a no gain/no loss transfer (ie a

73

disposal to which any of the provisions listed in *TCGA 1992, s 35(3)(d)* applies – see (d) in **3.70**), he is treated as having held the asset himself on 31 March 1982 (*TCGA 1992, Sch 3, para 1*).

If the taxpayer ('the transferee') acquired the asset after 5 April 1988 and *TCGA 1992, s 58* or *TCGA 1992, s 171* (no gain/no loss transfers between spouses and group companies respectively) applied to the acquisition, then:

(a)   any rebasing election made by the transferee does not cover his disposal of that asset;

(b)   any rebasing election made by the transferor causes the disposal to fall outside the exceptions listed above, so that rebasing applies on the transferee's disposal whether or not the transferee makes a rebasing election.

If the transferor in this situation acquired the asset after 5 April 1988, and *TCGA 1992, s 58* or *s 171* applied to his acquisition, a rebasing election made by him will not have the effect noted in (b) above. However, an election made by either of the following people will have that effect:

●   the last person to acquire the asset after 5 April 1988 on a transfer outside *TCGA 1992, ss 58* and *171*; or

●   if there is no such person, the person who held the asset on 5 April 1988 (*TCGA 1992, Sch 3, para 2*).

Assets held on 6 April 1965 and 31 March 1982

3.74   Special rules (set out in *TCGA 1992, Sch 2*, see **3.76**), apply to a disposal of an asset held on 6 April 1965 in a case where:

●   the rebasing rule in **3.69** does not apply; and

●   the no gain/no loss rule in **3.70** does not apply.

Deferred charges on gains before 31 March 1982

3.75   A special rule applies to the 'deferred charge' arising where gains accruing on the disposal before 6 April 1988 of an asset held on 31 March 1982 were rolled over or held over and deducted from allowable expenditure on a new asset (or, in some cases, on the same asset). In the absence of any adjustment, the effect of this deduction arising from the claim would be to bring into charge a pre-1982 element of the deferred gain on the occasion of a post-1988 disposal.

In broad terms, and subject to certain exceptions, the deferred gain is halved when it crystallises after 5 April 1988 (*TCGA 1992, s 36, Sch 4*).

ASSETS HELD ON 6 APRIL 1965

3.76 There are special rules for computing gains and losses arising on the disposal of assets held on 6 April 1965, the date on which CGT was introduced. The calculation generally involves the disposal being calculated by reference to the original cost of the asset or its market value at 6 April 1965. The lower gain (or loss) is then compared with the gain or loss arising under 31 March 1982 rebasing. If a 1982 rebasing election is in force, the gain or loss is computed using the 31 March 1982 value instead.

Quoted shares and securities

3.77 A gain or loss on disposal of quoted shares or securities is computed by reference to both the original cost and the market value of the asset as at 6 April 1965. The lower gain (or loss) arising is taken. If one computation produces a gain and the other produces a loss, the disposal is treated as giving rise to no gain and no loss. An irrevocable election (similar to the 31 March 1982 rebasing election, see **3.71**) can be made to use the 6 April 1965 market value of quoted shares and securities instead of their original cost (*TCGA 1992, Sch 2, Pt I*).

Land reflecting development value

3.78 The gain or loss on the disposal of land reflecting development value that was held at 6 April 1965 is computed as described for quoted shares and securities above if special provisions relating to development land apply (*TCGA 1992, Sch 2, Pt II*).

Other assets held on 6 April 1965

3.79 Where an asset other than quoted shares or land with development value was acquired before 6 April 1965, the general rule is that gains are calculated on the basis of original cost but are then time-apportioned. Only that part of the gain relating to the period falling after 6 April 1965 is chargeable. Any period of ownership before 6 April 1945 is ignored for time-apportionment purposes. The gain is reduced by any indexation allowance before being time-apportioned. However, the calculation using the 31 March 1982 value (see rebasing, **3.69**) should normally give rise to a lower gain and this time-apportionment method is now likely to be used only rarely.

The taxpayer may make an irrevocable election to ignore the original cost and compute the gain by reference to the asset's market value on 6 April 1965. Alternatively, where a rebasing election has been made, the asset's market value at 31 March 1982 replaces the original cost and no time-apportionment of the gain is necessary (*TCGA 1992, Sch 2, Pt III*).

DOUBLE TAX RELIEF

3.80   Relief for foreign tax suffered on gains that are chargeable to UK CGT or corporation tax may be obtained under the terms of a double taxation agreement between the UK and the relevant overseas territory (see **3.81**); or by means of a 'unilateral' tax credit granted under UK domestic tax law (see **3.82**); or by means of a deduction in computing the gain chargeable to UK tax (see **3.85**). See **5.22** with regard to the application of double tax relief where gains are assessed on the remittance basis. Anti-avoidance provisions were introduced in 2005 to counter schemes designed to create tax credit relief (*FA 2005, s 87* and *Sch 5*).

Double taxation agreements

3.81   The UK has more than a hundred double tax agreements or treaties with overseas territories, designed to limit the taxing rights of the contracting states in order to prevent double taxation, and to assist in countering evasion by means of exchange of information between tax authorities. The agreements contain articles to determine the residence status of persons who are resident in both territories under their respective domestic tax law. Many agreements have articles setting out how capital gains are to be taxed. Where a UK-resident taxpayer suffers foreign tax on a gain that is subject to CGT or corporation tax, the agreement itself may provide for a credit in respect of the foreign tax to be given against any UK liability (*ICTA 1988, s 788*).

Unilateral tax credit relief

3.82   Where chargeable gains are subject to tax in a territory that has no double taxation agreement with the UK, credit for any foreign tax liability is given 'unilaterally' unless the taxpayer elects for a deduction instead (see **3.85**) (*ICTA 1988, s 790*). The provisions of *ICTA 1988, Pt XVIII, Chs I* and *II* are modified for this purpose so that 'capital gains' and 'capital gains tax' are to be read in place of 'income' and 'income tax' (*TCGA 1992, s 277(1)*). The provisions are also applied to corporation tax on chargeable gains (*ICTA 1988, s 797*).

The UK tax and the foreign tax must be chargeable on the same chargeable gain, although there is no requirement that the respective liabilities arise at the same time or are charged on the same person (*ICTA 1988, s 790(4)*). A liability may arise in the UK but not in the overseas territory.

In some cases it may be difficult to ascertain the amount of the gain that is subject to 'double taxation' in the absence of any relief. HMRC practice in this regard is set out in the Capital Gains Manual at CG 14395–14400 and summarised below. Although the authority for this practice is unclear, HMRC provide a working sheet to assist taxpayers along with the tax return helpsheet IR 261:

(a)   Where the whole period of ownership of the asset is considered in arriving at both the UK assessment and the foreign assessment and the amount of the UK assessment is equal to or greater than the foreign assessment, the whole of the foreign tax is allowable for tax credit relief. However, the credit cannot exceed the amount of the UK tax liability arising on the gain and no deduction is available in the computation for any foreign tax that is not allowed as a tax credit.

(b)   Where the whole period of ownership is considered for both assessments as stated in (a), but the amount of the UK assessment is less than the foreign assessment, the whole of the gain is treated as doubly taxed but the tax credit is restricted to the fraction A/B, where A is the amount of the UK assessment and B is the amount of the foreign assessment.

(c)   Tax credit relief is restricted (i) when the same period of ownership is considered in arriving at both assessments but the amount of the UK assessment is less than the foreign assessment, and (ii) when the foreign assessment relates to a longer period of ownership than the period forming the basis of the UK assessment (eg as a result of the March 1982 rebasing of UK CGT, see **3.69**).

3.83   HMRC consider that tax credit relief is available in the following circumstances:

●   the foreign tax liability charges capital gains as income;

●   foreign tax is payable on a no gain/no loss disposal between group companies (within *TCGA 1992, s 171*) and a UK tax liability arises on a subsequent disposal;

●   an overseas trade carried on through a branch or agency or permanent establishment is domesticated (ie transferred to a non-resident subsidiary), relief is given under *TCGA 1992, s 140*, a later event gives rise to a

UK liability, and foreign tax is charged wholly or partly by reference to the gain accruing at the date of domestication; or

• foreign tax is payable by reference to increases in the value of assets although there is no disposal for UK tax purposes, and a UK liability arises on a later disposal (HMRC statement of practice SP 06/88).

HMRC have listed in their Double Taxation Relief Manual (at D 2140 onwards) the taxes that they consider to be admissible (or inadmissible) for tax credit relief. Statement of practice SP 07/91 (revised in August 2005) sets out how HMRC interpret the requirement in *ICTA 1988, s 790(12)* that the foreign tax must 'correspond' to the UK tax in order for relief to be available. Broadly, the question would be determined by examining the tax within its legislative context in the foreign territory and deciding whether it serves the same function as the UK tax.

EU savings directive: special withholding tax

3.84 Where the consideration for the disposal of an asset giving rise to a chargeable gain consists of or includes an amount of 'savings income', and 'special withholding tax' is levied in respect of that consideration (or a part of it), then credit relief is available for the amount found by the formula:

$$SWT \times [GUK/(G - SWT)]$$

where:

• SWT is the special withholding tax levied;

• GUK is the amount of the chargeable gain received in the UK; and

• G is the amount of the chargeable gain accruing on the disposal.

'Special withholding tax' means a withholding tax (however described) levied under the law of an EU member state territory outside the UK implementing *article 11* of the *EU Savings Directive*, or levied under a 'corresponding provision of international arrangements' in the case of a territory other than an EU member state (*TCGA 1992, s 277*).

'Savings income', in the case of special withholding tax levied under the law of an EU member state, has the same meaning as 'interest payment' has for the purposes of the *EU Savings Directive*. If the tax is levied elsewhere, 'savings income' has the same meaning as the corresponding expression has for the purposes of the relevant international arrangements. To the extent that it cannot be set off, special withholding tax is repayable (*FA 2004, s 107*).

Relief by deduction

3.85   Relief for foreign tax may be given by deduction if no tax credit relief is available or the taxpayer elects to forego any credit (as provided in *ICTA 1988, s 805*). The effect of the election may be to create or increase an allowable loss. Where foreign tax is suffered on a gain that is the subject of a UK roll-over relief claim (see **Chapter 14**) no tax credit relief is available because there is no UK liability, but relief by deduction reduces both the gain accruing and the amount to be deducted from the acquisition cost of the replacement asset as a result of the roll-over relief claim (*TCGA 1992, s 278*).

Chapter 4

Particular assets

Various exemptions for certain assets, gains or persons are examined in **Chapter 2**. This chapter discusses particular types of asset to which special rules apply. Private residences are examined in **Chapter 12** and options and deposits are discussed at **2.22**.

SHARES AND SECURITIES

4.1   Special rules apply to determine how shares and securities are identified with particular acquisitions for the purpose of calculating allowable expenditure in the CGT computation. Broadly, 'pooling' of shares, etc does not apply for acquisitions after 5 April 1998 (but it continues to apply for corporation tax on the chargeable gains of companies).

'Securities' means shares or securities (ie loan capital) of a company and any other assets (eg units in a unit trust) that are dealt in without identifying the particular assets concerned. These are 'fungible' assets in that they all answer to the same definition; the separate components of a holding cannot be identified and distinguished from each other. (This definition of 'securities' is separate from – and wider than – the definition in *TCGA 1992, s 132*, which determines whether loan capital is a chargeable asset.)

However, 'securities' here do not include 'relevant securities' (see **4.7**). Shares or securities of a company are treated as being of the same class only if they are treated as such by a recognised stock exchange, or would be so treated if they were dealt in on a recognised stock exchange (*TCGA 1992, s 104(3)*).

Securities held by a person who acquired them as an employee on terms that restrict his right to dispose of them – known as 'clogged shares' – are treated as being of a different class from other securities (*TCGA 1992, s 104(4)*).

Identification: general rules for CGT

4.2   The general rules that apply for CGT (not corporation tax) purposes are summarised below. These rules apply to disposals after 5 April 1998, when taper relief was introduced for individuals, trustees and personal representatives. The amount of taper relief due depends partly on the length of the period of ownership, so the earlier 'pooling' of shares was replaced in 1998 by a last-in, first-out system. Special rules apply to enterprise investment scheme or venture capital trust shares (see **16.6** and **17.4**).

'Shares' in the following summary includes securities that are within the definition 'securities' set out in **4.1**. Shares disposed of are identified with shares of the same class acquired by the person making the disposal, and earlier disposals are identified before later ones. The shares disposed of are identified with acquisitions in the following order:

(a)   any shares acquired on the same day as the disposal (*TCGA 1992, ss 105(1)(b), 106A(9)*);

(b)   any shares acquired in the period of 30 days after the disposal, taking earlier acquisitions first (*TCGA 1992, s 106A(5)*);

(c)   other shares acquired after 5 April 1998, identified on a last-in, first-out basis (*TCGA 1992, s 106A(6)*);

(d)   shares in a 'section 104 holding' (see **4.5**) (without identifying any particular shares comprised in it) (*TCGA 1992, s 106A(6), (7)*);

(e)   shares in a '1982 holding' (see **4.6**) (without identifying any particular shares comprised in it) (*TCGA 1992, s 106A(6), (7)*);

(f)   shares held on 6 April 1965, identified on a last-in, first-out basis (*TCGA 1992, s 106A(6)*); and

(g)   any shares acquired more than 30 days after the disposal, ie acquisitions not already identified in (b) above, taking earlier acquisitions first (*TCGA 1992, s 105(2)*).

With regard to (a), shares of the same class that are acquired (or disposed of) by the same person on the same day and in the same capacity are treated as acquired (or disposed of) in a single transaction. However, the taxpayer may elect for this rule to be modified, for acquisitions after 5 April 2002, where some of the shares acquired on the same day were acquired under an approved employee share option scheme or an enterprise management incentive scheme. This election may be beneficial if the allowable expenditure relating to the scheme shares is higher than the averaged cost computed under the 'same day' rule (*TCGA 1992, ss 105(1)(a), 105A, 105B*).

The 30-day rule in (b) was introduced in March 1998 to remove the tax advantage gained by 'bed and breakfasting' shares (see **10.17**) in order to realise losses or utilise the CGT annual exemption.

4.3 *Particular assets*

4.3   **Example 4.1**

Judith sold 5,000 ordinary shares in BBH Plc on 1 December 2006 for £40,000 and had the following share history for ordinary shares in that company:

Holding	Transaction	Date	Cost	Indexed cost
5,000	s 104 holding	5 April 1998	£12,000	£18,000
2,000	bought	1 October 1998	£10,000	
1,000	bought	1 January 1999	£6,000	

The 5,000 shares disposed of are identified with the following holdings:

- 1,000 bought on 1 January 1999, with taper relief for seven years.

- 2,000 bought on 1 October 1998, with taper relief for eight years.

- 2,000 from the 'pool' at 5 April 1998 with taper relief for nine years (including bonus).

Judith does not work for BBH Plc, so her holding is treated as a non-business asset for taper relief. The capital gain on the disposal of 5,000 shares, identified as shown above, must be calculated in three parts:

	Pro-ceeds	Cost	Gain	Gain
	£	£	£	£
1 1,000 shares from January 1999	8,000	6,000	2,000	
Less taper relief at 25%			(500)	1,500
2 1,000 shares from October 1998	16,000	10,000	6,000	
less taper relief at 30%			(1,800)	4,800
3 2,000 shares from pool at April 1998	16,000			
(2,000/5,000) x indexed cost £18,000		7,200	8,800	
less taper relief at 35%			(3,080)	5,720
Total proceeds	40,000			
Total chargeable gain				12,020

82

4.4   There are special rules to cater for reorganisations and stock dividends. Broadly, shares issued on the occasion of a bonus or rights issue are treated as acquired at the same time as the original shares. If the original shares were acquired at different times (eg before and after 5 April 1998) the bonus or rights shares are apportioned pro rata between each acquisition. Where a company offers its shareholders (after 5 April 1998) a dividend in the form of additional shares (ie a stock or scrip dividend) as an alternative to cash, the new shares are treated as a free-standing acquisition – they are not related back to the time when the original shares were acquired (*TCGA 1992, ss 104–106A, 127, 142*).

Example 4.2

Duncan bought 500 shares in Anywhere Plc for £5,000 on 17 May 2000. Anywhere Plc announced a 1 for 1 rights issue of new ordinary shares at £1 each in June 2006. Duncan sold his rights when they were worth £600 and the original holding of 500 shares was worth £8,000.

	Total £	Sold £	Retained £
Proceeds	600	600	
Market value of shares retained	8,000		8,000
	8,600		
Cost allocated in proportion	(5,000)	(349)	(4,651)
	3,600		
Gain on disposal of shares		251	
Allowable expenditure for retained shares			3,349

The realised gain of £251 is chargeable to CGT, subject to taper relief.

Section 104 holding – shares held at 5 April 1998

4.5   The section 104 holding mentioned in (d) of **4.2** comprises shares of the same class that were acquired after 5 April 1982 and before 6 April 1998 by the same person in the same capacity. Such shares are treated as indistinguishable parts of a single asset. This single asset was initially called a 'new holding'. A disposal of some of the shares in a section 104 holding is treated as a part disposal of an asset (*TCGA 1992, s 104(1), (3), (6); FA 2006, Sch 12, para 17*).

The section 104 holding is treated as acquired when the holding first came into existence. If this was before 17 March 1998 the holding is eligible for the 'bonus year' in computing the non-business asset rate of taper relief (*TCGA 1992, s 106A(8); CG 50574*).

There are special rules for calculating indexation allowance in respect of a section 104 holding (*TCGA 1992, ss 110, 110A*). These provide for the gain to be computed by reference to the averaged indexed cost (with indexation frozen at April 1998) of each share disposed of. HMRC provide detailed guidance on this and other aspects of the section 104 holding at CG 50590–50801.

The 1982 holding

4.6 This comprises, broadly, all shares of the same class in the same company that were acquired between 6 April 1965 and 5 April 1982. The holding is treated as acquired on 31 March 1982 (*TCGA 1992, s 109*).

Identification: general rules for corporation tax

4.7 The change made in 1998 on the introduction of taper relief (see **4.2**) was of no relevance for corporation tax. Companies are not entitled to taper relief. This means that the 'pooling' arrangement described in **4.5** continues for corporation tax. The identification rules for companies are summarised below.

All shares of the same class in the same company that are acquired after 31 March 1982 are 'pooled', ie treated as a single asset with a single average indexed cost per share. Each disposal of shares out of the pool represents a part disposal of a single asset and the chargeable gain or allowable loss is computed by reference to the averaged indexed cost of the shares sold.

Shares disposed of are identified with acquisitions in the following order:

(a)   acquisitions on the same day as the disposal;

(b)   for disposals before 5 December 2005 (see below), where the company held at least 2% of the issued share capital of the same class prior to the disposal, acquisitions of quoted company shares in the previous month (or six months for unquoted companies) (later acquisitions first), then acquisitions in the following month (or six months) (earlier acquisitions first);

(c)   acquisitions during the nine days before the disposal date (earlier acquisitions first);

(d)   shares acquired after 31 March 1982 and comprised in the 'section 104 holding', see **4.5**;

(e)   shares acquired before 1 April 1982 (the '1982 holding', see **4.6**);

(f)   shares acquired before 6 April 1965 (taking later acquisitions first); and

(g) acquisitions after the disposal (taking earlier acquisitions first) (*TCGA 1992, ss 105–107*; CG 50562).

With regard to (b) above, the provision in *TCGA 1992, s 106* was repealed by *FA 2006, s 72* as a consequence of new anti-avoidance provisions relating to allowable losses and contained in *TCGA 1992, s 8* (see **Chapter 9**).

Special rules apply to 'relevant securities', ie qualifying corporate bonds, securities within the accrued income provisions, deep discount securities and material interests in non-qualifying offshore funds (*TCGA 1992, s 108*).

LAND

4.8 Land (including any building situated on it), or an interest in or right over land, is an asset for CGT purposes. However, in certain circumstances land transactions can give rise to a charge to income tax (or corporation tax) as trading or other income. This may apply where the land is acquired with the intention of selling it for profit, or holding it as trading stock, or developing it prior to disposal at a profit. *Tottel's Income Tax 2006/07* discusses the relevant anti-avoidance provisions.

The legal owner of land will not always be the person who has the beneficial interest in it. In most cases it is the beneficial owner who is chargeable to CGT. HMRC regard the following factors as indicative of beneficial ownership, although each case is considered on its particular facts:

- legal title (in the absence of any contrary evidence the legal owner will normally also be the beneficial owner);

- occupation of the land;

- receipt of any rental income from the land;

- provision of the funds used to purchase the land; and

- receipt of the sale proceeds from a disposal of the land (CG 70230).

Part disposals of land

4.9 Special rules apply to small part disposals of land. Where certain conditions are satisfied, the taxpayer may claim that the part disposal does not constitute a disposal for CGT purposes. The disposal proceeds are instead deducted from the cost of the land when calculating a gain on its subsequent disposal (see **2.5**).

The grant of a lease is a part disposal and the CGT treatment depends on the term of the lease (see **4.14**).

Leases of land

4.10   It is important to distinguish between the grant of a new lease by a landlord, and the assignment of an existing lease. A leasehold interest entitles the holder to exclusive possession of the property for a fixed term. A lease includes, for this purpose:

- an underlease, sublease, tenancy or licence;

- an agreement for a lease, underlease, sublease, tenancy or licence; and

- a corresponding interest in land outside the UK (*TCGA 1992, Sch 8, para 10(1)(a)*).

There are special rules to determine the duration of a lease for these purposes, for example, where the terms of the lease include a provision (i) allowing the landlord to terminate the lease before the end of the stated term, or (ii) allowing the tenant to extend the term.

Any term of a lease that makes it unlikely that it will continue beyond a certain time – for example, a provision for an increase in rent to an amount greatly in excess of a commercial rent – is treated as granted for a period ending at that time (*TCGA 1992, Sch 8, para 8*).

Assignment of a lease

4.11   The assignment of a lease is treated as a disposal (not a part disposal) of an interest in the property. The CGT treatment depends on how long the lease has to run at the time of the assignment:

- the assignment of a long lease is subject to the normal CGT rules;

- the assignment of a short lease (ie one that has no more than 50 years to run at the time of the disposal) is a disposal of a 'wasting asset', and only a percentage of the original cost is allowable for CGT purposes, as set out below.

A lease does not become a wasting asset until its duration does not exceed 50 years. Once it has become a wasting asset, its value does not waste away at a uniform rate (as described in **4.25** in relation to other wasting assets). The rate of decline in the value of the lease increases towards the end of its term and the allowable expenditure is restricted by reference to the table in *TCGA 1992, Sch 8, para 1*, as explained below.

Exclusion from acquisition expenditure

4.12 A fraction of the acquisition expenditure (within *TCGA 1992, s 38(1)(a)*) that is equal to:

$$\frac{P(1) - P(3)}{P(1)}$$

is excluded, where

- P1 is the percentage shown in the table for the duration of the lease at the beginning of the period of ownership; and
- P3 is the percentage shown in the table for the duration of the lease at the time of the disposal (*TCGA 1992, Sch 8, para 1(4)*).

Exclusion from enhancement expenditure

4.13 A fraction of the enhancement expenditure (within *TCGA 1992, s 38(1)(b)*) that is equal to:

$$\frac{P(2) - P(3)}{P(2)}$$

is excluded, where

- P2 is the percentage shown in the table for the duration of the lease at the time when the expenditure is first reflected in the nature of the lease; and
- P3 is the percentage shown in the table for the duration of the lease at the time of the disposal (*TCGA 1992, Sch 8, para 1(4)*).

Grant of a lease

4.14 The owner of a freehold interest may grant a lease, or a leaseholder may grant a sublease for all or a part of the remaining term of his leasehold interest.

The grant of a lease or sublease is a part disposal because the taxpayer retains an interest in the property. Part of the lease premium is chargeable to income tax as additional rent if the lease is for 50 years or less (see **4.16** and **4.17**). The part that is not treated as rent represents the proceeds of a part disposal for CGT purposes.

If a lease is granted to a connected person, or otherwise granted in a transaction not made at arm's length (see **3.5**), the market value is taken to be the premium received (*TCGA 1992, s 17*).

4.15   *Particular assets*

Grant of a long lease

4.15   Where a long lease is granted out of either a freehold interest or a long lease, the computation of the gain accruing follows the normal part disposal rules, using the formula [A/(A+B)], as described in **3.46**. In this situation:

* A is the amount of the premium received; and
* B is the value of the interest retained by the landlord plus the value of the right to receive rents payable under the lease (*TCGA 1992, Sch 8, para 2*).

Grant of a short lease out of freehold or long lease

4.16   Where a short lease is granted out of a freehold interest, or a short sublease is granted out of a long lease, the following rules apply.

First, part of the premium is treated as rent and is chargeable to:

* income tax under *ITTOIA 2005, s 276*; or
* corporation tax under *ICTA 1988, s 34*.

This amount is excluded from the consideration for the disposal (*TCGA 1992, Sch 8, para 5(1)*). It is calculated using the formula set out in the relevant income tax or corporation tax provision.

Secondly, the [A/(A+B)] part disposal formula in **4.15** is modified so that:

* A in the numerator is not the whole of the premium received but only the part of it that is not treated as rent, but
* A in the denominator (A + B) is unchanged because (A + B) has to represent the value of the whole interest before the lease was granted (*TCGA 1992, s 42(2)*; CG 70961).

Grant of a short sublease out of a short lease

4.17   Where a short sublease is granted out of a short lease, the part disposal formula in *TCGA 1992, s 42* does not apply. A short lease is a wasting asset and the allowable expenditure to be set against the premium in computing the gain is restricted so as to allow, as a deduction, the expenditure that will waste away during the term of the sublease (*TCGA 1992, Sch 8, para 4*).

The amount of the premium that is treated as rent is, in this case, deducted in arriving at the chargeable gain. It is not excluded from the consideration for the disposal (as shown in **4.16**) (*TCGA 1992, Sch 8, para 5(2)*).

Exchange of joint interests in land

4.18   If the proceeds received on the compulsory acquisition of land by an authority are reinvested in acquiring new land, a form of CGT roll-over relief may be available – see **17.21**.

By concession, HMRC may allow relief on similar lines where there is an exchange of interests in land that is in joint ownership (ESC D26). The relief is available where:

* a holding of land is held jointly and, as a result of the exchange, each joint owner becomes the sole owner of part of the land formerly owned jointly; or

* a number of separate holdings of land are held jointly and, as a result of the exchange, each joint owner becomes the sole owner of one or more holdings.

There are no restrictions on the use of the land, either before or after the exchange. However, the relief is denied or restricted where land acquired on the exchange is, or becomes subsequently, a dwelling house (or part of a dwelling house) eligible for private residence relief within *TCGA 1992, ss 222–226* (see **Chapter 11**).

On the other hand the relief may be claimed where, as a result of the exchange, individuals who were joint beneficial owners of their respective residences become sole owners of their homes, providing that any gain accruing on a disposal of each dwelling house immediately after the exchange would be exempt by virtue of private residence relief.

Furnished holiday lettings

4.19   Special rules apply to the 'commercial letting of furnished holiday accommodation' in the UK (*TCGA 1992, s 241*). This expression takes its meaning for CGT purposes from the definition given in:

* *ITTOIA 2005, Pt 3, Ch 6* for income tax; or

* *ICTA 1988, s 504* for corporation tax.

A UK property business that consists of such lettings is treated as a trade, and all such lettings made by a particular person (or partnership or body of persons) are treated as one trade, for all of the following purposes:

(a)   roll-over relief on replacement of business assets (*TCGA 1992, s 152*);

(b)   hold-over relief for gifts of business assets (*TCGA 1992, s 165*);

(c)   relief for loans to traders (*TCGA 1992, s 253*);

(d)   taper relief (*TCGA 1992, Sch A1*); and

(e)   the substantial shareholdings exemption for companies (*TCGA 1992, Sch 7AC*).

The accommodation is taken to be used, in the relevant chargeable period, only for the purposes of the trade. The trade is regarded as carried on throughout that chargeable period.

However, if the property is neither let commercially nor available to be so let for a part of the period, and it is not prevented from being so let by construction or repair work, then the trade is not treated as carried on during that part of the period (*TCGA 1992, s 241(3)–(5)*).

A 'just and reasonable' apportionment is to be made where accommodation is let and only a part of it is holiday accommodation (*TCGA 1992, s 241(6)*).

Where roll-over relief is obtained on a disposal – by virtue of (a) above – and private residence relief is available on a disposal of the replacement asset, the gain eligible for private residence relief is reduced by the amount of the reduction in allowable expenditure to take account of the roll-over relief claim. The effect is that the private residence relief is restricted to the part of the gain that exceeds the amount of the earlier gain that was rolled over (*TCGA 1992, s 241(7)*; CG 61453).

CHATTELS

4.20   An asset is a chattel if it is tangible, moveable property, ie a physical object that is not permanently attached to land or a building and can be moved easily without damaging its surroundings. Examples would include paintings and small items of plant and machinery.

A gain accruing on the disposal of a chattel that is not a wasting asset (see **4.22**) is not a chargeable gain if the amount or value of the consideration is £6,000 or less (*TCGA 1992, s 262(1)*).

Where the consideration exceeds £6,000, a marginal relief is deducted in arriving at the chargeable gain. The chargeable gain is restricted to five-thirds of the amount by which the consideration exceeds £6,000 (*TCGA 1992, s 262(2)*).

If a loss accrues on the disposal and the consideration does not exceed £6,000, the allowable loss is restricted by substituting £6,000 for the actual consideration. There is no such restriction if the consideration exceeds £6,000 (*TCGA 1992, s 262(3)*).

The chattels exemption does not apply to disposals of currency of any description, or disposals of commodities dealt with on a terminal market (*TCGA 1992, s 262(6)*).

Example 4.3

Hannah sells a painting for £7,200. The gain accruing, before deduction of the chattels exemption, is £5,500. Marginal relief is available so that the chargeable gain is restricted to 5/3 x (£7,200 – £6,000) = £2,000.

Parts of a set

4.21   Special rules are designed to prevent the taxpayer splitting a set of articles worth more than £6,000 into individual assets and selling them for less than £6,000 in order to secure the chattel exemption.

They apply where the taxpayer has disposed of two or more assets that have formed part of a set of articles, all of which he has owned at one time, and the disposals were made (either on the same occasion or on different occasions) to:

(a)   the same person;

(b)   persons acting 'in concert' (see below); or

(c)   persons who are connected persons (see **3.16**).

In these circumstances, the transactions are treated as a single transaction disposing of a single asset. The chattels exemption, as described in **4.20**, is applied to the deemed single transaction and apportioned accordingly among the various assets (*TCGA 1992, s 262(4)*).

HMRC take the view that a number of articles will form a set only if they are essentially similar and complementary and their value taken together is greater than their total individual value (CG 76632).

With regard to (b) above, they consider that if persons not connected with each other acquire assets forming part of a set, the fact that they have done so is not sufficient. There must be evidence that they have previously agreed to act together to acquire the assets (CG 76634).

WASTING ASSETS

Exemption for wasting chattels

4.22   As a general rule, no chargeable gain accrues on a disposal of a 'wasting chattel', ie an asset that is both tangible moveable property (see **4.20**)

91

and a wasting asset (see **4.23**). See **4.24**, however, regarding assets qualifying for capital allowances (*TCGA 1992, s 45(1)*).

Wasting asset: definition

4.23 A 'wasting asset' is generally an asset with a predictable life of no more than 50 years. In the case of tangible moveable property, 'life' means useful life having regard to the taxpayer's purpose in acquiring or providing the asset. Freehold land is never a wasting asset, irrespective of the nature of the land itself or the buildings on it.

Plant and machinery is always regarded as having a predictable life of less than 50 years. It is assumed, in estimating its predictable life, that:

- the asset's life will end when it is finally put out of use as being unfit for further use; and

- the asset will be used in the normal manner and to the normal extent throughout its estimated life.

A life interest in settled property is not regarded as a wasting asset until the predictable expectation of life of the life tenant is 50 years or less. Actuarial tables approved by HMRC are used to estimate the predictable life of such life interests (*TCGA 1992, s 44*).

Wasting assets qualifying for capital allowances

4.24 The wasting chattels exemption (see **4.22**) does not apply – but the allowable expenditure deducted in the CGT computation may be restricted (see **4.25**) – if the taxpayer:

(a) used the asset solely for the purposes of a trade, profession or vocation from the beginning of his period of ownership and either claimed or could have claimed capital allowances for expenditure that is also allowable expenditure in the CGT computation; or

(b) incurred any expenditure on the asset (or interest in it) that has otherwise qualified in full for capital allowances (*TCGA 1992, s 45(2)*).

Separate CGT computations are required where:

- the taxpayer has used the asset partly for the purposes of the business and partly for other purposes;

- he has used it for business purposes for only part of the period of ownership; or

- the asset has qualified in part only for capital allowances.

In these circumstances both the consideration for the disposal and the allowable expenditure are apportioned by reference to the extent to which the expenditure qualified for capital allowances, and the exemption is not given for the part of the gain apportioned to the use or expenditure described in (a) or (b) above (*TCGA 1992, s 45(3)*).

The exemption does not apply to a disposal of commodities that is made by a person dealing on a terminal market (*TCGA 1992, s 45(4)*).

Example 4.4

Victor bought an aircraft on 31 May 1997 at a cost of £90,000 for use in his air charter business. It has been agreed that Victor's non-business use of the aircraft amounts to 1/10th, on a flying hours basis, and capital allowances and running costs have accordingly been restricted for income tax purposes.

On 1 February 2007, Victor sells the aircraft for £185,000. The aircraft is agreed as having a useful life of 20 years at the date it was acquired. The indexation factor for May 1997 to April 1998 is 0.036.

	£
Relevant portion of consideration 9/10 x £185,000	166,500
Relevant portion of expenditure 9/10 x £90,000	(81,000)
Unindexed gain	85,500
Indexation £81,000 x 0.036	(2,916)
Gain (subject to taper relief)	82,584

Restriction of allowable expenditure

4.25   The gain accruing on the disposal of a wasting asset that is not exempt (see **4.22**) is computed on the assumption that an equal amount of expenditure on the asset is written off every day. This restriction does not apply, however, to certain wasting assets qualifying for capital allowances (see **4.29**).

Acquisition costs

4.26   The asset's residual or scrap value is deducted from the amount of expenditure incurred on its acquisition (including incidental costs) and the balance remaining is written off – from its full cost down to nil – at a uniform rate from the time of the acquisition of the asset to the end of its life. The residual or scrap value in this calculation is adjusted for any enhancement expenditure (see below) that increases that value.

This writing down of the allowable expenditure is achieved by excluding from the acquisition costs the fraction:

$$\frac{T(1)}{L}$$

where

- L is the predictable life of the asset at the time when it was acquired or provided by the person making the disposal; and

- T(1) is the period from that time to the time of disposal (*TCGA 1992, s 46(2)(a)*).

Enhancement costs

4.27   Enhancement expenditure is written off, in the same way, from the time when it is first reflected in the asset's state or nature to the end of the asset's life (*TCGA 1992, s 46(1), (3)*).

The allowable expenditure to be excluded from the enhancement costs is given by the fraction:

$$\frac{T(2)}{L - [T(1) - T(2)]}$$

where

- L is the predictable life of the asset at the time when it was acquired or provided by the person making the disposal; and

- T(2) is the period from the time when the enhancement expenditure is first reflected in the state or nature of the asset to the time of disposal (*TCGA 1992, s 46(2)(b)*).

Residual or scrap value

4.28   The 'residual or scrap value' of a wasting asset is the value that the asset is predicted to have at the end of its predictable life. Where the nature of an asset does not determine immediately its predictable life and its residual or scrap value, such questions are determined on the basis of facts that were known or ascertainable at the time when the person making the disposal acquired or provided the asset (*TCGA 1992, s 44(2), (3)*).

Wasting assets qualifying for capital allowances

4.29   The restriction of allowable expenditure (see **4.25**) does not apply if the taxpayer:

(a)   used the asset solely for the purposes of a trade, profession or vocation from the beginning of his period of ownership and either claimed or could have claimed capital allowances for expenditure that is also allowable expenditure for the purpose of the CGT computation (see **3.37**); or

(b)   incurred any expenditure on the asset (or interest in it) that has otherwise qualified in full for capital allowances (*TCGA 1992, s 47(1)*).

Separate CGT computations are required where:

- the taxpayer has used the asset partly for the purposes of the business and partly for other purposes;

- he has used it for business purposes for only part of the period of ownership; or

- the asset has qualified in part only for capital allowances.

In these circumstances both the consideration for the disposal and the allowable expenditure are apportioned having regard to the extent to which the expenditure qualified for capital allowances. The consideration for the disposal is apportioned in the same proportions as the allowable expenditure is apportioned, except that any apportionment used in computing a balancing allowance or balancing charge by reference to the disposal is to be used for this purpose.

The restriction described in **4.25** does not apply to the part of the gain apportioned to the use or expenditure described in (a) or (b) above (*TCGA 1992, s 47(2)*).

DEBTS

4.30   A debt is an asset for CGT purposes. However where a person (A) incurs a debt to another person (B), no chargeable gain accrues to the original creditor (B) on a disposal of the debt, except in the case of (i) a debt on a security, and (ii) money held in a foreign currency bank account that does not represent currency acquired for personal expenditure outside the UK (*TCGA 1992, ss 21(1), 251, 252*).

For individuals, trustees and personal representatives, a debt is, therefore, not normally subject to CGT unless it is a 'debt on a security' (meaning, broadly, marketable loan stock).

Most loan stock is a type of 'qualifying corporate bond', which is an exempt asset (*TCGA 1992, s 115*).

As a general rule, therefore, gains on simple debts are exempt from CGT and no relief is available for losses. However, relief is available for losses incurred (or guarantee payments made) in respect of loans made after 11 April 1978 to UK traders, where the loan has become irrecoverable and certain conditions are met. This relief is discussed at **17.16**.

Profits and losses on loans by companies are generally dealt with under the 'loan relationship' rules. Corporate debt is, therefore, outside the scope of corporation tax on chargeable gains but is otherwise included in the calculation of profits chargeable to corporation tax. See *Tottel's Corporation Tax 2006/07*.

ASSETS APPROPRIATED TO OR FROM TRADING STOCK

Assets appropriated to trading stock

4.31   If the taxpayer acquires an asset otherwise than as trading stock of a trade that he carries on, and he subsequently appropriates that asset for the purposes of the trade as trading stock, then in the absence of any election (see below) he is treated as if, at the time of the appropriation, he sold the asset for its market value. This is the case providing that a chargeable gain or allowable loss would have accrued on an actual sale at market value (*TCGA 1992, s 161(1)*).

Election

4.32   This deemed disposal rule does not apply where the asset is appropriated for the purposes of a trade carried on wholly or partly in the UK, the income of which is chargeable to income tax or corporation tax (and the taxpayer makes an election (*TCGA 1992, s 161(3)*)).

The effect of the election is that the asset's market value at the time of the appropriation is treated as reduced, in computing the trading income, by the amount of the chargeable gain that would have accrued on the deemed sale mentioned above. If an allowable loss would have arisen, then the market value is increased by the amount of that loss. An election made by a person carrying on a trade in partnership at the time of the appropriation is effective only if the other partners concur in the election (*TCGA 1992, s 161(3), (4)*).

The election time limit is fixed by reference to the year of assessment in which the period of account covering the time of the appropriation ended. The election must be made within 12 months after 31 January following that year of assessment. For corporation tax purposes the election must be made within two years after the end of the accounting period in which the appropriation took place (*TCGA 1992, s 161(3A)*).

Assets appropriated from trading stock

4.33   If the taxpayer appropriates for another purpose an asset forming part of his trading stock, or he retains the asset on the cessation of his trade, he is treated as having acquired it at that time for a consideration equal to the amount brought into the accounts as a trading receipt (*TCGA 1992, s 161(2)*).

Chapter 5

Residence, ordinary residence and domicile

This chapter focuses on the CGT implications of an individual's residence and domicile status. The residence status of trustees is examined in **Chapter 8**. See **Chapter 9** and *Tottel's Corporation Tax 2006/07* regarding companies.

BASIS OF THE CHARGE TO CGT

5.1   A person is chargeable to CGT in respect of chargeable gains accruing to him on the disposal of assets in a year of assessment:

- during any part of which he is 'resident' in the UK; or

- during which he is 'ordinarily resident' in the UK (*TCGA 1992, ss 1, 2(1)*).

'Accruing' here means realised or deemed to be realised, rather than accumulated over a period. Anti-avoidance rules provide for a person to be chargeable to CGT on gains accruing to others in certain circumstances. For example:

- a non-resident person carrying on a business in the UK through a branch or agency (or through a permanent establishment, in the case of a company) is chargeable to CGT (or corporation tax) on gains arising from assets in the UK that are used for the purposes of the business (see **5.11**);

- a person who is a 'temporary non-resident' of the UK may be chargeable on gains accruing during years of non-residence (see **5.16**); and

- the gains of a non-resident trust (see **8.1**) or company (see **5.23**) may be attributed to a UK-resident individual.

Meaning of residence, etc

5.2   'Resident' and 'ordinarily resident' have the same meanings in *TCGA 1992* as they have in the Income Tax Acts (ie the enactments relating to income tax, including any provisions of the Corporation Tax Acts which relate to income tax) (*TCGA 1992, s 9(1); ICTA 1988, s 831(1)*).

An individual's domicile is also a key factor in determining a person's liability to CGT. An individual who meets the residence tests outlined above and is domiciled in any part of the UK is chargeable to CGT on gains accruing on the disposal of assets situated anywhere in the world. However, the liability of a non-domiciled individual in respect of gains accruing on the disposal of non-UK assets is limited to gains remitted to the UK (see **5.20**).

Since domicile is a matter of general law rather than tax law, it has the same meaning for CGT as it has for income tax. The meaning of the terms residence, ordinary residence and domicile is examined further in *Tottel's Income Tax 2006/07*.

HMRC's Centre for Non-Residents handles matters relating to a taxpayer's residence status: see www.hmrc.gov.uk/cnr. Detailed guidance is available in HMRC's leaflet IR 20.

Territorial limits of CGT

5.3   The UK comprises Great Britain and Northern Ireland. It includes the UK's territorial seas but excludes the Isle of Man and the Channel Islands. CGT is not limited to gains on the disposal of UK assets. However, gains accruing on non-UK assets are chargeable, in the case of an individual who is not domiciled in any part of the UK, only if and to the extent that the gains are remitted to the UK.

Presence in UK for temporary purposes only

5.4   As a general rule, an individual who is present in the UK for some temporary purpose only and not with any view or intent to establish his residence here is charged to CGT on chargeable gains accruing in a year of assessment if (and only) if he is resident in the UK in that year of assessment for a period (or periods) amounting to more than six months.

Any living accommodation available in the UK for the individual's use is disregarded for this purpose. For years prior to 1993/94, an individual who had living accommodation available to him in the UK was generally treated as UK resident in any year of assessment during which he visited the UK, regardless of the length of his visit (*TCGA 1992, s 9(3), (4)*).

Visiting armed forces

5.5   A member of the visiting armed force of a designated country is not treated as resident in the UK for CGT purposes, and is not treated as changing his residence or domicile status, for any period to which the income tax exemption in *ITEPA 2003, s 303(1)* applies solely because he is a member of that force (*TCGA 1992, s 11(1)*).

Diplomatic staff

5.6   UK-resident 'agents-general' (representatives of certain foreign governments) and certain members of their staff are entitled to the same immunity from CGT as that conferred on a UK-resident head of a diplomatic mission under the *Diplomatic Privileges Act 1964* (*TCGA 1992, s 11(2)–(4)*).

Disputes as to residence, etc status

5.7   Any dispute as to whether a person is (or has been) ordinarily resident or domiciled in the UK for CGT purposes is to be referred to and decided by the Commissioners for HMRC. If a person who has been given notice of the decision is aggrieved by the decision he may, within three months of receipt of the notice, appeal to the Special Commissioners (*TCGA 1992, s 9(2)* applying *Income Tax (Earnings and Pensions) Act 2003, ss 42* and *43*).

Appeals relating to residence status (as opposed to ordinary residence and domicile) and claims to relief are made to the General Commissioners or to the Special Commissioners (HMRC leaflet IR 20, Ch 10).

ARRIVING IN OR LEAVING THE UK

Arriving in the UK

5.8   An individual who is not ordinarily resident in the UK and arrives in the UK with the intention of settling here is treated as UK resident from the date of arrival. He is, therefore, resident for a part of the year of assessment in which he arrives and is chargeable to CGT for that year (see **5.1**).

An individual who is present in the UK for a temporary purpose only (see **5.4**) but spends more than six months in the UK in a year of assessment becomes chargeable to CGT on the basis that he is resident for that part of the year in which he is present here.

The rule set out in **5.1** means that strictly speaking an individual who is resident in the UK during any part of the year of assessment is chargeable to CGT on all chargeable gains accruing during that year, including those accruing before he became resident.

By concession, however, HMRC will split the year in which UK residence begins, so that gains accruing before the change of status are not chargeable, so long as the taxpayer has not been resident or ordinarily resident here at any time during the five preceding years of assessment (HMRC concession ESC D2, reproduced below).

HMRC will consider withholding the benefit of this concession where the taxpayer 'has entered into arrangements in an attempt to use the terms of ESC D2 to avoid liability to CGT which would otherwise arise'. See, for example, **5.10** with regard to *Regina v HM Inspector of Taxes, Reading ex parte Fulford-Dobson* (CG 25981).

HMRC concession ESC D2

Residence in the UK: year of commencement or cessation of residence: CGT

1. An individual who comes to live in the United Kingdom and is treated as resident here for any year of assessment from the date of arrival is charged to capital gains tax only in respect of chargeable gains from disposals made after arrival, provided that the individual has not been resident or ordinarily resident in the United Kingdom at any time during the five years of assessment immediately preceding the year of assessment in which he or she arrived in the United Kingdom.

2. An individual who leaves the United Kingdom and is treated on departure as not resident and not ordinarily resident here is not charged to capital gains tax on gains from disposals made after the date of departure, provided that the individual was not resident and not ordinarily resident in the United Kingdom for the whole of at least four out of the seven years of assessment immediately preceding the year of assessment in which he or she left the United Kingdom.

3. This concession does not apply to any individual in relation to gains on the disposal of assets which are situated in the United Kingdom and which, at any time between the individual's departure from the United Kingdom and the end of the year of assessment, are either:

(i) used in or for the purposes of a trade, profession or vocation carried on by that individual in the United Kingdom through a branch or agency; or

(ii) used or held for, or acquired for use by or for the purposes of, such a branch or agency.

4. This concession does not apply to the trustees of a settlement who commence or cease residence in the United Kingdom or to a settlor of a settlement in relation to gains in respect of which the settlor is chargeable under Sections 77–79 TCGA 1992, or Section 86 and Schedule 5 TCGA 1992.

5. This revised concession applies to any individual who ceases to be resident or ordinarily resident in the United Kingdom on or after 17 March 1998, or becomes resident or ordinarily resident in the United Kingdom on or after 6 April 1998.

The split-year treatment provided by paragraph 1 of the concession does not apply, therefore, where a taxpayer arriving in the UK was previously resident here and there are less than five complete tax years between the time of his departure and his return to the UK. In this situation, gains accruing at any time in the tax year of arrival are chargeable.

Leaving the UK

5.9   An individual leaving the UK during a year of assessment may be treated as not resident and not ordinarily resident in the UK from the day after his departure. However, his UK resident status for the period up to the date of departure means, as indicated in **5.1**, that strictly speaking he is chargeable to CGT on all chargeable gains accruing during the year, including those accruing after he became not resident and not ordinarily resident.

By concession, HMRC will split the year of departure so that gains accruing after the change of status are not chargeable, so long as the taxpayer has been not resident and not ordinarily resident in the UK for the whole of at least four out of the seven preceding years of assessment (HMRC concession ESC D2, reproduced in **5.8**).

The split-year treatment provided by paragraph 2 of the concession does not apply, therefore, where a taxpayer leaving the UK has been UK resident or ordinarily resident in any part of four or more of the seven preceding years of assessment. In this situation, gains accruing at any time in the tax year of departure are chargeable.

HMRC guidance indicates that cases will be examined where the date of disposal of an asset appears to be soon after the date of emigration, with a view to establishing whether a CGT liability arises, because:

- there was a binding agreement or contract for sale on or before the date of emigration;

- a business was carried on in the UK through a branch or agency in the period from the date of emigration to the date of disposal; or

- an attempt has been made to use ESC D2 for tax avoidance (CG 25805).

See **5.13** regarding the exception in paragraph 3 of the concession for gains on the disposal of assets used in or for the purposes of a trade, etc carried on in the UK through a branch or agency.

5.10   As indicated above, HMRC may seek to withhold the concession if the taxpayer tries to use it for tax avoidance purposes. In *Regina v HM Inspector of Taxes, Reading ex parte Fulford-Dobson* [1987] 60 TC 168 (QB), the taxpayer's wife (W) inherited a farm in 1977. She was considering selling it during 1980, at a time when the taxpayer (H) was negotiating employment with a German firm. H's contract of employment was signed on 18 August, requiring him to live and work in Germany and to commence work on 15 September. W transferred the farm to H by deed of gift on 29 August; H left for Germany on 13 September; and the farm was sold by auction on 17 September.

H admitted that one of the reasons for W's transfer of the farm to him was to ensure that the sale would be outside the scope of CGT by virtue of ESC D2, because at the time of the sale he would not be UK resident. HMRC took the view that there was an attempt to use the concession for tax avoidance and denied the benefit of the concession. The taxpayer sought a judicial review of that decision and the High Court held that:

- concession D2 was lawful, falling within the proper exercise of managerial discretion;

- HMRC was entitled, in giving a concession, to take reasonable steps to prevent its abuse; and

- the transactions undertaken by the taxpayers amounted to tax avoidance within the terms of HMRC's general 'health warning' about the use of concessions for tax avoidance.

HMRC do not regard a genuine postponement of the disposal on its own as an attempt to use the concession for avoidance, although they may regard it as such if it is combined with other arrangements (CG 25982).

They accept that the benefit of the no gain/no loss rule for transfers between spouses and civil partners (under *TCGA 1992, s 58*, see **3.67**) is available on the transfer to a non-resident spouse or civil partner (i) after that spouse or civil partner has become non-resident, and (ii) in a year throughout the whole of which that spouse or civil partner is non-resident. This reflects the majority decision of the House of Lords in *Gubay v Kington* [1984] 57 TC 601, HL. HMRC guidance says (CG 22304):

> 'There is no longer any authority to treat a non-resident spouse as separated from a resident spouse merely because of their residence status. Similarly a non-resident civil partner may not be treated as separated from a resident civil partner merely because of their residence status. So the possibility of passing assets outside the UK tax net remains.'

A taxpayer who becomes neither resident nor ordinarily resident in the UK may become chargeable to CGT, as a result of his change of status, on a gain that was held over following a claim to hold-over relief for gifts of business assets (see **13.2**) or gifts immediately chargeable (or exempt from) inheritance tax (see **13.37**).

NON-RESIDENTS DOING BUSINESS IN THE UK

5.11   Non-residents are, broadly, chargeable to tax on gains arising (i) on the disposal of UK assets used to carry on a business in the UK (see **5.13**), or (ii) on a deemed disposal when the assets are removed from the UK or the business ceases (see **5.14**).

Individuals

5.12   A person who is not resident and not ordinarily resident in the UK in a year of assessment remains chargeable to CGT in respect of certain gains accruing to him in that year if he is carrying on a trade, profession or vocation in the UK through a branch or agency in that year. See **5.15** regarding companies chargeable to corporation tax.

Disposal of assets

5.13   The charge applies to gains accruing on the disposal of any of the following assets, where the disposal is made at a time when the person is carrying on the trade, etc in the UK through a branch or agency:

- assets situated in the UK and used in, or for the purposes of, the trade, etc either at the time when the capital gain accrued or before that time;

- assets situated in the UK and used, or held, for the purposes of the branch or agency either at or before that time; and

- assets situated in the UK and acquired for use by, or for the purposes of, the branch or agency (*TCGA 1992, s 10(1), (2), (5)*).

'Branch or agency' means any factorship, agency, receivership, branch or management. There is no charge under this rule if the taxpayer is exempt from income tax on the profits or gains of the branch or agency by virtue of double tax relief arrangements (*TCGA 1992, s 10(4), (6)*).

The split-year concession ESC D2, discussed in **5.9**, does not apply (see paragraph 3 of the concession) to an individual in relation to gains on the disposal of assets situated in the UK that are used as set out in (a) or (b) below at any time between his departure from the UK and the end of the year of assessment:

(a)   used in or for the purposes of a trade, profession or vocation carried on by that individual in the UK through a branch or agency; or

(b)   used or held for, or acquired for use by or for the purposes of, such a branch or agency.

For an individual seeking to sell a UK business as a going concern and emigrate from the UK, the combined effect of *TCGA 1992, s 10* and HMRC's denial of concession ESC D2 is broadly as set out below:

- delaying the contract until after the taxpayer's departure is likely to involve making arrangements for the business to continue in his absence – HMRC consider that in most cases such as this they could argue that the activity is carried on in the UK through a branch or agency in the period between departure and the date of the contract;

- a disposal after the date of emigration but before the end of the year of assessment would be within the charge to CGT as set out in *TCGA 1992, s 2* and ESC D2 would not apply (as already indicated); and

- a disposal in the year of assessment following the year of emigration would also be within the charge to CGT, by virtue of *TCGA 1992, s 10* (CG 25900–25903).

Deemed disposals

5.14   A chargeable gain is deemed to accrue in the circumstances described below. This rule was introduced to prevent a taxpayer avoiding the charges on an actual disposal, described in **5.13**, by (i) transferring assets abroad before the disposal, or (ii) discontinuing the branch activities in one year of assessment and disposing of the assets in the following year of assessment.

There is a deemed disposal and reacquisition at market value where 'chargeable assets' (see below) are:

(a)   transferred abroad (*TCGA 1992, s 25(1)*); or

(b)   cease to be 'chargeable assets' because the individual ceases to carry on the trade, etc in the UK through a branch or agency (*TCGA 1992, s 25(3)*).

For this purpose, assets are 'chargeable assets' only if the individual is not resident and not ordinarily resident in the UK and a chargeable gain on their disposal would be chargeable under *TCGA 1992, s 10(1)* as described above (*TCGA 1992, s 25(7)*).

There is no deemed disposal within (a) if:

•   the transfer occurs on the cessation of the trade, etc; or

•   the asset is an exploration or exploitation asset, as defined (*TCGA 1992, s 25(2)*).

There is no deemed disposal within (b) if the asset is used, before the end of the chargeable period in which the cessation occurs, in another trade, etc carried on by the same individual in the UK through a branch or agency (*TCGA 1992, s 25(5)*).

Companies

5.15   A company that is not resident in the UK is nonetheless chargeable to corporation tax in respect of chargeable gains accruing to it if the company is carrying on a trade (including for this purpose a vocation, office or employment) in the UK through a permanent establishment in the UK (*TCGA 1992, s 10B*). See **Chapter 9** and *Tottel's Corporation Tax 2006/07*.

TEMPORARY NON-RESIDENCE

5.16   Special rules apply to individuals who realise capital gains during a period of temporary absence from the UK, during which their residence status would otherwise mean that they escaped CGT (*TCGA 1992, s 10A*). Broadly, an individual who leaves the UK and subsequently returns is chargeable to CGT on gains arising during his absence on the disposal of assets owned prior to departure, if:

- he was UK resident for at least four of the seven years of assessment prior to departure; and

- the period of non-residence is less than five complete years of assessment.

Gains arising in the year of departure are chargeable in that year and gains arising during the period of absence are chargeable in the year in which UK residence is resumed (*TCGA 1992, s 2*). Gains on assets acquired abroad that are realised in the intervening years of non-residence are outside the charge, subject to certain anti-avoidance provisions.

The following summary relates to the provisions of *TCGA 1992, s 10A* as amended by *F(No 2)A 2005*. These apply, broadly, where the 'year of departure' (see below) is 2005/06 or later (or, in some cases, 2004/05).

5.17   The charge arises in the following circumstances, a 'year' being a year of assessment:

(a)   the taxpayer satisfies the 'residence requirements' (ie broadly speaking, he is resident or ordinarily resident in the UK, see below) for a year (the 'year of return');

(b)   he did not satisfy the residence requirements for one or more years immediately preceding the year of return, but there are prior years for which he did satisfy them;

(c)   there are fewer than five 'intervening years', ie years falling between the year of departure (see below) and the year of return; and

(d)   he satisfied the residence requirements for at least four out of the seven years immediately preceding the year of departure (*TCGA 1992, s 10A(1)*).

All of these conditions must be met before the charge can arise. If any of these conditions is not met, no charge arises on any gains accruing in the intervening years (and any losses accruing in those years are not allowable).

With regard to (a), the taxpayer satisfies the residence requirements for a year of assessment:

- if he is resident in the UK and not 'treaty non-resident' (see below) during any part of that year; or

- if he is ordinarily resident in the UK during that year (unless he is treaty non-resident during that year) (*TCGA 1992, s 10A(9)*).

The 'year of departure' in (c) is the last year of assessment, before the year of return, for which the taxpayer satisfied the residence requirements. An 'intervening year', where conditions (a) to (d) above apply, is a year of assessment falling between the year of departure and the year of return (*TCGA 1992, s 10A(8)*).

An individual is 'treaty non-resident' at any time if, at that time, he is regarded as resident in a territory outside the UK for the purposes of double taxation relief arrangements (*TCGA 1992, s 10A(9A); s 228(7B)* inserted by *FA 2006, s 74 (3), (4)* with effect from 22 March 2006).

Gains, etc treated as accruing in year of return

5.18   In the circumstances outlined above, the taxpayer is chargeable to CGT as if the following gains or losses accrued to him in the year of return:

(a)   all the chargeable gains and losses which, apart from this rule, would have accrued to him – had he been resident and ordinarily resident in the UK – in an intervening year;

(b)   all the chargeable gains which, under *TCGA 1992, s 13* (see **5.23**) or *TCGA 1992, s 86* (see **8.1**), would be treated as accruing to him in an intervening year if he had been resident in the UK throughout that intervening year; and

(c)   any losses which, by virtue of *TCGA 1992, s 13(8)* (see **5.23**), would have been allowable in an intervening year if he had been resident in the UK throughout that intervening year (*TCGA 1992, s 10A(2), (6)*).

Chargeable gains and allowable losses are not to be brought into account in the year of return if they are gains or losses accruing in an intervening year and they fall to be taken into account under *TCGA 1992, s 10* or *TCGA 1992, s 16(3)* (non-residents carrying on a trade, etc through a UK branch or agency, see **5.11**) (*TCGA 1992, s 10A(5)*).

The normal time limits for assessments are modified where *TCGA 1992, s 10A* applies. Any assessment for the year of departure may be made at any time up to two years after the 31 January following the year of return (*TCGA 1992, s 10A(7)*).

Exclusion for assets acquired after departure from UK

5.19   The gains and losses treated as accruing to the taxpayer in the year of return (see **5.18**) exclude (except as mentioned below) any gain or loss accruing on his disposal of an asset if:

(a)   he acquired the asset at a time in the year of departure or any intervening year when (i) he was neither resident nor ordinarily resident in the United Kingdom, or (ii) he was resident or ordinarily resident in the UK but was 'treaty non-resident' (see below);

(b)   the acquisition did not take place by means of a 'relevant disposal' (see below) treated as a no gain/no loss transfer by virtue of *TCGA 1992, ss 58, 73* or *258(4)* (transfers between spouses or civil partners, property reverting to settlor on the death of a life tenant, and transfers of heritage property);

(c)   the asset is not an interest created by or arising under a settlement; and

(d)   the amount or value of the consideration for the taxpayer's acquisition of the asset is not reduced by any of the CGT roll-over reliefs provided by *TCGA 1992, ss 23(4)(b), (5)(b), 152(1)(b), 153(1)(b)* (with effect for disposals after 15 March 2005), *162(3)(b), 247(2)(b)* or *247(3)(b)*.

The 'relevant disposal' above is a disposal of an asset acquired by the person making the disposal at a time when he was resident or ordinarily resident in the UK and was not 'treaty non-resident' (*TCGA 1992, s 10A(3), (8)*).

However, a gain is not excluded from the charge (ie it is chargeable as described in **5.18**) if:

•   it has accrued or would have accrued on the disposal of any asset (the 'first asset');

•   it is treated as accruing on the disposal of the whole or part of another asset (the 'other asset') by virtue of *ss 116(10), (11), 134* or *154(2), (4)* (reorganisations, compensation stock and roll-over relief for depreciating assets); and

•   paragraphs (a) to (d) above apply to that other asset but not to the first asset (*TCGA 1992, s 10A(4)*).

The exclusion for assets acquired after departure from the UK applies only to the special charge under *TCGA 1992, 10A*. It does not have any bearing on any liability under the basic charging provision of *TCGA 1992, s 2*, which may give rise to a liability in the year of departure or the year of return to the UK where the split-year concession (ESC D2) is not available.

Nothing in any double tax relief treaty is to be read as preventing the taxpayer from being chargeable to CGT in respect of chargeable gains treated as accruing to him in the year of return (*TCGA 1992, s 10A(9C)*).

Example 5.1

Pedro came to live permanently in the UK on 5 January 1994. He left the UK to live in Cuba on 1 April 2002 and returned on 16 March 2006. During the period of absence he sold shares he acquired in a UK company in 1996 and made a gain of £40,000. Pedro is treated as being a temporary non-resident as the period of non-residence amounted to less than five complete tax years, and he was UK resident for at least four of the seven tax years before he left on 1 April 2002. The gain of £40,000 realised while he was living in Cuba is chargeable to CGT in 2005/06 and the CGT due is payable on 31 January 2007.

FOREIGN ASSETS OF NON-UK DOMICILED TAXPAYERS

5.20   CGT is not charged (except as stated below) on gains accruing on the disposal of assets situated outside the UK to an individual who is:

- resident or ordinarily resident in the UK (ie within the charge to CGT), but
- not domiciled in any part of the UK.

Where this exemption applies and amounts are remitted to the UK in respect of such gains, however, CGT is charged on the amounts received in the UK. Remittances are treated as gains accruing when they are received in the UK. The remittance basis does not apply, however, to remittances of gains that accrued before the individual became resident or ordinarily resident in the UK (*TCGA 1992, s 12(1)*).

HMRC take the view that if a non-domiciled individual acquires a UK domicile, the remittance basis applies to gains accruing before the change of domicile that are remitted to the UK after the change (CG 25311).

A non-domiciled individual who meets the residence tests in **5.1** remains chargeable on all gains accruing on the disposal of UK assets. The location of assets is examined in **5.34**.

Remittances

5.21   An amount is treated as received in the UK in respect of a gain if it is:

- an amount paid, used or enjoyed in the UK; or
- an amount transmitted or brought in any manner or form to the UK.

It is also provided that the anti-avoidance rules in *ITTOIA 2005, ss 833* and *834* (dealing with the repayment of UK-linked debts) apply as they would apply for the purpose of *ITTOIA 2005, s 832* if the gain were 'relevant foreign income' (*TCGA 1992, s 12(2)*). These rules are designed to counter arrangements involving loans, the proceeds of which are used or enjoyed in the UK, that are repaid out of gains that are not otherwise remitted to the UK.

Where a gain is not remitted directly but is invested in other assets, the gain is traced through those assets in order to establish whether the gain has been remitted to the UK. HMRC take the view that such tracing can take place through 'any number of investments, deposits to bank accounts, transfers between accounts, etc' (CG 25352).

HMRC's approach to remittances from 'mixed funds' – eg a bank deposit comprising deposits representing (i) income, (ii) capital, and (iii) capital gains – is set out in CG 25380–25440.

If the disposal giving rise to the gain is the gift of a non-UK asset, the donor has nothing to remit to the UK and the gain cannot be assessable on the remittance basis.

Remittance basis: computation of gains

5.22 Once gains remitted to the UK have been identified, the computation of the chargeable gain (in sterling) follows the normal rules applying at the time of the disposal, with indexation allowance (frozen at April 1998) being given where appropriate. Any delay between the time of the disposal and the remittance to the UK does not change the qualifying holding period for taper relief (see Example 5.2). HMRC practice regarding the application of double tax relief where gains are assessed on the remittance basis is explained at CG 14385–14427.

A loss accruing on the disposal of non-UK assets to an individual who is resident or ordinarily resident but not domiciled in the UK is not an allowable loss (*TCGA 1992, ss 12(1), 16(4)*).

Example 5.2

Arno is a non-domiciled but UK-resident taxpayer. He acquired shares in ABN, a foreign quoted company, in May 2002 and disposed of them in August 2006. The gain was remitted to the UK in January 2008. Arno held the shares for four complete years from May 2002 to May 2006 so that taper relief is available at the non-business asset rate of 10%. The delay in remitting the gain does not affect the qualifying holding period.

APPORTIONMENT OF NON-RESIDENT COMPANY'S GAINS

5.23 Chargeable gains accruing to certain non-UK resident companies may be treated as accruing to UK-resident individuals who have an interest in the company. The rules in *TCGA 1992, s 13* apply to chargeable gains accruing to a company that is not resident in the UK but would be a close company if it were UK resident. Gains apportioned to participators in this way are not eligible for taper relief (see **11.35**) (*TCGA 1992, s 13(10A)*). HMRC guidance on the application of these rules is set out in CG 57200–57411.

Apportionment to UK-resident participator

5.24   When a chargeable gain accrues to the company, a part of it is treated as accruing to every person who:

- is resident or ordinarily resident in the UK when the chargeable gain accrues to the company;
- is (in the case of an individual) domiciled in the UK; and
- is a participator in the company.

The company's gain is computed as if the company were within the charge to corporation tax on capital gains. Transfers between members of a group of non-resident companies are treated as if the group was UK resident for this purpose. The part of the gain that is attributed to each participator is based on the extent of his interest as a participator in the company. However, there is no charge where the amount apportioned to the taxpayer and to persons connected with him is not more than 10% of the gain (*TCGA 1992, ss 13(1)–(4), 13(11A), 14*).

If the company to which the gain accrues pays the participator's tax liability, that payment is ignored for the purposes of income tax, CGT and corporation tax but is not allowable as a deduction in computing the participator's gain on a disposal of shares (*TCGA 1992, s 13(11)*).

'Participator' and 'close company' take their meaning from *ICTA 1988, ss 417* and *414* respectively (*TCGA 1992, ss 13(12)* and *288(1)*), but see also **5.30** regarding participators.

Exceptions

5.25   There is no charge in respect of a chargeable gain:

- accruing on the disposal of an asset used only for the purposes of (i) a trade carried on by the company wholly outside the UK, or (ii) the part carried on outside the UK of a trade carried on by the company partly within and partly outside the UK;

- accruing on the disposal of either currency or a debt within *TCGA 1992, s 252(1)*, where the currency or debt is (or represents) money in use for the purposes of a non-UK trade carried on by the company; or

- in respect of which the company is chargeable to tax under *TCGA 1992, s 10B* (see **5.15**) (*TCGA 1992, s 13(5)*).

The assets of a pension scheme are ignored in determining a person's interest as participator for this purpose, if a gain accruing on disposal of the scheme's assets would be exempt from CGT (*TCGA 1992, s 13(10B)*).

Set-off on distribution of gain

5.26 Where a charge arises (see **5.24**) and tax is paid accordingly, and there is a distribution in respect of the chargeable gain within a specified period (see below), the tax is set against the taxpayer's liability to income tax, CGT or corporation tax on the distribution.

The distribution may be made by means of a dividend or distribution of capital, or on the dissolution of the company. The set-off is reduced to the extent that the tax is reimbursed by the company or applied as a deduction (see below).

The specified period is the period of three years from the earlier of:

- the end of the company's period of account in which the chargeable gain accrued; or

- the end of the period of 12 months from the date when the chargeable gain accrued (*TCGA 1992, s 13(5A), (5B)*).

Deduction on disposal of interest in the company

5.27 If the taxpayer pays the CGT charged as mentioned in **5.24** above and the tax is neither reimbursed by the company nor set-off as mentioned in **5.26**, it is allowable as a deduction in computing a gain accruing on his disposal of any asset representing his interest as a participator in the company (*TCGA 1992, s 13(7)*).

Calculation of the income tax or CGT chargeable

5.28 For the purpose of calculating any income tax or CGT chargeable for any year on the distribution or disposal, the following rules apply:

113

(a)   a distribution treated as the person's income for that year forms the highest part of his chargeable income;

(b)   a gain accruing in that year on the person's disposal of any asset representing his interest as a participator forms the highest part of his chargeable gains;

(c)   where a distribution falls to be treated as a disposal giving rise to a chargeable gain, the gain forms the next highest part of his chargeable gains, after any gains within (b); and

(d)   a gain apportioned to him as mentioned in **5.24** and treated as accruing to him in that year is regarded as the next highest part of his chargeable gains, after any gains within (c) (*TCGA 1992, s 13(7A)*).

Losses

5.29   Losses accruing to the non-resident company are not attributed to participators. However, in arriving at the amount of gains accruing to a company that can be apportioned to participators, a loss may be deducted if it would be an allowable loss in the hands of a UK-resident company (*TCGA 1992, s 13(8)*).

Participators

5.30   'Participator' takes its meaning from *ICTA 1988, s 417*. Broadly, any person who has a share or interest in the capital or income of the company is a participator. However, it is also provided for the purpose of the apportionment of gains under *TCGA 1992, s 13*, that:

(a)   a person's interest as a participator in a company is the interest in the company that is represented by all the factors contributing to his treatment as a participator; and

(b)   the 'extent' of that interest is the proportion of all participators' interests that the person's interest represents.

The apportionment in (b) is made on a just and reasonable basis and takes account of interests of participators who are neither resident nor ordinarily resident in the UK (*TCGA 1992, s 13(13)*).

Any appeal as to the extent of a person's interest as a participator for this purpose is made to the Special Commissioners (*TCGA 1992, s 13(15)*).

If a person's beneficial interest under a settlement is a factor in determining whether he has an interest as a participator in a company, the interest as a participator is deemed to be the trustees' interest to the extent that it is represented by the beneficial interest (*TCGA 1992, s 13(14)*).

Corporate participators

5.31   If the participator (A) in the non-UK resident company (B) is itself a non-UK resident company, but would be a close company if it were UK resident, then the amount apportioned to A is further apportioned among A's participators according to the extent of their respective interests as participators. Since A's participators may include companies, and those companies' participators may also include companies, the rule is applied through any number of companies (*TCGA 1992, s 13(9)*).

Trustees

5.32   Gains may be attributed to trustees of a settlement who are participators in the company, even if they are neither resident nor ordinarily resident in the UK. Such gains may be attributed to UK-resident beneficiaries under the provisions of *TCGA 1992, Ch II* (see **8.1**) (*TCGA 1992, s 13(10)*; *FA 2006 Sch 12, para 8*).

DOUBLE TAX RELIEF

5.33   Double tax relief is described in detail at **3.80**. Relief may be available by virtue of double tax relief arrangements to taxpayers who are not resident in the UK but are chargeable to UK tax under any of the provisions discussed in this chapter. See, however, **5.19** regarding double tax relief arrangements to be disregarded in relation to gains accruing in a period of temporary non-residence, and **5.22** regarding the application of double tax relief where gains are assessed on the remittance basis.

LOCATION OF ASSETS

5.34   It is often unnecessary to establish the location of an asset for CGT purposes, but in some circumstances the asset's location will determine the extent of any liability. For example:

- non-residents are chargeable to tax on gains arising on the disposal or deemed disposal of UK assets used to carry on a business in the UK (see **5.11**); and

- a remittance basis applies to non-domiciled individuals, but only in relation to non-UK assets (see **5.20**).

The territorial limits of the UK are set out in **5.3**. Most of the rules fixing the location of assets for CGT purposes are contained in *TCGA 1992, s 275* and the main rules are summarised briefly in Table 5.1. Note also the changes enacted in *F(No 2)A 2005* and summarised below.

Table 5.1

Asset	Location
1. Immovable property	Where the property is situated
2. Tangible movable property or chattels	Where the property is situated
3. Debts (secured or unsecured)	Where the creditor resides
4. Shares or securities of a local or governmental authority	The country of that authority
5. Other shares or securities	See below
6. Ships or aircraft	The country in which the owner is resident
7. Goodwill	Where the trade, etc is carried on
8. Patents, trademarks and registered designs	Where they are registered
9. Copyright, design right and franchises	Where the right or design is exercisable
10. A judgment debt	Where the judgment is recorded
11. Futures, options and intangible assets	See below

With regard to item 5, anti-avoidance legislation applies to assets such as bearer shares in a UK company with effect from 16 March 2005. Shares in or debentures of a company incorporated in the UK (other than shares, etc within item 4) are treated as situated in the UK. Subject to that rule, registered shares or debentures are situated where they are registered. If they are registered in more than one register, they are situated where the principal register is situated (*TCGA 1992, s 275(1)* as amended by *F(No 2)A 2005, s 34 and Sch 4, para 4*).

New rules for determining the location of futures, options and underlying intangible assets (item 11) were also introduced with effect from 16 March 2005. The basic rule is that such assets are located in the UK if they are subject to UK law (*TCGA 1992, ss 275A–C* inserted by *F(No 2)A 2005, s 34 and Sch 4, para 5*).

LIABILITY TO CGT ON GAINS FROM UK OR OVERSEAS ASSETS

5.35   Table 5.2 summarises the effect of an individual's residence, ordinary residence and domicile status and the location of assets in determining CGT liability. It is necessarily of general application and the detailed provisions should be examined in each case.

Table 5.2

Residence and domicile	UK asset	Overseas assets
UK resident and ordinarily resident and UK domiciled	Chargeable	Chargeable
UK resident and ordinarily resident but not UK domiciled	Chargeable	Chargeable if received in UK
UK resident but not ordinarily resident and UK domiciled	Chargeable	Chargeable
UK resident but not ordinarily resident and not UK domiciled	Chargeable	Chargeable if received in UK
Not UK resident but ordinarily UK resident and UK domiciled	Chargeable*	Chargeable*
Not UK resident but ordinarily UK resident and not UK domiciled	Chargeable*	Chargeable if received in UK*
Not UK resident, not ordinarily UK resident but UK domiciled	Not chargeable**	Not chargeable
Not UK resident, not ordinarily UK resident and not UK domiciled	Not chargeable**	Not chargeable

Notes:

* Relief under a double tax treaty may be possible.

** Subject to the rules for temporary non-residents (see **5.16**). Immediate liability arises if the assets were used or held for the purposes of a trade or profession carried on in the UK through a branch or agency (see **5.11**).

Chapter 6

Partnerships

INTRODUCTION

6.1 Partnerships, including limited liability partnerships, are treated as transparent entities for CGT purposes. This means that:

(a) where two or more persons carry on a trade or business in partnership, a disposal of a chargeable asset owned by the partnership is treated as a disposal by the partners, and not as a disposal by the partnership itself; and

(b) CGT is charged on each partner separately in respect of any chargeable gain accruing to him on the disposal of a partnership asset, and that gain is charged in the same way as other chargeable gains accruing to him in the same chargeable period (and if a loss accrues on the disposal each partner's share of the loss becomes an allowable loss which he can set against his own chargeable gains) (*TCGA 1992, s 59*).

A partner making such a disposal may be eligible for hold-over relief (see **Chapter 13**) or roll-over relief for replacement of business assets (see **Chapter 14**). If the disposal was made before 6 April 2003 he may be entitled to retirement relief (see **17.22**).

A partner treated as disposing of a partnership asset (or a share in it) can roll over a chargeable gain accruing against the acquisition of an asset for the purpose of another trade, whether that trade is carried on by him as a sole trader or by a partnership in which he is a partner.

The CGT legislation does not define 'partnership' but the *Partnership Act 1890* defines it as 'the relation which subsists between persons carrying on a business in common with a view to profit'. A partnership is a separate legal person in Scotland, but this rule is overridden for CGT purposes so that there is no difference in treatment between, for example, a Scottish partnership and an English one (*TCGA 1992, s 59(1)(a)*).

Although a partnership's dealings are treated as dealings by the partners and not by the partnership itself, the partnership is required to provide details of disposals of partnership property. For this purpose the partnership tax return is to include the particulars that would be required if the partnership itself were liable to tax on a chargeable gain accruing on the disposal (*TMA 1970, s 12AA(7)*).

It may not always be clear whether, for CGT purposes, arrangements amount to a partnership or merely joint ownership of the assets concerned. HMRC provide guidance on this issue in their Business Income Manual (BIM 72000).

Several points of practice in relation to partnerships are set out in HMRC's statement of practice D12 (reproduced in the appendix to this chapter), supplemented by statements of practice 1/79 and 1/89. These apply in principle to corporate partners as well as individuals, although companies are chargeable to corporation tax on their chargeable gains (see **Chapter 9**). Statement of practice D12 was extended following the creation of limited liability partnerships as bodies corporate in 2001 (see **6.19**). See **6.20** regarding partnerships residing outside the UK or carrying on a business controlled and managed outside the UK.

PARTNERSHIP ASSETS AND 'OTHER' ASSETS

6.2   A 'partnership asset' is an asset owned by all of the partners. An asset that is owned by only some of the partners is not a partnership asset – HMRC guidance refers to such assets as 'other assets' and says:

> 'There are no hard and fast rules to tell you what are partnership assets and what are other assets. You have to have regard to the facts of the particular case, any documentary evidence and the intentions of the partners. For example, the fact that only one of the partners paid for, and took title to, the assets would suggest these would be other assets. However, if all the partners intended them, or some of them, to be partnership assets then we would regard them as such.' (CG 27142).

Roll-over relief for replacement of business assets (see **Chapter 14**) is available to the owner of assets that are let to a partnership in which he is a partner, if those assets are used for the purposes of the partnership's trade or profession and the other conditions for the relief are met (HMRC statement of practice D11).

FRACTIONAL SHARE IN A PARTNERSHIP ASSET

6.3   When a partnership buys an asset, each partner is treated as acquiring a fractional share in it. In order to compute the gain or loss accruing to a partner on either the disposal of a chargeable asset owned by the partnership (see **6.6**) or a change in asset surplus sharing arrangements (see **6.9**) it is necessary to calculate each partner's disposal consideration and allowable expenditure by reference to his fractional share in the partnership asset.

HMRC guidance sets out a series of tests to determine a partner's fractional share of a partnership asset. Where there is actual consideration for the disposal, HMRC will apply the following tests in the order shown:

- any specific written agreement setting out the allocation of capital assets;
- any written agreement or other evidence setting out how capital profits are to be shared; and
- any written agreement or other evidence setting out how income profits are to be shared.

In the absence of any such agreements or evidence (eg treatment in the accounts) the assets are treated as held equally by all the partners (CG 27121).

Where the market value of a partner's share in a partnership asset is to be ascertained for CGT purposes it is taken as a fraction of the value of the partnership's entire interest in the asset. There is no discount to take account of the size of the partner's share. For example, if a partner has a one-tenth share in the partnership assets and the partnership owns all of the shares in a company, the value of the partner's interest in the shareholding is one-tenth of the partnership's interest (HMRC statement of practice D12, para 1).

Allowable expenditure: multiple acquisitions

6.4   Where a partner has built up his fractional share in stages since 6 April 1965, his acquisition cost of the various assets is calculated by pooling the expenditure relating to each asset. Where all or a part of the partner's share was acquired before 6 April 1965 the disposal will normally be identified with shares acquired on a 'first in, first out' basis, but HMRC may accept a different approach where this produces an unreasonable result (eg where there is a temporary change in the shares in a partnership due to a delay between the departure of one partner and the arrival of a new one) (HMRC statement of practice D12, para 10).

Partnership goodwill

6.5   Where the value of goodwill generated by a partnership is not recognised in the balance sheet and it is customary not to place a value on that goodwill in dealings between the partners, HMRC practice on a disposal of a partner's interest in that goodwill for actual consideration is to regard that interest as the same asset as was acquired by the partner when he first became entitled to a share in it.

This practice is also applied to purchased goodwill that is not recognised in the balance sheet asset at a value greater than cost and is not otherwise taken into account in dealings between partners. However, this purchased goodwill is treated as a separate asset from the partnership's self-generated goodwill for the purpose of computing CGT taper relief. The interest in purchased goodwill is, therefore, treated as acquired on the later of:

- the date of purchase by the partnership; or
- the date when the disposing partner first became entitled to a share in that purchased goodwill (HMRC statement of practice D12, para 12).

DISPOSAL OF PARTNERSHIP ASSETS

6.6 When a partnership disposes of an asset to an outside party, each partner is treated as making a disposal of his fractional share (see **6.3**) in that asset. The proceeds of disposal are allocated to the partners in the ratio of their share in asset surpluses at the time of disposal.

If this ratio is not specifically laid down, the allocation follows the destination of the surplus as shown in the partnership accounts but regard is also had to any agreement outside the accounts. If the surplus is put to a common reserve, the asset surplus sharing ratio is taken. If no such ratio is specified, regard is had to the ordinary profit sharing ratio (HMRC statement of practice D12, para 2).

Example 6.1

Each of the following partnerships disposes of its chargeable asset to outside parties at arm's length, realising a gain of £90,000. The gain is apportioned among the partners as follows:

Arthur & Co

The partnership agreement states that each of the three partners shall be entitled to share equally in any surplus arising from assets disposed of by the partnership. Each partner is therefore treated as if he had made a gain of £30,000.

Binder & Co

The three partners in Binder & Co have no formal agreement, but interest on capital contributed to the partnership is shown in the accounts at the same sum for each. The inference is that the capital has been equally contributed and can be equally withdrawn, so that the apportioned gain is £30,000 to each partner.

Cooper & Co

The three partners, Abby, Chris and Kate, have no formal agreement and the capital is shown in the accounts as a global sum. The profit-sharing ratio is 3:2:1. Thus the gain is apportioned:

Abby   £45,000

Chris   £20,000

Kate   £10,000

Part disposals

6.7   If a partnership makes a part disposal, the part disposal rules (see **2.4**) are applied before the gain is divided among the partners. Where the relief for small part disposals of land is available (see **2.5**) the conditions are applied separately in relation to each partner.

Partnership assets distributed in kind

6.8   Where a partnership asset is distributed to one or more partners (eg on a dissolution of the partnership), the disposal is treated as being made for a consideration equal to the market value of the asset. The gain accruing to each individual partner is computed but the gain accruing to the partner receiving the asset is deducted from his allowable expenditure on a subsequent disposal of the asset. The same principle applies where a loss arises (HMRC statement of practice D12, para 3).

CHANGE IN FRACTIONAL SHARE OF ASSETS

6.9   A reduction in an individual partner's fractional share of a partnership asset is a disposal for CGT purposes, and an increase in that share is an acquisition. Such a change can arise from:

- the actual disposal or acquisition of a partnership asset (see **6.6**);
- the partners varying the terms of the partnership agreement or reaching a separate agreement with regard to the asset concerned (see **6.10**); or
- a partner joining or leaving the partnership (see **6.13**).

Transfers of fractional shares between spouses or civil partners living together are, however, subject to the no gain/no loss rule laid down for such transfers and outlined in **3.67** (*TCGA 1992, s 58*).

Change in asset surplus sharing ratios

6.10   An individual may introduce capital when joining a partnership, which is credited to his capital account. The partnership's retained profits may subsequently increase his capital account balance. No CGT liability arises when those amounts of capital are subsequently withdrawn, for example, on retirement.

However, if consideration in money or money's worth passes between the partners on a change in asset surplus sharing ratios, that consideration represents:

- the disposal consideration received by the partner whose share is reduced; and

- acquisition expenditure incurred by the partner whose share is increased.

The CGT treatment of a merger of two or more partnerships to form one partnership follows the treatment for a change in partnership asset surplus sharing ratios. Roll-over relief on replacement of business assets (see **Chapter 14**) may be available where a partner disposes of part of his share in the assets of the old partnership and acquires a share in other assets put into the merged partnership (HMRC statement of practice D12, paras 4, 9).

Consideration within the accounts

6.11 If there is no direct payment of consideration outside the partnership, then the consideration for the disposal is the fraction of the asset's current balance sheet value that corresponds to the fractional share passing between the partners. The normal part disposal rule (see **2.4**) is not applied in this situation.

If the firm's assets have not been revalued, a reduction in an existing partner's capital profit-sharing ratio is treated as a disposal on which no gain or loss arises. No taper relief is available on such a disposal and the acquiring partner's qualifying holding period for taper relief begins on the date of his acquisition (CG 27612, CG 27616).

HMRC have agreed that such a disposal may be treated as a no gain/no loss disposal for the purpose of the 31 March 1982 rebasing rules (*TCGA 1992, Sch 3*) and the partial relief for deferred charges on gains accrued before 31 March 1982 (*TCGA 1992, Sch 4*). Where indexation allowance is available the consideration for the disposal is calculated on the assumption that an unindexed gain equal to the indexation allowance accrued, so that there is no gain and no loss after deducting the indexation allowance (HMRC statement of practice 1/89).

Example 6.2

[Example based on the scenario in HMRC's Capital Gains Manual para CG 27185]

123

A & B are in partnership and the only chargeable asset is a property. If the fractional shares change from 50:50 to 40:60, A has disposed of a 10/50 of his share in the assets and B has acquired a 10/50 share.

The current balance sheet value of the property is £50,000. A's disposal proceeds, and B's acquisition cost, will be (10/50 x £50,000) x 1/2 = £5,000.

A's disposal gives rise to no gain and no loss so long as the asset has not been revalued – see below – because his acquisition cost is also (10/50 x £50,000) x 1/2 = £5,000.

If assets (such as land and buildings) are revalued to a higher amount, the surplus is credited to the existing partners' capital accounts. No chargeable gain accrues on that event. However, the partner has effectively realised a proportion of the partnership's assets. A chargeable gain therefore arises upon a subsequent disposal (which results in all or part of the capital account being paid to him).

In summary, an upward revaluation of the partnership asset in the balance sheet gives rise to a potential gain on a future change in asset surplus sharing ratios, although the revaluation itself does not represent a disposal for CGT purposes (HMRC statement of practice D12, para 5).

Consideration outside the accounts

6.12   Any payment made outside the partnership accounts on a change of asset surplus sharing ratios represents consideration for the disposal of the whole or part of a partner's share in partnership assets. This consideration is in addition to the consideration by reference to balance sheet value (see **6.11**). It may be paid directly or via a transfer between capital accounts.

Such a payment may represent consideration for goodwill that is not included in the balance sheet. In such cases:

- the partner receiving the payment will have no allowable expenditure to set against it unless he made a similar payment for his share in the asset; and

- the partner making the payment will only be allowed to deduct it in computing gains or losses on a subsequent disposal of his share in the asset (HMRC statement of practice D12, para 6).

Example 6.3

David, Edward and Fiona are partners in a firm of accountants who share all profits in the ratio 7:7:6. George is admitted as a partner in May 2006 and pays the other partners £10,000 for goodwill. The new partnership shares are: David

3/10, Edward 3/10, Fiona 1/4 and George 3/20. The book value of goodwill is
£18,000, being its cost on acquisition of the practice from the predecessor in
1988. The table below shows the calculation of the chargeable gains accruing to
David, Edward and Fiona and George's acquisition costs. In practice, the
calculations must be adjusted for indexation allowance to April 1998 which is
added to the notional consideration and then deducted from the unindexed gain.
Any chargeable gains remaining after indexation are eligible for taper relief.

David	£	£
Fractional share disposed of 7/20 – 6/20 = 1/20		
Disposal consideration:		
Notional: 1/20 x £18,000	900	
Actual: 7/20 x £10,000	3,500	
		4,400
Allowable expenditure 1/20 x £18,000		(900)
Unindexed gain		3,500
Edward		
Fractional share disposed of 7/20 – 6/20 = 1/20		
Unindexed gain (computed as for David)		3,500
Fiona		
Fractional share disposed of 6/20 – 5/20 – 1/20		
Disposal consideration:		
Notional: 1/20 x £18,000	900	
Actual: 6/20 x £10,000	3,000	
		3,900
Allowable expenditure 1/20 x £18,000		(900)
Unindexed gain		3,000
George		
Allowable expenditure on share of goodwill:		
Actual consideration paid		10,000
Notional consideration paid 3/20 x £18,000		2,700
		12,700

Partners joining and leaving the partnership

6.13   Changes in asset surplus sharing arrangements on the occasion of one or more partners joining or leaving the partnership are treated for CGT purposes in a similar way to the changes outlined in **6.9**.

For example, a partner leaving the partnership reduces his share to nil. The capitalised value of an annuity paid to a retiring partner may represent consideration in money's worth but HMRC practice is to disregard annuities meeting certain conditions (see **6.14**).

Annuities to retiring partners

6.14   The capitalised value of an annuity paid to a retiring partner represents consideration in money's worth for the disposal of the retiring partner's share of the partnership assets. This is the case whether or not the partnership buys a life annuity for the benefit of the retiring partner. The potential CGT charge on this consideration is not precluded by the general exclusion of money or money's worth charged to income tax from the consideration for a disposal of assets (*TCGA 1992, s 37(3)*).

However, HMRC practice is to treat that capitalised value as consideration only if the amount of the annuity is 'more than can be regarded as a reasonable recognition of the past contribution of work and effort made by the partner to the partnership'. HMRC's measure of 'reasonable' recognition is based on a fraction of the partner's share of the partnership's profits. That fraction depends on how long the taxpayer has been a partner, as indicated below. See **6.17** regarding the treatment of a lump sum paid in addition to an annuity.

Partner for at least ten years

6.15   A reasonable recognition of the partner's contribution will be no more than two-thirds of his average share of profit in the 'best three' of the last seven years of assessment in which he devoted substantially the whole of his time to acting as a partner. The share of profit is computed before deducting any capital allowances, charges, or losses.

Partner for less than ten years

6.16   If the retiring partner was a partner for less than ten years, the fraction of his average share of profit – to be used instead of two-thirds – is found in the following table.

Complete years in partnership	Fraction
1–5	1/60 for each year
6	8/60
7	16/60
8	24/60
9	32/60

The annuity may be stated as a percentage of future partnership profits. HMRC guidance indicates that they are unlikely to spend time enquiring about the level of future payments in cases that are 'clearly marginal'. In most cases, a reasonable estimate of the amount likely to be paid would fall within the above limits (CG 27366).

However, the full capitalised value of the annuity is taken as consideration for the partner's disposal (and will represent allowable acquisition expenditure on the part of the remaining partners) if it exceeds the limits. HMRC will take advice from an actuarial advisor where necessary, but their guidance indicates that the response to any request from the taxpayer for an advance clearance will be limited to providing a general outline of their published practice (CG 27368).

Lump sum paid in addition to annuity

6.17   Where a lump sum is paid in addition to an annuity:

- the lump sum is treated as consideration for the disposal; and

- one-ninth of the lump sum is added to the capitalised value of the annuity and if the total exceeds the fraction of the retired partner's average share of the profits (ie the fraction given in either **6.15** or **6.16**) then the capitalised value of the annuity is treated as additional consideration (HMRC statement of practice 1/79; CG 27392).

MARKET VALUE RULE

6.18   Partners are connected persons (see **3.19**) for CGT purposes. However, where an interest in a partnership asset is transferred between partners on a commercial basis, market value is not substituted for the actual consideration passing unless the partners are otherwise connected.

HMRC guidance makes it clear that this practice applies to:

- 'normal disposals and acquisitions' of fractional shares in partnership assets between partners who are otherwise acting at arm's length and connected solely by partnership; and

- acquisitions made by an incoming partner and disposals made by the existing partners (*TCGA 1992, s 286(4)*; CG 27296).

HMRC may seek to apply the market value rule where 'there have been direct payments between partners and these appear to have been artificially contrived to produce a tax advantage' (CG 27297).

Where the partners are connected otherwise than by partnership, or where they are not so connected but may not be acting at arm's length, HMRC will consider whether any consideration passing is of an amount that might reasonably have been expected to pass had they been (i) unconnected except by partnership, and (ii) acting at arms length (CG 27298; HMRC statement of practice D2, para 7).

LIMITED LIABILITY PARTNERSHIPS

6.19   A limited liability partnership (LLP) carrying on a trade or business with a view to profit is treated in the same way as a conventional partnership for CGT purposes, ie it is 'fiscally transparent'. Although an LLP is a corporate body, for CGT purposes its assets are treated as held by its members as partners and the LLP's dealings are treated as dealings by the members in partnership rather than by the LLP itself. Tax is charged on the members of the LLP separately, in respect of chargeable gains accruing to them as members, on a disposal of any of the LLP's assets (*TCGA 1992, s 59A(1)*).

The CGT provisions applying to partnerships other than LLPs are generally extended to LLPs and it is provided that references to members of a partnership include members of an LLP. However, references to a company or its members do not include an LLP or its members (*TCGA 1992, s 59A(2)*).

The members of an LLP are entitled to the same reliefs as partners in a conventional partnership. All HMRC concessions and statements of practice apply to an LLP in the same way as they apply to a conventional partnership while it is carrying on a trade or business. However, they do not apply to the members of an LLP that has ceased to be 'fiscally transparent' (see below) (HMRC statement of practice D12, introduction; CG 28001).

The 'transparency' treatment outlined above continues on the temporary cessation of a trade or business carried on with a view to profit. It also continues during a period of winding up following a permanent cessation of the trade or business, so long as that period is not unreasonably prolonged and the winding up is not done for reasons connected with tax avoidance. Transparency ceases to apply, however:

- on the appointment of a liquidator; and

- where a court makes a winding-up order or there is a corresponding event under the law of an overseas territory (*TCGA 1992, s 59A(3), (4)*).

Where transparency does end, and tax is charged on the LLP as a company in respect of chargeable gains accruing on a disposal of its assets (or on the members in respect of chargeable gains accruing on a disposal of their capital interests in the LLP) then the liability is computed and tax is charged as though the rules outlined above never applied (*TCGA 1992, s 59(5)*).

There is no deemed disposal of assets by the LLP or any member as a result of transparency beginning or coming to an end (*TCGA 1992, s 59(6)*).

However, when transparency ends and a member of the LLP holds an asset that he acquired for a consideration that was treated as reduced by virtue of a claim to roll-over relief (under *TCGA 1992, s 152* or *s 154*) he is treated as if a gain equal to the amount of that reduction accrued at that time. There is a similar provision for clawback of hold-over relief on gifts (under *TCGA 1992, s 165* or *s 260*) (*TCGA 1992, ss 156A, 159A*).

RESIDENCE, ETC

6.20 A partnership's fiscal transparency (see **6.1**) means that special rules applying to partnerships controlled abroad are (with the exception mentioned below) no longer relevant. Each partner's CGT position depends on his own residence and domicile status (see **Chapter 5**). For example:

- a partner who is resident, ordinarily resident and domiciled in the UK is chargeable on gains accruing to him on the disposal of partnership assets irrespective of where they arise; and

- a partner who is neither resident nor ordinarily resident in the UK is chargeable only in relation to gains accruing on the disposal of assets used for the purpose of a trade carried on via a UK branch or agency (see **5.11**).

Any double taxation agreement providing relief from CGT in the UK for a partnership's capital gains does not affect the CGT liability on a UK resident partner's share of those gains where the partnership carries on a trade, profession or business whose control and management are situated outside the UK (*TCGA 1992, s 59(2), (3)*).

APPENDIX: HMRC STATEMENT OF PRACTICE D12

6.21 *The full text of the statement of practice is reproduced below.*

This statement of practice was originally issued by the Board of Inland Revenue on 17 January 1975 following discussions with the Law Society and the Allied Accountancy Bodies on the capital gains tax treatment of partnerships. This statement sets out a number of points of general practice which have been agreed in respect of partnerships to which *TCGA 1992, s 59* applies.

The enactment of the Limited Liability Partnership Act 2000 has created, from April 2001, the concept of limited liability partnerships (as bodies corporate) in UK law. In conjunction with this, new capital gains tax provisions dealing with such partnerships have been introduced through *TCGA 1992, s 59A. TCGA 1992, s 59A(1)* mirrors *TCGA 1992, s 59* in treating any dealings in chargeable assets by a limited liability partnership as dealings by the individual members, as partners, for capital gains tax purposes. Each member of a limited liability partnership to which *s 59A(1)* applies has therefore to be regarded, like a partner in any other (non-corporate) partnership, as owning a fractional share of each of the partnership assets and not an interest in the partnership itself.

This statement of practice has therefore been extended to limited liability partnerships which meet the requirements of *TCGA 1992, ss 59, 59A(1)*, such that capital gains of a partnership fall to charged on its members as partners. Accordingly, in the text of the statement of practice, all references to a 'partnership' or 'firm' include reference to limited liability partnerships to which *TCGA 1992, ss 59, 59A(1)* applies, and all references to 'partner' include reference to a member of a limited liability partnership to which *TCGA 1992, ss 59, 59A(1)* applies.

For the avoidance of doubt, this statement of practice does not apply to the members of a limited liability partnership which ceases to be 'fiscally transparent' by reason of its not being, or its no longer being, within *TCGA 1992, ss 59, 59A(1)*.

1 Valuation of a partner's share in a partnership asset

Where it is necessary to ascertain the market value of a partner's share in a partnership asset for capital gains tax purposes, it will be taken as a fraction of the value of the total partnership interest in the asset without any discount for the size of his share. If, for example, a partnership owned all the issued shares in a company, the value of the interest in that holding of a partner with a one-tenth share would be one-tenth of the value of the partnership's 100% holding.

2 Disposals of assets by a partnership

Where an asset is disposed of by a partnership to an outside party each of the partners will be treated as disposing of his fractional share of the asset. In computing gains or losses the proceeds of disposal will be allocated between the partners in the ratio of their share in asset surpluses at the time of disposal. Where this is not specifically laid down the allocation will follow the actual destination of the surplus as shown in the partnership accounts; regard will of course have to be paid to any agreement outside the accounts. If the surplus is not allocated among the partners but, for example, put to a common reserve, regard will be had to the ordinary profit sharing ratio in the absence of a specified asset-surplus-sharing ratio. Expenditure on the acquisition of assets by a partnership will be allocated between the partners in the same way at the time of the acquisition. This allocation may require adjustment, however, if there is a subsequent change in the partnership sharing ratios (see paragraph 4).

3 Partnership assets divided in kind among the partners

Where a partnership distributes an asset in kind to one or more of the partners, for example on dissolution, a partner who receives the asset will not be regarded as disposing of his fractional share in it. A computation will first be necessary of the gains which would be chargeable on the individual partners if the asset has been disposed of at its current market value. Where this results in a gain being attributed to a partner not receiving the asset the gain will be charged at the time of the distribution of the asset. Where, however, the gain is allocated to a partner receiving the asset concerned there will be no charge on distribution. Instead, his capital gains tax cost to be carried forward will be the market value of the asset at the date of distribution as reduced by the amount of his gain. The same principles will be applied where the computation results in a loss.

4 Changes in partnership sharing ratios

An occasion of charge also arises when there is a change in partnership sharing ratios including changes arising from a partner joining or leaving the partnership. In these circumstances a partner who reduces or gives up his share in asset surpluses will be treated as disposing of part of the whole of his share in each of the partnership assets and a partner who increases his share will be treated as making a similar acquisition. Subject to the qualifications mentioned at 6 and 7 below the disposal consideration will be a fraction (equal to the fractional share changing hands) of the current balance sheet value of each chargeable asset provided there is no direct payment of consideration outside the partnership. Where no adjustment is made through the partnership accounts (for example, by revaluation of the assets coupled with a corresponding increase or decrease in the partner's current or capital account at some date between the partner's acquisition and the reduction in his share) the disposal is treated as made for a consideration equal to his capital gains tax cost and thus there will be neither a chargeable gain nor an allowable loss at that point. A partner whose share reduces will carry forward a smaller proportion of cost to set against a subsequent disposal of the asset and a partner whose share increases will carry forward a larger proportion of cost.

The general rules in *TCGA 1992, s 42* for apportioning the total acquisition cost on a part-disposal of an asset will not be applied in the case of a partner reducing his asset-surplus share. Instead, the cost of the part disposed of will be calculated on a fractional basis.

5   Adjustment through the accounts

Where a partnership asset is revalued a partner will be credited in his current or capital account with a sum equal to his fractional share of the increase in value. An upward revaluation of chargeable assets is not itself an occasion of charge. If, however, there were to be a subsequent reduction in the partner's asset-surplus share, the effect would be to reduce his potential liability to capital gains tax on the eventual disposal of the assets without an equivalent reduction of the credit he has received in the accounts. Consequently at the time of the reduction in sharing ratio he will be regarded as disposing of the fractional share of the partnership asset represented by the difference between his old and his new share for a consideration equal to that fraction of the increased value at the revaluation. The partner whose share correspondingly increases will have his acquisition cost to be carried forward for the asset increased by the same amount. The same principles will be applied in the case of a downward revaluation.

6   Payments outside the accounts

Where on a change of partnership sharing ratios payments are made directly between two or more partners outside the framework of the partnership accounts, the payments represent consideration for the disposal of the whole or part of a partner's share in partnership assets in addition to any consideration calculated on the basis described in 4 and 5 above. Often such payments will be for goodwill not included in the balance sheet. In such cases the partner receiving the payment will have no capital gains tax cost to set against it unless he made a similar payment for his share in the asset (for example, on entering the partnership) or elects to have the market value at 6 April 1965 treated as his acquisition cost. The partner making the payment will only be allowed to deduct the amount in computing gains or losses on a subsequent disposal of his share in the asset. He will be able to claim a loss when he finally leaves the partnership or when his share is reduced provided that he then receives either no consideration or a lesser consideration for his share of the asset. Where the payment clearly constitutes payment for a share in assets included in the partnership accounts, the partner receiving it will be able to deduct the amount of the partnership acquisition cost represented by the fraction he is disposing of. Special treatment, as outlined in 7 below, may be necessary for transfers between persons not at arm's length.

7 Transfers between persons not at arm's length

Where no payment is made either through or outside the accounts in connection with a change in partnership sharing ratio, a Capital Gains Tax charge will only arise if the transaction is otherwise than by way of a bargain made at arm's length and falls therefore within *TCGA 1992, s 17* extended by *TCGA 1992, s 18* for transactions between connected persons. Under *TCGA 1992, s 286(4)* transfers of partnership assets between partners are not regarded as transactions between connected persons if they are pursuant to genuine commercial arrangements. This treatment will also be given to transactions between an incoming partner and the existing partners.

Where the partners (including incoming partners) are connected other than by partnership (for example, father and son) or are otherwise not at arm's length (for example, uncle and nephew) the transfer of a share in the partnership assets may fall to be treated as having been made at market value. Market value will not be substituted, however, if nothing would have been paid had the parties been at arm's length. Similarly if consideration of less than market value passes between partners connected other than by partnership or otherwise not at arm's length, the transfer will only be regarded as having been made for full market value if the consideration actually paid was less than that which would have been paid by parties at arm's length. Where a transfer has to be treated as if it had taken place for market value, the deemed disposal will fall to be treated in the same way as payments outside the accounts.

8 Annuities provided by partnerships

A lump sum which is paid to a partner on leaving the partnership or on a reduction of his share in the partnership represents consideration for the disposal by the partner concerned of the whole or part of his share in the partnership assets and will be subject to the rules in 6 above. The same treatment will apply when a partnership buys a purchased life annuity for a partner, the measure of the consideration being the actual costs of the annuity.

Where a partnership makes annual payments to a retired partner (whether under covenant or not) the capitalised value of the annuity will only be treated as consideration for the disposal of his share in the partnership assets under *TCGA 1992, s 37(3)* if it is more than can be regarded as a reasonable recognition of the past contribution of work and effort by the partner to the partnership. Provided that the former partner had been in the partnership for at least ten years an annuity will be regarded as reasonable for this purpose if it is no more than two-thirds of his average share of the profits in the best three of the last seven years in which he was required to devote substantially the whole of this time to acting as a partner. In arriving at a partner's share of the profits regard will be had to the partnership profits assessed before deduction of any capital allowances or charges. The ten-year period will include any period during which the partner was a member of another firm whose business has been merged with that of the present firm. For lesser periods the following fractions will be used instead of two-thirds:

Complete years in partnership	Fraction
1–5	1/60 for each year
6	8/60
7	16/60
8	24/60
9	32/60

Where the capitalised value of an annuity is treated as consideration received by the retired partner, it will also be regarded as allowable expenditure by the remaining partners on the acquisition of their fractional shares in partnership assets from him.

9 Mergers

Where the members of two or more existing partnerships come together to form a new one, the capital gains tax treatment will follow the same lines as that for changes in partnership sharing ratios. If gains arise for reasons similar to those covered in 5 and 6 above, it may be possible for roll-over relief under *TCGA 1992, ss 152–158* to be claimed by any partner continuing in the partnership insofar as he disposes of part of his share in the assets of the old firm and acquires a share in other assets put into the 'merged' firm. Where, however, in such cases the consideration given for the shares in chargeable assets acquired is less than the consideration for those disposed of, relief will be restricted under *TCGA 1992, s 153*.

10 Shares acquired in stages

Where a share in a partnership is acquired in stages wholly after 5 April 1965, the acquisition costs of the various chargeable assets will be calculated by pooling the expenditure relating to each asset. Where a share built up in stages was acquired wholly or partly before 6 April 1965 the rules in *TCGA 1992, Sch 2, para 18* will normally be followed to identify the acquisition cost of the share in each asset which is disposed of on the occasion of a reduction in the partnership's share; that is, the disposal will normally be identified with shares acquired on a 'first in, first out' basis. Special consideration will be given, however, to any case in which this rule appears to produce an unreasonable result when applied to temporary changes in the shares in a partnership, for example those occurring when a partner's departure and a new partner's arrival are out of step by a few months.

11 Elections under TCGA 1992, Sch 2, para 4

Where the assets disposed of are quoted securities eligible for a pooling election under *TCGA 1992 Sch 2, para 4* partners will be allowed to make separate elections in respect of shares or fixed interest securities held by the partnership as distinct from shares and securities which they hold on a personal basis. Each partner will have a separate right of election for his proportion of the partnership securities and the time limit for the purposes of *Schedule 2* will run from the earlier of:

(a)   the first relevant disposal of shares or securities by the partnership; and

(b)   the first reduction of the particular partner's share in the partnership assets after 19 March 1968.

12 Partnership goodwill and taper relief

This paragraph applies where the value of goodwill which a partnership generates in the conduct of its business is not recognised in its balance sheet and where, as a matter of consistent practice, no value is placed on that goodwill in dealings between the partners. In such circumstances, the partnership goodwill will not be regarded as a 'fungible asset' (and, therefore, will not be within the definition of 'securities' in *TCGA 1992, s 104(3)*) for the purpose of capital gains tax taper relief under *TCGA 1992, s 2A*. Accordingly, on a disposal for actual consideration of any particular partner's interest in the goodwill of such a partnership, that interest will be treated as the same asset (or, in the case of a part disposal, a part of the same asset) as was originally acquired by that partner when first becoming entitled to a share in the goodwill of that partnership.

The treatment described in the preceding paragraph will also be applied to goodwill acquired for consideration by a partnership but which is not, at any time, recognised in the partnership balance sheet at a value exceeding its cost of acquisition nor otherwise taken into account in dealings between partners.

However, such purchased goodwill will continue to be treated for the purpose of computing capital gains tax taper relief as assets separate from the partnership's self-generated goodwill. On a disposal or part disposal for actual consideration of an interest in such purchased goodwill by any particular partner, that interest shall be treated for taper relief purposes as acquired either on the date of purchase by the partnership or on the date on which the disposing partner first became entitled to a share in that goodwill, whichever is the later.

Chapter 7

Administration of an estate

INTRODUCTION

7.1   In the event of death, the property included in the deceased's estate does not automatically pass to the beneficiaries, but passes to the personal representatives or executors whose duty is to administer the estate. The executors' or personal representatives' duty includes getting in the property, discharging the deceased's debts and finally distributing the assets to the beneficiaries under the will or according to the rules of intestacy.

In relation to CGT, the personal representative will be concerned with:

- capital gains arising in the period to the date of death; and
- capital gains arising in the administration of the estate.

CAPITAL GAINS TAX IN THE PERIOD TO THE DATE OF DEATH

General provisions

7.2   Generally, the deceased will be liable to tax on any capital gains made in the period up to the date of death and it is the duty of the personal representative to ensure that his tax liability is discharged or provisions are made prior to the distribution of the estate. The normal self-assessment procedure has to be followed, however, *TMA 1970, s 40(1)* has extended the self-assessment time limits and the assessment now must be made by the end of the third year after 31 January following the year of assessment in which the death took place.

Example 7.1—Time limits

John died on 1 July 2006. The tax return for the period from 6 April 2006 to the date of death has not yet been completed.

The date of death occurred in the year of assessment ending 5 April 2007, for which the filing date is 31 January 2008. Therefore, assessment in respect of the period to date of death may be made at any time up to 31 January 2011.

CGT losses of the deceased

7.3   Special provisions in relation to capital losses made in the tax year in which a person dies are introduced by *TCGA 1992, s 62(2)*. These rules provide that allowable losses sustained by an individual in the year of assessment in which he dies may, so far as they cannot be deducted from chargeable gains accruing in that year, be deducted from chargeable gains accruing to the deceased in the three years of assessment preceding the year of assessment in which his death occurs, taking chargeable gains accruing in a later year before those accruing in an earlier year.

Example 7.2—Capital losses

John (see Example 7.1), in the period 6 April 2006 to the date of death, made capital losses of £10,000. In 2005/06 he made capital gains of £12,000, on which CGT was paid.

His executors can make a claim under *TCGA 1992, s 62(2)* and obtain a tax refund, which will fall into John's estate for IHT purposes.

CAPITAL GAINS TAX IN THE ADMINISTRATION OF AN ESTATE

General provisions

7.4   The general rule is that the 'assets of which a deceased person was competent to dispose' are deemed to have been acquired by his personal representatives for a consideration equal to their market value at the date of death. These assets are not deemed to be disposed of by the deceased on death, and therefore there is no charge to CGT on the deceased's unrealised gains (*TCGA 1992, s 62(1)*).

'Assets of which the deceased was competent to dispose of' are defined in *TCGA 1992, s 62(10)* as assets of the deceased, which he could, if of full age and capacity, have disposed of by will, assuming that the assets were situated in England, and, if he was not domiciled in the United Kingdom, that he was domiciled in England, and include references to his severable share in any assets to which, immediately before his death, he was beneficially entitled as joint tenant.

The provisions of *TCGA 1992, s 73* extend the general rule to settlements with an interest in possession, in that on the death of a life tenant, the gains within the fund will be exempt from CGT. However, following the *Finance Act 2006* these provisions will not apply to interest in possession settlements which were established after 22 March 2006, as the assets within such trusts will no longer form part of the estate of the deceased.

If on death the property within the trust reverts to the settlor, the disposal and reacquisition shall be deemed to be for such consideration so that neither a loss nor a gain accrues to the trustee (*see TCGA 1992, s 73(1)(b)*).

The exception to the rule in *s 73* is that, where gains were held over on the transfer of assets into a trust, such held-over gains will now be chargeable to CGT on the death of the life tenant (see *TCGA 1992, s 74*).

Example 7.3—Tax-free uplift on death

John's estate includes a seaside cottage, which he purchased in 1990 for £50,000. The property is worth £250,000.

On John's death the gain of £200,000 on the seaside cottage is not chargeable to tax, instead John's executors acquire the seaside cottage at a new base value of £250,000.

John was also the life tenant of an interest in possession trust which includes assets which were valued at £150,000. The settlor of the trust was John's father who transferred assets valued at £50,000 into the trust in 1982. The gain held over in 1982 was £20,000.

On John's death, the held-over gain of £20,000 becomes chargeable, unless it is possible to make another hold-over claim. The tax-free uplift only applies to the balance of the gain which is £80,000 (ie £150,000 – £50,000 – £20,000).

Personal representatives

7.5   Personal representatives are treated as a single and continuing body of persons, and they are treated as having the deceased's residence, ordinary residence and domicile at the date of death (*TCGA 1992, s 62(3)*). They are liable to capital gains tax on disposals made by them during the administration of the estate. For the year of assessment in which the death occurs and the following two years of assessment, the personal representatives are entitled to the same annual exempt amounts as individuals with the same general provisions applying (*TCGA 1992, s 3(7)*).

As personal representatives are deemed to take the deceased's residence status, UK personal representatives of a non-resident deceased are not chargeable to CGT. However, this exception does not apply to trustees, and therefore if there are ongoing trusts, for example, because there are minor beneficiaries, the residence status of the trustees will determine whether the trust is UK resident for CGT purposes (see **8.39** and **8.40**).

Valuation of chargeable asset at the date of death

7.6   When considering a potential charge to CGT during the administration of an estate, any computation of a capital gain must start with a consideration of the market value, ie 'the price which the asset might reasonably be expected to fetch on a sale in the open market' (*TCGA 1992, s 272(1)*).

Where, on the death of any person, IHT was chargeable on the value of the estate immediately before death and where the value of an asset as part of that estate has been 'ascertained' by any means for the purposes of IHT, that value is taken to be the market value for CGT purposes (*TCGA 1992, s 274*).

Care has to be taken in cases where the deceased's estate does not attract a charge to IHT, as the value of the asset will not be 'ascertained' for IHT, and so the personal representatives' base value will not be fixed. This can happen in the following situations:

- All the assets pass to a surviving spouse and the entire estate is IHT exempt.

- All the assets pass to charities or political parties and the estate is thus IHT exempt.

- The estimated value of the estate is well below the threshold on which tax is to be payable and therefore the estate is not subject to IHT charges.

- The assets of the estate are all subject to agricultural and business property relief for IHT at the rate of 100%.

- Some combination of the above factors and/or other exemptions makes the estate non-taxpaying.

If the value of an asset is not ascertained for inheritance tax, the normal rules of *TCGA 1992, s 272* will apply to determine the capital gains tax acquisition value of the beneficiary. The acquisition cost of each asset must be negotiated with HMRC when the asset is sold. The taxpayer *must* supply information about the transactions to which the valuations relate, as specified on CG 34, together with any relevant tax computations. The taxpayer *may* use form CG 34, but this is not mandatory. Costs *may* be subject to negotiations if HMRC decide to open an enquiry.

HMRC Capital Gains Tax Manual in CG 32269 to CG 32271 explains the procedure to be adopted when either: values have been ascertained for IHT and there are queries; or the values have not been ascertained.

Occasionally it transpires during the administration of an estate that the market value on death of an asset for IHT is too high and relief from IHT may be available. The personal representatives may substitute a lower figure for the market value on death where property valued on death as 'related property' is sold within three years after the death (*IHTA 1984, s 161*), or if quoted securities are sold within 12 months of death for less than their market value on death (*IHTA 1984, ss 178* ff) and land is sold within four year for less than its market value on death (*IHTA 1984, ss 190* ff). See *Tottel's Inheritance Tax Annual 2006/07, Chapter 10*. This lower figure will then also be used to form the personal representatives' base value for CGT.

Alternatively, it may be advantageous for the personal representatives to claim a CGT loss on the disposal. The example below illustrates this point:

Example 7.4—IHT revaluation

William died on 1 January 2006. His main asset is his home which is valued at £240,000. He also owns (quoted) shares in Green plc which on his death were valued at £60,000. His estate is worth £300,000 and the executors paid IHT of £10,000 ((£300,000 – £275,000) @ 40%).

Scenario 1

During the first year of administration of William's estate it transpires that the shares in Green plc have fallen in value and are now only worth £20,000 and the executors decide to sell. The executors could consider claiming relief under *IHTA 1984, s 178* to reduce the estate below the nil rate band threshold for IHT of £275,000. The IHT repayment would be £10,000.

Alternatively, the executors could claim a CGT loss of £40,000 on the sale of the shares. As the property was subject to a gain of £60,000, this will reduce the overall gain to £20,000 (£60,000 – £40,000). This will result in a CGT saving of £16,000.

The executors, if they decide to use the capital loss on the shares, rather than reclaiming IHT, could save tax of £6,000.

Scenario 2

Assuming that the market value on death of William's property was £300,000 and his overall IHT liability was £34,000 ((£300,000 + £60,000) – £275,000) @ 40%). The property was sold for £300,000, while the sale proceeds of the shares were only £20,000.

A claim for relief under *s 178* will result in a repayment of IHT of £16,000 (£40,000 @ 40%). As the estate made no other capital gains, they cannot claim a capital loss on the disposal of the shares.

It therefore will be advantageous to make a *s 178* relief claim rather than to rely on capital loss relief.

Scenario 3

Assuming the facts are similar to *Scenario 2*, however, William's estate also included a painting which was valued at £20,000 on his death. His overall IHT liability therefore would have been £42,000 ((£300,000 + £60,000 + £20,000) – £275,000) @ 40%). The painting has risen in value from £20,000 to £60,000 between the date of death and the sale of the shares.

While a claim for relief under *s 178* on the sale of the shares will result in a repayment of IHT of £16,000 (£40,000 @ 40%), at the same time there will be a capital gains tax charge on the sale of the painting of £16,000 (£40,000 @ 40%). The use of the capital loss on the shares against the gain on the painting will achieve the same overall tax outcome. The decision whether to opt for an IHT repayment or to use capital losses depends on the costs and the practicalities of making the claim.

Transactions during the administration period

7.7   Sales of assets comprised in the deceased's estate by the personal representatives are disposals for capital gains tax purposes. Capital gains tax, subject to the deductions and allowances mentioned below, will have to be paid on the difference between the sale consideration and the market value at the date of death. The rates of tax are as follows:

- Transactions until 5 April 2004   34%
- Transactions since 6 April 2004   40%

Allowable expenses

7.8   Following the decision in *Richards' Executors HL 1971* 46 TC 626 personal representatives can deduct an appropriate proportion of the cost of acquiring the assets from the testator (ie legal and accountancy costs that are involved in preparing the inheritance tax account and obtaining the grant of probate) from the sales proceeds.

The Revenue Statement of Practice 02/04 has suggested a scale for deaths after 5 April 2004 (for deaths prior to 6 April 2004 see Inland Revenue Statement of Practice 8/94).

Table 7.1—Statement of Practice 02/04—Allowable expenditure

Gross value of estate	Allowable expenditure
A. Up to £50,000	1.8% of the probate value of the assets sold by the personal representatives
B. Between £50,001 and £90,000	A fixed amount of £900, to be divided between all the assets in the estate in the proportion to the probate values, and allowed in those proportions on assets sold by the personal representatives
C. Between £90,001 and £400,000	1% of the probate value of all assets sold
D. Between £400,001 and £500,000	A fixed amount of £4,000, divided as at B above
E. Between £500,001 and £1,000,000	0.8% of the probate value of the assets sold
F. Between £1,000,001 and £5,000,000	A fixed amount of £8,000, divided as at B above
G. Over £5,000,000	0.16% of the probate value of the assets sold, subject to a maximum of £10,000

Personal representatives may claim to deduct more, when higher expenses have been occurred. Note that this relief is available only to the personal representatives, and not, for example, to a beneficiary to whom the asset may have been appropriated.

Taper relief and indexation

7.9   For death before April 1998, any assets comprised within an estate may attract both indexation allowance and taper relief. See **3.59** for the application of indexation allowance. As with individuals, the indexation allowance now has been replaced by taper relief, which is available to the personal representatives and legatees.

As explained in **Chapter 12** the rate of taper relief depends on whether the asset disposed of is a business asset or non-business asset. Generally a capital gain on a disposal of non-business assets by personal representatives is treated the same as the disposal by an individual.

The application of business asset taper relief in relation to disposals by personal representatives has been substantially extended over the last few years and the rules are as follows:

- In the case of disposals before April 2000, shares were business assets if the company was a trading company and the personal representative had 25% of the voting rights.

- Following the changes introduced in the *Finance Act 2000*, for disposals after 6 April 2000 all shareholdings in unlisted trading companies held by personal representatives are now business assets (see *TCGA 1992, Sch A1, para 6(3)*).

- The *Finance Act 2000* extended business asset taper to land and buildings let to an unquoted trading company, even if the personal representative has no connection with the company.

- With effect from 6 April 2004 business asset taper relief has been extended to all trading structures. Therefore, letting property to a sole trader, trustees or a partnership, as long as they carry on a trade, now qualifies for business asset taper.

The definitions of taper relief, as explained in **Chapter 12**, also apply here.

Annual exemption

7.10   Personal representatives have the same annual exemption from CGT as individuals (£8,800 for 2006/07) in the tax year of death and in each of the two following tax years.

With some foresight it may be advantageous to transfer assets to the legatees prior to a sale and use the legatees' annual exemptions to reduce the CGT burden. Therefore, the personal representatives should carefully consider the tax consequences of any sale (see **7.11**).

Example 7.5—Sale of property by personal representatives

Alice died leaving a property worth £1,000,000. Alice's will left her estate to her six children. The personal representatives now wish to sell the property.

	£
Sale proceeds	1,100,000
Probate value	1,000,000
Capital gain	100,000
Allowable expenses (0.8% of probate value)	8,000
Annual exemption	8,800
Taxable gain	83,200
Tax @ 40%	33,280

Transfers to legatees

7.11 Where a person disposes of an asset to which he became absolutely entitled as legatee, any incidental expenditure incurred by that person or by the personal representative in relation to the transfer of the asset to him is allowable as a deduction in the computation of the gain arising on the disposal (*TCGA 1992, s 64(1)*).

A 'legatee' includes any person taking under a testamentary disposition or on intestacy or partial intestacy, whether he takes beneficially or as trustee (*TCGA 1992, s 64(2)*).

On a transfer of an asset to a legatee, the personal representatives neither make a gain nor a loss for capital gains tax purposes. The legatee acquires the asset at the personal representative's base cost, which usually is the probate value. If there is more than one legatee receiving an asset, the base costs have to be apportioned accordingly.

Where the asset disposed of is a dwelling house that has at some time in the period of administration been a residence of a person who is a legatee in respect of that dwelling house, private residence exemption may, in certain circumstances, be available under the terms of Extra-Statutory Concession D5 and, for disposals after 9 December 2003, *TCGA 1992, s 225A*.

A *donatio mortis causa* (a gift in anticipation of death) is treated as a testamentary disposition and not a gift, so that the donee acquires the asset at its market value on the date of death and the asset therefore is subject to a tax-free uplift on death (*TCGA 1992, s 62(5)*).

Example 7.6—Sale of property by legatees

The example is the same as in **7.5**, but the personal representatives recognised that a sale by the legatees may be advantageous.

(CGT position of each legatee)	£
1/6th share in sale proceeds	183,333
Proportionate probate value	166,667
Capital gain	16,666
Expenses of sale (1/6th share of £8,000)	1,333
Annual exemption	8,800
Taxable gain	6,533

Capital gains tax can be saved by using each legatee's annual exemption. In addition, further tax can be saved if any of the legatees are not higher rate taxpayers or if their entitlement is not subject to CGT, because they are non-UK resident.

Exempt legatees

7.12   Certain legatees are exempt from capital gains tax and the personal representative therefore has to consider carefully the capital gains tax position prior to selling any assets within the estate which are subject to a capital gain. The following legatees are exempt:

●   UK charities under *TCGA 1992, s 256*.

●   Legatees which are not resident, nor ordinarily resident in the UK.

Problems may arise in situations where the estate is divided among several charities or where the personal representatives need part of the sale proceeds to cover administration expenses. In order for the *charity* exemption or the non-resident exemption to apply, the personal representatives should consider the following options:

●   to appropriate the assets to the charities or to the non-UK resident individual in partial or total satisfaction of their entitlement and then, having received instructions from the beneficiary, sell the assets as bare trustees for those charities; or

●   to appropriate the assets to charities or to the non-UK resident individual subject to a lien in favour of the personal representative.

LEGATEE OR BENEFICIARY

7.13   It is often difficult to determine whether someone receives assets as a legatee or as a beneficiary absolutely entitled under the terms of a trust. If assets are appointed by trustees of a trust, this will be a deemed disposal under *TCGA 1992, s 71* and a charge to CGT may arise (see **8.11**). In contrast, as explained above, there will not be any CGT consequences under *TCGA 1992, s 62* if personal representatives pass assets to legatees.

If a trust is created by a will or on intestacy, the trustees of that trust are legatees in precisely the same way as, for example, an individual taking an absolute interest in an asset. This is confirmed by *TCGA 1992, s 64(2)*. As a result the personal representatives are not liable to capital gains tax for disposals after assets have vested in the trustees, and the trustees acquire the assets at market value.

Problems often arise in situations where the same persons are appointed as executors and trustees under a will or on intestacy. The question then arises in what capacity those persons acted. In order to answer this question it is important to consider whether the administration period has come to an end. This will be the case once all the assets of the estate have been determined and the liabilities have been discharged or adequate provisions have been made. It will then be possible to ascertain the residue, ie the assets which will pass to the residuary beneficiaries, which signals the end of the administration period. Once the administration period has ended, it is likely that the beneficial interests have vested in trustees rather than being retained by the personal representatives. Any acts carried out after that time will therefore be carried out by those persons acting as trustees rather than the personal representatives.

DEEDS OF APPOINTMENT, VARIATIONS OR DISCLAIMERS

7.14   The devolution of the estate may be varied in a number of ways:

- *Deeds of appointment*: if a will directs that after completion of the administration period, some or all of the assets of the estate are to be held on trust and that trust contains powers enabling the trustees to appoint assets out of the trust, a deed of appointment may be executed so that those assets pass direct to the appointee on vesting rather than entering the trust. For a discussion of the capital gains tax consequences of deeds of appointment see **8.11**.

- *Disclaimers*: if a legatee wishes to give up his or her entitlement to assets of the estate without directing how those assets should be dealt with thereafter, a deed of disclaimer may be executed.

- *Deeds of variation*: if a legatee wishes to give up his or her entitlement to certain assets of the estate but wishes to direct to whom those assets should devolve in place of that legatee, a deed of variation may be executed.

Disclaimers

7.15 A disclaimer operates in much the same way as a deed of variation, however, it is a much simpler document. A legatee can terminate his entitlement to an inheritance by executing a disclaimer. However, unlike with a variation, the legatee cannot redirect his interest. The benefit disclaimed will pass in accordance with the terms of the will relating to the residue in an estate or on intestacy.

Therefore, if the disclaimed interest was an absolute interest, either in specific assets or in residue, after the disclaimer those assets are added to the remaining residual entitlements. The residue is then distributed in accordance with the pre-existing terms of the will. If an interest in residue has been disclaimed, residue is divided between the other persons entitled to residue ignoring the bequest to the disclaimer, or if there are no other residuary beneficiaries, according to the rules of intestacy.

If under the terms of a will a person would have received a life interest, a disclaimer by that person will result in the acceleration of the interests of other persons having successive interests.

Example 7.7—Disclaimer

Alice's will leaves her husband William a pecuniary legacy of £50,000 with a life interest in residue. On William's death their children Hannah and Imogen will receive absolute interests in residue in equal shares.

William is elderly and financially secure, and he wishes to help Hannah and Imogen, who both are in the process of purchasing their first property. He therefore wishes to disclaim his interest in the pecuniary legacy and the life interest. If he executes such a disclaimer, the estate will pass to Hannah and Imogen in equal shares absolutely.

Deeds of variation

7.16 A person who executes a deed of variation gives up his or her rights to receive an interest that he or she would otherwise have received under the terms of a will or intestacy. However, in contrast to disclaimers, the person who decides to vary his interest gives directions as to how the assets subject to the variation shall devolve. Variations are very flexible tools which usually remove certain clauses from the will and replace them with other clauses redirecting the original legatee's interest. For intestacies variations deem to pass assets under a will having clauses containing the new conditions.

A deed of variation may be used to:

- vary certain clauses in a will;

- create a trust that was not in the original will, which often is used in estate planning to create a nil rate band discretionary trust to safeguard the nil rate band of a deceased spouse;

- vary the terms of a trust created by the will without varying the assets passing from the estate to the trustees;

- delete a trust that was in the will; or

- sever a joint tenancy to allow jointly held assets to pass under the terms of the will or the variation.

Example 7.8—Deed of variation

Using the scenario in Example 7.7, William is worried about passing the assets to Hannah and Imogen absolutely. Hannah is about to get married. William never liked her future husband, who has little job prospects and spends most of his spare time gambling. He is worried that Hannah's inheritance will rapidly be whittled away.

Under a deed of variation, William could consider passing some of the assets to the two daughters outright to help them to purchase property, while passing the remainder on trust to retain some control over the use of these assets.

Effect of disclaimers and deeds of variations

7.17   A variation or disclaimer shall not constitute a disposal for capital gains tax purposes and it will be treated as if the dispositions have been effected by the deceased if:

- the variation or disclaimer was made within the period of two years after a person's death; and

- the variation or disclaimer was made by an instrument in writing made by the persons who benefit or would benefit under the dispositions (*TCGA 1992, s 62(6)*).

In other words, the effects of the disclaimer or variation are treated as being retrospective to the date of death. The assets are therefore deemed to have been acquired by the person at market/probate value at the date of death. A future gain therefore is calculated by reference to the probate value and not to the value at the time the variation or disclaimer was executed. It sometimes may be beneficial not to elect for *s 62(6)* to apply, which is discussed at **7.18**.

The provisions of *s 62(6)* do not apply to a variation or a disclaimer that is made 'for any consideration in money or money's worth other than consideration consisting of the making of a variation or disclaimer in respect of another of the dispositions (*TCGA 1992, s 62(8)*).

The *Finance Act 2002, s 52* amended *s 62(7)* in that for a variation to be effective for capital gains tax purposes, the deed of variation now has to contain a statement by the persons making the instrument to the effect that they intended *s 62(7)* to apply to the variation. This in effect means that for deeds executed after 31 July 2002, it will not be necessary to give notice to HMRC within six months of the date of execution of the instrument, for *s 62(6)* to apply. As long as the variation expressly states that the provisions of *s 62(6)* are to apply to the deed of variation, the provisions automatically apply without further notices to HMRC. Note, however, that although for the purposes of trust law a deed of variation may give effect to many changes, as described at **7.16**, it will be retrospective for CGT only if it varies the dispositions of the estate of the deceased.

Care has to be taken if the variation creates a settlement, as following the case of *Marshall v Kerr* [1994] 3 All ER 106, (1994) STC 638, HL the settlor for the purposes of CGT is the original beneficiary who made the variation and not the deceased. Therefore, if the variation establishes a UK settlement, *TCGA 1992, s 77* provides that if the settlor retains an interest he is taxed on all gains realised by the trustees. This will be the case where a surviving spouse executes a deed of variation to create a nil rate band discretionary trust to safeguard the nil rate band of the deceased spouse, but is included in the list of beneficiaries.

The *Finance Act 2006* inserted a new section to determine the identity of the settlor of a trust following a *s 62(6)* election. These new rules apply to variations occurring on or after 6 April 2006 irrespective of the date on which the deceased person died. Therefore the person who gives up part or all of their entitlement to property under the will or intestacy will be regarded as a settlor for capital gains tax purposes (*TCGA 1992, s 68C*).

To elect or not to elect?

7.18   As explained above, if the deed of variation or disclaimer expressly elects for *s 62(6)* to apply, the new beneficiaries are deemed to acquire the assets at market/probate value at the date of death. Sometimes, however, there may be capital gains tax advantages in not electing for *s 62(6)* to apply, and for the new beneficiary to acquire the assets based on the market value at the date of execution of the variation or disclaimer, rather than at probate value. This can best be illustrated with the following examples.

Example 7.9— To elect or not to elect?

Scenario 1

Isabella's will, amongst other assets, leaves shares worth £100,000 to her daughter Julie. Julie wishes to vary her mother's will and to pass the shares to her son Stuart. The value of the shares has now increased to £108,000.

If Julie decides not to elect for *s 62(6)* to apply, Julie will be subject to a capital gain of £8,000 which will be covered by her annual exemption. However, Stuart will acquire the shares at the higher base cost of £108,000, which will reduce a possible future capital gains tax liability when he decides to sell the shares.

Scenario 2

Alice's estate includes shares which have a probate value of £400,000. Alice's son James, the sole legatee, wishes to pass these shares to his daughter Isabella. In the meantime the shares have risen in value to £440,000. James will have to decide whether to opt to elect for *s 62(6)* apply. If James elects for *s 62(6)* to apply, he will pass the shares to Isabella at the base value of £400,000, otherwise James will be subject to a capital gain of £40,000.

SALES BY LEGATEES

7.19   During the administration period, until assets are vested in the beneficiaries or residue has been ascertained, the legatee only holds a 'chose in action' ie a right to have the estate properly administered (see *Cochrane's Executors v CIR CS1974 49 TC 299* and *Prest v Bettinson Ch D 1998 53 TC 437*).

The disposal of such a 'chose in action' by the legatee is the same as when the legatee executes a deed of variation for full consideration which is not retrospective to the date of death. The disposal consideration is the price received rather than the market value of the expectation.

Chapter 8

Capital Gains Tax – Settlements

INTRODUCTION

8.1   Trustees of certain settlements are liable to capital gains tax on disposals and deemed disposals. The legislation distinguishes between UK-resident trusts and non-resident trusts. In addition there are separate rules for settlor-interested trusts and bare trusts which charge any capital gain tax arising either:

- on the settlor, in the case of settlor-interested trusts; or

- on the beneficiary, in the case of bare trusts.

The *Finance Act 2006* introduced a new tax regime for interest in possession trusts and accumulation and maintenance trusts with the effect that such settlements now are chargeable transfers for inheritance tax. Therefore, in relation to interest in possession trusts, it will be necessary to ascertain whether the settlement was created prior to 22 March 2006, and in relation to accumulation and maintenance trusts, it will be necessary to ascertain whether a beneficiary has become entitled to an interest in possession prior to 22 March 2006.

The *Finance Act 2006* also introduced changes to the definition of settlor-interested settlements in *TCGA 1992, s 77* by extending these provisions to parental trusts for minor children who are unmarried or not in a civil partnership. Capital gains tax hold-over relief for settlements where children or stepchildren are potential beneficiaries is not available from 22 March 2006.

When determining the tax position of a settlement, it is important to determine whether one deals with the creation of a settlement, or a disposal or deemed disposal by the trustees. In addition it will be necessary to determine whether the trustees will be assessed on any capital gains tax arising or whether one of the special rules, listed below, apply:

- *TCGA 1992, s 60* provides for a number of situations in which the 'settled property' is treated for tax purposes as belonging to the beneficiary and taxed as such (see **8.2**).

- In settlor-interested settlements gains accruing to the trustees are not chargeable on them, but are treated as accruing to the settlor (see **8.36**).

- Special capital gains tax rules apply to overseas resident settlements (see **8.39**).

- The *Finance Act 2005* created a new trust tax regime for 'vulnerable persons' (see **8.42**).

DEFINITION OF 'SETTLEMENT' AND 'SETTLED PROPERTY'

General considerations

8.2   Prior to *FA 2006* the legislation did not define the term 'settlement' and one had to look to *TCGA 1992, s 68* which stated that 'settled' property means any property held in trust other than property to which *s 60* applies. The changes are in *Sch 12* and were introduced as part of the Trusts Modernisation initiative. These represent the proposals that were discussed with professional bodies, in sharp contrast to the IHT changes, which were introduced, clumsily, without that benefit and had to be revised to be workable and to hit their intended target. This group of changes have the effect that, from 6 April 2006, the definitions of 'settled property', 'settlement', 'settlor' and the tests as to residence of trustees are the same for income tax and CGT.

In outline:

- new *s 68A* defines 'settlor';

- new *s 68B* looks at transfers of property between settlements, to determine who is the settlor of them;

- new *s 68C* introduces new rules in relation to instruments of variation to determine who is the settlor;

- *s 69* is substantially revised by the insertion of subsections (*1*), (*2*) and (*2A*) to 2(*E*) which address residence issues;

- *s 77* is also substantially amended so as to widen the concept of 'settlor-interest' to include benefits for minor dependent children (including stepchildren) who are unmarried and do not have a civil partner.

'Bare trusts' and 'absolute entitlement'

8.3   *Section 60(1)* provides that, although there is a trust of property, the property is not 'settled property' and is treated as belonging to the beneficiary, where:

- assets are held by a person as nominee for another person, or as trustee for another person absolutely entitled as against the trustee, which includes nomineeships and simple or bare trusts;

- property is held on trust 'for any person who would be absolutely entitled but for being an infant or other person under a disability';

- property is held for two or more persons who are or would be jointly entitled, which, for example, includes joint ownership of land in England or Wales where trustees hold the legal title upon 'trust for sale' for the joint tenants or tenants in common (see *Kidson v Macdonald (1974) STC 54*).

If a person is 'absolutely entitled against the trustee' and he has the 'exclusive right' to direct how that asset shall be dealt with, the property will not be 'settled property' for capital gains tax and any gains will be assessed on the beneficiary personally (*TCGA 1992, s 60(2)*).

Example 8.1—bare trust

Sven holds shares for his son Matthew who is 26 years old. As Matthew can direct Sven at any time to either transfer the shares to him or to sell the shares and to pass the proceeds to him, this is a bare trust.

For capital gains tax the shares will be treated as belonging to Matthew and a transfer of the shares to Matthew will not incur a charge to capital gains tax. Any capital gain on the sale of the shares will be attributed to Matthew personally.

Example 8.2—minor beneficiaries

Scenario 1

Max is nine years old and is therefore not allowed to own property. His parents hold the property for him absolutely. As a minor he cannot demand the property from his parents, the trust therefore is not a bare trust, however, following *s 60(1)* for capital gains tax purposes he is treated as owning the asset absolutely. When he attains the age of 18 and his parents transfer the property to him, his parents will not be subject to capital gains tax charges.

Scenario 2

The property was passed to Max under his father's will contingent upon Max attaining the age of 18. Max is only nine years old. As his entitlement is contingent upon his attaining the age of 18, the property will be settled property for capital gains tax purposes and *s 60(1)* does not apply. Therefore, when he attains the age of 18, the trustees will be subject to capital gains tax, when the trustees transfer the property to him.

'Exclusive right'

8.4   'The exclusive right ... to direct how that asset shall be dealt with' may cause problems where there is more than one beneficiary entitled to the fund and the assets within the fund are indivisible assets like land, paintings, an item of antique furniture or a single share in a company. Therefore, apart from the terms of the settlement, the type of property held will determine when a beneficiary can direct the trustees to deal with his or her share in the trust asset and when such assets may be assessed to capital gains tax. One has to look towards the case of judgment of Goff J in *Crowe v Appleby* [1976] 2 All ER 914 and HMRC Capital Gains Tax Manual on CG 37540 to find the answer to when a beneficiary becomes absolutely entitled in an indivisible asset as against the trustees.

The rule in *Crowe v Appleby* states that in relation to indivisible assets, a beneficiary, among a group of beneficiaries, might have to wait for his absolute entitlement until the last beneficiary has fulfilled a possible contingency, for example, reached a specified age.

Example 8.3—absolute entitlement to trust assets

Under James' will his estate passes to his three children Sophie, Max and Saskia contingent upon them attaining the age of 21. James' estate comprises a property and 90,000 shares in Pharmaceuticals plc. Sophie has just turned 21 and the issue now arises whether she will be able to claim her one-third share in her father's estate and whether the trustees will be charged to capital gains tax.

Sophie now can claim her one-third share in the shares, as they are divisible assets and the trustees now can pass these shares to her subject to any capital gains tax charges, which may arise.

Following the rule in *Crowe v Appleby*, however, she will only become entitled to her one-third share in the property, once all her siblings have turned 21 or die before they are 21. Any capital gain, therefore, will be assessed, once the last sibling has become absolutely entitled. The assessment will be on the market value of the property when the last beneficiary turned 21.

The rule in *Crowe v Appleby* ceases to apply if the trustees sell the land in question after the first contingency, even if the proceeds are used to buy further land. Once the sale has taken place the trust fund, or the relevant part, consists of cash and the beneficiaries with absolute interests can call upon the trustees to hand over their share of the money. If further land is bought then there is a tenancy in common with the tenants in common being the trustees of the original settlement and the absolutely entitled beneficiaries.

THE CREATION OF A SETTLEMENT

General provisions

8.5   *Section 70* provides that a transfer into a settlement, whether revocable or irrevocable, is a disposal of the entire property thereby becoming settled property notwithstanding that the settlor has some interest as a beneficiary (ie the settlement is settlor-interested) and notwithstanding that he is a trustee, or the sole trustee of the settlement.

The transfer into the trust is made at market value. If the transfer is a chargeable transfer for inheritance tax purposes, or would be but for the annual inheritance tax exemption (of currently £3,000), the settlor could elect hold-over relief to hold any capital gain over as against the trustees under *s 260* or, in the case of business assets, under *s 165*, unless the trust is settlor-interested, which pre-cludes the application of hold-over relief.

Example 8.4—creation of a settlement

Alice decides, after the coming into force of *FA 2006*, to settle her shares in X plc on her son Boris, who is 19 years old. She acquired the shares in 2000 for £100,000. The market value of the shares now stands at £200,000.

Deemed disposal consideration:	£200,000
Cost	£100,000
Capital gain	£100,000

Alice will be subject to capital gains tax on her gain of £100,000 when she transfers the shares into the settlement. Alice can use her annual exemption and taper relief to reduce her tax liability. Alternatively, since the creation of a lifetime settlement is now nearly always a chargeable transfer, Alice could elect for hold-over relief under *s 260*, as Boris is not a dependent child under *TCGA 1992, s 77(2A)*.

The 'connected persons' rule

8.6   The settlor and the trustees are connected persons, therefore any gains on a transfer from the settlor to the trustees of a settlement can only be offset against losses on a transfer to the same settlement (*TCGA 1992, s 81(3)*). This can best be illustrated by the following example:

Example 8.5—connected persons

James wishes to benefit his two children Louis and Lily, who have three children each. Ideally he would like to set up two trusts – one for each branch of the family. His assets include a property worth £200,000 which he acquired many years ago for £50,000 and a share portfolio which is also worth £200,000, but which he originally acquired for £250,000.

He discusses the capital gains tax position with his accountant. If James decides to create two new settlements, one which will receive the property, the other which will receive the share portfolio, he will not be able to offset the loss on the shares against the gain on the property.

His accountant therefore advises him to transfer his assets into the same settlement. Subsequently it will be possible to create two sub-funds, one for each branch of the family, which will not be a disposal under *s 71(1)*, unless the trustees elect for the new sub-fund rules to apply (see **8.17**).

ACTUAL AND DEEMED DISPOSALS BY TRUSTEES

General considerations

8.7   The general rule is that gains arising from the disposal, whether an actual disposal or a deemed disposal of trust assets, whether of assets originally settled or acquired subsequently by the trustees, are chargeable on the trustees. Exceptions to this rule apply to the disposal of trust assets of settlor-interested trusts (see **8.36**), non-UK resident trusts (see **8.39**) and trusts for 'vulnerable persons' (see **8.42**).

Following *s 69(1)* when new trustees are appointed, this is not treated as a disposal for capital gains tax, as trustees are treated as a single and continuing body. However, care has to be taken when appointing a non-UK resident trustee to not inadvertently export the trust, which may trigger a charge to capital gains tax. Following the *Finance Act 2006* changes to the residence rules of trusts, practitioners are advised to review certain offshore arrangements which may be affected (see **8.41**).

Person becoming absolutely entitled to settled property (s 71)

8.8   There are many ways in which a beneficiary may become absolutely entitled as against the trustee. The main examples are:

- the termination of the trust after a term of years;

- when a beneficiary reaches a particular age;

- the happening of any other contingency;

- the termination of a prior life interest;

- the exercise by the trustee of a discretionary power to release capital;

- an order of the Court;

- an agreement by the beneficiaries to terminate the trust; and

- the merger of interests.

Termination of the trust after a term of years and/or happening of a contingency

8.9   *Section 71(1)* provides that there is a deemed disposal by the trustees when the beneficiary of a settlement 'becomes absolutely entitled to any settled property as against the trustees'. The trustees are treated as disposing of that property at market value and immediately reacquiring it for the same value. A charge to capital gains tax may arise on the capital gain.

After the reacquisition of the assets the trustees will hold the property in question at market value as bare trustees. The beneficiary then is treated as the owner of the property and anything done by the trustees afterwards is treated as if it had been done by the beneficiary. When the trustees actually transfer the property to the beneficiary entitled to it, this is disregarded for capital gains tax purposes. If they sell it on behalf of the beneficiary, that is treated as a disposal by him or her, and the gain or loss is the difference between the sale proceeds and the market value on the occasion of the deemed acquisition.

Example 8.6—see HMRC Capital Gains Tax Manual at 37040

The case of *Stephenson v Barclays Bank Trust Co Ltd* (1975) STC 151 illustrates the general principles for determining when absolute entitlement occurs.

The facts (simplified) are as follows. Under the will of W, his daughters C, D and E were entitled to annuities of £300 a year during widowhood. Subject to the annuities the property was to be held in trust for such of his grandchildren as should reach the age of 21. There were two grandchildren, A and B, who both reached 21 before CGT was introduced in 1965.

In 1969 the trustees, the daughters and the grandchildren entered into a deed under which specific funds should be set aside to meet the annuities and the rest of the property should be paid over to the grandchildren. In fact, however, the trustees held onto this property.

The Revenue argued that A and B became absolutely entitled only when the deed was executed.

The trustees' arguments were that an individual grandchild merely had to be entitled to specific property, not to possess it. The judge agreed: he considered that the two grandchildren together were entitled to the whole of the settled property prior to 1965. Therefore, they were 'jointly' absolutely entitled as against the trustees when the deed was executed. Thus, there was no charge to capital gains tax on the trustees when the property was handed over to the beneficiary some time later.

Where trustees sell assets after the occasion of charge under *s 71(1)* but before assets are appropriated to the beneficiaries, charges on the beneficiaries should be calculated under *s 60(1)* in proportion to their entitlement on the gain arising between absolute entitlement and sale by the trustees.

Life interest released in favour of remaindermen

8.10   It is very common for a deed to give a person a life interest, with the property going absolutely to one or more individuals, or to the members of a class of persons, on the death of that person. Sometimes the life interest can be contingent upon the happening of a certain event, ie until the life tenant remarries.

On the termination of the life interest, when the property passes absolutely to one or more beneficiaries (also called the 'remaindermen'), the trustees will be subject to capital gains tax charges on the gain arising on any assets which now pass absolutely to these beneficiaries. *Section 71(1)* also applies where a life tenant releases his or her interest in favour of any remainderman who then becomes entitled to an absolute interest as against the trustees.

If, however, the termination is due to the death of the person entitled to the life interest, which was created prior to 22 March 2006, the trustees may, subject to certain exceptions, escape a charge to capital gains tax under *s 72* and *s 73* (see **8.14**).

Exercise of power to advance or appoint capital

8.11   A beneficiary may become absolutely entitled as against the trustees on the following occasions:

● Following a power within the trust document, the trustees pay a capital sum (rather than interest) to a beneficiary of a discretionary trust or they use their overriding powers in an interest in possession trust.

- The trustees exercise their powers under the *Trustee Act 1925, s 32* (the statutory power of advancement for England and Wales) which permits trustees to pay or apply one half of a beneficiary's presumptive or vested share for his or her 'advancement' or benefit. In many cases the deed authorises payment of the full share instead of limiting it to the statutory one half.

Section 71(1) applies to such an advance and/or appointment and the trustees will be chargeable to any capital gains arising on the advanced/appointed assets.

A charge to capital gains tax under *s 71(1)* also may arise when the trustees, in the exercise of their express powers in the trust document, resettle property on a new, different settlement.

Termination of life interest on death of the person entitled (s 73)

8.12   For inheritance tax purposes, if a person has a life interest in possession in settled property, which was created prior to 22 March 2006 and this person dies, the value of the settled property in which he or she has the interest is treated as part of his or her property on death.

Section 73 was amended by *FA 2006* to include a new *s 73(2A)* so that from 22 March 2006 the capital gains tax-free uplift on death applies only to an interest in possession that is:

- 'immediate post-death interest' ('IPDI');
- 'transitional serial interest' ('TSI'); or
- 'bereaved minor trust' ('BMT').

The expressions IPDI, TSI and BMT refer to categories of trust that were formerly treated as interests in possession prior to the coming into force of *FA 2006* and which are still so treated. For a full exposition of the subject the reader is referred to *Tottel's Inheritance Tax Annual 2006/07*, Chapters 7 and 8.

Therefore, if a life interest settlement has been created after 22 March 2006 and does not fall into one of the three categories of trusts mentioned above, the *Finance Act 2006* provides that the settled property will not be treated as part of the deceased's estate, as the creation of such a life interest is now treated as a chargeable event for inheritance tax.

Following *s 72* for life interests created prior to 22 March 2006 or transitional serial interests, no chargeable gain accrues on the death of the life tenant, unless there was a hold-over election on the acquisition of the property by the trustees (**8.23**), or where the property reverts to the settlor.

Example 8.7—death of life tenant

Scenario 1

Alice has an interest in possession in her husband's estate for life or until she remarries. The remainderman is her son William.

Alice's husband died on 5 June 2005 which was prior to the changes introduced by the *Finance Act 2006*.

On Alice's death, there will not be a charge to capital gains tax following *s 73* and the value of the assets subject to the life interest will form part of her estate for inheritance tax.

However, if Alice's interest is terminated following a remarriage *s 73* will not apply, and there will be a charge to capital gains tax on William's absolute entitlement following *s 71(1)*.

Scenario 2

Alice's husband died on 5 June 2006 which was after the changes introduced by the *Finance Act 2006*. Unfortunately Alice dies a month later so William becomes absolutely entitled to the trust assets.

On Alice's death, following the changes introduced by the *Finance Act 2006*, her life interest will be 'an immediate post-death interest', and there will not be a charge to capital gains tax (*TCGA 1992, s 73(2A)(a)*).

Scenario 3

Alice is the life tenant of an interest in possession trust, which was created on 1 May 2006, which was after the introduction of the *Finance Act 2006* changes. Alice, unfortunately, dies a few weeks later. The fund now passes to William.

Section 73(2A) applies here. Alice's interest in possession does not fall within the restricted class of interests in *s 72(1B)*. As a result, the charge that would have applied under *s 73(1)* or *73(2)* is disapplied. Therefore, on her death there will be no capital gains tax-free uplift; and if the trust had continued there would have been no disposal for CGT; as the trust now comes to an end on the vesting of William's interest, any capital gains within the fund will be subject to a charge under *s 71(1)* because the remainderman now becomes absolutely entitled. The trustees ought to consider a hold-over election under *s 260*.

Termination of life interest on death of the person entitled (s 72), where settlement continues

8.13   The rule prior to 22 March 2006 was that if the life interest on the death of the life tenant was terminated and the property continued to be settled property, the trustees were treated as disposing of the settled property and reacquiring it at market value on the date of death, but without any charge to capital gains tax.

In relation to new settlements, ie those created after the *Finance Act 2006* came into force, the rule is that, as noted above, the tax treatment will depend on whether the fund remains with the trustees. The ending of the prior (post-*FA 2006*) life interest is not treated as an occasion of charge, see *s 72(1A)*, because it is not an interest within *s 72(1B)*, ie neither an IPDI nor a TSI nor a BMT.

DISPOSAL OF BENEFICIAL INTERESTS

General considerations

8.14   The general rule is that there is no charge to CGT when a beneficial interest in trust property is disposed of and the disposal was made:

- by the person for whose benefit the interest was created; or
- by any other person except one who acquired the interest for a consideration in money or money's worth (*TCGA 1992, s 76(1)*).

Therefore, once a beneficial interest has been purchased, a future disposal is chargeable to CGT.

The capital gains tax exemption in *s 76(1)* used to offer CGT planning opportunities for individuals who placed assets in trust subject to a CGT hold-over election, but retaining an interest in the trust asset which was subsequently sold. The sale of the interest did not attract a charge to CGT. However, as of 21 March 2000 trustees of settlor-interested trusts will be treated as disposing of the asset and re-acquiring it at market value. Any tax will be charged on the settlor, if the trust is still settlor-interested, or at the trust tax rate. The trustees can then recover the tax charge from the beneficiary who sold his interest (*TCGA 1992, s 76A* and *Sch 4A*).

Example 8.8—disposal of beneficial interest

William is the remainderman in a life interest trust set up under his father's will. He sells his interest to his friend Fred. Under the rule in *s 76(1)* there is no charge to CGT.

However, Fred's subsequent sale of the beneficial interest in the trust is outside the protection of the rule in *s 76(1)* and any capital gain therefore will be taxable under general principles.

Purchase by one beneficiary of other interest

8.15   The general rule in *s 76(1)* does not apply where an original life tenant of settled property makes a payment to the original remainderman for the sale of his or her interest to the original life tenant, as the life tenant now becomes absolutely entitled to the property as against the trustees. The gain will be chargeable under *s 71(1)* and the property is deemed to have passed to the original life tenant at market value.

The same applies if the original remainderman acquires a life interest from the original life tenant.

Purchase of life interest and reversion

8.16   Where a person acquires a life interest or remainder in settled property for a consideration in money or money's worth and subsequently also acquires the other interest and therefore becomes absolutely entitled as against the trustees to the settled property, a charge to CGT will occur on the trustees under both *s 71(1)* and a charge under *s 76(2)* will occur.

Example 8.9—purchase of life interest and reversion

Alice has a life interest and William is the remainderman; both are original beneficiaries. Fred buys Alice's life interest and, before it terminates, he also buys the remainder interest from William.

Fred therefore becomes absolutely entitled to the settled property as against the trustees and a charge to CGT will arise on the trustees. As Fred is not the original life tenant, a charge under *s 76(2)* will arise on him.

SUB-FUND ELECTIONS

8.17   Where a settlement has been divided into one or more sub-funds which are administered by either the same, or different, trustees for different beneficiaries, the main settlement and any sub-funds are treated as a single settlement for capital gains tax purposes.

The *Finance Act 2006* introduced provisions which allow trustees of a settlement to elect that a sub-fund or portion of the settlement shall be treated as a separate settlement, called a 'sub-fund' settlement for capital gains tax purposes as of 6 April 2006 (*TCGA 1992, Sch 4ZA*).

Making a sub-fund election will give rise to a charge to capital gains tax, as it is considered to be a deemed disposal under *s 71(1)* (*TCGA 1992, Sch 4ZA, para 20*).

In order to make the election, a number of conditions have to be satisfied:

- Condition 1 is that the principal settlement is not itself a sub-fund (TCGA *1992, Sch 4ZA, para 4*).

- Condition 2 is that the sub-fund does not comprise the whole of the property of the principal settlement (*TCGA 1992, Sch 4ZA, para 5*).

- Condition 3 is that, if the sub-fund election had taken effect, the sub-fund settlement would not consist of or include an interest in an asset which would be comprised in the principal settlement (*TCGA 1992, Sch 4ZA, para 6*).

- Condition 4 is that, once the sub-fund election had taken effect, no person would be a beneficiary under both the sub-fund settlement and the principal settlement.

As making the election gives rise to a disposal for capital gains tax purposes, the trustees would be in the same position as trustees who had used their powers to transfer property out of the principal settlement into a new settlement, thereby triggering a charge to capital gains tax. A sub-fund election therefore only will be useful in relation to settlements which were drafted without wide powers of advancements. A sub-fund election is unlikely to be attractive where trust assets are subject to substantial gains.

RATES OF TAX

General considerations

8.18   Following *ICTA 1988, s 686*, the rate of capital gains tax applicable to the trustees of any settlement who are liable in respect of disposals of settled property is equivalent to the 'rate applicable to trusts'. This rate is as follows:

- From 6 April 2005   40%
- From 6 April 1998 to 5 April 2005   34%

Trustees are treated as a single and continuing body of persons regardless of any changes in the persons acting. Assessments are to be made on those in office at the time of the assessment, not those in office when the gain is made.

In settlor-interested trusts any chargeable gains will accrue to the settlor rather than to the trustees (see **8.36**).

If tax assessed on the trustees of a settlement in respect of a chargeable gain accruing to the trustees is not paid within six months from the date when it becomes payable by the trustees, and the asset in respect of which the chargeable gain accrued, or any part of the proceeds of sale of that asset, is transferred by the trustees to a beneficiary, that person may at any time within two years from the time when the tax became payable be assessed and charged (in the name of the trustees) to capital gains tax (*TCGA 1992, s 69(4)*).

Actual disposals and losses

8.19   Where a beneficiary becomes absolutely entitled to settled property as against the trustees, any allowable loss which arises on the deemed disposal by the trustees on the asset transferred and which cannot be deducted from gains accruing to the trustees, is treated as a loss of the beneficiary (*TCGA 1992, s 71(2)*).

Where the beneficiary has become absolutely entitled to an asset on or after 16 June 1999, and he is treated as if he had incurred an allowable loss on that occasion, that loss can only be set against chargeable gains accruing on the same asset or, where the asset is an estate, interest or right in or over land, that asset or any asset deriving from that asset.

Example 8.10—allowable losses

William becomes absolutely entitled to a trust set up by his late father. The trust assets are a portfolio of shares. At this time the trustees have unused trust losses of £15,000. The share portfolio to which William becomes absolutely entitled to is worth £25,000 less than when it was acquired.

The unused losses of £15,000 belong to the trustees and cannot be passed on to William.

The capital loss of £25,000 on the share portfolio can only be used by William on a future gain of the disposal of the same share portfolio, unless the trustees could use it against gains realised earlier or gains arising on William's absolute entitlement.

Allowable expenditure by trustees

8.20   *TCGA 1992, s 38* sets out the basic types of expenditure regarded as 'incidental costs … of making and acquisition or disposal' (see **3.37**), which can be deducted from capital gains. *Section 38* also applies to trustees.

In addition, there are a number of cases which directly refer to allowable expenses by trustees:

- Expenses in varying and/or ending settlements are allowable and they may include the costs of legal and actuarial services including stamp duty on transfers and ancillary expenses incurred in varying or ending a settlement (see *CIR v Chubb's Trustee* 1972 SLT 81).

- Fees in respect of discharges and commission on the transfer of assets to beneficiaries, but not insurance premiums, see *Allison v Murray* [1975] 3 All ER 561.

Where property is transferred to a person absolutely entitled to that property as against the trustees of a settlement, then, on any subsequent disposal of that property, the person to whom the property is transferred may be allowed a deduction for the expenses involved in the transfer of this asset.

Inland Revenue statement of practice SP 2/04, updating SP 8/94, lists the amount of expenditure allowable to be deducted for expenses incurred by personal representatives and corporate trustees. Note, however, that this allowance is not available to a beneficiary to whom an asset has been appropriated or assented, because the expenses in question were incurred not by the beneficiary but by the personal representative/trustee, even though in reality it may be the beneficiary who eventually foots the bill.

The deductibility of valuation costs and costs of appeal was reviewed in *Caton's Administrators v Couch* [1997] STC 970 and disallowed by the Court of Appeal, affirming the judgment of the High Court. The costs of the initial valuation were allowable but not the litigation costs, since that would deter taxpayers from 'reaching a sensible agreement with the Revenue as to the quantum of liability'.

EXEMPTIONS AND RELIEFS

Annual exemption

8.21 *TCGA 1992, Sch 1*, modified by the *Finance Act 2006*, determines the level of the annual exemption.

Trustees of a settlement are entitled to one-half of the annual exemption available to an individual for any year of assessment during the whole or part of which any property is 'settled property' as defined in *TCGA 1992, s 68*. Thus, the trustees' exemption for 2006/07 is £4,400. Trustees of settled property held for people with disabilities and others are entitled to the full annual exemption.

Where two or more 'qualifying settlements' comprise a 'group' (see definitions below) then each qualifying settlement is entitled to an annual exemption equal to the greater of:

- one-tenth of the annual exemption for an individual (ie £880 for 2006/07); or

- one-half of that exemption divided by the number of settlements in the group.

For these purposes:

- a 'qualifying settlement' is any settlement (other than an 'excluded settlement', see below) made after 6 June 1978 where these rules apply to the trustees for the year of assessment; and

- all qualifying settlements that have the same settlor (see below) comprise a group.

A settlement may feature in more than one group by virtue of having more than one settlor. In such a case the number by which one-half of the annual exemption for an individual is to be divided is the number of settlements in the largest group.

Following the new sub-fund election rules, *Finance Act 2006* introduced *TCGA 1992, Sch 1, para A1*, which states that in relation to the annual exemption, the principal settlement and its sub-fund settlements shall be treated as if no sub-fund election has been made.

8.22   'Settlor' has the meaning given by *ITTOIA 2005, s 620* and includes the testator in the case of a settlement arising under a will and the intestate under an intestacy. Thus a settlor, in relation to a settlement, is any person by whom the settlement was made. A person is treated as having made a settlement if he has made or entered into it directly or indirectly. In particular, he is treated as having made the settlement if he has:

- provided funds directly or indirectly for the purpose of the settlement;

- undertaken to provide funds directly or indirectly for the purpose of the settlement; or

- made a reciprocal arrangement with another person for the other person to make or enter into the settlement.

'Excluded settlement' means:

- any settlement where the trustees are not, for the whole or any part of the year of assessment, treated under *TCGA 1992, s 69(1)* as resident and ordinarily resident in the UK;

167

- any settlement where the property comprised in it is held for charitable purposes only and cannot become applicable for other purposes;

- with effect from 6 April 2006, subject to transitional rules, any settlement where the property comprised in it is held for the purposes of a registered pension scheme, a superannuation fund to which *ICTA 1988, s 615(3)* applies or an occupational pension scheme within the meaning of *FA 2004, s 150(5)* that is not a registered pension scheme; and

- prior to 6 April 2006, any settlement where the property comprised in it is held for the purposes of a fund to which *ICTA 1988, s 615(3)* applies, schemes and funds approved under *ICTA 1988, s 620* or *s 621*, sponsored superannuation schemes as defined in *ICTA 1988, s 624* and exempt approved schemes and statutory schemes as defined in *ICTA 1988, Pt XIV, Ch I.*

Hold-over relief

8.23   Hold-over relief may, subject to the exceptions discussed below, be available in two circumstances:

- On a transfer of assets into a trust, it may be possible to make a claim for gifts hold-over relief under *s 260* where, for the purposes of inheritance tax, there is a chargeable transfer or there would be a chargeable transfer but for the application of an inheritance tax exemption or the availability of the nil rate band.

- Hold-over relief also applies to gifts of business assets to a settlement under *s 165(1)(b)*.

Where both reliefs are available, *s 260* takes priority. A claim has to be made on helpsheet IR 295.

As an election for hold-over relief 'kills' any accrued taper relief, such election has to be considered carefully, especially if the trustees or the beneficiary anticipate to sell the asset transferred in the near future.

Hold-over relief under *s 260*

8.24   Prior to 22 March 2006, hold-over relief under *s 260* only used to be available for:

- gifts to discretionary trusts;

- when a discretionary trust was terminated; or

- when assets were appointed/advanced to beneficiaries of discretionary trusts.

Gifts to accumulation and maintenance trusts and interest in possession trusts used to be potentially exempt transfers rather than chargeable transfers for inheritance tax, therefore *s 260* hold-over relief did not apply.

The *Finance Act 2006* changed the inheritance tax treatment of interest in possession trusts and accumulation and maintenance trusts in that transfers into such settlements are now treated as chargeable transfers for inheritance tax. Therefore all transfers into trusts, whether discretionary or not, now allow the election of *s 260* hold-over relief.

A planning opportunity existed for accumulation and maintenance trusts where a beneficiary became entitled to income at the age of 18 and capital at the age of 25. If the beneficiary, once he turned 18, but before the age of 25, resettles his interest away from himself so that he will not become entitled to capital until the age of 25, capital gains tax hold-over relief under *s 260* will be available when he becomes absolutely entitled. Despite the changes introduced by the *Finance Act 2006*, this planning opportunity is still available for beneficiaries who have obtained an interest in possession in the accumulation and maintenance trust prior to 22 March 2006. All other beneficiaries are subject to the new inheritance tax charging regime for accumulation and maintenance trusts in any event, which allows for the application of *s 260* hold-over relief, when a beneficiary becomes absolutely entitled to trust assets.

The *s 260* relief extends to actual and deemed disposals of trustees of settlements which are subject to ongoing inheritance tax charges or exit charges, or would be if the value of the assets were above the nil rate band for inheritance tax. Such settlements are as follows:

- discretionary settlements, whether created prior to 22 March 2006 or afterwards; and

- interest in possession trusts and accumulation and maintenance trusts created after 22 March 2006.

Hold-over relief under *s 165*

8.25   *Section 165(1)(b)* extends the application of hold-over relief for business assets (as discussed in detail in **Chapter 13**) to settled property.

Anti-avoidance measures

8.26   There are two main anti-avoidance provisions:

- The first anti-avoidance measure can be found in *TCGA 1992, s 169B* to *169G* on a transfer into settlor-interested settlements. For this purpose a settlor has an interest in a settlement where any property within the settlement may be used for the benefit of the settlor or his spouse. This anti-avoidance measure has been amended by the *Finance Act 2006, s 77(2A)* to extend the settlor-interested definition to include minor unmarried children who are not in a civil partnership, which also includes stepchildren. Hold-over relief under *s 260* or *s 165* will not be available for trusts set up by a parent where minor children and/or stepchildren are potential beneficiaries. Hold-over relief remains available for grandparents' trusts.

- *Section 226A* has been introduced by the *Finance Act 2004* and prevents the application of principal private residence relief under *TCGA 1992, s 223* in cases where hold-over relief has been claimed under *s 260*, when property was transferred into the settlement. This measure applies from 9 December 2003 and principal private residence relief is not available from this date, and any subsequent gains will have to be apportioned.

Taper relief

8.27   **Chapter 11** discusses the operation of taper relief on disposals by individuals. While the same principles and definitions apply to taper relief on disposals by trustees, when determining whether business asset taper applies, the rules vary from those applying to individuals.

Disposal of shares before April 2000

8.28   As to whether an asset was a business asset at any time before 6 April 2000, a company was a 'qualifying company' by reference to trustees if at that time it was a trading company or holding company of a trading group, and either:

- the trustees could exercise at least 25% of the voting rights in that company; or

- the trustees could exercise at least 5% of the voting rights in that company and an eligible beneficiary was a full-time working officer or employee of the company or of a company which at that time had a relevant connection with it.

Disposal of shares after 5 April 2000

8.29   In determining whether an asset is a business asset at any time after 5 April 2000, a company is a qualifying company by reference to trustees if at that time it is a trading company or holding company of a trading group, and:

- the company is unlisted;

- an eligible beneficiary is an officer or employee of that company or a company having a relevant connection with it; or

- the trustees can exercise at least 5% of the voting rights in that company.

A non-trading company (or a holding company of a non-trading group) is a qualifying company in relation to trust shareholdings, if:

- an eligible beneficiary is an officer or employee of the company in which the trust holds shares or a company having a relevant connection with it; and

- neither the trustees of the settlement nor any person connected with them have a material interest in the company or any company which controls it.

Disposals of assets other than shares

8.30   For a disposal after 5 April 2000, an asset other than shares is also a business asset if at that time it is used wholly or partly for the purposes of any office or employment held by an eligible beneficiary with a person carrying on a trade. There is no requirement here that the eligible beneficiary must work as an employee on a full-time basis. Therefore at any time before 6 April 2000, an asset was a business asset if at that time it was used wholly or partly for the purposes of either:

- any qualifying office or employment to which the eligible beneficiary was at that time required to devote substantially the whole of his time; or

- any other office or employment with a trading company in respect of which the eligible beneficiary was a full-time working officer or employee.

For periods of ownership before 6 April 2004, in respect of disposals of an asset other than shares by trustees of a settlement, the asset is a business asset at any given point in time if at that time it was used wholly or partly for the purposes of a trade carried on at that time by one or more of the following:

- the trustees (with effect for determining whether an asset was a business asset at any time after 5 April 2000, the legislation makes it clear that this includes a trade carried on by a partnership in which the trust is a partner, as well as a trade carried on by the trustees as sole traders);

- an eligible beneficiary;

- a partnership of which an eligible beneficiary was a partner;

- a company which at that time was a qualifying company of either the trustees or an eligible beneficiary; or

- a company which at that time was a member of a trading group where the holding company was either the trustees' or eligible beneficiary's qualifying company.

8.31   For periods of ownership after 5 April 2004 the rules are relaxed so that a wider range of assets will qualify. Assets used wholly or partly for the purposes of trades carried on by individuals, trustees of settlements, personal representatives or certain partnerships will qualify as business assets irrespective of whether the owner of the assets is involved in carrying on the trade concerned. Everything that qualifies as a business asset under the current rules will qualify as a business asset under the new rules.

Accordingly, for periods of ownership after 5 April 2004, to qualify as a business asset at any point in time, the asset in question must be used wholly or partly for the purposes of a trade being carried on by:

- any individual;

- any body of trustees;

- the personal representatives of any deceased person; or

- any partnership which includes as a member any individual, body of trustees or personal representatives.

Where at any time the use of the asset is for the purposes of a trade carried on by a company, the conditions for treatment as a business asset for trustees of a settlement applying to periods of ownership after 5 April 2004 are as follows. The company must be:

- a qualifying company in relation to the trustees or an eligible beneficiary;

- a company which at that time was a member of a trading group where the holding company was at that time a qualifying company by reference to the trustees or an eligible beneficiary; or

- a partnership whose members at that time included a company.

When calculating the gain on a disposal of an asset which will have become a business asset after 5 April 2000, it will be necessary to calculate the gain on an apportionment basis, as the asset qualifies for business asset taper relief for only part of the relevant period. This is known as 'tainted' taper (see **11.25**).

Property settled by a company

8.32   An asset does not qualify for business asset taper if:

- it is held by the trustees of a settlement;

- the settlor was a company;

- the settlor company, or an associated company, is within the charge to corporation tax in respect of the chargeable gains for the accounting period in which the chargeable gain accrues; and

- the settlor company, or an associated company, is an actual or potential beneficiary or enjoys a benefit.

This rule is intended to prevent companies transferring their assets to settlements in which they retain an interest in order to obtain taper relief at the higher rates for business assets. As the provisions do not disallow taper relief entirely, gains on property settled by companies may be tapered at the rate for non-business assets.

Furthermore, HMRC have stated that as the meaning of the terms 'settlement' and 'settlor' for these purposes is defined by *ITTOIA 2005, s 620*, the measures apply to settlements made by a company where there is no element of bounty.

A company is associated with another company, for the purposes of business asset taper relief, if at any time, or within a period of one year previously, it is controlled by the other or both are under the control of the same person or persons.

Roll-over relief

8.33   Trustees may claim reinvestment roll-over relief to roll the gain realised on a business asset into the purchase of another asset (*TCGA 1992, ss 152–158*). The rules are explained in detail in **Chapter 14**.

However, as one of the requirements for the application of roll-over relief is that the asset on which roll-over relief is to be claimed, and the trade in which the asset is used, must be within the same ownership, the availability of roll-over relief to the trustees is likely to be rare. It only would apply where a trust owns the asset and is a partner in the trade.

Example 8.11—roll-over relief

Julian is a life tenant in a settlement and runs a restaurant from premises owned by the trust. If the premises were sold to purchase bigger premises, roll-over relief will not be available.

Roll-over relief would only be available if the trust was a partner in the restaurant.

Principal private residence relief

8.34   The disposal by trustees of a dwelling house which has been the only or main residence of a beneficiary or beneficiaries entitled to occupy it under a settlement may well give rise to a chargeable gain or allowable loss.

Section 225 extends the scope of private residence relief to gains or losses accruing to trustees on the disposal of settled property. The property must be a dwelling house, and/or its garden or grounds if it has any, which has been occupied as the only or main residence of a person entitled to occupy it under the terms of the settlement during the period of ownership of the trustees.

If these conditions are fulfilled, private residence relief is applied in the same way as it would be applied on a gain accruing to an individual. Further relief may also be available to the trustees under *s 223(4)* if that dwelling house has been let, in the same way as it would be available to an individual.

If a life tenant or other beneficiary, who has satisfied those conditions from the time of acquisition of the house by the trustees, or 31 March 1982 if later, subsequently becomes the absolute owner of the residence, no chargeable gain or allowable loss will arise on that event under *s 71(1)*.

If the asset to which the beneficiary becomes absolutely entitled was previously occupied as an only or main residence by another beneficiary under the terms of the settlement, then *s 225* also may apply.

CGT small disposal rule

8.35   As explained in **4.20** in relation to individuals, a gain is not chargeable if it arises on the disposal of an asset which is tangible moveable property (a chattel) and the consideration does not exceed £6,000.

For the application of marginal relief, where the consideration exceeds £6,000, see **4.20**.

The same rules apply to disposals made by trustees.

SETTLOR-INTERESTED SETTLEMENTS

General considerations

8.36   There are special capital gains tax rules to deal with the case where the person who made the settlement (the 'settlor'), the settlor's spouse or the settlor's minor unmarried children who are not in a civil partnership retain an interest in the settlement (see *ss 77–78*). These provisions apply to disposals by trustees on or after 6 April 1988 if:

- both the settlor and the trustees are resident in the UK during any part of the year (or ordinarily resident in the UK during the year); and

- the settlor, the settlor's spouse or the settlor's unmarried minor children who are not in a civil partnership, at any time during the year of assessment have an interest in the settlement, or enjoy a benefit deriving from the settlement income or property (see *ITTOIA 2005, s 265*).

A settlor has an interest in the settlement if the settlor, his spouse or minor children have a present or future interest in income or capital under the settlement, whether vested or contingent, even if they never have or will actually receive any income or capital from the trust.

8.37 'Benefit' is a rather vague concept, but it will include the use of trust income or property on non-commercial terms, which may include a low or nil interest loan, rent-free occupation of trust property, or appointments of trust income or capital (including the writing off of a loan to the settlor).

It is accepted that a small *de minimis* benefit will not bring the settlement within *s 77*.

Following *s 77(3)* a 'spouse of the settlor' does not include the following:

- a person to whom the settlor is not presently married but might marry later;

- a person of whom the settlor is not for the time being a civil partner but of whom he may later be a civil partner;

- a spouse from whom the settlor is separated under a court order, under a separation agreement or in other circumstances such that the separation is likely to be permanent;

- a widow or widower of the settlor. (In other words, if the person who is presently the spouse of the settlor can only benefit after the settlor is dead, he or she is disregarded.)

Following *s 77(4)* certain interests are to be disregarded when determining whether someone has an interest in the settlement if the settlor can only benefit on:

- the bankruptcy of a beneficiary;

- any assignment of, or charge on, the beneficiary's interest in the property or income;

- the failure of a marriage settlement or civil partnership settlement by reason of both parties to the marriage or civil partnership and all or any of the children of the marriage or civil partnership;

- the death of a child of the settlor who had become beneficially entitled to the property or the income at an age not more than 25; or

- so long as a person is alive and under 25, during whose lifetime none of the property or income may become payable to the settlor unless that person becomes bankrupt or assigns, etc his interest.

Computation of trust gains

8.38   The chargeable gains of the settlement are computed in the normal way subject to allowable reliefs and exemptions, but any charge to capital gains tax accrues to the settlor. The trustees' own annual exempt amount is not taken into account in these computations.

Any tax paid by the settlor as a result of these provisions can be recovered from the trustees of the settlement.

OFFSHORE SETTLEMENTS

General considerations

8.39   The capital gains tax rules applying to offshore settlements are complex and are beyond the scope of this book.

Offshore settlements are used to offer substantial capital gains tax advantages, as they are not liable to capital gains tax on gains accruing to them on disposals of the trust property. Therefore they were much reviled by the Inland Revenue which tightened the rules and closed many tax planning loopholes. Consequently there are special provisions to charge the gains accruing to such trustees to capital gains tax in so far as they are reflected in payments made to beneficiaries domiciled within the UK.

While it will be necessary to consult a tax practitioner or a specialist text on offshore tax planning, an inadvertent export of the trust may catch the unwary and trigger a charge to capital gains tax. Practitioners therefore will have to have an understanding of the residence rules of trusts and the ensuing consequences of the inadvertent export of a trust.

Residence of trust

8.40   Prior to *FA 2006* the rules for residence of trustees were different depending upon whether it was income tax or capital gains tax that was under consideration. For capital gains tax a trust was considered as non-resident if its administration was ordinarily carried on outside the UK and the trustees for the time being, or a majority of them, were neither resident nor ordinarily resident in the UK. A resident professional trustee may be treated for this purpose as not resident in the UK if the settled property was provided by a settlor who was not domiciled, resident, or ordinarily resident when he settled the property.

FA 2006 introduced new rules which will become effective as of 5 April 2007, ie only for 2007/08 and later years, which will allow trustees to alter their arrangements if required. The new rules are modelled on the old income tax test based initially on the residence status of the trustees and using the residence and domicile status of the settlor as a tiebreaker where the body of trustees contains a mixture of UK resident and non-UK resident trustees. Therefore:

- If all the persons who are the trustees of the settlement are UK resident, the trust is both UK resident and ordinarily UK resident (new *s 69(2A)*).

- If all the persons who are the trustees of the settlement are non-UK resident, the trust is both non-UK resident and not ordinarily UK resident.

- If at least one trustee is UK resident and at least one is non-UK resident then the residence and ordinary residence of the trust is treated as UK resident if a settlor in relation to the settlement meets the conditions specified below (new *s 69(2B)*):

  - a settlor in relation to a settlement was UK resident, ordinarily UK resident or domiciled in the UK when the settlement was established;

  - if the settlement arises on the death of the settlor (whether by will, intestacy or otherwise), the settlor was UK resident, ordinarily UK resident or domiciled immediately before his death;

  - in any other case the settlor was UK resident, ordinarily UK resident or domiciled when the settlor makes, or is treated as making, the settlement.

Thus, if a settlement has both resident and non-resident trustees, irrespective of whether the majority are either resident or non-resident, then if the settlor is UK resident, etc at the relevant time then the settlement is UK resident.

Example 8.12—residence of trustees

A trust has three trustees. All three are resident in the United Kingdom; two of them are partners in a firm of solicitors in London. The settlor is resident and domiciled in Switzerland. The administration of the trust was carried out in Guernsey.

Under the old rules the trustees are resident in the United Kingdom because a majority are so resident, however, as two of the trustees are professional trustees, they are treated as non-resident, which means that a majority of the trustees are non-resident. In addition, the administration of the trust was carried on in Guernsey, which makes the trust non-resident under *s 69(1)*. If the administration of the trust had been carried out in London, the trust would have been treated as a resident trust.

Under the new rules, however, all the trustees are treated as resident in the UK: as the professional trustee exemption under *s 69(2)* does not exist any longer, the trust will be treated as a UK trust for capital gains tax purposes.

The trustees have until 5 April 2007 to introduce a non-UK resident trustee, to ensure that the trust remains offshore.

Charge to tax on emigration of trust under s 80

8.41   If the trustees cease to be resident in the UK, even if this happens inadvertently, a charge to capital gains tax may arise on the deemed disposal and reacquisition of the settled property at its market value on the date of emigration (*TCGA 1992, s 80*).

TRUSTS AND VULNERABLE BENEFICIARIES

General considerations

8.42   *Finance Act 2005, ss 23* to *45* create a new trust tax regime for 'vulnerable person' which was backdated to 6 April 2004.

A 'vulnerable person' is a 'disabled person' or a 'relevant minor'. A 'vulnerable persons' election' has to be made to HMRC in writing on the requisite form for the beneficial tax treatment to apply (*FA 2005, s 37*).

'Disabled person'

8.43   A 'disabled person' is defined in the *Finance Act 2005, s 38* as a person who:

- by reason of mental disorder within the meaning of the *Mental Health Act 1983* is incapable of administering his property or managing his affairs;

- is in receipt of attendance allowance;

- is in receipt of a disability living allowance by virtue of entitlement to the care component at the highest or middle rate; or

- satisfies HMRC that, if he were to satisfy the residence allowances, he would be entitled to either the attendance allowance or disability allowance.

Where property is held on trust for the benefit of a disabled person, those trusts are 'qualifying trusts' if any property is applied for the benefit of the disabled person and either the disabled person is entitled to all the income arising from the property or no such income may be applied for the benefit of any other person (*FA 2005, s 34*).

'Relevant minor'

8.44   A person under the age of 18 is a 'relevant minor' if at least one parent has died (*FA 2005, 39*).

Where property is held on trust for the benefit of a relevant minor, those trusts are 'qualifying trusts', if they are statutory trusts for the relevant minor under the *Administration Act 1925*, or they are established under the will of a deceased parent of the relevant minor, or trusts established by the Criminal Injuries Compensation Scheme (*FA 2005, s 35*).

Capital gains tax treatment

8.45   Following *FA 2005, s 30* special capital gains tax treatment applies for a tax year if:

- chargeable gains accrue in that tax year to the trustees of a settlement from the disposal of settled property which is held on qualifying trusts for the benefit of a vulnerable person;

- the trustees would be chargeable to capital gains tax in respect of those gains;

- the trustees are UK resident; and

- a claim for special tax treatment has been made by the trustees for this tax year.

The special tax treatment determines that a UK-resident vulnerable person will be treated as the settlor of the settlement in that tax year. He therefore is able to use his full annual exemption and will be taxed at his marginal tax rate. The vulnerable person then is able to reclaim any tax paid back from the trustees.

If the vulnerable person is not resident in the UK during the tax year the vulnerable persons' liability has to be calculated according to the formulae described in *FA 2005, ss 32* and *33*, which is complex and is beyond the scope of this book.

Chapter 9

Companies

INTRODUCTION AND BASIS OF CHARGE

9.1   Companies are chargeable to corporation tax in respect of chargeable gains accruing to them. The relevant legislation is contained in *Income and Corporation Taxes Act 1988 (ICTA 1988), s 6* and elsewhere in the corporation tax acts (*TCGA 1992, s 1(2)*).

For further information on the general scheme of corporation tax, including the basis of assessment of profits and the rates of tax, see *Tottel's Corporation Tax 2006/07*. Generally, the amount included in a company's profits for an accounting period in respect of chargeable gains is the total amount of chargeable gains accruing to the company in that accounting period, less:

• any allowable losses accruing to the company in the period; and

• any allowable losses that (i) accrued to the company in earlier periods when it was within the charge to corporation tax, and (ii) have not already been allowed as a deduction from chargeable gains (*TCGA 1992, s 8(1)*).

A loss is not an allowable loss for this purpose if a gain accruing to the company on the disposal would be exempt from corporation tax. A loss accruing on a disposal made on or after 5 December 2005 is not an allowable loss if it is disqualified by anti-avoidance rules enacted in *FA 2006* (see **9.17**) (*TCGA 1992, s 8(2); FA 2006, s 69*).

The rate of corporation tax payable on chargeable gains is the rate appropriate to the accounting period in which the gains accrued. Companies are not entitled to the annual CGT exemption available (see **1.16**) to individuals, trustees and personal representatives.

The total amount of the chargeable gains is computed in accordance with CGT principles, and the CGT provisions are used to determine questions as to:

• the amounts taken into account as chargeable gains or as allowable losses, or in computing gains or losses, or charged to tax as a person's gain; and

9.1 *Companies*

● the time when any such amount is treated as accruing.

These questions are determined as if accounting periods were years of assessment (*TCGA 1992, s 8(3)*).

As a general rule, references in CGT legislation to income tax or the income tax acts (except those restricted, for example, to individuals) are to be read, in relation to a company, as references to corporation tax or to the corporation tax acts. The income tax acts are the enactments relating to income tax, including any provisions of the corporation tax acts which relate to income tax (*TCGA 1992, s 8(4), (5)); ICTA 1988, s 831(1)*).

The acts of a liquidator in whom the assets of a company have been vested are treated as if they were the acts of the company, and the assets are treated as remaining vested in the company. Transfers of assets between the liquidator and the company are ignored (*TCGA 1992, s 8(6)*).

Tottel's Corporation Tax 2006/07 has detailed coverage of corporation tax on chargeable gains. Various matters relevant to disposals by companies are discussed in this chapter or elsewhere in this book, as shown in Table 9.1.

Table 9.1

Chapter 2	**Disposal**
2.7	No gain/no loss disposals
2.10	Assets lost, destroyed or becoming of negligible value
2.21	Deemed disposal by non-resident
Chapter 3	**Computation**
3.10	Disposals to connected persons
3.15	Assets disposed of in a series of transactions
3.20	Connected persons
3.23	Delayed or irrecoverable consideration
3.30	Election to carry back loss on disposal of right
3.59	Indexation allowance
Chapter 4	**Particular assets**
4.7	Shares and securities: identification rules
4.19	Furnished holiday lettings
4.30	Debts
Chapter 5	**Residence**
5.15	Non-residents doing business in the UK
5.23	Apportionment of non-resident company's gains
Chapter 6	**Partnerships**
6.19	Limited liability partnerships

Chapter 2	**Disposal**
Chapter 14	**Roll-over relief for replacement of business assets**
14.6	Non-residents with UK branch, etc
14.14	Groups of companies
14.20	Intangible assets
14.34	Transfer to a European Company or Societas Europaea ('SE')
14.39	Claims
Chapter 17	**Other reliefs**
17.11	Relief for loans to traders
17.16	Losses on shares in unlisted trading companies

COMPUTATION

9.2   The gain accruing on the disposal of a company's chargeable asset is computed according to normal capital gains tax principles (see **9.1** and **Chapter 3**).

The rules setting out the consideration for the disposal (see **3.3**) and the expenditure allowable as a deduction (see **3.37**) in the computation apply to companies except where otherwise stated. Companies continue to be eligible for indexation allowance, introduced in 1982 in order to eliminate 'paper gains' attributable to inflation (see **3.59**). This allowance was replaced by taper relief with effect from April 1998 for individuals, trustees and personal representatives only.

As a general rule, capital losses may only be set against capital gains of the current accounting period or carried forward to be set against future capital gains. There are no provisions allowing for the carry back of capital losses or the surrender of capital losses between group companies. However, a capital loss on the disposal by an investment company of shares, for which it subscribed, in an unlisted trading company may be set against income for corporation tax purposes (see **17.20**).

The effect of a claim to relief for trading losses under *ICTA 1988, s 393A* may be to set such losses against chargeable gains, because the losses are set against profits including chargeable gains.

Example 9.1

The West End Trading Co Ltd prepares accounts to 31 March each year. The company disposes of an office block on 3 December 2007 for £40m. The incidental costs of sale are £1m. The block was purchased in January 2002 for

£15.5m. Costs of acquisition amounted to £0.5m. In January 2003 a new frontage at a cost of £2m was added to the building that was deemed to be capital expenditure. The chargeable gain to be included within the corporation tax computation for the year ended 31 March 2008 is calculated as follows:

		£000	£000
December 2007	Gross sale proceeds		40,000
	Less: Incidental costs of sale		1,000
	Net sale proceeds		39,000
	Less: Relevant allowable expenditure:		
January 2002	Acquisition cost	15,500	
January 2002	Incidental costs of acquisition	500	
January 2003	Enhancement expenditure	2,000	
			18,000
	Unindexed gain		21,000
	Less: Indexation allowance		
	Cost 16,000 × 0.183	2,928	
	Enhancement 2,000 × 0.150	300	
			3,228
	Chargeable gain		17,772

Workings: calculation of indexation factor

RPI	December 2007	*205.1
RPI	January 2002	173.3
RPI	January 2003	178.4
Factor		
Cost	(RPI December 2007 − RPI January 2002) ÷ RPI January 2002	0.183
Enhance-ment	(RPI December 2007 − RPI January 2003) ÷ RPI January 2003	0.150
* assumed		

ROLL-OVER RELIEF FOR REPLACEMENT OF BUSINESS ASSETS

9.3   The effect of roll-over relief is to defer a chargeable gain where the proceeds of disposal of business assets (the 'old assets') are used to invest in new business assets. The old and the new assets must be used in the business. The detailed rules are discussed in **Chapter 14** (and see Table 9.1 at **9.1**, listing matters contained in that chapter that are of particular relevance to companies). See also **9.13** regarding groups of companies (*TCGA 1992, ss 152–158*).

GROUPS OF COMPANIES

Definitions

9.4   For the purpose of corporation tax on chargeable gains a group broadly consists of a company (known as the principal company) and all of its 75% subsidiaries. If any of those subsidiaries have 75% subsidiaries of their own, the group includes them and their 75% subsidiaries. Any subsidiary that is not an effective 51% subsidiary of the principal company of the group is excluded.

A company that is a 75% subsidiary of another company cannot be the principal company of a group. The principal company can be UK or overseas resident and the inclusion of a non-resident subsidiary does not disturb the group relationship.

Example 9.2

A Ltd owns 75% of the ordinary share capital of B Ltd.

B Ltd owns 80% of the ordinary share capital of C Ltd.

A Ltd and B Ltd are a group, as A Ltd owns 75% of B Ltd.

A Ltd and C Ltd are a group because A Ltd effectively owns 60% (75 × 80%) of C Ltd.

9.5   A company cannot be a member of more than one group. Where a company would be a member of two or more groups but for this rule, the group to which it is treated as belonging is determined by reference to its links to the principal company. If the group conditions are not met the links should then be established with the next group – see Example 9.3 (*TCGA 1992, s 170*).

Example 9.3

A Ltd owns 75% of the ordinary share capital of B Ltd.

B Ltd owns 80% of the ordinary share capital of C Ltd.

C Ltd owns 75% of the ordinary share capital of D Ltd.

D Ltd owns 75% of the ordinary share capital of E Ltd.

A Ltd and B Ltd are a group.

A Ltd and C Ltd are a group.

A Ltd and D Ltd are not a group because A Ltd effectively owns 45% (75 × 80% × 75%) of D Ltd.

D Ltd and E Ltd are a group.

Transfers within a group of companies

9.6   For chargeable gains purposes, intra-group transfers of assets are deemed to be made at a price that results in neither a gain nor a loss accruing to the transferee company (*TCGA 1992, s 171*) (*Innocent v Whaddon Estates Ltd* (1981) 55 TC 476, [1982] STC 115).

The no gain/no loss rule is applied automatically – no claim is required. It does not apply to a disposal:

- arising on the satisfaction of a debt due from the transferee company;
- arising on the redemption of redeemable shares in a company;
- by or to an investment trust, a venture capital trust, a qualifying friendly society, or a dual resident investing company; or
- by or to a real estate investment trust (*TCGA 1992, s 171(2)* as amended by *FA 2006, s 135*)).

On a company reconstruction where *TCGA 1992, s 135* applies, that provision takes preference so that *s 171* does not apply (*TCGA 1992, s 171(3)*).

The effect of this no gain/no loss rule is that when the transferee company eventually disposes of the asset to a third party, its allowable acquisition expenditure in the chargeable gains computation will comprise (i) the original base cost of the asset to the group, plus (ii) indexation allowance for the period to the date of the transfer. The transferee company will be eligible for indexation on this deemed acquisition expenditure as well as any allowable enhancement expenditure that it incurs.

Although a non-UK resident company can be a member of the group, it cannot take part in a no gain/no loss transfer unless it trades in the UK through a permanent establishment in the UK. The asset must be in the UK and be used for the purposes of that trade (*TCGA 1992, s 171(1A)*).

Election to treat a disposal as if made by another group member

9.7   In order to fully utilise the group's capital losses, a group company may treat a disposal of an asset outside the group as though it were made by another group member that has the capital losses available to set against the gain accruing on the disposal. The group companies must make a joint election for this treatment within two years of the end of the accounting period (of the company actually making the disposal) in which the transfer takes place (*TCGA 1992, s 171A*).

Company leaving the group

9.8   If a company leaves a group within six years of an intra-group transfer that was treated as a no gain/no loss disposal (see **9.6**) and the company still owns the asset when it leaves the group, a chargeable gain arises on that occasion (*TCGA 1992, s 179*). The gain is calculated on the basis that the company leaving the group sold and repurchased the asset at its market value at the time of the no gain/no loss transfer, but the gain is charged in the accounting period in which the company leaves the group (*TCGA 1992, s 179(3)*).

The transferee company and another group company may elect jointly that this 'degrouping charge' be treated as accruing to the other company (*TCGA 1992, s 179A*). Roll-over relief (see **Chapter 14**) may be available if the relevant conditions are met (*TCGA 1992, s 179B*).

Example 9.4

In 1988 N Ltd acquired a freehold property for £280,000. In 2001 when the market value was £500,000, and the indexation to date was £20,000, N Ltd transferred the freehold property to P Ltd (a fellow group member). P Ltd leaves the group on 1 January 2007. Both companies prepare accounts to 30 June each year.

The *TCGA 1992, s 179* gain for the year ended 30 June 2007 is calculated as follows:

P Ltd	£
Market value	500,000
Indexed cost	300,000
Capital gain	200,000

If P Ltd purchases another qualifying asset, P Ltd will be able to make a roll-over relief claim under *TCGA 1992, s 152*.

If N Ltd and P Ltd jointly elect for the gain to be treated as accruing to N Ltd, then N Ltd may be able to make a roll-over relief claim against its acquisition of a qualifying asset.

9.9   HMRC confirmed that a degrouping charge will not be imposed on assets transferred to the parent of a two company group which disposes of its single subsidiary (CG 45450).

Transfers of assets to trading stock

9.10   Where one group member acquires a capital asset from another member and appropriates that asset to trading stock, the intra-group asset transfer will be treated as a no gain/no loss disposal (see **9.6**) but as soon as the asset is transferred to stock a chargeable gain will arise in the hands of the transferee. The transferee adopts the transferor's asset base cost and indexation to the date of the transfer (*TCGA 1992, ss 171, 173*).

Alternatively, the transferee can elect under *TCGA 1992, s 161(3)* to treat the asset as acquired at market value less the capital gain arising. The gain will therefore be taken as part of the trading profit on the asset.

Example 9.5

O Ltd transfers a fixed asset to its holding company N Ltd. N Ltd appropriates the asset to its trading stock. The indexed cost of the asset was £12,500 to O Ltd and the market value on transfer is £20,000. N Ltd eventually sells the asset to a third party for £30,000.

Without a *TCGA 1992, s 161(3)* election the position is as follows:

N Ltd	£
Market value	20,000
Indexed cost	12,500
Capital gain	7,500
Sale proceeds	30,000
Deemed cost	20,000
Trading profit	10,000

With a *TCGA 1992, s 161(3)* election the position is as follows:

N Ltd	£
Sales proceeds	30,000
Indexed cost	12,500
Trading profit	17,500

9.11   There is the potential here to turn a capital loss into a trading loss. The loss will only be allowed if there is a true trading intention (*Coates v Arndale Properties Ltd* (1984) 59 TC 516, [1984] STC 637, [1984] 1 WLR 1328, [1985] 1 All ER 15).

Transfers of assets from trading stock

9.12   Where a group company transfers an asset that it holds as trading stock to another group company, and the transferee holds it as a capital asset, the asset is deemed to be transferred at market value giving rise to a trading profit in the hands of the transferor. When the transferee company sells the asset outside the group it adopts as its base cost the market value of the asset at the time of the transfer, plus indexation allowance.

Example 9.6

N Ltd transfers a chargeable asset from its trading stock to its subsidiary company O Ltd. O Ltd will hold the asset as an investment. The cost of the asset was £10,000 and the market value on transfer is £30,000. O Ltd then sells the asset to a third party for £40,000. The indexation from the time of transfer is £500.

N Ltd	£	£
Market value		30,000
Cost		10,000
Trading profit		20,000
O Ltd		
Sale proceeds		40,000
Deemed cost	30,000	
Indexation	500	
		30,500
Capital gain		9,500

Roll-over relief and groups

9.13   Roll-over relief (see **9.3**) is extended to group situations. For this purpose all trades carried on by the members of a group are treated as a single trade. The new assets must be purchased outside the group (*TCGA 1992, s 175*).

Losses attributable to depreciatory transactions

9.14   A transfer of assets between group companies for a consideration other than market value may have the effect of deflating the value of a group company. Any capital loss accruing on the sale of the shares in that company may not be an allowable loss to the extent that it is attributable to the 'depreciatory transaction'. The detailed rules are set out in *TCGA 1992, s 176*.

Dividend stripping

9.15   The rule in **9.14** may also apply in a non-group situation. Where a company (A) owns 10% or more of all holdings of the same class of shares of another company (B), and company A is not a dealing company in relation to the holding, then if company B makes a distribution which materially reduces the value of the holding an adjustment is made for that distribution in calculating the chargeable gain or loss accruing on a disposal of the shares (*TCGA 1992, s 177*).

Pre-entry losses and gains

9.16   There are provisions to restrict:

(a) the set-off of 'pre-entry losses' (broadly, losses accruing to a company before the time when it became a member of a group and losses accruing on assets held by a company at that time) (*TCGA 1992, s 177A, Sch 7A*); and

(b) the losses that may be set against the chargeable gains accruing to a company in the accounting period in which it joins a group (*TCGA 1992, s 177B, Sch 7AA*).

The provisions in (b) do not apply, broadly, to the computation of chargeable gains for an accounting period ending on or after 5 December 2005 (*FA 2006, s 70(4), (6)*). They are replaced by measures enacted in *FA 2006* (see **9.17**).

CAPITAL LOSSES

9.17 Three targeted anti-avoidance rules ('TAARs') were introduced with effect, broadly, from 5 December 2005. The legislation is aimed at:

• the buying of capital losses and gains (*TCGA 1992, ss 184A, 184B*);

• the conversion of an income stream into capital and the use of capital losses to create a deduction against it (*TCGA 1992, s 184G*); and

• the artificial generation of capital losses (*TCGA 1992, s 184H*).

A company's allowable losses now exclude losses generated as part of a tax avoidance scheme. A loss will not now be an allowable loss if it accrues in 'disqualifying circumstances', ie if it accrues directly or indirectly in consequence or in connection with any arrangements of which the main purpose is to secure a tax advantage (*TCGA 1992, s 8(2), (2A)* as amended by *FA 2006, s 69*).

Measures to counter bed and breakfast arrangements existed up to 5 December 2005 and are superseded by the new anti-avoidance rules (*TCGA 1992, s 106* repealed by *FA 2006, s 72*).

The detailed rules are discussed in *Tottel's Corporation Tax 2006/07*.

RELIEF ON DISPOSAL OF SHARES

9.18 Three important reliefs are available in relation to a company's disposal of shares. These relate to:

• losses on shares in unlisted trading companies (see **9.19**);

• substantial shareholdings (see **9.20**); and

● the corporate venturing scheme (see **9.24**).

Losses on shares in unlisted trading companies

9.19   Relief against income is available to an investment company incurring an allowable loss for corporation tax purposes on the disposal of shares, for which it subscribed, in a qualifying trading company (see **17.20**).

Substantial shareholdings exemption

9.20   A gain accruing on a company's disposal of shares in another company is not a chargeable gain where the conditions set out below are met. On the other hand, a loss accruing on a qualifying disposal is not an allowable loss (*TCGA 1992, s 192A, Sch 7AC*). This relief does not apply where the disposal is deemed to be a no gain/no loss transfer for capital gains under *TCGA 1992, s 171* (see **9.6**). Broadly, the investing company must hold at least 10% of the investee company's share capital and be entitled to at least 10% of the profits and assets available for distribution to equity holders. The investing company must have held the shares for a continuous period of at least 12 months beginning not more than two years before the disposal (*TCGA 1992, Sch 7AC, para 7*).

Group member holdings can be aggregated in order to calculate whether the 10% holding condition is met (*TCGA 1992, Sch 7AC, para 9*). The capital gains tax group definition is used (see **9.4**) but a 51% relationship is required rather than a 75% relationship.

The period of ownership may be extended to take account of earlier no gain/no loss transfers and share reorganisations. There are provisions dealing with deemed disposals and reacquisitions, repurchase agreements, stock-lending arrangements, demergers and liquidations (*TCGA 1992, Sch 7AC, paras 10–16*).

Conditions affecting the investing company

9.21   The investing company must have been a sole trading company or a member of a trading group throughout the 12-month period (see **9.20**) and immediately after the disposal. The relief also applies in a group situation where the company holding the shares does not qualify but, assuming an intra-group transfer under *TCGA 1992, s 171*, another company would qualify. Where completion takes place after the time of disposal (as provided by *TCGA 1992, s 28*) the investing company must qualify at the time of completion (*TCGA 1992, Sch 7AC, para 18*).

Conditions affecting the investee company

9.22   The investee company must have been a trading company or the holding company of a trading group during the 12-month period (see **9.20**), and it must also be a qualifying company immediately after the disposal of the shares. The responsibility for determining whether a company in which shares (or an interest in shares or assets related to shares) were held and since disposed of was a qualifying company lies with the investor company concerned (HMRC Tax Bulletin 84, August 2006).

Where completion takes place after the time of disposal (as provided by *TCGA 1992, s 28*) the investee company must qualify at the time of completion (*TCGA 1992, Sch 7AC, para 19*).

Trading company

9.23   A trading company for these purposes is a company that carries on trading activities (see below) and whose activities do not include to a 'substantial extent' (see below) activities other than trading activities.

Trading activities include activities carried on by a company:

(a)   in the course of, or for the purposes of, a trade it is carrying on;

(b)   for the purposes of a trade it is preparing to carry on;

(c)   with a view to its acquiring or starting to carry on a trade; or

(d)   with a view to its acquiring a significant interest in the share capital of a trading company, or the holding company of a trading group or subgroup (subject to the restrictions outlined below).

With regard to (c) and (d), the company must make the acquisition, or start to trade, as soon as is reasonably practical in the circumstances. It is understood that HMRC regard 'substantial' in this context as meaning 20% or more (*TCGA 1992, Sch 7AC, para 20*).

Example 9.7

Atlantic Ltd is a trading company, with two wholly-owned subsidiary companies, India Ltd and China Ltd.

On 1 July 2006, Atlantic Ltd acquired 25% of the ordinary share capital of Pacific Ltd.

On 1 September 2006 Pacific Ltd is taken over by Adriatic Ltd.

Atlantic Ltd received an exchange of shares under the no gain/no loss treatment (*TCGA 1992, s 135* applied *TCGA 1992, s 127*). As a result Atlantic Ltd now owns 20% of Adriatic Ltd.

On 1 March 2007 Atlantic Ltd transfers its holding in Adriatic Ltd on a no gain/no loss basis so that *TCGA 1992, s 171* applies to its 100% subsidiary India Ltd.

On 1 July 2007 India Ltd sells the holding to a third party.

The holding was bought on 1 July 2006 and sold on 1 July 2007. It is necessary to look back through the period of ownership to ascertain whether the substantial shareholdings exemption applies (*TCGA 1992, Sch 7AC, para 10*). The holding throughout has remained within the group. India Ltd is treated as owning the shares for 12 months prior to disposal and so the exemption applies.

Corporate venturing scheme

9.24   Relief under the corporate venturing scheme is available for investments in qualifying shares issued during the period from 1 April 2000 to 31 March 2010. The detailed rules are set out in *FA 2000, s 63* and *Sch 15*. HMRC guidance is available at http://www.hmrc.gov.uk/guidance/cvs.htm.

Tax reliefs

9.25   Three types of relief are available:

- investment relief – relief against corporation tax of up 20% of the amount subscribed for the full-risk ordinary shares held for three years;

- deferral relief – any gain on the sale of shares can be rolled into the cost of new shares acquired under the scheme; and

- loss relief – any loss on the sale of the shares can be relieved against income or chargeable gains.

The investing company

9.26   Broadly, the investing company's interest in the investee company must not be more than 30% and the investing company must not be in a position to control the investee company. The interests of connected persons (as defined in *ICTA 1988, s 839*) are taken into account for this purpose. No reciprocal arrangements must exist regarding the investment. The investing company must be a trading company or the holding company of a trading group. Financial activities (eg banking, money lending and insurance) are excluded. Further conditions are set out in *FA 2000, Sch 15, paras 5–14*).

The issuing company

9.27   The investee or 'issuing' company must be an unquoted trading company or the holding company of a trading group when the shares are issued (AIM and OFEX shares are unquoted for this purpose). The company can be preparing to carry on a trade. It must not have made any arrangements to become a quoted company.

The company must have gross assets of no more than £7m immediately before and £8m immediately after the issue. If the issuing company is the parent company of a group, this test is applied to the group as a whole. For shares issued before 6 April 2006, the limits are £15m before and £16m after the issue of shares.

Throughout the 'qualification period' the issuing company must not be a 51% subsidiary of another company or under the control of another company. In addition, at least 20% of the issuing company's ordinary share capital must be held by 'independent individuals', ie individuals other than directors or employees (or their relatives) of an investing company or any company connected with it. Further conditions are set out in *FA 2000, Sch 15, paras 15–33*).

The investment

9.28   The investment must be in cash and the shares must be fully paid-up at the time they are issued. There can be no arrangement in force to protect investors from normal commercial investment risk.

The investing company must use at least 80% of the funds it receives from issuing the shares for the purposes of a qualifying trade, or for research and development intended to lead to or benefit a qualifying trade. The funds must be used no later than the end of the period of 12 months starting with the issue of the share or the 12 months following the commencement of the trade if later. The remaining 20% of the funds must be used within the following 12 months (*FA 2000, Sch 15, para 36*).

Obtaining clearance

9.29   The investee company can obtain HMRC clearance before the shares are issued. If the issue goes ahead the issuing company should complete form

CVS 1 confirming it has met all the necessary conditions with which it must comply. The company must submit the form to HMRC and, if satisfied, HMRC will authorise the issuing company to provide the investing company with a compliance certificate to enable it to claim investment relief (and, where applicable, deferral relief). The compliance certificate can only be issued after the issuing company has been carrying on the trade (or, where appropriate, research and development) for which the funds were raised for at least four months (*FA 2000, Sch 15, para 89*).

Investment relief

9.30   The investing company claims investment relief against its corporation tax liability by completing the corporate venturing scheme CT600G supplementary pages and including the relief claimed in box 71 of the main return. Loss relief is included in CT600 box 22.

The necessary conditions must be complied with for three years or else the relief is withdrawn. The relief is only available during the accounting period for which the investment is made. It is given against corporation tax after marginal relief but before any double taxation relief.

Example 9.8

If during an accounting period an investing company subscribes £30,000 for 3,000 shares in company A and £90,000 for 6,000 shares in company B, then the maximum investment relief available is £24,000 (20% of £30,000 + £90,000).

If the investing company's corporation tax liability for the accounting period is £18,000 before taking account of any investment relief, then only three-quarters of the available investment relief can be used.

So, the amount attributable to the shares in A is:

£30,000 × £18,000/£120,000 = £4,500

The amount attributable to the shares in B is:

£90,000 × £18,000/£120,000 = £13,500

It would also be possible for the investing company to claim investment relief only in respect of the shares in company B, so all the investment relief would be attributable to those shares. But this would prevent shares in company A from qualifying for CVS loss relief and deferral relief because there would be no investment relief attributable to the shares in company A immediately before any future disposal.

9.31   If the investing company receives value, other than insignificant value, from the investee company, relief equal to 20% of the value received is withdrawn. There are detailed rules setting out when value is received.

An amount is insignificant if it does not exceed £1,000 or the amount is insignificant in relation to the amount subscribed for the shares (*FA 2000, Sch 15, paras 47–58*).

Deferral relief

9.32   The investing company may claim deferral relief in respect of the gain accruing on a disposal of qualifying shares if it reinvests the gain in a 'qualifying investment' in a different company (see below).

This relief is available only if investment relief was attributable to the shares immediately before the disposal and the investing company held the shares continuously from the time they were issued until the time of the disposal.

The qualifying investment must comply with the investment relief conditions and must be made within the period beginning four years before the gain accrued.

The gain is deferred until the qualifying investment is disposed of, or an event occurs (such as a receipt of value) that causes investment relief attributable to the shares to be withdrawn or reduced.

The investing company claims deferral relief on the corporate venturing scheme supplementary pages. It may do so after it has received a compliance certificate relating to the qualifying investment. The amount of the deferral must be shown on the claim (*FA 2000, Sch 15, paras 73–79*).

Relief for losses

9.33   A loss accruing on a disposal of shares that have attracted investment relief (see **9.30**) may be set against a chargeable gain, or carried forward to set against future chargeable gains, in the normal way. Alternatively, the investing company may claim that the loss be set against its income for the accounting period in which the disposal was made, with any excess carried back to periods ending in the 12 months before that period. Several conditions are set out in *FA 2000, Sch 15, paras 67–72*.

Example 9.9

An investing company subscribes £100,000 for 100,000 shares (obtaining investment relief of £20,000).

It retains the shares for four years before disposing of them all for £55,000.

The allowable loss is calculated as follows:

Disposal proceeds £55,000 – £80,000 (consideration given for shares less investment relief given and not withdrawn) giving an allowable loss of £25,000.

Any unutilised loss cannot be carried forward as a trading loss but may be carried forward as a capital loss.

Chapter 10

Capital gains tax planning

10.1   This chapter provides an overview of some of the matters that should be considered by taxpayers seeking to ensure that they do not pay more CGT than the law requires. It does not examine every possible legal step that could be taken to reduce or eliminate a potential tax liability and, as indicated below, taxpayers and their advisers need to bear in mind the implications of recent developments in relation to tax avoidance. These are discussed briefly below.

PLANNING AND AVOIDANCE:
RECENT DEVELOPMENTS

10.2   The new system for disclosure of tax avoidance schemes, introduced in the *Finance Act 2004* and modified in August 2006 (see **10.3**), has led to the disclosure of a large number of schemes to HMRC and an increase in targeted anti-avoidance legislation. The government has made it clear that it is prepared to introduce retrospective legislation in areas where it identifies a threat of significant loss of revenue.

Recent developments have also indicated that a general anti-avoidance rule (GAAR) is being considered once again. The Inland Revenue consulted on the possibility of GAAR in 1998 but the government decided not to go ahead with the proposal. HMRC director general Dave Hartnett told the House of Lords Economic Affairs Committee on 22 May 2006 that HMRC were carrying out a 'legal study' of GAARs and similar rules around the world. He observed that they were used in a number of countries including Canada, Australia, New Zealand and Spain with mixed results. The study 'may or may not, in time, lead to advice to our ministers', he said.

Some leading tax experts have suggested that a GAAR may be preferable to the present complex system of anti-avoidance legislation. In July 2005 the Institute of Chartered Accountants of Scotland (ICAS) wrote to the Chancellor of the Exchequer to encourage the government to consult on the possibility of introducing a GAAR. However, the ICAS warned that such a rule 'must be accompanied by the repeal of most existing tax avoidance provisions and the launch of a new pre-transaction ruling system to give certainty'. Hartnett told the Lords committee in May 2006 that a number of countries had pre-transaction clearance systems, but he questioned how sensible it would be to offer clearances for what were 'very clearly tax avoidance arrangements'.

The ICAS's reference to tax avoidance provisions relates to the ever-growing body of specific anti-avoidance legislation – much of it bolted on to tax reliefs in response to perceived abuse of those reliefs.

DISCLOSURE OF TAX AVOIDANCE SCHEMES

10.3   The regime requiring disclosure of tax avoidance schemes (DOTAS) is designed to alert HMRC to certain schemes or arrangements that are intended to provide a tax advantage when compared to a different course of action. It is not intended to catch mainstream tax planning.

HMRC said in June 2006 that the new regime appeared to have led to a sharp decline in marketed schemes without affecting 'legitimate' tax planning. The scope of the regime was widened in August 2006 by *SI 2006/1543*. It is no longer restricted to employment or financial products and is not limited by 'filters'.

The DOTAS regime now applies generally to income tax, corporation tax and CGT. It was extended to VAT and stamp duty land tax in 2005. Disclosure is required for any arrangements if any one of a series of 'hallmarks' applies.

Detailed guidance is available on the HMRC website: www.hmrc.gov.uk/aiu/index.htm. This includes the following summary (as at 31 August 2006) of the disclosure requirements for income tax, corporation tax and CGT:

A tax arrangement must be disclosed when:

- it will, or might be expected to, enable any person to obtain a tax advantage;

- that tax advantage is, or might be expected to be, the main benefit or one of the main benefits of the arrangement; and

- it is a tax arrangement that falls within any description ('hallmarks') prescribed in the relevant regulations.

In most situations where a disclosure is required it must be made by the scheme 'promoter' within 5 days of it being made available. However, the scheme user may need to make the disclosure where:

- the promoter is based outside the UK;

- the promoter is a lawyer and legal privilege applies; or
- there is no promoter.

The hallmarks are:

- wishing to keep the arrangements confidential from a competitor;
- wishing to keep the arrangements confidential from HMRC;
- arrangements for which a premium fee could reasonably be obtained;
- arrangements that include off market terms;
- arrangements that are standardised tax products;
- arrangements that are loss schemes; and
- arrangements that are certain leasing arrangements.

Upon disclosure, HMRC issue the promoter with an 8-digit scheme reference number for the disclosed scheme. By law the promoter must provide this number to each client that uses the scheme, who in turn must include the number on his or her return or form AAG4.

A person who designs and implements their own scheme must disclose it within 30 days of it being implemented.

Source: HMRC Anti-Avoidance Group: http://www.hmrc.gov.uk/aiu/index.htm

'RAMSAY' AND ANTI-AVOIDANCE LEGISLATION

10.4 A series of appeals heard by the courts during the 1980s established the principle that one or more steps in a pre-ordained tax avoidance scheme could be ignored, with the result that the scheme did not have the intended tax consequences. See, in particular, *W T Ramsay Ltd v CIR* [1981] 54 TC 101, HL and *Furniss v Dawson* [1984] 55 TC 324, HL. Subsequent cases have scaled back the impact of the *Ramsay* (or *Furniss v Dawson*) principle but the possibility of an HMRC challenge on these grounds should always be borne in mind.

The ever-increasing length and complexity of recent Finance Acts is largely due to the addition of detailed legislation to counter artificial or contrived arrangements designed to obtain a tax advantage, and to close loopholes (ie flaws in the legislation which mean that it did not work as intended). They include:

	TCGA 1992
Temporary non-residents	s 10A
Attribution of gains to members of non-resident companies	s 13
Transactions between connected persons	s 18
Assets disposed of in a series of transactions	ss 19–20
Value shifting	ss 29–34
Shares in close company transferring assets at an undervalue	s 125
Company reconstructions	s 137
Emigration of donee	s 168
Concessions that defer a charge	s 284A
	ICTA 1988
Transactions in securities	ss 703–709
Transactions in land	ss 776–780

Other anti-avoidance measures specific to particular situations or tax reliefs are discussed where appropriate in the relevant chapter of this book.

TAX PLANNING

10.5   It is important to distinguish between mainstream tax planning from the use of artificial or contrived schemes to avoid tax. HMRC regard the former as legitimate but appear determined to eliminate the latter. This section focuses on some of the matters to be considered by, or on behalf of, taxpayers wishing to make the most of exemptions or reliefs provided by the legislation. The matters most likely be of concern to most potential payers of CGT are mentioned first. Unfortunately, many tax reliefs introduced by government, for example, those designed to encourage investment in business, have been complicated by voluminous – and often tortuous – anti-avoidance rules.

Residence and domicile

10.6   In most cases it is the residence and domicile status of the taxpayer, rather than the location of the assets, that determines liability to CGT. Non-residents are generally not chargeable except in relation to gains on assets used in connection with a UK business.

UK resident individuals who retain a non-UK domicile are chargeable only on the remittance basis in respect of gains accruing outside the UK, and in this respect they have a distinct advantage over UK-domiciled taxpayers. The government continues to keep this anomaly under review, but speculation that a change is imminent appears to be a thing of the past.

The scope for avoiding CGT by attaining non-resident status for a relatively short period and making disposals during the period of absence from the UK was significantly reduced by the special rules for temporary non-residents, introduced in 1998 (see **5.16**).

Exemptions

10.7   The next question to consider is whether a gain is going to be exempt as a result of a specific provision or because it falls within the annual CGT exemption. Exemptions for specific persons, assets or gains are listed at **1.6**. An outright exemption is clearly better than a deferral of CGT.

The annual CGT exemption is discussed at **1.16**. The main point to bear in mind here is that the exemption – currently worth £8,800 to an individual and, in effect, £17,600 for a couple – cannot be carried forward from one year of assessment to the next. Any part of it that is unused is lost for good.

The benefit of the annual exemption may be maximised by careful timing of the disposal of assets, but as ever it is important to remember that personal and commercial considerations will often be more important than saving tax. The taxpayer should also bear in mind that HMRC may wish to examine the timing of disposals stated to fall shortly before or after the end of a tax year (see **2.8**). The practice of 'bed and breakfasting' shares was made ineffective by a change in the identification rules but variations on the theme remain possible (see **10.12**).

A member of a married couple or civil partnership who has already used their annual exemption might consider transferring an asset such as a shareholding to the other spouse or partner, leaving the transferee free to sell the asset and utilise their own annual exemption. Care is needed to safeguard against a possible HMRC challenge here. They may seek to establish that the transferor has made a transfer of sale proceeds rather than the asset itself.

A deferral relief claim, made on the basis that a gain has been reinvested in enterprise investment scheme shares (see **Chapter 16**) operates by reducing the allowable expenditure on the shares. The claim may be limited in order to set the annual exemption against a part of the gain that would otherwise be deferred and subject to a potential CGT charge in the future.

The structure of hold-over relief for gifts, roll-over relief for replacement of business assets and incorporation relief (see **Chapters 13, 14** and **15**) is such that some gains may be left in charge to be absorbed by the annual exemption.

The general CGT exemption that applies to deemed disposals on a taxpayer's death should not be overlooked in any tax planning exercise. Assets that the taxpayer was competent to dispose of are deemed to be acquired by the personal representatives or legatees at their market value (see **Chapter 7**). The absence of a CGT charge, on what may well be significant capital appreciation in many cases, means it is worthwhile considering retention of an asset rather than, for example, making a lifetime gift.

Hold-over relief for gifts effectively transfers the potential CGT liability to the transferee. It is worth noting that this liability is based on the market value of the asset gifted at the time of the transfer – regardless of any later reduction in value – and that a loss of taper relief may well make a hold-over relief claim less attractive than it appears at first. The inheritance tax position may point towards lifetime giving, but in many cases the potential IHT bill is substantially reduced or eliminated by business property relief or agricultural property relief.

The computation

10.8   In the absence of any exemption it is useful to estimate a potential CGT liability in order to establish whether any claim or other action to reduce or defer the liability is appropriate or desirable. Recent reductions in the effective CGT rate on disposals of business assets – due largely to the generous rate of taper for business assets (see **11.6**) – mean that in many cases the taxpayer may regard the liability as acceptable.

It is important to check for any reduction in allowable expenditure that may be required as a result of a claim to roll-over or hold-over relief, increasing the chargeable gain on the disposal being considered.

Where the 31 March 1982 value is substituted for the actual cost of an asset (see **3.68**), the benefits of obtaining a professional valuation and ensuring that all items of allowable enhancement expenditure are identified can be substantial. The value at that date will determine the level of any indexation allowance (for the period to April 1998) as well as the amount of the gain, although the effect of the allowance may be significantly reduced where business asset taper relief is set against the indexed gain.

Where the disposal has already taken place and a valuation is required, it may well be useful to take advantage of HMRC's post-valuation service using form CG 34 (see **1.34**) before the end of the tax year to allow time for consideration of any other possible action as part of a pre-year end planning review.

Taper relief

10.9   This relief replaced indexation allowance in 1998 and for individuals (it is not available to companies, for which indexation continues) it can result in a substantial reduction in the effective rate of CGT. Detailed anti-avoidance rules apply to taper relief and are summarised at **11.29** onwards.

The taxpayer's qualifying holding period begins on the later of 6 April 1998 and the date of acquisition of the asset. The maximum rate of taper relief is available for a business asset after a qualifying holding period of only two years. The percentage of the gain that is chargeable is reduced to 25%. For a 40% taxpayer this reduces the maximum CGT rate to 10% of the gain. Gains falling between the starting rate and basic rate limits are charged at 20%, giving an effective rate after the maximum taper relief of only 5%.

Taper relief is, therefore, a key consideration for an individual who finds himself likely to make chargeable gains in excess of the annual exemption. However, the availability of the higher rate for business assets depends on the relevant asset having been a business asset (as defined) throughout the qualifying holding period.

Taper relief for non-business assets is much less valuable. A non-business asset has to be owned for at least three years before any taper relief is obtained and the rate of relief increases by only 5% per annum. A taxpayer who still owns a non-business asset acquired before 17 March 1998 will have a nine-year qualifying holding period by 6 April 2007, and that period will be increased to ten years by the 'bonus year' mentioned at **11.4**. This means that 40% of his gain will be chargeable.

The qualifying holding period comprises complete periods of 12 months, so the taxpayer may be able to achieve a significant reduction in CGT by ensuring that a disposal takes place after the end of the current 12-month period. Other factors to consider, preferably before a disposal, include:

- the effect of 'tainting', ie the loss of business asset status for part of the period of ownership (see **11.26**);

- the interaction of losses with taper relief and the annual exemption (see **11.41**);

- the impact of other reliefs (see **10.10**).

Impact of roll-over and other reliefs

10.10   Claims to any of the following deferral reliefs can have a significant impact on the availability of taper relief, as explained in **11.43**, on the ultimate disposal:

- hold-over relief for gifts (see **13.36**);

- roll-over relief for replacement of business assets (see **14.44**);

- incorporation relief on the transfer of a business to a company (see **15.18**); and

- deferral relief for gains reinvested in enterprise investment scheme shares (see **16.25**).

Allowable losses should be allocated against gains on the basis that maximises taper relief. This means broadly that losses should be set first against the gains attracting the lower rate of taper. The legislation itself provides for this order of set-off (see **11.41**).

Securing business asset status

10.11 As indicated in **Chapter 11**, the conditions for business asset status are complex and there are conditions attaching to both the owner of the asset and the use to which it is put. In the case of shares there may be uncertainty surrounding, for example, the effect on a company's 'qualifying company' status of activities other than trading (see **11.10**). It is important to monitor the company's activities and examine the possible impact of, for example, a reduction in trading activity and the letting of surplus property.

Losses

10.12 Allowable losses must be set against chargeable gains arising in the same year of assessment. There is no facility to restrict the set off of losses against such gains (see **1.19**). A taxpayer who is contemplating a disposal on which a loss will accrue might, therefore, consider deferring the disposal until after 5 April if the gains would be covered in any event by the annual exemption. The delay would avoid wasting the exemption, and having the loss accruing in the following tax year might have the effect of reducing a potential CGT liability on other gains. Relief for allowable losses carried forward is more flexible. It may be restricted in order to preserve the benefit of the annual exemption.

Spouses or civil partners may consider a transfer of assets under the no gain/no loss rule (see **3.67**) where one spouse or partner has an unrealised loss that he or she is unlikely to use. The transferee may be able to realise the loss on a later disposal to an unconnected third party and set it against chargeable gains in excess of the annual exemption. Care is needed to safeguard against a possible HMRC challenge on the lines mentioned in **10.7**.

Monitoring unrealised gains and losses, and planning to make the best use of the annual exemption, are key features of basic CGT planning. It is also important to identify any allowable losses that might be generated by means of, for example:

- realising a loss on quoted shares;

- making a negligible value claim (see **2.10**); or

- claiming relief on a loan to a trader, where the loan has become irrecoverable (see **17.11**).

The possibility of setting any unused trading losses against capital gains (see **3.52**) might also be considered, although care is needed in assessing the interaction of this relief with CGT taper relief and the annual exemption. A capital loss on an investment in an unlisted trading company may be relieved against income tax where certain conditions are met (see **17.16**).

Spouses and civil partners

10.13   Each member of a married couple is taxed independently of the other and is required to make a separate return of his or her own chargeable gains. There is no joint assessment and losses borne by one spouse cannot be set against gains accruing to the other. However, chargeable assets transferred from one spouse to the other are treated as taking place on a no gain/no loss basis (see **3.67**).

This treatment was extended to partners in a civil partnership with effect from 5 December 2005. Civil partners are of course taxed independently of one other, and many of the tax planning opportunities available to married couples are now open to them.

Private residence relief

10.14   The CGT exemption for an individual's only or main residence can be very valuable, especially in the light of recent increases in house prices. The relief is extended to cover certain periods of absence and periods during which a house is let. It is examined in detail in **Chapter 12**.

Connected persons

10.15   The possible impact of the market value rule outlined in **3.5** should be considered where, for example, there are transactions within a family and the no gain/no loss rule mentioned in **10.12** does not apply.

Losses accruing on a disposal to a connected person cannot be set against gains other than those accruing on a disposal to the same connected person (see **3.21**). On the other hand, the gift of a chargeable asset showing a gain may be eligible for hold-over relief (see **Chapter 13**) so in some cases care in choosing which asset to give away can be worthwhile. Other provisions that may be relevant to transactions between connected persons include those applying to:

- assets disposed of in a series of transactions (see **3.11**);

- the disposal of chattels forming part of a 'set of articles' in order to secure the chattels exemption (**4.21**); and

- the value shifting provisions (*TCGA 1992, s 29*).

Ownership of assets

10.16   There may be some flexibility as to who should be the beneficial owner of an asset, for example, where a family company is involved. Factors that might be considered, preferably before an asset is acquired, include:

- whether the value of the asset is likely to increase significantly in the future;

- the effect of any deferral relief on the new owner's allowable expenditure for CGT purposes;

- the potential 'double charge' to tax on gains (i) accruing on a disposal of assets owned by a company, and then (ii) realised by the shareholder in the form of increased gains on sale of the shares or on a liquidation;

- the availability of private residence relief (note that it is not available to companies);

- the respective income tax and CGT marginal rates of spouses or civil partners;

- whether the conditions for business asset taper relief are going to be met;

- the potential tax and other benefits of having business property owned by a pension scheme; and

- the merits of any trust arrangements (bearing in mind that the inheritance tax advantages previously available to accumulation and maintenance trusts and interest in possession trusts have been reduced substantially following *FA 2006*).

Bed and breakfast transactions

10.17   'Bed and breakfasting' is the practice of selling shares and repurchasing them the following day. This used to be a common year-end tax planning technique, undertaken for many years by taxpayers wishing to:

- utilise their annual CGT exemption;

- realise gains that could be covered by unused capital losses; or

- realise losses and set them against gains that would otherwise give rise to a tax liability.

The cost of the new acquisition would represent the allowable expenditure on its future disposal. The exercise would, therefore, achieve an uplift in the CGT base cost of the investment.

However, the effect of the 30-day rule introduced in April 1998 (see **4.2**) was to negate the effect of such transactions. The disposal on day 1 would now be matched with the acquisition on day 2, leaving a small loss in most cases where there was little movement in the share price.

'Bed and spousing' is the rather undignified term for a technique that is sometimes suggested as an alternative to a bed and breakfast arrangement. One spouse sells the shares and the other spouse buys a similar holding shortly afterwards. Alternatively, the taxpayer might:

- identify shares in the same industry sector that would make a suitable replacement for the initial investment; or

- sell the shares in one capacity and buy the new holding in another capacity – shares bought within an individual savings account are free of CGT in the hands of the investor (see **1.8**).

Part B

Reliefs

Chapter 11

Taper relief

INTRODUCTION

11.1   Taper relief replaced indexation allowance in April 1998 for individuals, trustees and personal representatives. Assets held before April 1998 may attract both indexation allowance (see **11.42** and **3.59**) for the period up to April 1998 and taper relief for later periods of ownership. Companies and other bodies within the charge to corporation tax continue to be eligible for indexation allowance and are not entitled to taper relief.

Whereas indexation allowance was designed specifically to eliminate 'paper gains' attributable to inflation, taper relief provides a percentage reduction in the amount of the capital gain that is chargeable. In general, the rate of taper relief is higher (so the percentage chargeable is smaller) the longer an asset is held. Allowable enhancement expenditure will reduce a gain but its timing has no bearing on the rate of taper relief. The reduction in the percentage of the gain that is chargeable is significantly greater for business assets than it is for non-business assets. However, taper relief, unlike indexation allowance, cannot eliminate a gain entirely.

TRUSTEES, PERSONAL REPRESENTATIVES AND LEGATEES

11.2   This chapter discusses taper relief as it applies to disposals made by individuals only. It does not deal with individuals' disposals of assets acquired as legatee, or disposals by personal representatives. These are discussed in **Chapter 7**. Taper relief for trustees is discussed in **Chapter 8**.

OPERATION OF THE RELIEF

11.3   Taper relief is available to individuals where, for a year of assessment, chargeable gains exceed any allowable losses and those gains include gains that are eligible for taper relief. Losses are to be set against gains in the order that maximises taper relief (see **11.41**). Taper relief then reduces this excess by:

11.3   *Taper relief*

- applying taper relief to the gain(s) eligible for that relief;

- aggregating the tapered gains; and

- adding to this aggregate any gains that are not eligible for taper relief.

A chargeable gain is eligible for taper relief if it is a gain on the disposal of:

- a business asset with a 'qualifying holding period' (see below) of at least one year; or

- a non-business asset with a qualifying holding period of at least three years.

The relief is obtained by multiplying the amount of the gain by the percentage, given by the table in *TCGA 1992, s 2A(5)* (reproduced below), for the number of whole years in the qualifying holding period. This table applies to disposals after 5 April 2002. For earlier disposals of business assets, the rate of taper relief was lower than shown (so that a higher percentage of the gain was chargeable).

A year is a continuous period of 12 months. HMRC will not try to determine the time of day of an acquisition or disposal. Instead, they assume that where a disposal takes place on the anniversary of the asset's acquisition, a whole year of ownership has been completed. If the asset is acquired on 29 February in a leap year, the anniversary date is 1 March in the following years (or 29 February in leap years) (*TCGA 1992, s 2A*; CG 17900).

Table 11.1

Gains on disposal of business assets		Gains on disposal of non-business assets	
Number of whole years in qualifying holding period	Percentage of gain chargeable	Number of whole years in qualifying holding period	Percentage of gain chargeable
1	50	–	–
2 or more	25	–	–
		3	95
		4	90
		5	85
		6	80
		7	75
		8	70
		9	65
		10 or more	60

214

Qualifying holding period

11.4   The 'qualifying holding period', measured at the time of disposal, is the period after 5 April 1998 for which the asset had been held at the time of its disposal. In the case of a non-business asset held at both 17 March 1998 and 6 April 1998 a 'bonus year' is added, except where the qualifying holding period is reduced because of an anti-avoidance rule stipulating that a period does not count for taper relief (see **11.29**) (*TCGA 1992, s 2A(8)*).

Example 11.1

The following table illustrates the calculation of the qualifying holding period.

Asset	Acquired on	Disposed of on	Qualifying holding period (whole years)
Business	1 June 2004	1 November 2006	2
Non-business	1 March 1998	1 May 2006	8 + 1 = 9
Either	6 May 2006	5 April 2007	None

Example 11.2

Jill realised a gain of £40,000 on disposal of an asset that was a business asset throughout the period of ownership. She acquired the asset on 1 September 2003 and sold it on 31 January 2007. The qualifying holding period is three years and 25% of the gain, ie £10,000, is chargeable.

Example 11.3

Alan realised a gain of £10,000 on disposal of an asset that was a non-business asset throughout the period of ownership. He acquired the asset on 1 August 2000 and sold it on 31 October 2006. The qualifying holding period is six years and 80% of the gain, ie £8,000, is chargeable.

In *O'Sullivan v Philip* (*Inspector of Taxes*) [2005] EWHC 2130 Ch D it was held that there was no basis for the taxpayer's argument that 'the period after 5 April 1998 for which the asset had been held at the time of its disposal' should be taken to include the whole of the period from the taxpayer's acquisition of shares in 1989.

Transfers between spouses or civil partners

11.5   Where an asset is transferred between spouses living together and the transfer is treated under *TCGA 1992, s 58(1)* as giving rise to no gain and no loss, then on a subsequent disposal the transferee spouse is treated, for taper relief purposes, as having acquired the asset when the transferor spouse acquired it. This means that the qualifying holding period will be the entire period of ownership of both spouses falling after 5 April 1998. A similar rule applies with effect from 5 December 2005 to transfers between civil partners living together.

Example 11.4

Mr Fox acquired an asset on 1 January 2003. On 15 September 2003 he transferred it to Mrs Fox and the no gain/no loss rule applied. Mrs Fox sold the asset on 31 January 2007. The assessable gain before taper relief is £10,000 and the asset was used throughout the combined period of ownership as a non-business asset. The amount of the gain that is chargeable is £9,000, being 90% of £10,000 (*TCGA 1992, Sch A1, para 15*).

BUSINESS ASSETS

11.6   The conditions determining whether an asset was a business asset at a particular time before its disposal are set out in *TCGA 1992, Sch A1* and summarised below. There are separate rules for (i) shares and securities (see **11.7**) and (ii) other assets (see **11.21**).

Shares and securities

11.7   Any reference in the taper relief rules (and in the commentary below) to shares of a company includes any securities of the company and any debentures that are deemed by *TCGA 1992, s 251(6)* to be securities of the company. An 'interest in' shares or securities or debentures is an interest as a co-owner (as either joint tenant or tenant in common).

A holding of shares in a company, or an interest in such shares, was a business asset at a time before its disposal if the company was a 'qualifying company' by reference to that individual. Where business asset status depends on the taxpayer being able to exercise a certain percentage of the voting rights in a company, HMRC do not regard this requirement having to be satisfied by virtue of the particular class of shares disposed of. For example, non-voting preference shares in a company could qualify as a business asset if the holder could exercise at least 5% (or 25% prior to 6 April 2000) of the voting rights through other shareholdings (*TCGA 1992, Sch A1, paras 4(1), (2), 22*; CG 17951).

Periods of ownership after 5 April 2000

11.8   The following definitions apply to determine whether an asset was a business asset at any time after 5 April 2000. See **11.19** regarding earlier periods of ownership.

Qualifying company

11.9   A company is taken to have been a qualifying company by reference to an individual at any time when either (a) or (b) below applied:

(a)   the company was a trading company (see below) or the holding company of a trading group (see below) and at least one of the following conditions was met:

  - the company was unlisted, meaning that none of its shares were listed on a recognised stock exchange and it was not a 51% subsidiary of a company whose shares, or any class of whose shares, was so listed,

  - the individual was an officer or employee of the company (or of a company having a relevant connection with it), or

  - the individual was able to exercise at least 5% of the voting rights;

(b)   the company was a non-trading company or the holding company of a non-trading group, the individual was an officer or employee of the company (or of a company having a relevant connection with it), and the individual did not have a material interest (see below) in either the company or in any company which at that time had control of it.

A company has a 'relevant connection' with another company at any time if they are both members of the same group of companies or of the same commercial association of companies.

A taxpayer disposing of shares who is unsure as to whether a company was a qualifying company for taper relief purposes may apply to HMRC for a post-transaction ruling under the procedures set out in HMRC code of practice COP 10. HMRC suggest that the taxpayer should seek advice from the company in the first instance. A company wishing to establish its status so that it can inform non-corporate shareholders may also ask HMRC for an opinion in accordance with COP 10 (*TCGA 1992, Sch A1, paras 6(1)*, *(1A)* (as amended by *FA 2000*), *22*; CG 17953).

Trading company

Periods from 17 April 2002

11.10   The following definitions apply to disposals on or after 17 April 2002 and periods of ownership from that date:

217

- 'Trading company' means a company carrying on 'trading activities' whose activities do not include to a substantial extent (see below) activities other than trading activities. HMRC interpret 'activities' as meaning 'what a company does'. Activities would include 'engaging in trading operations, making and holding investments, planning, holding meetings and so forth'.

- 'Trading activities' include activities carried on by the company in the course of, or for the purposes of, a trade that it is carrying on or is preparing to carry on. HMRC regard such activities as including (i) certain activities that a company has to carry out before it can start trading, and (ii) cases where an existing trade is to be acquired from another person, where trading activities may include developing a business plan, acquiring premises, hiring staff, ordering materials and incurring pre-trading expenditure. HMRC also provide guidance at CG 17953i on the question whether the generation of investment income constitutes a trading or investment activity.

- 'Trading activities' also include activities undertaken with a view to the company acquiring or starting to carry on a trade, or with a view to its acquiring a 'significant interest' (see below) in the share capital of another company that is a trading company or the holding company (see below) of a trading group (so long as, where the acquiring company is a member of a group of companies, it is not a member of the target company's group). These activities qualify as trading activities only if the acquisition is made, or (as the case may be) the company starts to carry on the trade, as soon as is reasonably practicable. HMRC accept that a company that has disposed of its trade and invested the proceeds and is 'actively seeking' to acquire a new trade or trading subsidiary might still be a trading company if it does not have substantial non-trading activities. What is 'reasonably practicable in the circumstances' will depend on the particular facts of the case. See below regarding the letting of surplus business property.

- An acquisition by a company (A) of a 'significant interest' in the share capital of another company (B) is an acquisition of ordinary share capital in company B that would make company B a 51% subsidiary of company A, or would give company A a 'qualifying shareholding in a joint venture company' (see below) without making the two companies members of the same group of companies. Ordinary share capital takes the meaning given by *ICTA 1988, s 832(1)*. A 51% subsidiary takes its meaning from *ICTA 1988, s 838*, so that for taper relief purposes a company (B) is a 51% subsidiary of another company (A) if company A owns directly or indirectly more than 50% of company B's ordinary share capital.

Where a company carries on activities other than trading activities, HMRC regard 'substantial extent' (see above) as meaning more than 20% and they indicate that the measures that might be taken into account in ascertaining a company's status include:

- income from non-trading activities;
- the company's asset base;
- expenses incurred, or time spent, by officers and employees of the company in undertaking its activities; and
- the company's history.

HMRC would weigh up 'the impact of each of the measures in the context of an individual case'. HMRC guidance also indicates that the following activities will not necessarily indicate non-trading activity where a company lets property surplus to its current requirements:

- letting part of the trading premises;
- letting properties that are no longer required for the purpose of the trade, where the company's objective is to sell them;
- subletting property where it would be impractical or uneconomic in terms of the trade to assign or surrender the lease;
- the acquisition of property (whether vacant or already let) where it can be shown that the intention is that it will be brought into use for trading activities (*TCGA 1992, Sch A1, para 22A* inserted by *FA 2002*; CG 17953, CG 17953p).

HMRC provided detailed guidance in issue 62 of their Tax Bulletin and said: 'The phrase substantial extent is used in various parts of the TCGA 1992 to provide some flexibility in interpreting a provision without opening the door to widespread abuse. We consider that substantial in this context means more than 20%'.

Periods prior to 17 April 2002

11.11   A trading company is a company which is either:

- a company existing wholly for the purpose of carrying on one or more trades; or
- a company that would fall within the above definition apart from any purposes capable of having no substantial effect on the extent of the company's activities.

HMRC regard 'wholly' above as meaning solely. In this context, there must be no purpose other than for the company to trade, but the generation of investment income does not automatically mean that a company's purpose is not wholly trading.

In assessing the purpose of a company's existence, HMRC take account of 'those purposes which are reflected in the activities, or intended activities, of the company' rather than the wider powers of the company. HMRC consider that the question whether any purposes are 'capable of having no substantial effect' on the extent of the company's activities requires an objective assessment as to whether it can be shown that those purposes were not so capable. HMRC's interpretation of 'substantial' here is discussed at CG 17953p and summarised at **11.10** (*TCGA 1992, Sch A1, para 22* (before amendment by *FA 2002*); CG 17953d–g, CG 17953p).

Trade

11.12 'Trade' means any trade, profession or vocation within the meaning of the Income Tax Acts which is conducted on a commercial basis with a view to the realisation of profits. An asset used for a business of letting furnished holiday accommodation that meets the conditions set out in *ICTA 1988, ss 503 and 504* is regarded as an asset used for a trade (*TCGA 1992, Sch A1, para 22*).

Holding company

Periods from 17 April 2002

11.13 A holding company is a company that has one or more 51% subsidiaries (*TCGA 1992, Sch A1, para 22(1)* as substituted by *FA 2002*).

Periods prior to 17 April 2002

11.14 A holding company is a company whose business (disregarding any trade that it carries on) consists wholly or mainly of the holding of shares in one or more companies which are its 51% subsidiaries. Such companies might be investment companies for corporation tax purposes but that does not prevent them from being holding companies for taper relief purposes. HMRC regard 'wholly or mainly' as meaning more than half of 'whatever measure is reasonable in the circumstances of the case' (*TCGA 1992, Sch A1, para 22(1)* (before amendment by *FA 2002*); CG 17953, CG 17953h).

Trading group

Periods from 17 April 2002

11.15 The following definitions apply to disposals on or after 17 April 2002 and periods of ownership from that date:

- 'Trading group' means a group of companies in which one or more members of the group carry on trading activities (see below), where the activities of the members, taken together, do not include to a substantial extent (see below) activities other than trading activities. A group of companies is a company that has one or more 51% subsidiaries, together with those subsidiaries.

- 'Trading activities' include activities carried on by a group company in the course of, or for the purposes of, a trade that a group company is carrying on or is preparing to carry on.

- 'Trading activities' also include activities carried on by a group company with a view to any group company acquiring or starting to carry on a trade, or with a view to any group company acquiring a 'significant interest' (see below) in the share capital of another company that is (i) a trading company or the holding company of a trading group and (ii) not a member of the same group as the acquiring company. These activities qualify as trading activities only if the acquisition is made, or (as the case may be) the group company concerned starts to carry on the trade, as soon as is reasonably practicable.

- An acquisition by a company (A) of a 'significant interest' in the share capital of another company (B) is an acquisition of ordinary share capital in company B that would make company B a member of the same group of companies as company A, or would give company A a 'qualifying shareholding in a joint venture company' (see below) without making the joint venture companies members of the same group of companies as company A.

- The activities of the members of a group are treated as one business for these purposes, so that intra-group activities are disregarded.

HMRC's interpretation of 'substantial' is discussed at CG 17953p and summarised at **11.10** (*TCGA 1992, Sch A1, para 22B*; CG 17953).

Periods prior to 17 April 2002

11.16   A trading group is a group of companies the activities of which (if all the activities of the companies in the group are taken together) do not, or do not to any substantial extent, include activities carried on otherwise than in the course of, or for the purposes of, a trade. HMRC would disregard all intra-group activities, so that, for example, a letting of property from one group company to another would be disregarded. However, this 'netting off' approach would not be extended to transactions with qualifying joint venture companies other than 51% subsidiaries. HMRC's interpretation of 'substantial' is discussed at CG 17953p and summarised at **11.10** (*TCGA 1992, Sch A1, para 22* (before amendment by *FA 2002*); CG 17953).

11.17 *Taper relief*

Material interest

11.17 The following rules determine whether an individual had a material interest in a company in order to establish whether a non-trading company or the holding company of a non-trading group is a qualifying company (see **11.9**). An individual is taken to have a material interest in a company if he, together with one or more persons connected with him (as determined in accordance with *TCGA 1992, s 286*), has a material interest. He is also taken to have a material interest if any person connected with him, with or without any other such persons, has a material interest.

A material interest in a company for these purposes is defined as possession of, or the ability to control directly or indirectly:

• more than 10% of the issued shares of any particular class;

• more than 10% of the voting rights;

• rights that would give entitlement to receive more than 10% of the amount distributed if the whole of the company's income were distributed among the participators (without regard to any rights of loan creditors); or

• rights that would give entitlement to receive more than 10% of the assets available for distribution among the participators in the event of a winding up of the company or in any other circumstances.

'Loan creditor' and 'participator', where mentioned above, have the same meaning as in *ICTA 1988, s 417*. A right to acquire shares or rights is treated as a right to control them, and a person is treated as having a right to acquire any shares or rights which (a) he is entitled to acquire at a future date, or (b) he will at a future date be entitled to acquire. Where the rights are to shares that have not been issued yet, then for the purpose of the material interest test those unissued shares are added to both the person's holdings and the total number of issued shares of the company. There are similar rules for voting rights, rights to income and rights to distributions in the event of a winding up. Shares or rights conferred by a conditional contract are treated as acquired when that conditional contract is made (*TCGA 1992, Sch A1, paras 6(4), 6A*).

Qualifying shareholdings in joint venture companies

11.18 The following rules apply to determine whether an asset is a business asset at any time after 5 April 2000:

• A company is a 'joint venture company' if, and only if, it is a trading company or the holding company of a trading group, and 75% or more of its ordinary share capital (in aggregate) is held by no more than five persons (the shareholdings of members of a group of companies being treated as held by a single company for this purpose).

- A company has a 'qualifying shareholding' in a joint venture company if (i) it holds at least 10% of the joint venture company's ordinary share capital, or (ii) it is a member of a group of companies, it holds ordinary share capital of the joint venture company and the members of the group between them hold at least 10% of that share capital.

- Where an investing company does have a qualifying shareholding in a joint venture company under these rules, then for the purpose of determining whether the investing company is a trading company any shares that it holds in the joint venture company are disregarded. The investing company is treated as carrying on an 'appropriate proportion' (see below) of the activities of the joint venture company or, where the joint venture company is the holding company of a trading group (see below), an appropriate proportion of the activities of the group.

- The question whether a group of companies is a trading group is determined in the following manner except in cases where the joint venture company is a member of the group. Every holding of shares in the joint venture company that is held by a member of the group having a qualifying shareholding in that company is disregarded. Each member of the group having such a qualifying shareholding is treated as carrying on an 'appropriate proportion' (see below) of the activities of the joint venture company, or where the joint venture company is the holding company of a trading group, of that group.

- The 'appropriate proportion' corresponds to the percentage of the ordinary share capital of the joint venture company held by the investing company or, as the case may be, by the group company concerned.

- For the purposes of the above rules the activities of a joint venture company that is a holding company and its 51% subsidiaries are treated as a single business, so that intra-group activities are disregarded (*TCGA 1992, Sch A1, para 23* (inserted by *FA 2003, s 67*)).

Periods of ownership before 6 April 2000

11.19 The following definition applies to determine whether a company was a qualifying company at any time before 6 April 2000.

Qualifying company

11.20 A company is taken to have been a qualifying company by reference to an individual at any time when either (a) or (b) below applied:

(a)   the company was a trading company or the holding company of a trading group and the voting rights in that company were exercisable, as to not less than 25%, by that individual; or

(b)   the company was a trading company or the holding company of a trading group, the voting rights in that company were exercisable, as to not less than 5%, by that individual, and that individual was a full-time working officer or employee of that company or of a company which at the time had a relevant connection with that company (*TCGA 1992, Sch A1, para 6* before amendments by *FA 2000*).

Assets other than shares, etc

11.21   The rules governing the status of assets other than shares and securities are set out below. The rules that apply to periods of ownership up to 5 April 2004 remain relevant to disposals after that date. The receipt of rent, where, for example, the owner lets property to a partnership or qualifying company which uses it for the purpose of a trade, profession or vocation, does not necessarily prevent an asset from being a business asset (CG 17940a).

Periods of ownership after 5 April 2004

11.22   Where the disposal is made by an individual, an asset, other than a holding of (or an interest in) shares, was a business asset at a time before its disposal if it was being used, wholly or partly, for the purposes of a trade (see below) carried on by:

(a)   an individual, or a partnership of which an individual was at that time a member;

(b)   the trustees of a settlement or a partnership whose members at that time included either (i) the trustees of a settlement, or (ii) any one or more of the persons who at that time were the trustees of a settlement (so far as acting in their capacity as trustees);

(c)   the personal representatives of a deceased person or a partnership whose members at that time included (i) the personal representatives of a deceased person, or (ii) any one or more of the persons who at that time were the personal representatives of a deceased person (so far as acting in their capacity as personal representatives);

(d)   a company which at that time was a qualifying company by reference to that individual;

(e)   a company which at that time was a member of a trading group, where the group's holding company was at that time a qualifying company by reference to that individual; or

(f)   a partnership whose members at that time included a company within (d) or (e) above.

In addition, the asset was a business asset if it was being used, wholly or partly, for the purposes of any office or employment held by the individual with a person carrying on a trade.

'Trade' means any trade, profession or vocation within the meaning of the Income Tax Acts which is conducted on a commercial basis with a view to the realisation of profits. An asset used for a business of letting furnished holiday accommodation that meets the conditions set out in *ICTA 1988, s 504* (for companies) or *ITTOIA 2005, ss 323–326* (for individuals) is regarded as an asset used for a trade (*TCGA 1992, Sch A1, para 5* (as amended by *FA 2003*); *TCGA 1992, s 241(3)*).

Periods of ownership between 6 April 2000 and 5 April 2004

11.23   Where the disposal is made by an individual, an asset, other than a holding of (or an interest in) shares, was a business asset at a time before its disposal if it was being used, wholly or partly, for:

(a)   the purposes of a trade carried on at that time by that individual or by a partnership of which he was a member at that time;

(b)   the purposes of any trade carried on by a company which at that time was a qualifying company by reference to him;

(c)   the purposes of any trade carried on by a company which at that time was a member of a trading group, where the group's holding company was at that time a qualifying company by reference to him; or

(d)   the purposes of any office or employment that he held with a person carrying on a trade (*TCGA 1992, Sch A1, para 5(2)* (before amendment by *FA 2003*)).

Periods of ownership between 6 April 1998 and 5 April 2000

11.24   Where the disposal is made by an individual, an asset, other than a holding of (or an interest in) shares, was a business asset at a time before its disposal if at that time it was being used, wholly or partly, for:

(a)   the purposes of a trade carried on at that time by either that individual or a partnership of which he was a member at that time;

(b)   the purposes of any trade carried on by a company which at that time was a qualifying company by reference to him;

(c)   the purposes of any trade carried on by a company which at that time was a member of a trading group, where the group's holding company was at that time a qualifying company by reference to him;

(d)   the purposes of any qualifying office or employment (ie an office or employment with a person who was at that time carrying on a trade) to which that individual was at that time required to devote substantially the whole of his time; or

(e)   the purposes of any office or employment, not falling within (d), where the taxpayer fell to be treated as a full-time working officer or employee of a trading company. A full-time working officer or employee for this purpose is an officer or employee of that company, or of that company and one or more other companies with which it has a 'relevant connection', who is required in that capacity to devote substantially the whole of his time to the service of that company, or to the service of those companies taken together. In practice, HMRC regard this test as satisfied if the taxpayer is required to devote at least three-quarters of normal working hours to the service of the company. A company has a 'relevant connection' with another company at any time when they are both members of the same group of companies, or of the same 'commercial association of companies'. A commercial association of companies is defined as a company together with such of its associated companies (defined in *ICTA 1988, s 416*) as carry on businesses which are of such a nature that the businesses of the company and the associated companies, taken together, may be reasonably considered to make up a single composite undertaking (*TCGA 1992, Sch A1, paras 5(2)* (before amendment by *FA 2000*), *22*; CG 17937, CG 17953).

THE RATE OF TAPER RELIEF

11.25   The rate of taper relief depends on whether the asset disposed of has been a business asset or a non-business asset. A chargeable gain accruing on the disposal of an asset is a gain on the disposal of a business asset if the asset was a business asset throughout its 'relevant period' of ownership. Two key definitions are provided for the purpose of fixing the rate of taper relief:

- The 'relevant period of ownership' is whichever is the shorter of the period after 5 April 1998 for which the asset had been held at the time of disposal, and the period of 10 years ending with the time of disposal.

- The period for which an asset has been held at the time of its disposal begins with the later of (i) 6 April 1998, and (ii) the time when the asset was acquired, and ends with the time of the disposal.

Thus the relevant period of ownership cannot exceed 10 years. Where an asset has been held for more than 10 years, the relevant period of ownership is the last 10 years of ownership.

The relevant period is not increased by the 'bonus year' that may be added to the qualifying holding period (see **11.4**). Any period that is not counted for the purposes of taper relief because of an anti-avoidance rule (see below) is excluded from the qualifying holding period; does not count towards the period of 10 years ending with the disposal; and is not included in the relevant period of ownership.

Example 11.5

Maxine acquired an asset on 1 January 1999 and disposed of it on 1 January 2012. The relevant period of ownership is the shorter of (i) 13 years, being the whole period of ownership, and (ii) the period of 10 years ending with the time of the disposal. The relevant period of ownership is, therefore, the period of 10 years from 1 January 2002 to 1 January 2012.

Example 11.6

Robert acquired an asset on 1 June 1994 and used it for non-business purposes until he sold it on 6 April 2007. The relevant period of ownership is the shorter of (i) 9 years, being the whole period of ownership after 5 April 1998, and (ii) the period of 10 years ending with the time of the disposal. The relevant period of ownership is, therefore, 9 years. The qualifying holding period will be 10 years, including the 'bonus year'.

If the person making the disposal did not acquire the asset but created it, the date of acquisition for taper relief is the date on which the asset was created. HMRC consider that this date is to be determined as a question of fact on the basis of the available evidence (*TCGA 1992, Sch A1, paras 1–3*; CG 17900).

Business asset status for only part of the relevant period

11.26　Where the asset met the conditions for business asset status (see **11.6**) for only part of that period, then (assuming for simplicity's sake that there is only one period of business use and one period of non-business use):

- The gain is divided into two parts. One part is taken to be a gain on the disposal of a business asset and the remainder is taken to be a gain on the disposal of a non-business asset.

- This is achieved by dividing the relevant period of ownership into two parts and apportioning the overall gain accordingly (see below regarding the basis of apportionment).

- In this way, one deemed gain is treated as accruing on the disposal of a business asset and the other deemed gain is treated as accruing on the disposal of a non-business asset.

- Each of these two deemed separate assets is treated as owned for the whole of the relevant period of ownership.

The apportionment here is to be made on a just and reasonable basis, and on the assumption that any amount to be apportioned by reference to a period of time arose or accrued at the same rate throughout the period during which it is treated as having arisen or accrued (*TCGA 1992, Sch A1, paras 3, 21*).

Example 11.7

Nichola acquired shares on 1 March 1997. They did not meet the conditions for business asset status until 6 April 2000, when the rules were relaxed. She disposed of the shares on 6 April 2007, realising a gain of £90,000. Nichola held the shares for nine whole years after 5 April 1998; this is the relevant period of ownership. During that period her holding was a non-business asset for two years and a business asset for the remaining seven years.

Non-business asset

Gain £90,000 x 2/9ths = £20,000

Qualifying holding period is ten years (nine years plus a 'bonus year')

Percentage of gain chargeable is 60%, ie £12,000

Business asset

Gain £90,000 x 7/9ths = £70,000

Qualifying holding period is nine years

Percentage of gain chargeable is 25%, ie £17,500

Total amount chargeable is £12,000 + £17,500 = £29,500

Mixed use

11.27   The relevant period of ownership of an asset may include one or more periods of 'mixed use'. This is a period throughout which the asset was a business asset, because it met the conditions set out above (see **11.6**), but at the same time it was being put to non-qualifying use, ie use that would not secure business asset status. In such a case it is necessary to find the 'relevant fraction' representing the proportion of use, during the mixed-use period, that is non-qualifying. The relevant fraction of the mixed-use period is treated as a period throughout which the asset was not a business asset. The asset is taken to have been a business asset for the remainder of the period. The relevant fraction is to be recalculated where the proportion of non-qualifying use varies (*TCGA 1992, Sch A1, para 9*).

Example 11.8

Edward sold a property on 5 April 2007. Throughout the four-year period of ownership he used three-quarters of the property for the purpose of his retail trade and he let the remaining quarter to private tenants. The letting did not qualify for business asset taper relief (see **11.22**). The 'relevant fraction' is one quarter. A gain of £80,000 arose on the disposal. Edward needs to split this gain into two parts, one deemed to accrue on the disposal of a non-business asset and the other deemed to accrue on disposal of a business asset.

Non-business asset

Gain £80,000 x relevant fraction 1/4 = £20,000

Qualifying holding period is four years

Percentage of gain chargeable is 90%, ie £18,000

Business asset

Gain £80,000 x 3/4 = £60,000

Qualifying holding period is four years

Percentage of gain chargeable is 25%, ie £24,000

Total amount chargeable is £18,000 + £24,000 = £42,000

Transfers between spouses or civil partners

11.28   Where an asset is transferred between spouses living together and the transfer is treated under *TCGA 1992, s 58(1)* as giving rise to no gain and no loss, then on a subsequent disposal the transferee spouse is treated, for taper relief purposes, as having acquired the asset when the transferor spouse acquired it. As already indicated, this means that the qualifying holding period will be the entire period of ownership of both spouses falling after 5 April 1998. A similar rule applies with effect from 5 December 2005 to transfers between civil partners living together.

There are separate rules for shares, etc and other assets to determine whether the asset was a business asset before and after the transfer:

- An asset other than shares or securities in a company is treated as a business asset at any time before the transfer if the business asset conditions were satisfied by either spouse or civil partner at that time. For the period after the transfer, business asset status depends entirely on whether the conditions are met in relation to the transferee.

- Where the asset comprises shares or securities, the question whether the asset is a business asset depends on whether the company was a 'qualifying company' of the transferee spouse or civil partner only, throughout the combined period of ownership after 5 April 1998. If it was not a qualifying company throughout the combined period, then an apportionment is required (*TCGA 1992, Sch A1, para 15*).

ANTI-AVOIDANCE RULES

Limited exposure to fluctuations in value

11.29   The purpose of this rule is to counter attempts by a taxpayer to take advantage of taper relief while retaining an asset where the risk attached to the asset has been reduced as a result of a transaction. A period does not count for taper relief if the holder of the asset, or his predecessor, had a 'limited exposure', during that period, to fluctuations in the asset's value.

The holder of the asset is taken to have had such limited exposure at any time when a transaction entered into at any time by him had the effect that he:

- was not exposed (or not exposed to any substantial extent) to the risk of loss from such fluctuations; and

- was not able to enjoy (or to enjoy to any substantial extent) any opportunities to benefit from such fluctuations.

HMRC regard 'substantial' as meaning greater than 20%, so that a person who has divested himself of at least 80% of the exposure will have 'limited exposure'. A similar rule applies where a transaction entered into by a 'relevant predecessor' has had the same effect. A 'relevant predecessor' is any other person who held the asset at any time during the period treated for taper relief purposes as the whole period during which the asset had been held at the time of the disposal. This period would include a spouse or civil partner's period of ownership where the asset was acquired under the 'no gain/no loss' rule (see **3.67**). In such a case the relevant predecessor would be the spouse or civil partner of the person making the disposal. For this purpose a period of ownership prior to 5 April 1998 is not ignored, even though taper relief is available only with effect from that date.

There are exemptions for transactions that provide:

• insurance against loss of (or damage to) the asset, where the holder of the asset might reasonably have been expected to enter into such insurance; and

• protection from fluctuations in the value of the asset resulting from fluctuations in the value of foreign currency.

HMRC consider that this anti-avoidance rule does not apply to loan notes (other than qualifying corporate bonds) where the loan notes are issued in exchange for shares as part of the normal commercial arrangements in a take-over. However, they may seek to apply the rule in 'more complex or non-commercial circumstances, where the loan notes are issued to exploit the operation of taper' (*TCGA 1992, Sch A1, para 10*; CG 17916, CG 17917, CG 17928).

Company is not active

11.30   This rule is designed to counter an advantage that might be gained by a taxpayer holding shares in a company when the company was inactive. In the absence of this rule, when the company became active the qualifying holding period for taper relief would include the 'inactive' period. There is no 'motive test'. With effect for disposals on or after 17 April 2002, any period after 5 April 1998 during which the asset consisted of shares in a close company that was not active does not count for the purposes of taper relief.

Such a period does not count towards the qualifying holding period or the relevant period of ownership, and this rule should be considered before ascertaining whether an asset is a business asset. However, the rule does not affect the availability of the 'bonus year' to be added in calculating the qualifying holding period for a non-business asset held at 17 March 1998. The rules at *ICTA 1988, ss 414* and *415* apply to determine whether a company is close. A period when a company is inactive but is not close will count for taper relief purposes.

This rule replaced provisions that applied where there was a 'relevant change of activity' involving a close company. *TCGA 1992, Sch A1, para 11* was repealed with effect for disposals on or after 17 April 2002, even if a relevant change of activity occurred before that date (*TCGA 1992, Sch A1, para 11A*).

Example 11.9

Francis disposed of shares in a close company on 1 November 2006. He acquired the shares on 1 May 2001 but the company was close and inactive throughout the period of 12 months from 1 May 2001 to 30 April 2002. The company became active on 1 May 2002 and remained active until 1 November 2006. His qualifying holding period is the period from 1 May 2002 to 30 November 2006, ie four whole years.

Business activities

11.31   A company is regarded as active at any time when it is carrying on (or preparing to carry on) a business of any description – including holding and managing assets, and any business that is not conducted on a commercial basis or with a view to the realisation of a profit – or the company or another person is winding up the affairs of a business that the company has ceased to carry on.

'Business' has a wider meaning than trade and HMRC accept that it may include property investment and rental. However, HMRC guidance also points to cases where it has been held that a trading company that has ended its main activities but retained an investment portfolio is not carrying on a business of holding investments. Mr Justice Park said in *Jowett v O'Neill and Brennan Construction Ltd* [1988] 70 TC 566, Ch D that ' ... although the normal conclusion when a company lays out its assets and earns an income return is that it is carrying on a business, that is not inevitably so as a matter of law'. In any event, as HMRC point out, business activities have to extend 'beyond just holding money on deposit' because this is one of the activities listed in **11.32** which, by itself, does not render the company active.

In *Revenue and Customs Commissioners v Salaried Persons Postal Loans Ltd* [2006] EWHC 763 (Ch), which concerned small companies' relief for corporation tax purposes, the High Court upheld the Special Commissioner's decision that an associated company receiving rent from property it had previously occupied for the purposes of its trade was not carrying on an investment business (or any other business).

Lawrence Collins J said the Special Commissioner was entitled to come to the decision of fact that the rents did not come from a source which amounted to a business. The letting was the continuation of the letting of former trading premises, a state of affairs that had continued for nearly 30 years while the company was trading, and which merely continued after the cessation of trading.

Whether a company is preparing to carry on a business is a question of fact. HMRC guidance says: 'At one extreme the directors of a company may simply get together once a year to agree that the company will do nothing in the coming year unless a business opportunity arises. That company would not be "active" ... By comparison, the directors of another company may have identified a specific business opportunity and be in negotiation to finance and start up or acquire a business. This would be an active company ...'

Liquidation, etc

11.32   HMRC regard a company as unlikely to be active if it is in liquidation and there are 'no winding-up activities' and no other activities. However, a company will be treated as active where:

- the directors, or some other person, are dealing with the company's post-cessation business affairs (eg paying off creditors, closing bank accounts or selling off assets) and the company remains in being;

- the company is intended to remain in being in order to start another business later and there is a gap between winding up the first business and starting the next. The time spent winding up the affairs of the first business 'counts as active'.

Where a company's business ceases and there is a period in which the company is neither settling the affairs of that business nor preparing to start a new one, that period is regarded as a time when the company is 'inactive'.

A company is not regarded as active if it does nothing more than all, or any, of the following:

(a)   holding money, in any currency, in cash or on deposit;

(b)   holding other assets whose total value is insignificant;

(c)   holding shares in or debentures of a company that is not active;

(d)   making loans to an associated company (as defined in *ICTA 1988, s 416*), or to a participator, or to an associate of a participator (as defined in *ICTA 1988, s 417*);

(e)   carrying out administrative functions to comply with requirements of certain company law provisions or other regulations, eg filing an annual return at Companies House.

Shares in, or debentures of, a company include for this purpose an interest in, or option in respect of, such shares or debentures. HMRC regard 'insignificant' in (b) above as taking its 'normal dictionary meaning of trifling or completely unimportant', and they consider that in most cases it is 'unlikely to cover any assets with a value in excess of £1,000', but whether or not the holding of assets is insignificant is a question of fact.

11.33   *Taper relief*

HMRC guidance provides the following examples:

1   A company may issue 100 £1 ordinary shares (fully paid). If that is all the company has done to date it will not be active. Or, it may simply be a repository for funds which are held in cash or on deposit without indulging in any other activity. Only where there is a structured commercial activity beyond the holding of money on deposit which the company is carrying on, or is preparing to carry on, would it count as active.

2   A company may have invested the £100 it received on the issue of the ordinary shares in an option to buy an asset. The value of the option would normally be insignificant at that time (CG 17915, CG 17921).

Groups, etc

11.33   A company is treated as active regardless of the above rules if:

• it is the holding company of a group of companies that contains at least one active company;

• it has a qualifying shareholding in a joint venture company; or

• it is the holding company of a group of companies any member of which has a qualifying shareholding in a joint venture company.

Value shifting

11.34   This rule is designed to counter the advantage that could be obtained by a taxpayer bringing about a transfer of value from shares held for a short period of time into shares held for a longer period, to take advantage of a longer qualifying holding period and a correspondingly higher rate of taper relief. There is no 'motive test'.

Taper relief may be restricted where the taxpayer, having control of a close company, has exercised his control so that value passed into shares or securities, or rights over the company. The rules at *ICTA 1988, ss 414* and *415* apply to determine whether a company is close. This restriction applies where:

• there is a disposal of an asset consisting of shares or securities in a close company, and

• at least one 'relevant shift of value' involving those shares or securities has occurred between the 'relevant time' and the time of the disposal.

Where the restriction applies, the period prior to the time of the latest shift of value does not count for taper relief. The 'relevant time' is the beginning of the period after 5 April 1998 for which that asset had been held at the time of its disposal. A 'relevant shift of value' involving an asset is taken to have occurred whenever:

- a person having control of a close company exercised his control of that company so that value passed into that asset out of a 'relevant holding'; or

- effect was given to any other transaction that resulted in value passing into that asset out of a relevant holding.

A 'relevant holding' is a holding of shares or securities in the same company (or in a company under the control of the same person or persons as that company) that is held by the taxpayer or a person connected with him.

'Insignificant' shifts of value are ignored. A shift of value is ignored if, when it took place, the qualifying holding period for taper relief purposes of the relevant holding was at least as long as the qualifying holding period of the shares, etc into which the value was shifted. For this purpose, the qualifying holding period is taken to be what it would have been had the holding been disposed of at that time (*TCGA 1992, Sch A1, para 12*).

Gains of non-resident company attributed to an individual

11.35   A gain is not eligible for taper relief if it accrues to a non-UK resident company and is assessable on a UK resident participator in the company under *TCGA 1992, s 13*. The benefit of indexation allowance is available, however, in that the gain is computed as if the non-resident company were a UK resident company within the charge to corporation tax (*TCGA 1992, s 13(10A), (11A)*).

SPECIAL RULES

Options

11.36   The acquisition and subsequent exercise of an option are treated for CGT purposes as one transaction, where *TCGA 1992, s 144* applies. In such a case the date of acquisition for taper relief purposes is the later of 6 April 1998 and the time the option is exercised. There is an exception for options granted under an Enterprise Management Incentive scheme, where the qualifying holding period normally begins on the date the option is granted.

So far as the person who granted the option is concerned, the time of the asset's disposal for taper relief purposes is the time of the following disposal:

- if the option binds the grantor to sell, the disposal made in fulfilment of the grantor's obligations under the option; or

- if the option binds the grantor to buy, the disposal made to the grantor in consequence of the exercise of the option.

The question whether the asset disposed of or acquired was a business asset is determined by reference to the asset to which the option related, and not the option itself (*TCGA 1992, Sch A1, para 13, Sch 7D, para 15*).

Example 11.10

Alison was granted an option over land in September 2001. She exercised the option in May 2002 and sold the land in November 2006. The qualifying holding period for taper relief purposes began in May 2002.

Assets derived from other assets

11.37 If the value of the asset disposed of was derived, as a result of a merger or division of assets, from one or more assets acquired previously by the taxpayer, then the asset disposed of is deemed for taper relief purposes to have been acquired at the time of the earlier acquisition (*TCGA 1992, Sch A1, para 14*).

Example 11.11

John acquired a lease of land on 1 June 2001. He acquired the freehold on 1 December 2002, extinguishing the lease, and sold the freehold on 1 November 2006. The qualifying holding period runs from 1 June 2001, giving five whole years.

Share reorganisations

11.38 Where *TCGA 1992, s 127* applies to a share reorganisation such as a scrip or rights issue, or a take-over, there is no disposal and the original shares and the new holding are treated as the same asset, acquired as the original shares were acquired. The taper relief qualifying holding period for the new holding begins with the later of (i) the date of acquisition of the original holding, and (ii) 6 April 1998.

The question whether a company is close and inactive at any time, for the purpose of the anti-avoidance rule in *TCGA 1992, Sch A1, para 11A* (see **11.30**), is determined by reference to the status of the company in which the shares are held at that time.

Postponed gains

11.39   Where a gain is deemed under certain provisions to accrue at a time later than the disposal or other event giving rise to the gain, taper relief is available only for the period up to the date of that disposal or other event. It is not available for the period following the disposal or other event. The relevant provisions are set out in Table 11.2.

Table 11.2

TCGA 1992:	
s 10A	Temporary non-residents
s 116(10)	Reorganisations, etc
s 134	Compensation stock
s 154(2) or (4)	New assets which are depreciating assets
s 169C(7)	Clawback of hold-over relief
Sch 5B or 5C	Enterprise investment schemes and venture capital trusts
FA 1996:	
Sch 15, para 27	Loan relationships: qualifying indexed securities

With regard to the enterprise investment scheme, the Special Commissioner in *Daniels v Revenue and Customs Commissioners* [2005] SpC 489 held that deferral relief under *TCGA 1992, Sch 5B* should be deducted from the chargeable gains accruing in the year of assessment before applying taper relief, because 'taper relief only applies to chargeable gains that the 1992 Act treats as accruing in the particular year of assessment'. The taxpayer may restrict the amount of his deferral relief claim to take account of taper relief and any unused part of the annual exemption. There are special rules for EIS deferral relief, examined in **Chapter 16** (*TCGA 1992, Sch A1, para 16(1)*).

Non-UK domiciled taxpayer disposing of foreign assets

11.40   The rules deferring assessment of CGT in *TCGA 1992, s 12* (foreign assets of person with foreign domicile) and *s 279* (foreign assets: delayed remittances) are disregarded for taper relief purposes, so that taper relief is calculated by reference to the period to the time of the disposal (*TCGA 1992, Sch A1, para 16(4)*).

Example 11.12

Pierre is a non-UK domiciled taxpayer. He acquired a non-business asset located outside the UK in December 2000 and sold it in November 2004. He did not remit the gain to the UK until March 2007. Although the gain accrued in

237

March 2007, the qualifying holding period for taper relief runs from December 2000 to November 2004, ie three whole years, so that 95% of the gain is chargeable.

INTERACTION WITH OTHER CGT RELIEFS, ETC

Losses

11.41   Allowable losses are not subject to taper relief but they are set off against 'untapered' chargeable gains (see **3.48**). Where the taxpayer has more than one chargeable gain arising in a year of assessment, any allowable losses (whether realised in the current year, or carried forward or back to the current year) are to be set against untapered gains in the order that results in the largest reduction in those gains, ie the order that maximises the available taper relief. See **1.19** regarding the interaction between losses carried forward and the CGT annual exemption.

Example 11.13

Adam has unrelieved capital losses of £20,000 available to carry forward to 2006/07. His gains for that year are as set out in the following table:

	Disposal 1 Business asset	Disposal 2 Non-business asset	Disposal 3 Non-business asset
Gains	£20,000	£30,000	£14,000
Qualifying holding period in years	2	7	4
Percentage of gain chargeable	25%	75%	90%
Loss set-off	Nil	£6,000	£14,000
Net gains before taper relief	£20,000	£24,000	Nil
Chargeable gain	£5,000	£18,000	Nil

The losses are allocated first against the gain accruing on disposal 3, which qualifies for the lowest rate of taper relief. Taper relief is most valuable in relation to disposal 1, so the remaining losses are allocated against disposal 2. Total chargeable gains, after losses and taper relief, are £23,000 (*TCGA 1992, s 2A(6)*).

Indexation allowance

11.42   Indexation allowance, where it is available (see **3.59**), is given before taper relief. This is because indexation allowance is given in calculating the chargeable gain, while taper relief is not given until a person's chargeable gains and allowable losses for a year of assessment have been established (*TCGA 1992, ss 2A, 15, 53*).

Roll-over relief for replacement of business assets

11.43   Roll-over relief under *TCGA 1992, s 152* (see **Chapter 14**) is applied before taper relief. The period of ownership of the old asset is ignored in calculating the qualifying holding period of the new asset for taper relief. This means that where roll-over relief is claimed on disposal of the old asset and that relief is obtained without restriction, any taper relief that would otherwise be due on that disposal is lost.

Transfer of a business to a company

11.44   A similar problem arises on the transfer of a business to a company, where the conditions for roll-over relief under *TCGA 1992, s 162* (see **15.2**) are met. However, the taxpayer may elect under *s 162A* for the relief not to apply where the transfer takes place after 5 April 2002. See Example 15.1 in **Chapter 15** (*TCGA 1992, s 162A*).

Chapter 12

Main Residence Relief

WHAT CONSTITUTES RESIDENCE?

Quality of occupation

12.1   Relief is allowed under *TCGA 1992, s 222* in respect of a gain that accrues to an individual (or, see at **12.24** to trustees and personal representatives) on the disposal of an interest in 'a dwelling house or part of a dwelling house which is, or has at any time in his period of ownership been, his only or main residence'. The legislation does not define 'residence' though there is guidance in the decided cases and, from the standpoint of HMRC, in CG 64236 and CG 64427–64456. Lord Widgery described it well in *Fox v Stirk, Ricketts v Registration Officer for the City of Cambridge* [1970] 3 All ER 7 as 'the place where he sleeps and shelters and has his house'.

There are many cases: see, for example, *Goodwin v Curtis* (*Inspector of Taxes*) [1996] STI 1290, which concerned the redevelopment of a farmhouse and its outbuildings. One of the two partners engaged in the development purchased the farmhouse for his own use. He took up occupation and had the services and telephone connected. After only a matter of days the property was offered for sale. A few weeks later contracts were exchanged at a very substantial profit. The taxpayer then moved to another property which was much smaller. The Inland Revenue considered that his residence at the farmhouse lacked the necessary permanence for him to claim relief under *s 222* on the gain that he had realised. The taxpayer appealed.

At the hearing it was revealed that, at the time of his purchase, the taxpayer was separated from his wife and family and had no need of a house as large as the farmhouse. That was supported by the evidence of the size of property to which he later moved. It also appeared that the property had been placed on the market before the taxpayer even took up 'residence'. There was little evidence that he intended to make the property his permanent home. He was denied relief on the gain. However, that case is not decisive: there is actually no minimum period – what matters is the quality of the occupation: see *Moore v Thompson* (61TCIS).

12.2   In *Jones v Wilcox* (*Inspector of Taxes*) [1996] STI 1349 the argument was all the other way. The taxpayer had made a gain unconnected with property

240

and was hoping to set against that gain a loss which he had sustained on the sale of the house because the market had gone against him. The taxpayer therefore argued that main residence relief should not apply, because of the anti-avoidance provisions in *s 224(3)* which provide that relief is not available to shelter a gain where the acquisition of the dwelling house 'was made wholly or partly for the purpose of realising a gain from the disposal of it'.

Again, the taxpayer's case fell down on the evidence. He and his family had lived in the property for a number of years. Children had been born and brought up there. The taxpayer and his wife had considered a number of properties. The only reasonable inference was that this particular house had been chosen, not to make a profit, but because they wanted to live there. Whilst making a gain from the eventual disposal of the house might have been a hope or even an expectation, everyone has to live somewhere and the main purpose of the purchase had been as a residence. There was no evidence that profit was the main motive for the purchase. As a result, in the same way that a gain would not have been chargeable, the loss was not relievable.

Lynch v Edmondson (*Inspector of Taxes*) [1998] STI 968 also illustrates some of the principles. A bricklayer purchased two plots of land. He developed them into two flats. One of them was immediately let at a premium for a term of 99 years. The Inland Revenue considered that, taken together, the transactions amounted to dealing in land. Evidence before the Special Commissioner of the way in which the property had been financed, and transactions between the bricklayer and the woman with whom he was living, all tended to support that interpretation.

Helpfully the Special Commissioner summarised the various tests that led to the final decision. Thus:

- this was a single transaction that could nevertheless amount to trading;

- it was a transaction in land, which was certainly a commodity in which it was possible to trade;

- the way that the taxpayer went about developing the land pointed towards trading, in that he realised substantial money from one of the units by letting it as soon as it was built;

- the way that the project was financed was consistent with trading, in that much of the cost of the development was repaid from the premium that was taken on the grant of the lease of the first unit to be finished;

- the fact that the bricklayer himself carried out the work was consistent with trading;

- the fact that the original purchase of the land was divided up into units for sale was consistent with trading; and

241

- it was relevant to consider the motive of the taxpayer. He had told the bank that had leant him the money that he would sell one of the flats. That was consistent with trading.

On the other hand there were factors that tended to point the other way, such as the fact that one of the units was not immediately disposed of on a long lease but was instead let in a manner that was more consistent with investment than with trade. Also, the way that the asset was used in the overall circumstances was ambiguous. Nevertheless, on balance, the taxpayer was held to be trading.

12.3   Some general principles emerge from these cases. The average person who buys a property, takes up occupation and later sells it will fall within the decision in *Jones v Wilcox*. The obsession of the British with owning property and the plethora of television programmes on the purchase, improvement, decoration and resale of houses does not make the average purchaser a property speculator. Discussion of house prices is second in popularity only to discussion of the weather. Subject to the many qualifications that are discussed in this chapter in relation to the extent of property and periods of absence, most transactions affecting property that has been occupied by the taxpayer will escape taxation. No entry is required on a tax return in such cases: see CG 64206.

It is, however, different where a clear pattern of dealing can be discerned and a person buys properties, renovates them and resells them on a regular basis. As a rule of thumb, to renovate one run down property or perhaps two is no more than 'nest building' for a young couple; but by the time the taxpayer(s) embark on a third renovation project it becomes easier to infer that they are engaged in a trade. The speed with which a taxpayer moves from one property to another is relevant, as was clear from the decision in *Goodwin v Curtis*. The statute stipulates nothing. Residence in a property for a full year is probably long enough to establish relief.

Usually a careful examination of the facts will show the truth of the position and never more so than where a taxpayer has more than one residence available to him, a situation that is discussed at **12.18**. If, perhaps because no notice has been filed under *s 222(5)(a)*, the taxpayer is forced to show where he is resident, it will be relevant where the taxpayer claims to live for the purposes of:

- voting;

- letters to friends;

- bank and building society accounts and investments;

- registration to vote; and

- tax returns.

Evidence will be examined including, see CG 64552, the way that a property is furnished and where the family spend their time.

Homeworkers: the use of a residence partly for business purposes

12.4   Relief under *s 222* is available in respect of the entirety of a dwelling house or of part only. As will be seen at **12.6**, the main apportionment of a residence required, where it does not all qualify for relief, is between the part that is within the 'permitted area' and the part that is not; but a separate apportionment is recognised by *s 224(1)* where, as will now increasingly be the case, a person works from home.

The distinction to be drawn is a fine one. If the taxpayer, wishing to pay as little income tax as possible, claims that a proportion of the expenses of the building in which the business is carried on should be deductible from profits, there is an inference that that part of the building is not also the residence of the taxpayer. The result is a matter of fact and degree. HMRC may be aware that a house is used as a business: see CG 64209.

Example 12.1—Soft furnishings business

Alice lives in a former council house in Thetford. Immediately adjoining the property is a small row of lock-up garages which have for a number of years been used by various tenants, mainly for drug dealing. Alice buys the garages for two reasons: she wants more peace at night and in any case she runs a small business from home, making curtains. She needs extra space for her stock. Following the purchase of the garages, she uses one for her domestic car, one for her delivery van, one for the stock of finished goods and she lets the remainder. For convenience she continues to run the business itself from the house. Customers like to sit in her kitchen over a mug of tea to discuss their requirements and she has set up the living room so that she can make curtains, watch television and keep an eye on her young children all at the same time.

On disposal of the house and the garages at a gain, Alice must apportion the gain between the different parts of the property. The garages that were let are a simple investment and taxable as such. The garages used respectively for the storage of stock and to house the delivery van have really been used exclusively for the business and not for any domestic purpose and are therefore outside the scope of *s 222*. The remainder of the property, however, does qualify for relief, see CG 64663, even though Alice may have claimed costs of services, etc against her business. There is only one kitchen. It is not used exclusively for the business. There is only one living room and the family spend their spare time in there. The garage for the family car is not used for business. Any reasonable apportionment should be accepted by HMRC: see CG 64672.

The extent of the 'curtilage' of the dwelling house

12.5 There is usually little difficulty, on the disposal of urban properties, in claiming that the whole of the gain realised on a residence should qualify for relief. The 'curtilage' is, in layman's terms, the property that obviously 'goes with' the house, the part that, if the layman had to describe the extent of the property, he would not treat such parts as extra or needing specific mention. The curtilage is the house, not the grounds.

We have a slight difficulty here: HMRC at CG 64248 and CG 64255 describes the test as being what would be included in a legal description of the property for conveyancing purposes. That was fine when most land was unregistered: each conveyance had to set out a description of the extent of the land conveyed, perhaps by reference to an earlier conveyance and plan. Now, however, most land is registered. Lawyers transfer it simply by reference to a Title Number at the Land Registry. As a result, it would be difficult now to apply the test in the Manual. However, the Manual applies some reasonable tests: thus an off-lying garage may be included: see CG 64292.

The 'permitted area'

12.6 The rules in *s 222(1)(b)* and following often create difficulties in relation to suburban and country properties. Relief is allowed in respect of 'land which [the taxpayer] has for his own occupation and enjoyment with that residence as its garden or grounds up to the permitted area'. That area is defined as being an area, which includes the house, of up to 0.5 of a hectare (about 1.25 acres; see CG 64816 for an explanation for this limit) being, in case of dispute, the part of the grounds that is 'the most suitable for occupation and enjoyment with the residence'.

Section 222(3) recognises that the size and character of a dwelling house may make some larger area than 0.5 of a hectare appropriate as 'required for the reasonable enjoyment of the dwelling house' or of the part of the dwelling house with which the transaction is concerned. There are many cases on the subject. It is possible that, over time, our perception of how much of this planet we should each occupy may have changed. Some of the earlier cases on 'permitted area' are redolent of a more leisured and spacious age. The phrase 'garden or grounds' in *s 222(1)(b)* carries its normal meaning: it is a question of fact.

Lewis v Lady Rook [1992] STC 171 is a fairly recent case and a good starting point, being of high authority. A woman had purchased an eight-bedroomed house. The land extended to over 10 acres. There were two cottages, one of which she sold many years later. It had been occupied by a gardener and it stood 190 yards from the main house. When assessed on the gain she appealed, claiming main residence relief.

The Court of Appeal held that the true test was whether the cottage was within the 'curtilage' of, and appurtenant to, the main property. For relief to be allowed the cottage must be part of the entity which, together with the main house, constituted the dwelling house for the purposes of *s 222* as being occupied by the taxpayer as her main residence. The cottage was too far away from the main building. It was separated by a large garden. It was not part of the main residence.

Another recent example of the principle is *Longson v Baker* [2000] SpC 08.05 2000. The Longsons were keen on riding. He purchased a property amounting to just over 7.5 hectares which included a farmhouse, some stables and an outhouse. A building was added for use as a riding school. As part of settlement between husband and wife the interest in the property was transferred to her. It became necessary to decide the extent of the 'permitted area'. He argued that 'required' in *s 222(3)* meant 'called for', whereas the inspector argued that it meant no more than 'necessary'. Thus, whilst it was certainly convenient for a family interested in riding to enjoy the whole of the land that was available that was not actually necessary for the enjoyment of the property. The Special Commissioner agreed with the Revenue, allowing relief only in respect of a much smaller area, observing that to hold otherwise might tend to encourage widespread interest in riding to shelter gains on properties with substantial amenities.

Land which is separated from a house may not be its garden or grounds, though the Manual, at CG 64370, fairly recognises that cottage gardens may lie across the village street.

Surplus land

12.7   In practice there is a difficult argument for the taxpayer to resist where the disposal is of only part of the property. It is addressed in CG 64832 and following.

Example 12.2—Stable block conversion

Belinda for many years occupied the Old Coach House, built in 1850 as part of a much more extensive property and still enjoying 1 hectare of garden with access, down an unmade track 20 feet wide at the rear, to a side road. Belinda owns the track and uses it occasionally because there are, at the end of the garden, old stables, formerly used by Belinda's children as a play area and later for car repairs. The character of the neighbourhood has changed in the last 150 years. Belinda secures planning permission to convert the stable block into a mews residence, which she sells with 0.25 of a hectare of land.

It is difficult for Belinda to resist the HMRC argument that, if she is now selling the stable block and a parcel of land, that land is not 'required for the reasonable enjoyment of the (retained) dwelling house'. Clearly, if Belinda goes on living at the Old Coach House, the land is not now so required. An argument may perhaps be advanced that times have changed. Originally the Coach House itself was part of a much larger property. For most of the time that Belinda has owned it properties in that area have enjoyed large gardens and she has actually with her family occupied the whole property as a single unit. It is only recently, with changes in the locality, that it has been possible for her to obtain planning permission and therefore, for most of her period of ownership of the stables, the requirements of *s 222* have been met.

Note that if the land is within the permitted area, relief automatically extends to all of it, whether sold as one or with a plot sold off separately. In such a case the issue of 'surplus' land, or the plot sold later (see below) does not apply: CG 64815.

Care should be taken where land exceeding the permitted area is owned before a residence is built on it. In *Henke and another v HMRC* (2006) SpC 550, the taxpayers bought 2.66 acres of land in 1982. In 1993, they built their main residence on part of the land. They later sold some of the land, on which houses were built. The taxpayers appealed against HMRC's refusal to allow main residence relief on the whole gain arising from the disposal of the land. The Special Commissioner considered that the permitted area should extend to 2.03 acres, based on the circumstances at the time of disposal. It was also held that because the land was owned for a period before the house was built, main residence relief should be apportioned (under *s 223(2)*), as the 'throughout the period of ownership' requirement in *s 223(1)* was not satisfied.

The problem of the residual building plot

12.8   A common pitfall is illustrated by the case of *Varty v Lynes* [1976] STC 508. See the following example.

Example 12.3—Sale of land delayed

Charles owned and occupied a suburban property with an extensive (over 5 hectare) corner plot. Work forced him to relocate. He obtained planning permission for a single dwelling on the plot and, as a temporary measure, purchased a residence nearer his new work. In the end, the sale of his former house goes through before the sale of the adjoining plot. Any gain on the sale of the house itself, after apportionment, is covered by main residence relief.

Unfortunately for Charles, in general there can be no relief on the eventual sale of the plot. At the time of the sale it is neither a dwelling house nor part of a dwelling house. It was, but is no longer: the legislation is precise in distinguishing the house from its grounds on this point. It would have been better for Charles to have sold the house and the plot together but with the benefit of the planning permission. Note, however, some relaxation of the strict rule in CG 64384 where all the land was formerly occupied as garden, which is only reasonable.

Other forms of accommodation

12.9 A mobile caravan does not qualify for relief, but a static one may do. A 'live aboard' yacht in a marina does not qualify even if on 'shore power' as many cruising yachts are, but a houseboat permanently located, and connected to all mains services, may do. It seems that the claim in such cases usually relates to the site, rather than the van or vessel.

PERIODS OF RESIDENCE

12.10 In a straightforward case this issue gives no difficulty. A person buys a house, moves in, lives there until some change of circumstances, finds a buyer and moves out. In such a situation no apportionment is necessary and, assuming no other complications, the entire gain qualifies for relief. Difficulties arise in more complicated situations.

Delay in taking up occupation

12.11 ESC D49 applies where an individual acquires land on which he has a house built which becomes his main residence or buys an existing property and before moving in:

- arranges for alterations or redecorations; or
- completes the necessary steps for disposing of his previous residence.

Provided that the delay is no more than one year, this period of non-residence is treated as if it were a period of residence. If a taxpayer needs more than one year, he may have a second year if there are good reasons for delay which are outside the control of the taxpayer. If, however, the individual fails to move into the property within the period of one year (or two if extended) no relief will be given at all for that period of non-occupation. There may be overlap between the period of deemed occupation under this concession and relief on another property in respect of the same period.

Example 12.4—Relocation plans undermined

David lives in Warwick. He buys a scruffy house in Markfield, Leicestershire, with a view to renovating it and living there because it will be near his work. In fact the property suffers from mining subsidence that was not revealed before the purchase and the renovation takes 18 months.

Meanwhile, David has been promoted by his employers, so Markfield will no longer be convenient to him. The house in Warwick has increased in value, as has that in Markfield. If David had moved into the renovated house, the delay would not prejudice relief because it was not his fault.

If he decides simply to sell the house in Markfield without taking up occupation, the whole of the gain will be taxable. It might have been better for him to consider the possibilities that are discussed below in connection with owning two or more residences. As will be seen below, an election in relation to residences need not be permanent. Even a short period residence at Markfield would serve to bring David within ESC D49.

'Overlap' relief

12.12   Occasionally the property market is so sluggish that homeowners experience significant delays in finding purchasers whilst personal circumstances compel them to move and to acquire a new residence before disposing of the old. Recognising this, *s 223(2)(a)* has the affect that, provided the taxpayer has been resident in the dwelling house at some point in his period of ownership, the last 36 months of ownership will qualify to be treated as a period of ownership 'in any event'. Apart from that, the basic rule is that main residence relief is calculated on a time-apportionment basis and is allowed in respect of periods of ownership but not of periods of absence.

Example 12.5—Last 36 months

Evan bought a scruffy property on 1 January 1999. He renovated it himself, but did not live onsite. He was so slow that the work took until 31 March 2001, so Evan was outside the terms of ESC D49. He lived in the property from 1 April 2001 to 31 December 2002. He sold on 31 March 2003 at a good profit even after the cost of the improvements.

Evan does not benefit from ESC D49 because the improvements took too long. He qualifies for main residence relief from 1 April 2001 to 31 March 2003 under general principles, giving him relief in respect of ownership of 24 months out of 51. However, by virtue of *s 223(2)(a)* main residence relief will be allowed in respect of 36 months out of 51.

'Sandwich' reliefs

12.13   *Section 223(3)* recognises individual circumstances where a person is unable to continue to live at a property throughout his period of ownership. For a period of absence to be treated as a period of occupation under *s 223(3)* the dwelling house must have been the only or main residence of the taxpayer both before and after the period of absence, ie sandwiched between periods of genuine occupation. If that condition is satisfied, the following periods of absence will be treated as if they were periods of occupation:

- Period during all of which the taxpayer worked outside the United Kingdom (without limit as to duration).

- Period, up to four years, or periods together not exceeding four years, during which the taxpayer could not live at the residence because of where he was working or as a result of any condition imposed by his employer that required him to live elsewhere. The condition must have been reasonable as to secure the effective performance of his duties by the employee.

- Any other period of absence up to three years or periods together not exceeding three years.

Example 12.6—No place like home

Frances worked in the gas industry and on 1 January 1985 purchased a property in Bacton, Norfolk where she lived until 31 December 1985. She was then seconded to Aberdeen, working there until 31 December 1988; then to Norway, where she remained until 31 December 1997. Tiring of life on gas rigs, Frances then took an extended holiday from 1 January 1998 to 31 December 1999, returning to Bacton and living there from 1 January 2000 to 30 June in that year, when she sold the property at a profit.

The whole of the gain qualifies for relief. There are periods of residence to satisfy the 'sandwich' requirement. The period in Scotland is less than the maximum stipulated by *s 223(3)(c)*. During all of her time in Norway, Frances was working: the absence therefore complied with *s 223(3)(b)*. The extended holiday is less than the maximum stipulated by *s 223(3)(a)*.

Job-related accommodation

12.14   Apart from the provisions of *s 223* treating a period of absence as if it were a period of residence, there is a separate rule under *s 222(8)* which can help the taxpayer. If a property or part of it has been purchased with the intention that it should eventually be a residence, but the owner for the time being lives in job-related accommodation, the owner is deemed to occupy the property. It does not matter that the house is never, in fact, occupied, provided that the intention to occupy can be proved: CG 64558.

Example 12.7—Getting away from work

Gemma is a prison officer on a low salary. She purchases at auction a terraced property in poor condition which is occupied by a tenant who is entitled to remain at the property for the rest of his life. Gemma meanwhile is required by the terms of her employment to live onsite, though not always at the same secure establishment.

The tenant dies. Gemma is still employed as a prison officer but uses her holidays to renovate the property. That takes time and it is seven years from the date of the purchase before Gemma is actually able to start to use the property as her home when she is on leave. Although she has always intended to use the property as her home a change in her circumstances involves a move to a completely different part of the country and she sells the property.

She can show that she always intended, once the property was available and fit for her use, to occupy it as her only or main residence. She can also show, in compliance with *s 222(8A)* and following, that her accommodation with the prison service is job-related (see below).

12.15   Accommodation is job-related where a person or his spouse or civil partner has some kind of work, whether employed or self-employed, that meets the following conditions.

Employment

If the taxpayer or spouse or civil partner is employed, there are three circumstances in which accommodation is job-related:

- it is necessary for the proper performance of the work to live in specific accommodation;

- accommodation is provided by the employer for the better performance by the employee of his duties and it is customary in that trade or employment to provide living accommodation for employees; or

- there is a special threat to the security of the employee and to meet it special security arrangements are enforced as part of which the employee lives in particular accommodation.

Freelance

The contract must be at arm's length. Two conditions must be satisfied:

- the taxpayer is required as part of the contract to carry on the work on premises that are provided by another person (who may, but need not, be the other party to the contract); and

- it is a term of the contract that the contractor should live on those premises or on some other premises provided by the other party to the contract.

Link to a company: anti-avoidance

Special rules apply where a company provides the accommodation to an employee who is a director. To avoid the situation where a person might artificially create job-related accommodation for his own benefit, the provisions as to job-related accommodation for employees described at **12.14** will not apply, see *s 222(8B)*, unless two further conditions are satisfied.

The first is that the employee/director must have no material interest in the company. The second condition is that one of three sub-conditions is satisfied namely:

- the taxpayer is a full-time working director;

- the company is non-profit making; or

- the company is established for charitable purposes only.

Again, see *s 222(8C)*, to avoid abuse, relief in respect of job-related accommodation for a self-employed person under *s 222(8A)(b)* described at **12.15** is not available where the living accommodation is wholly or partly provided by certain entities that have a link to the taxpayer. In this subsection the person who would otherwise claim relief is described as 'the borrower'. The relief will not apply where the accommodation has been provided either by a company in which the borrower or his spouse or civil partner has a material interest; or by anyone who, together with the borrower or his spouse or civil partner, carries on any trade or business in partnership.

These provisions as to job-related accommodation were tightened up by *FA 1999*. The references to matters such as 'employment', 'director', 'full-time working director' and 'material interest' are taken from *ITEPA 2003*. The changes relate to residence on or after 6 April 1983.

Residence in the context of trusts and estates

12.16   Situations are often encountered where main residence relief may be in point on the disposal of a property by trustees or in the administration of an estate. This is discussed more fully at **12.26** and will particularly apply where the 'debt or charge' scheme has been used. For a description of that scheme see *Tottel's Inheritance Tax Annual 2006/07*, Chapter 14, relating to the family home generally; and more specifically Chapter 13, Wills and Estate Planning, at **13.2** and following.

LETTINGS RELIEF

12.17   'Buy to let' properties do not as such qualify for main residence relief. There is, however, a specific relief which was no doubt designed to increase the availability of accommodation at moderate cost. It is in *s 223(4)* and can apply where a person lets all or part of his own home. For the relief to apply, the dwelling house, or the part on which the gain arises, must at some time in the ownership of the taxpayer have been a residence within the general terms of *s 222*, ie his only or main residence or a property that he owned whilst in job-related employment. The part in question must be let as residential accommodation. Up to a limit of £40,000 of the gain that would otherwise have been taxable is relieved.

Example 12.8—Money in the cellar

Henry buys as a single unit an urban terraced property for £480,000 of which 25% is represented by the value of accommodation in the basement that could be occupied separately; the remainder relates to the ground floor and upper floor. He lives there, allowing a lodger to occupy the basement, and later sells the entire property for £660,000. There is valuation evidence that the basement flat is still worth 25% of the whole. The gain on the ground floor and upper floor is exempt under general principles. The gain on the basement is £45,000 of which £40,000 is exempt under *s 223(4)(b)*. Note that if the basement had always been self-contained, it might have been regarded as a separate dwelling house and thus not part of Henry's estate.

Separate relief, up to £40,000, may be allowed where part of the gain relates to the letting, for example by time-apportionment. This is illustrated in CG 64737 and CG 64738.

TWO OR MORE RESIDENCES

12.18   It is arguable that, with the introduction of self-assessment, the law in this area may have changed slightly from what was established by the case of

Griffin v Craig-Harvey [1994] STC 54 discussed below. This is probably the area of main residence relief that gives the most difficulties and perhaps spawns more claims in negligence against advisers than the rest of the main residence relief code. HMRC may be aware that the taxpayer has more than one residence: see CG 64209.

Section 222(6) provides that 'a man and his wife living with him' (which expression should now be extended to include civil partners) can have only one main residence for both of them as long as they are living together. *Section 222(5)* applies where the taxpayer has two or more residences. If no action is taken by the taxpayer under the legislation, the question of which property is the main residence is one of fact.

Example 12.9—Home for the weekend

Ian, a VAT consultant, has a home at Empingham, overlooking Rutland Water, but the main demand for his services is from construction companies based in North London. He buys a studio flat in Hendon for use during the week. He and his family are keen on fishing and sailing. He spends as much time as possible in Empingham and the minimum in Hendon. On the balance of the facts, the property in Rutland is his main residence. Note that *Fox v Stirk, Ricketts v Registration Officer for the City of Cambridge* [1970] 3 All ER 7 contains the observation by Lord Denning MR that a man may have 'a flat in London and a house in the country. He is resident in both'.

Nomination of a property as the main residence

12.19   If a taxpayer has two properties that he could call home, *s 222(5)(a)* provides that, within two years of the date on which the second residence was available to him, he may give notice to HMRC identifying which property is his residence. If married or having a civil partner and living with that person, the notice binds them both. There is no precise form of notice, but see CG 64520, but it must be signed by the resident, not by his agent: see CG 64523.

Example 12.10—Timeous notice

Jessica buys her first home, a flat, on 1 January 1999 and lives there. On 1 July 2002 her aunt dies, leaving Jessica a bungalow which happens to be far more convenient for Jessica to live in. Jessica has from 1 July 2002 to 30 June 2004 in which she may serve notice under *s 222(5)(a)*. If she does serve notice, the property notified will be treated as Jessica's main residence whether in fact she lives there or not.

Difficulties for the taxpayer arise because it is not always possible to predict which of two properties will appreciate in value the most and which the taxpayer will want to retain long term. Particular problems arise where in fact both properties will be sold.

Example 12.11—Overlap and sandwich reliefs

Returning to the example of Jessica, she gives notice to treat the bungalow as her main residence for a period 1 January 2002 onwards. She serves the notice within the two-year period. She does in fact move there but keeps the flat until 31 December 2005 when she sells it.

The flat has not been her residence for two and a half years but there is no reduction in relief because that period of absence falls within the 36 months discussed at **12.12**. It might be thought that the fact that Jessica lives at the bungalow for the better performance of her work might help with relief but this is not a 'sandwich' period because Jessica never moves back to the flat. None of the 'sandwich' reliefs can therefore apply but fortunately they are not needed. In the event of a later sale of the bungalow all of the gain is relieved as well.

Varying the notice

12.20 The taxpayer may vary a notice given under s $222(5)(a)$ by giving further notice. The statute does not require any minimum period during which a person must reside at a property in order to claim relief. This is recognised by HMRC: see CG 64512.

Example 12.12—Well sheltered gains

Kylie, like Jessica, bought a studio flat on 1 January 1999. Like Jessica, she inherited on 1 July 2002 a sum of money which she immediately laid out on buying a second property, and which she let until 31 December 2002. Both properties were appreciating in value and Kylie gave notice to treat the second property as her main residence with effect from 1 January 2003 though in fact she continued to live at the original property. The second property was, as at 1 January 2003, available as a residence to Kylie. It was vacant.

Kylie later varied the notice so as to treat the original property as her residence again with effect from 31 March 2003. The second property was then let until its sale on 30 June 2006, realising a gain which is treated as accruing evenly over time (monthly in this example). The second property has, by virtue of the notice, been (for a time) Kylie's main residence. She has owned it for 48 months in all. During the first six months the property was no more than an investment. For three months it was Kylie's main residence under the terms of notice. For 36 months the property is treated as her main residence under *s 223(1)*. The other three months, from 1 April to 30 June 2003, qualify for relief under *s 223(4)* because the property has been Kylie's main residence and is let as residential accommodation.

As a result, 6/48 of the gain does not qualify for main residence relief but the remainder, 42/48, of the gain is covered. On the eventual sale of the original property main residence relief is available from 1 January 1999 to 31 December 2002 and from 1 April 2003 until sale. The period of non-residence is sandwiched between two periods of residence and does not exceed three years. It therefore qualifies to be treated as a period of occupation under *s 223(3)(a)*, so the entire period of ownership under the original property qualifies as occupation and therefore for relief.

12.21   Social mobility adds complications which impinge on seemingly unrelated transactions.

Example 12.13—Filing the notices

Lucy and Mary are artists. They met whilst working in Cornwall. Lucy had bought a small studio ('Cornwall 1') on 1 January 1999 whilst Mary bought a similar property ('Cornwall 2') on 1 January 2000. Their careers and, it must be said, their relationship flourished and on first January 2004 they jointly bought a flat in Highgate, London thereafter spending the summer months in Cornwall producing work which they sold in London during the winter months. Hurriedly completing tax returns for 2004/05 they each included, when lodging them on 31 January 2006, notice to treat Highgate as main residence from two years before. They registered their civil partnership on 31 Match 2006. In April 2006 they wished to sell one of the Cornwall properties to reduce the mortgage of Highgate.

The notices were sent with the tax returns. Mary's notice is effective but that of Lucy is out of time. Highgate has been available to her since 1 January 2004 so strictly she should have lodged her notice at least one month earlier. On the face of it, the question whether Lucy's main residence is Cornwall 1 or Highgate cannot be determined by the notice and must instead be decided according to the facts. Given the relationship between Lucy and Mary, it might at least be arguable that, at some time after Mary's purchase of Cornwall 2, by virtue of the relationship, Lucy had available to her a second residence. *Section 222(5)* does not require the taxpayer to own both residences for notice to be appropriate. That is not the outcome, see at **12.22**. The facts bring into play two extra considerations, set out below, respectively ESC D21 and RI89.

Special considerations in dual-residence cases

12.22   Revenue Interpretation 89 (RI 89) sets out the current thinking of HMRC in the situation where a person has available more than one residence. It was originally thought that any residence, including one's club in London, could trigger the need for an election but, since October 1994, the new advice has been to interpret *s 222(5)* purposively, within the context of that section as a whole. Since the relief relates to gains on property in which the taxpayer has a legal or equitable interest it is not appropriate to consider notice of election where the second residence is merely occupied under licence and the taxpayer has neither a legal nor an equitable interest in it.

Thus, in the example of Lucy and Mary above, the fact that Lucy might spend time at Cornwall 2 would not of itself be reason to serve notice because, absent any agreement to the contrary, Lucy would have neither a legal nor an equitable interest in Cornwall 2. RI89 specifically confirms that no notice of election under *s 222(5)*, which relies on a residence occupied only under licence and which is made after 16 October 1994, will be regarded as valid. Clearly, therefore, Lucy in the above example cannot use Cornwall 2 as a peg on which to hang a late election in respect of Cornwall 1.

ESC D21 addresses the issue of late claims in the very reasonable situation where a taxpayer becomes entitled to an interest in a second property without realising that by so doing time will begin to run against him or her under *s 222(5)(a)*. Where:

- the interest in the second property – or in each property if there is more than one – has a negligible capital value on the open market; and

- the individual is unaware that a nomination could be made,

there is an extension of the time limit. This will arise, for example, where the interest in the second property is no more than the tenancy of the flat or is accommodation provided by an employer. In each case the nomination to treat the other property, being the one in which the taxpayer does have a substantial interest, as the main residence may be made within a reasonable time of when the taxpayer first became aware of a possibility of making an election and it will be effectively backdated as far as is necessary.

Marriage or civil partnership

12.23 Where each party to a relationship has a residence, each may claim main residence relief unless and until they begin to be treated as living together within the context of marriage or a civil partnership. There can be only one residence for both parties to a marriage or a civil partnership by virtue of *s 222(6)(a)*. They must therefore do the sums and decide which property is to be home. If they give notice in time they can make the decision otherwise it will be based on the facts.

Returning to the example of Lucy and Mary, from 31 March 2006 they will have two years, see CG 64525, in which to decide whether their home together is to be Highgate, Cornwall 1 or Cornwall 2. Applying the rules relating to the last 36 months of ownership, they may decide to make sure that any property that is to be sold has been their main residence for a period so that, at the very least, the last 36 months of ownership qualify for relief.

RESIDENCES HELD BY TRUSTEES OR PERSONAL REPRESENTATIVES

12.24   The general rule is that, where trustees hold residential property and a beneficiary is 'entitled to occupy it under the terms of the settlement', main residence relief will be available. Specifically, *s 225* operates by substituting a reference to the trustees for a reference to the individual in *ss 222* to *224* and by providing that a notice under *s 222(5)(a)*, where there is more than one residence, is to be a joint notice by the trustees and the beneficiary.

The enactment of *FA 2006* will, over time, limit the number of life interest settlements. However, the amendments introduced in *FA 2006, Sch 20* do not specifically refer to main residence relief. As will be seen at **12.26**, this change may affect a situation, which has given difficulty in the past, where IHT and CGT interact. In a straightforward case the relief is valuable.

Example 12.14—Council house sold at a profit

Norma, widowed, was encouraged by her daughter Olive to buy the council house in which Norma had for many years lived. The open market value was £60,000 but Norma could buy it for £30,000. Olive agreed to help with the cost. Norma was advised that, if she entered into a deed of trust at the same time as buying the property, that would not contravene the restrictions on resale of council houses.

She therefore signed a Declaration of Trust, the first essential term of which was that she was entitled to live in the house and to any rents and profits of the house until sale or until her death, whichever should first occur. Subject to that prior interest, she declared herself trustee of the property for her only daughter Olive absolutely. The house sold, many years later, for £180,000.

The gain was entirely sheltered by relief under *s 225* because Norma was entitled to occupy the residence under the terms of the settlement. Had the property been retained until Norma's death, relief would have been available not only under the provisions of main residence relief but, this being a pre-2006 situation, by virtue of the tax-free uplift on death allowed by *s 73(1)(a)*.

Discretionary trusts

12.25   Where a trust instrument gives the trustees a complete discretion over what benefit may be enjoyed by any of the objects of the trust the effect is that, until the trustees take action, none of the beneficiaries actually has a right to any of the trust assets. This principle is seen in the rather specialist circumstances of *Judge and another (personal representatives of Walden, dec'd) v HMRC* (2005) SpC 506 which concerned the wording of a poorly-drawn will where it was held, on the particular facts, that the widow of the testator did not have an interest in possession in the former matrimonial home. The result was that the house was not treated as part of her estate for IHT, which was the main point at issue, but the collateral consequence was that, if there had been any increase in the value of the property during her period of occupation since her husband's death, no relief was available under *s 225*, because she did not have a right to occupy as required by that section.

The correct treatment of gains arising to trustees of discretionary trusts on properties occupied as residencies by beneficiaries was decided in *Sansom v Peay* [1976] STC 494. It had previously been thought, see CG 65443, that no beneficiary was entitled to occupy a dwelling house under the terms of the settlement, so as to benefit from *s 225*, unless the trust instrument specifically gave a right of occupation to that beneficiary.

The trust in *Sansom v Peay* was a discretionary one, allowing the trustees 'to permit any beneficiary to reside in any dwelling house or occupy any property or building … for the time being subject to the trust hereof upon such conditions … as the trustees … think fit'. Beneficiaries occupied a trust property and it was held that the occupations resulted from the exercise by the trustees of their powers under the deed. When the beneficiaries moved into the house they were entitled to stay there unless and until permission was withdrawn by the trustees. As at the date of the disposal of the house the beneficiaries were still entitled to occupy it and were occupying it under the terms of the trust deed. The gain was therefore sheltered by main residence relief.

Nil rate band discretionary will trusts

12.26   The issue will commonly arise in the context of will trusts. For a full discussion of the IHT implications the reader is referred to *Tottel's Inheritance Tax Annual 2006/07* at **13.1**. In outline, there are many families whose main wealth is the family home, the value of which exceeds the nil rate band for IHT (£285,000 for 2006/07). The family appreciate that any transfer between husband and wife is exempt but that, on the death of the survivor of them, any value in excess of the nil rate band attracts a charge to IHT at 40%. With a view to using the nil rate band on the first death, wills are drawn which give the nil rate band on discretionary trusts to beneficiaries including the surviving spouse, commonly with residue to that surviving spouse absolutely. The hope is that using the nil rate band on each death will combine to exempt the family property from IHT.

The argument runs that, where the house is occupied as tenants in common, each joint owner can occupy the entirety of it for the rest of their life, regardless of the fact that the other half of the property may have been given away. This argument is not always accepted by HMRC from the point of view of IHT. There may be circumstances which suggest that, even though the trustees were under no obligation to do so, they have actually so exercised their powers under the trust instrument that they have, in effect, created the situation that arose in *Sansom v Peay* and have therefore given the surviving spouse an interest in possession in the half of the property that that spouse does not own, with the result that, on the second death, the whole of the house becomes subject to IHT and the tax planning is thrown away.

Where the trustees can satisfy HMRC, from the standpoint of IHT, that in fact they have not exercised their powers in such a way as to grant the surviving spouse an interest in possession, the interest in the property that is held within the discretionary trust may escape IHT but, on any disposal of the property at a gain, CGT will become due because main residence relief is not available.

Example 12.15—Hit for CGT but not for IHT

Percy was married to Prudence. Their house was worth £360,000 and held by them as tenants in common in equal shares. Percy died on 5 April 2000, having by his will left the nil rate band on discretionary trusts for the benefit of his children, further issue and Prudence. At the time of his death the nil rate band was £231,000. His estate comprised the house and cash of £50,000, all of which passed to the trustees. There was no residue and IHT.

The trustees then held the half of the house on discretionary trusts but took no steps to grant Prudence any right of occupation of it. On 17 September 2005 the house was sold for £500,000. On her share of the property Prudence was able to take her gain tax-free. The gain of £70,000 on half of the house within the discretionary trust is, however, subject to CGT (after allowance for taper relief and the reduced annual exemption available to the trustees).

On the death of Prudence shortly after the sale, the matter is reopened for IHT purposes but it appears that the trustees have not handed over to her any part of the proceeds of sale that they received nor have they given Prudence benefit out of the trust fund. It also appears that they have met from time to time to consider their powers, so the trust has not just been 'in limbo'. The result for IHT purposes is that the estate of Prudence will be limited to her own share of the proceeds of sale of the house and to any other assets that she has and will not be deemed to include the half share in the house that sits within the discretionary trust.

Example 12.16—Hit the other way

Contrast the result in Example 12.15 with the situation where the trustees have either taken no steps at all since Percy's death or can be seen positively to have exercised their powers in favour of Prudence with regard to the house as, for example, taking unequivocal steps to show that they are unwilling to sell the house whilst Prudence is still alive even though other beneficiaries are in urgent need of money.

In such a case the argument by HMRC that Prudence has effectively an interest in possession in the half of the house that sits within the trust is very likely to succeed. The tax consequence is that, on a sale as already described, there will be no CGT. However, the trust fund, here meaning the part that is represented by the share in the house rather than the cash, will be treated as agreeable with the estate of Prudence on her death.

Disregarding expenses and the like, in the event of the death of Prudence at any time in the seven years after the time when her interest ceased, which will probably be the date of sale, the value of the half of the house in the trust will be added to her free estate to establish the chargeable transfer on death.

The IHT charge is at 40% of the capital value. The CGT charge would have been at 40%, but only on the gain and would have been subject to reliefs. It is nearly always better to structure these transactions so that the tax paid is CGT rather than IHT. The downside is of course that CGT becomes payable as soon as there is a disposal of the property, which is likely to reduce the money then available for alternative accommodation.

Estates in administration

12.27   Quite often there will be a substantial increase in the value of a dwelling house from the date of the death of its owner to the date on which the property can be sold. Delays can arise where there is a dispute about the terms of a will or where a claim is made under the *Inheritance (Provision for Family and Dependents) Act 1975* or where, quite simply, everything takes rather longer than it should.

Valuation issues

12.28   In the simple situation of a property that becomes vacant on death and is not thereafter occupied until sale, the normal rules will apply which are set out in **3.6**. However, so deep-rooted in the consciousness of the British public is the idea that a gain on a house is tax-free that families will go to considerable lengths, on the disposal of a house, to avoid suffering any tax on it. It is often fondly imagined that the property can, for probate and IHT purposes, be valued at an artificially low level and that it can later be sold for much more and tax-free.

That idea exhibits not only a cavalier attitude to the payment of tax but some fundamental errors of tax law. First, there is no such thing as 'probate value', meaning some artificially low value approximating to the lowest price that anyone could accept in the open market further discounted by the costs of sale. The correct value for IHT purposes, as is explained in *Tottel's Inheritance Tax Annual 2006/07*, is 'the price which the property might reasonably be expected to fetch if sold in the open market': see *ITA 1984, s 160*. That value is imported into the CGT code by *s 274* which provides that, where the value at the date of death has been 'ascertained' for the purposes of IHT, that value is the market value of the asset at the date of death for CGT purposes, with the knock-on effect that under *s 62* it is the value at which the personal representatives are deemed to acquire the property as at the date of death of the deceased.

Quick sale

12.29   Naturally, if sale on the open market takes place quite soon after death, this is a strong guide as to market value at the earlier date. If, however, the value is established as at the date of death on a proper basis and with full disclosure and a substantial time elapses until sale it will not be necessary to substitute the eventual sale price for the probate value at date of death.

In this context, some 'hope' value should be included in the value at date of death if there is, say, a potential building plot. The case of *Prosser v IRC* (DET/1/2000) suggests that hope value is no more than 25% of the full development value.

Example 12.17—IHT followed by CGT

Quentin died on 4 April 2006. His estate comprised his home and other assets that were exactly matched by liabilities. The fair open market value of the house at date of death was £276,000. The nil rate band at that date was £275,000 so IHT was payable of £400, being 40% of the excess. Probate is obtained quickly and the property is sold on 3 August 2006 for £300,000 less expenses (inclusive of VAT) of 3%.

CGT is calculated as under:	
	£
Net proceeds of sale	291,000
Less probate value	276,000
Less allowance available under SP 2/04	
(band C) at 1%	2,760
Gain after allowance	12,240
Deduct annual allowance*	8,800
Taxable gain	3,440
Tax at 40%	1,376

* This being a disposal within the year of assessment in which death occurred or one of the two years following, the executors may claim the full allowance of £8,800.

Ongoing residence by major beneficiary

12.30   It sometimes happens that the main asset of an estate is a house that is given by its owner on death to someone who has been living with the owner prior to death. In the past a tax liability could arise on the disposal of such a property during the administration of the estate and only by concession was it possible to shelter any of the gain using main residence relief. The position has been made statutory by *s 225A*. For the relief to apply there are two conditions. The first may be called the 'permanent dwelling house' condition. It is that, both before and after the death of the deceased, the property in question 'was the only or main residence of one or more individuals'.

The second condition, which may be called 'main beneficiary' condition, is that the individual (or group of individuals) who was/were living in the property before and after the relevant death is/are entitled to at least 3/4 of the proceeds of sale of the property in question. The entitlement may thus be shared among several beneficiaries if they can all show that they were resident before and after the death and that they have a 'relevant entitlement', meaning an entitlement as a legatee of the person who has died or an entitlement to an interest in possession in the whole or sum part of the net proceeds of the disposal of the house.

Section 225A(4) defines 'net proceeds of disposal' as the proceeds realised by the personal representatives less incidental costs as are allowable on computing the gain that would otherwise arise to the personal representatives, assuming, whether or not this be the case, that none of the proceeds of sale is needed to meet liabilities of the estate (including liability to IHT). Relief is available only if the personal representatives claim it.

Example 12.18—Requirements not satisfied

Robert, a widower, had at the date of his death on 3 April 2005, a house worth £300,000 and net cash of £100,000 after all liabilities. His son (and daughter-in-law) moved in with Robert to look after him after his wife died. They continued to live there after his death. Robert's will leaves his estate equally between the son who was living with him and his daughter.

Relief under *s 225* is not available. The estate benefits from the nil rate band of £263,000 but the excess, £137,000, attracts IHT of £54,800. The net estate to divide between the son and the daughter is £345,200, £172,600 each. Even though the son and his wife might like to take the house, if necessary providing money by way of equalisation, they are outside the requirements of *s 225A(3)(b)* because their entitlement under the will is less than 75% of the proceeds of the disposal, if it were now to take place, of the house.

Relief could have been available if the will had been otherwise.

Example 12.19—A better solution

The facts are as in Example 12.18 except that Robert, in recognition of the care provided by his daughter-in-law, had given her an equal share of residue with her husband and sister-in-law. The figures would work out differently. On his death the daughter would be entitled, net of IHT, to £115,667 whereas the son and daughter-in-law between them would be entitled to £230,133. That is more than 75% of the value of the house, unless it has risen substantially in value since the death. Relief may therefore be available.

Property as asset of beneficiary

12.31   Relief under *s 225A* is not very common because in many circumstances there will be a simpler solution. If the value of the estate is sufficient, and liquidity available, for a property in it to be transferred to a beneficiary outright there will be no need for *s 225A* relief. The beneficiary will acquire the property as 'legatee' within the meaning of *s 64(3)* and will, on acquiring the property, step into the shoes of the personal representatives and be deemed to have acquired it at probate value. If that beneficiary then occupies the property, giving notice as appropriate if already the owner of another property, main residence relief will be available under general principles and there will be no need for *s 225A* relief.

There is, however, often a problem: IHT. For an asset to be dealt with, and any gain realised, by the beneficiary in this way the asset must first be placed unreservedly at the disposal of the beneficiary. Appropriation 'in book form', as sometimes suggested by exempt beneficiaries, is not in truth appropriation at all. The desire to avoid the trouble and fees involved in 'doing the job properly' can threaten the relief. In theory at least, the house could be assented to the beneficiary subject to a lien or charge in favour of the personal representatives for unpaid IHT but that situation is far from ideal, especially in the light of the principles seen on *Howarth's Executors v IRC* [1997] STC (SCD) 162 relating to accountability of executors for tax after parting with estate assets. A compromise might be to assent to the vesting in the beneficiary of a share only in the house equal to the proportion that can be released free of any lien for tax. The rest of the gain would then sit (and be taxed) in the estate, but that might be better than tax on the whole gain.

ANTI-AVOIDANCE

Washing the gain through a trust

12.32   The discussion of the relief in this chapter has touched on various minor anti-avoidance provisions. The main provision is *s 226A*, which applies to transactions on or after 9 December 2003 and which was introduced by *FA 2004*. The background to this legislation was the perceived abuse of 'washing the holiday cottage gain'.

Example 12.20—The 'mischief'

A family owns a main residence and a country property which had been acquired cheaply many years earlier. The children become too old to want to take holidays with their parents and consider the holiday cottage far too uncool to take holidays there with their friends. It is time for the cottage to be sold.

Commonly the arrangement was that mother and father would settle the cottage on discretionary trusts, holding over the accrued gain under *s 260*. There were then two ways to proceed. The tax planning required one of the children to be over the age of 18 (but preferably unemployed or otherwise free for a reasonable time to live in the country cottage).

Under one version of the scheme, the property would then be appointed out entirely to that child and the gain held over under *s 260*. The child would occupy the property as his or her main residence and soon afterwards sell it, claiming main residence relief on the gain that then arose, which would include the gain that had been held over on the transfer of the property into the trust and any further gain that had arisen and was likewise held over, with the previous held

264

over gain, on removal of the property from the trust. Thus, within the space of a few months, the gain arising on the holiday cottage could be washed. The only disadvantage with this plan was that the entire proceeds of sale ended legally, if not actually, in the hands of the child.

A variant of the scheme involved the appointment by the trustees of an interest in possession in the cottage to the beneficiary child. Some time later the trustees would sell the property and, because it had been residence of a beneficiary entitled to occupy it under the terms of the settlement, part of the gain would be exempt under *s 225*. It did not matter too much that the trustees had not owned the property for very long; the period of ownership before the appointment of the life interest to the child would not qualify for main residence relief but, where the gain held over was substantial, the ability to shelter most of it by main residence relief made the exercise very worthwhile. Under this version, the money ended up in the 'right' place.

The statutory change

12.33   *Section 226A* nullified the scheme. The section is closely targeted. It applies where:

- main residence relief would otherwise apply to a gain or part gain accruing to an individual or trustees on the eventual disposal of a property;

- on the later disposal the amount of the gain would be reduced but for the effect of *s 223*; and

- the reduction would result, directly or indirectly, from a hold-over claim under *s 260* at an earlier stage in the arrangement.

Where a claim to hold over a gain under *s 260* was made on the earlier transaction (or any of them if more than one), main residence relief will not be available on the later disposal of the property. Where a hold-over claim is made under *s 260* after the later disposal of the property and provision just described does not apply, it is to be assumed for the purposes of CGT that main residence relief never was available in relation to the gain or part gain arising on the later disposal. The relief, if claimed, is withdrawn and adjustments are made that give effect to the anti-avoidance legislation.

It is possible for the taxpayer to be wise after the event. Where a gain was held over under *s 260* and it now appears that it would have been better to have relied on main residence relief and to have paid the tax on the earlier gain, the earlier claim for hold-over relief can be revoked and, if revoked, it is as if the claim had never been made.

There are exceptions from *s 226A* in connection with maintenance funds for heritage property. This is a complicated topic and readers are referred to specialist works on the subject.

Transitional relief

12.34   At the time of its introduction, *s 226A* was widely seen to be retrospective. The scheme described at Example 12.20 had been in quite common use and it is fair to say that taxation advisers were taken by surprise. Their indignation, righteous or otherwise, was not really defused by the transitional provisions of *FA 2004 Sch 22, para 8*, inserting extra provisions into *s 226A*. The effect was to confer limited transitional relief where the held-over disposal occurred before 10 December 2003.

The residence in question was deemed not to have been the only or main residence of the individual from 10 December 2003 and any gain was apportioned between the time before that date and the time after. The gain that was time-apportioned included both the held-over gain and any later gain even though all the held-over gain had accrued before 10 December 2003. The effect was that, unless action was taken very quickly after 10 December 2003 to ameliorate the situation, a very large proportion of the gain fell into the tax net. The difficulty for advisers at the time was that they had no legislation to go on, only the scant details in the Pre-budget Report of the Chancellor in December 2003. This was unfair: effectively advisers did not know what the law was until about August 2004, and by then it was too late to bring structures within acceptable bounds.

Effect of the Finance Act 2006

Trusts of houses

12.35   The subject of the *Finance Act 2006* changes affecting settlements is discussed in **Chapter 8**. There are few major changes of principle effecting main residence relief introduced by *FA 2006, Sch 20*. The incidental changes are those that arise from the way in which trusts will be treated in future. The fact that, with virtually no exceptions, the creation of a lifetime trust will in future be a chargeable transfer increases the number of occasions on which it will be possible to hold over gains under *s 260*; but in the light of the discussion of the effect of *s 226A* above, the ability to hold over a gain into a new trust is of limited value in a context of residences.

There are other changes introduced by *FA 2006* which may be relevant to trusts of houses, not because of main residence relief but because of those occasions where, on death, there is effectively a tax-free uplift. Thus, *s 72* is amended by *s 72(1A)* to *(1C)*, cutting down the availability of uplift on death so that it applies only to an immediate post-death interest ('IPDI'), a transitional serial interest ('TSI') or a bereaved minor's trust ('BMT').

DEPENDENT RELATIVE RELIEF

12.36   This relief has been left until last because, after 18 years, it is now seldom encountered in practice. The requirements are that, on or before 5 April 1988, an interest in a dwelling house or part of a dwelling house owned by the taxpayer was the sole residence of a dependent relative of that taxpayer and was provided rent free and without any other consideration. For this purpose 'dependent relative' means (see *s 226(6)*):

- any relative of the taxpayer or of his spouse or civil partner who is incapacitated by old age or infirmity from maintaining himself; or

- the mother of the taxpayer or spouse or civil partner who, whether or not incapacitated, is widowed or living apart from her husband, or who is a single woman in consequence of disillusion or annulment of marriage.

Relief is available only if claimed. If allowed, the 'dower house' that forms the subject matter of the claim is treated as if it had been the only or main residence of the taxpayer for as long as the dependent relative lived there and regardless of the fact that the taxpayer may have had another residence qualifying for relief. There is further apportionment so that a period of ownership after the 'dower house' ceases to be the sole residence of the dependent relative is disregarded and qualifies for no relief. The taxpayer may claim relief in respect of only one dower house at a time.

Chapter 13

Hold-over relief for gifts

INTRODUCTION

13.1   The gift of a chargeable asset, or the sale of a chargeable asset otherwise than at arm's length (see **13.13**), is treated for CGT purposes as a disposal at market value. See **3.5** regarding the market value rule (but note the special rules explained at **3.67** for transfers between spouses and civil partners). The person acquiring the asset is treated as acquiring it at its market value.

Two forms of hold-over relief are available to defer the CGT liability until there is a disposal by the transferee:

(a)   hold-over relief for gifts of business assets, see **13.2** (*TCGA 1992, s 165*); and

(b)   hold-over relief for gifts on which inheritance tax is either (i) immediately chargeable, or (ii) not chargeable because of a particular exemption, see **13.37** (*TCGA 1992, s 260*).

The relief in (b) takes precedence over the relief in (a). Certain gifts are exempt from CGT so that hold-over relief is not necessary – see the exemptions at **1.7**. Where neither an exemption nor any form of hold-over relief applies, it may be possible for the CGT to be paid in instalments. If the transferor does not pay the tax, it may be recovered from the transferee (*TCGA 1992, ss 281, 282*).

GIFTS OF BUSINESS ASSETS

13.2   Where an individual (or a trustee in some cases, see **13.26**) disposes of an asset otherwise than under a bargain at arm's length, any gain accruing may be deferred where the conditions in *TCGA 1992, s 165* are met. The gain held over is set against the transferee's acquisition cost in calculating the gain on a subsequent disposal. The potential CGT liability is, in effect, assumed by the donee. The date of an outright gift is the date on which it becomes effective. The date of a sale at a price below market value is, broadly, the date of the contract – see **2.8** regarding the time of a disposal.

Conditions

13.3   Hold-over relief is generally available where:

(a)   an individual ('the transferor') makes a disposal otherwise than under a bargain at arm's length of an asset mentioned in **13.5**;

(b)   both the transferor and the person acquiring the asset ('the transferee') make a claim to relief;

(c)   the transferee is UK resident (see **13.19**).

There is no requirement for the transferee to make a claim if the transferee is the trustee (or a body of trustees) of settled property (*TCGA 1992, s 165(1)*).

Exceptions

13.4   Relief is not available:

*   where a claim could be made to hold-over relief for gifts on which inheritance tax is chargeable (or not chargeable because of a particular exemption) (ie relief under *TCGA 1992, s 260*, see **13.37**);

*   on a transfer of shares or securities to a company; or

*   where a gain is deemed to accrue on the disposal of qualifying corporate bonds acquired in exchange for shares (*TCGA 1992, s 165(3)*).

Qualifying assets

13.5   An asset may be the subject of a hold-over relief claim if it falls within (a) to (d) below:

(a)   an asset (or an interest in an asset) used for the purposes of a trade, profession or vocation carried on by (i) the transferor (either alone or in partnership), or (ii) his personal company, or (iii) a member of a trading group whose holding company is his personal company (*TCGA 1992, s 165(2)*);

(b)   shares or securities of a trading company, or of the holding company of a trading group, where either (i) the trading company or holding company is the transferor's personal company, or (ii) the shares or securities are not listed on a recognised stock exchange (shares listed on the alternative investment market (AIM) being regarded as not listed) (*TCGA 1992, s 165(2)*);

(c)   farmland and buildings that would be eligible for inheritance tax agricultural property relief (*TCGA 1992, s 165(5), Sch 7*); and

(d)   certain settled property disposed of by the trustees of a settlement (see **13.26**) (*TCGA 1992, s 165(5), Sch 7*).

HMRC regard the condition in (a) as meaning that the asset has to have been in use for the trade, etc just before it was gifted (CG 66950). See **13.8** regarding partial relief where an asset other than shares has not been used wholly for the purposes of the trade, etc during the entire period of ownership.

Operation of TCGA 1992, s 165 relief

13.6   The effect of this relief, which must be claimed (see **13.34**), is that the 'held-over gain' (see below) is deducted from both:

●   the chargeable gain (if any) that would otherwise accrue to the transferor; and

●   the consideration which the transferee would otherwise be regarded as having given for the acquisition of the asset (or the shares or securities) (*TCGA 1992, s 165(4)*).

The 'held-over gain' on a disposal, where this relief is not restricted by reference to actual consideration received for the disposal, is the chargeable gain that would have accrued in the absence of hold-over relief (*TCGA 1992, s 165(6)*). The relief may be restricted where consideration is received (see **13.7**) or as described in **13.8**.

Example 13.1

Anthony has carried on a business as a sole trader since June 2001. His only chargeable asset is goodwill, which is now worth £150,000 although he paid only £10,000 for it.

He gives the business to his daughter Mary in December 2006, and they claim hold-over relief under *TCGA 1992, s 165*. There is no actual consideration so the whole of the gain accruing is held over. Anthony's gain of £140,000 is therefore reduced to nil, and Mary's allowable expenditure on any future disposal is reduced from £150,000 to £10,000. See **13.36** regarding the interaction between hold-over relief and taper relief.

Example 13.2

Barnaby purchased shares in Beach Plc, a listed company, in May 1999 for £50,000. In September 2006, when they are worth £60,000, he settles the shares

– which represent a non-business asset for taper relief – in a discretionary trust which is not settlor-interested (see **13.27**). Barnaby claims hold-over relief.

The held-over gain is £10,000 and the trustees' allowable expenditure is reduced from £60,000 to £50,000. The trustees sell the shares for £180,000 in February 2008. The gain accruing on their disposal is £180,000 – £50,000 = £130,000. No taper relief is due on the trustee's disposal because they have held the shares for less than three complete years.

Consideration received

13.7   Where a claim to hold-over relief is made and there is actual consideration for the disposal, the held-over gain becomes:

- the 'unrelieved gain' on the disposal (ie the chargeable gain that would have accrued in the absence of hold-over relief), *less*

- the excess of the actual consideration for the disposal over the allowable expenditure deductible in computing the gain (*TCGA 1992, s 165(7)*).

Where the actual consideration does not exceed the allowable expenditure, there is of course no gain and no need for hold-over relief.

Example 13.3

The facts are as in Example 13.1 but Mary pays £40,000 for the goodwill. The held-over gain becomes £110,000:

	£	Gain £
Unrelieved gain		140,000
less		
consideration received	40,000	
less allowable expenditure	(10,000)	(30,000)
Held-over gain		110,000

Therefore, Anthony's gain is reduced from £140,000 to £30,000 (being the consideration received less his allowable expenditure) and Mary's allowable expenditure on any future disposal is £150,000 less £110,000 = £40,000.

Partial relief

13.8   Hold-over relief is restricted if an asset other than shares has not been used wholly for the purposes of the trade, etc during the entire period of

271

ownership, or if part of a building was so used and part was not. In the case of shares, the gain eligible for hold-over relief may be restricted if the company's chargeable assets include non-business assets. These restrictions are examined below.

Asset not used for trade, etc throughout period of ownership

13.9   If the asset was not used for the purposes of the trade, etc throughout the transferor's period of ownership, the held-over gain is reduced by multiplying it by the fraction A/B, where:

- A is the number of days in that period of ownership during which the asset was so used; and

- B is the number of days in the entire period of ownership.

There is no restriction under this rule where the asset would qualify for inheritance tax agricultural property relief (*TCGA 1992, Sch 7, paras 4, 5*).

Partial use for trade, etc purposes of a building or structure

13.10   If the asset disposed of is a building or structure, and during the transferor's period of ownership (or any 'substantial part' of that period) only a part of the building or structure was used for the purposes of the trade, etc, the gain is apportioned on a just and reasonable basis and only the fraction of the gain apportioned to the part of the building so used is held over. Again, there is no restriction where the asset would qualify for inheritance tax agricultural property relief.

Where both this restriction and the time restriction above are appropriate, HMRC consider that the time restriction should be applied first (*TCGA 1992, Sch 7, paras 4, 6*; CG 66952).

Example 13.4

Julian bought a shop, with a flat above, for £80,000. He gave the property to his son James five years later, having used the shop for the purpose of his trade throughout the last three years of ownership. Market values at the time of the gift are agreed at £180,000 for the whole property and £120,000 for the shop.

Julian's unrelieved gain of £100,000 is multiplied by 3/5ths to reflect the period of trade use, giving £60,000. It is then apportioned for partial trade use of the building in that period, with 12/18ths (or 2/3rds) of the gain of £60,000 being apportioned to trade use. The held-over gain is therefore £40,000.

Shares: restriction for chargeable non-business assets

13.11   Where shares in a company are disposed of and non-business assets are included in the company's chargeable assets (or in the group's chargeable assets, where the company is the holding company of a trading group), hold-over relief is restricted as set out below if:

(a)   the transferor was able to exercise at least 25% of the voting rights at any time in the 12 months before the disposal; or

(b)   the transferor is an individual and the company is his personal company at any time in that 12-month period.

The held-over gain is reduced by multiplying it by the fraction A/B, where:

- A is the market value of the company's (or group's) 'chargeable assets' that are 'business assets' (see definitions below); and

- B is the market value of all the company's (or group's) chargeable assets.

In both cases the market value is taken at the date of the disposal. For the purpose of this restriction, an asset is a business asset if it is used for the purposes of a trade, profession or vocation carried on by the company (or member of the group). An asset is a chargeable asset if, on a disposal of it, a gain accruing to the company (or member of the group) would be a chargeable gain.

In the case of a disposal of shares in the holding company of a trading group, a holding by one member of the group of the ordinary share capital of another member is not counted as a chargeable asset. If the holding company (X) does not own, directly or indirectly, all of the ordinary share capital of a 51% subsidiary (Y), the value of company Y's chargeable assets is reduced by multiplying it by the fraction A/B, where:

- A is the amount of company Y's ordinary share capital owned directly or indirectly by company X; and

- B is the whole of company Y's share capital (*TCGA 1992, Sch 7, paras 4, 7*).

Partial claims

13.12   It is not possible to limit a claim to hold-over relief in order, for example, to utilise the donor's annual exemption. However, where several assets are transferred the parties may choose to claim relief on some assets and not others.

Definitions

Arm's length

13.13   A gift is not a bargain at 'arm's length'. Broadly, HMRC regard a bargain as made at arm's length if it is a normal commercial transaction and all the parties involved try to obtain the best deal for themselves in their particular circumstances (see **3.5**).

Personal company

13.14   A company is an individual's 'personal company' if he is able to exercise not less than 5% of the voting rights in the company (*TCGA 1992, s 165(8)*).

Trading company, etc

13.15   Broadly, a company is a trading company if its business does not include non-trading activities 'to a substantial extent'. 'Holding company', 'trading company' and 'trading group' take the definitions given for taper relief purposes (see **11.8**). These are found in *TCGA 1992, Sch A1, paras 22(1), 22A* and *22B* respectively (*TCGA 1992, s 165(8)*).

Trade, etc

13.16   'Trade', 'profession' and 'vocation' have the same meaning as in the Income Tax Acts. 'Trade' is taken to include the occupation of woodlands managed by the occupier on a commercial basis and with a view to the realisation of profits, both for the general purposes of hold-over relief and in determining whether a company is a trading company (*TCGA 1992, ss 165(8), (9)*).

Relief for inheritance tax

13.17   Where hold-over relief is obtained under *TCGA 1992, s 165* and the disposal is, or proves to be, a chargeable transfer for inheritance tax purposes, a deduction is allowed to the transferee in computing for CGT purposes the chargeable gain accruing on his disposal of the asset. The deduction is equal to the inheritance tax attributable to the value of the asset, except that it cannot exceed the amount of the chargeable gain before the deduction.

The deduction is adjusted in the event that the inheritance tax is varied after it has been taken into account in this way, and in the event that a disposal which is a potentially exempt transfer for inheritance tax purposes becomes a chargeable transfer (*TCGA 1992, s 165(10), (11)*).

Example 13.5

In July 2006 Barbara sold unlisted shares for £500,000. Her father gave her the shares in March 1993 when they were worth £150,000. He died shortly after the gift and inheritance tax of £60,000 was payable. He had purchased the shares in May 1982 for £40,000. The held-over gain and Barbara's chargeable gain on the 2006/07 disposal are computed as follows:

	£	£
Held-over gain on gift in March 1993:		
Market value in March 1993		150,000
Cost in May 1982		(40,000)
Unindexed gain		110,000
Indexation £40,000 x 0.707		(28,280)
Held-over gain		81,720
Gain on Barbara's disposal:		
Sale proceeds, July 2006		500,000
Market value in March 1993	150,000	
Less gain held over	(81,720)	(68,280)
		431,720
Indexation to April 1998 £68,280 x 0.167		(11,403)
		420,317
Deduction for inheritance tax		(60,000)
Chargeable gain 2006/07		360,317

Separation, divorce or dissolution of civil partnership

13.18   A transfer between spouses or civil partners is not subject to the no gain/no loss rule in *TCGA 1992, s 58* (see **3.67**) if it takes place after the end of the year of assessment in which the parties separate. Hold-over relief may be available, in principle, in either of the following circumstances:

- a disposal from one spouse or civil partner to the other after the end of the year of assessment in which they separate but prior to the divorce decree absolute (or prior to the final dissolution order); or

275

- a transfer made under a court order, whether or not by consent, after divorce or dissolution.

HMRC consider that such a disposal or transfer is, where there is no recourse to the courts, usually made in exchange for a surrender by the transferee of rights to obtain alternative financial provision. The value of the rights surrendered would represent actual consideration, reducing the potential hold-over relief claim to nil. However, relief may be available if the parties can demonstrate a 'substantial gratuitous element' in the transfer.

The position where certain court orders are made is viewed differently. A court order may reflect 'the exercise by the court of its independent statutory jurisdiction' rather than being the consequence of a party to the proceedings surrendering alternative rights in return for assets. In such a case HMRC consider that the spouse or civil partner to whom the assets are transferred does not give actual consideration for the transfer (CG 67190–67192).

Gifts to non-residents

13.19 Hold-over relief under *TCGA 1992, s 165* is denied where the transferee is:

(a) neither resident nor ordinarily resident in the UK; or

(b) an individual who is resident or ordinarily resident in the UK, where double taxation relief arrangements have the effect that he is regarded as resident in another territory and he would not be liable in the UK to tax on a gain arising on a disposal of the asset (*TCGA 1992, s 166*).

Emigration of transferee

13.20 Where hold-over relief has been given under either *TCGA 1992, s 165* or *TCGA 1992, s 260* on a disposal ('the relevant disposal') to an individual, and the transferee becomes neither resident nor ordinarily resident in the UK at a time when he has not disposed of the asset (see below), a chargeable gain equal to the held-over gain is deemed to accrue to the transferee immediately before that time.

The CGT annual exemption and any allowable losses available to the transferee at that time may be set against the deemed gain. However, the gain would not be eligible, for example, for roll-over relief on replacement of business assets (see **Chapter 14**) because it would not accrue on the actual disposal of an asset. Once the held-over gain has been clawed back in this way, the transferee's chargeable gain on a subsequent disposal is computed without any reduction in respect of the held-over gain.

There is no charge, however, where the transferee's change of residence status occurs more than six years after the end of the year of assessment in which the relevant disposal was made (*TCGA 1992, s 168(1), (4), (10)*).

Transferee's disposal of the asset

13.21 The transferee is taken to have disposed of the asset before the time of the change of residence status only if he has made one or more disposals on which the allowable expenditure, deducted in computing his gain, was reduced by the held-over gain on the relevant disposal. Where the transferee has made a disposal and only part of the transferor's gain went to reduce the transferee's allowable expenditure deductible on that disposal, the deemed chargeable gain accruing on the change of residence status is reduced accordingly (*TCGA 1992, s 168(2)*).

The transferee's disposal of an asset to his spouse or civil partner under a no gain/no loss transfer (under *TCGA 1992, s 58*) does not count as a disposal for this purpose, but a subsequent disposal by the spouse or civil partner is taken into account as if he (not the spouse or civil partner) made that disposal (*TCGA 1992, s 168(3)*).

Example 13.6

Hold-over relief is claimed on the transfer of an asset to H, who gives the asset to his wife W at a later date. If W then sells the asset, her disposal is treated as a disposal by H for these purposes.

A temporary change of residence status will not trigger a deemed chargeable gain where the transferee:

- becomes neither resident nor ordinarily resident in the UK because he works in an employment or office and all the duties are performed outside the UK;

- becomes resident or ordinarily resident in the UK once again within three years of losing that status; and

- has not disposed of the asset in the meantime.

With regard to this last condition, the transferee is taken to have disposed of an asset only if he has made a disposal on which the allowable expenditure, deducted in computing his gain, would have been reduced by the held-over gain on the relevant disposal if he had been UK resident (*TCGA 1992, s 168(5), (6)*).

Payment of tax

13.22   The tax on the chargeable gain deemed to accrue to the transferee may be assessed and charged on the transferor, in the name of the transferee, if it has been assessed on the transferee but not paid within 12 months of the due date. The transferor is entitled to recover the tax from the transferee. No such assessment may be made more than six years after the end of the year of assessment in which the transferor made the relevant disposal (*TCGA 1992, 168(7), (8), (9)*).

Gifts to foreign-controlled companies

13.23   Hold-over relief under *TCGA 1992, s 165* is denied where the transferee is a company that is controlled by one or more persons who are neither resident nor ordinarily resident in the UK but are connected with the person making the disposal.

A person who is resident or ordinarily resident in the UK is regarded as neither resident nor ordinarily resident in the UK for this purpose if:

- he controls a company – alone or with others – by virtue of holding assets relating to that company or another company; and

- double taxation relief arrangements have the effect that he is regarded as resident in another territory and would not be liable in the UK to tax on a gain arising on a disposal of the assets (*TCGA 1992, s 167*).

Gifts to dual-resident trusts

13.24   Where hold-over relief would otherwise be available under either *TCGA 1992, s 165* or *TCGA 1992, s 260* on a disposal ('the relevant disposal') to the trustees of a settlement, the relief is denied if:

(a)   at the 'material time' (ie the time of the relevant disposal) those trustees fall to be treated (under *TCGA 1992, s 69*), as resident and ordinarily resident in the UK, although the trust's general administration is ordinarily carried on outside the UK; and

(b)   on a notional disposal of the asset by the trustees immediately after the material time, they would be regarded under double taxation relief arrangements as resident in a territory outside the UK and not liable to UK tax on any gain arising (*TCGA 1992, s 169*).

With effect for relevant disposals after 5 April 2007, the condition in (a) is amended so that it applies where, at the material time, the trustees are resident and ordinarily resident in the UK. The reference to a gain 'arising' in (b) is replaced by a reference to a gain 'accruing' (*TCGA 1992, s 169(3)* as amended by *FA 2006, Sch 12, para 37*).

Agricultural property

13.25   Hold-over relief under *TCGA 1992, s 165* is available where the asset disposed of is, or is an interest in, agricultural property (as defined in the *Inheritance Tax Act 1984 (IHTA 1984), Pt V, Ch II)* if:

(a)   the disposal does not qualify for hold-over relief under the normal rules only because the agricultural property is not used for the purposes of a trade carried on as set out in **13.5**; and

(b)   agricultural property relief is obtained in respect of the transfer of value for inheritance tax purposes, or it would be obtained if the transfer was a chargeable transfer, or it would be obtained but for certain rules relating to transfers within seven years before the transferor's death (*TCGA 1992, s 165, Sch 7, para 1*).

Agricultural property relief for inheritance tax purposes is available in respect of the agricultural value only, ie it is not available for any 'hope or development value' inherent in the property. However, HMRC consider that CGT hold-over relief can be allowed on the whole of the gain (not just the part reflecting agricultural value) because hold-over relief is given by reference to the nature of the asset transferred rather than its value (CG 66962).

Trustees

13.26   Hold-over relief under *TCGA 1992, s 165* is available where the trustees of a settlement make a disposal of an asset mentioned in (a) or (b) below otherwise than under a bargain at arm's length:

(a)   an asset, or an interest in an asset, used for the purposes of a trade, profession or vocation carried on by (i) the trustees making the disposal, or (ii) a beneficiary who had an interest in possession in the settled property immediately before the disposal;

(b)   shares or securities of a trading company, or of the holding company of a trading group, where either (i) the shares or securities are not listed on a recognised stock exchange, or (ii) the trustees are able to exercise at least 25% of the voting rights.

Claims to hold-over relief in respect of disposals by trustees are made by trustees and the transferee (or by the trustees alone if the trustees of a settlement are also the transferee) (*TCGA 1992, Sch 7, para 2*).

The relief is extended to a disposal of agricultural property by trustees, as described in **13.25** in relation to non-settled property (*TCGA 1992, Sch 7, para 3*).

Hold-over relief under *TCGA 1992, s 260* is also available for transfers from certain trusts where an inheritance tax charge would arise but for their 'tax-favoured' status (see **13.38**).

Gifts to settlor-interested settlements

13.27 Hold-over relief is generally not available on a disposal after 9 December 2003 to the trustees of a settlement in which the settlor has an interest. The settlor here can be someone other than the person making the disposal.

Relief may also be denied where there is an 'arrangement' for the settlor to acquire an interest in the settlement, and relief may be clawed back or blocked if the settlement becomes settlor-interested in the period ending six years following the tax year in which the disposal was made.

Hold-over relief under either *TCGA 1992, s 165* or *TCGA 1992, s 260* is excluded where the disposal (the 'relevant disposal') is made by a person ('the transferor') to the trustees of a settlement and either of the following two conditions is satisfied in relation to the disposal:

- Condition 1 is that immediately after the relevant disposal there is a 'settlor' who has an 'interest in the settlement', or an 'arrangement' exists under which the settlor will (or may) acquire such an interest. The various terms are defined below.

- Condition 2 is that:

  (a) a chargeable gain would (in the absence of hold-over relief under either *TCGA 1992, s 165* or *TCGA 1992, s 260*) accrue to the transferor on the disposal to the trustees;

  (b) in computing the transferor's gain on that disposal, his allowable expenditure would be reduced directly or indirectly because of a hold-over relief claim made on an earlier disposal made by an individual; and

  (c) immediately after the relevant disposal (i) that individual has an interest in the settlement, or (ii) an arrangement exists under which that individual will or may acquire such an interest.

Relief is not available where either condition 1 or condition 2 is met. There are exceptions for maintenance funds for historic buildings and certain settlements for people with disabilities (*TCGA 1992, ss 169B, 169D*).

Clawback of relief: settlement becoming settlor-interested

13.28 Once obtained, hold-over relief may be clawed back where either condition 1 or condition 2 above is met at any time during the 'clawback period'. This is the period beginning with the relevant disposal and ending six years after the end of the year of assessment in which the disposal took place.

Example 13.7

Mervyn transfers to trustees an asset used for the purposes of a trade carried on by his personal company. The transfer takes place on 10 May 2006 and he claims hold-over relief. He is the only settlor and does not have an interest in the settlement (see the definitions below). The relief may be clawed back if he acquires an interest in the settlement before 6 April 2013.

Where the clawback is triggered, a chargeable gain of an amount equal to the held-over gain is treated as accruing to the transferor at the 'material time', ie the time when either condition 1 or condition 2 is first met – not at the time of the relevant disposal. If no claim to hold-over relief is made before the material time, then the relief may not be claimed in relation to that disposal.

Once again, there are exceptions for maintenance funds for historic buildings and certain settlements for people with disabilities (*TCGA 1992, ss 169C, 169D*).

Definitions

13.29 The following definitions are provided for the purpose of the rules governing gifts to settlor-interested settlements.

Settlor

13.30 A person is a settlor in relation to a settlement if he is an individual and the settled property consists of, or includes, property originating from him. Property is deemed to originate from him if he has provided it directly or indirectly, or it represents such property (or any part of it, or accumulated income from it). Property provided directly or indirectly by another person under reciprocal arrangements with the settlor is treated as provided directly or indirectly by the settlor (*TCGA 1992, s 169E*).

Interest in a settlement

13.31   Prior to 6 April 2006 (see below) an individual is regarded as having an interest in a settlement if either (a) or (b) below applies:

(a)   any property that may at any time be comprised in the settlement, or any 'derived property' (as defined below), is, or will or may become, in any circumstances, either payable to the individual or his spouse or civil partner or applicable for their benefit; or

(b)   the individual or his spouse or civil partner enjoys a benefit deriving directly or indirectly from property comprised in the settlement, or from 'derived property'.

A separated spouse or civil partner, and a widow (or widower or surviving civil partner), are ignored in determining whether an individual has an interest in a settlement (*TCGA 1992, s 169F*).

A future interest is ignored for this purpose if it could only arise:

•   in the case of a marriage settlement or civil partnership settlement, on the death of both parties to the marriage or civil partnership and of all or any of their children; or

•   on the death of a child of the individual where the child had become beneficially entitled to the property (or any derived property) by age 25 (*TCGA 1992, s 169F(5)*).

The following changes were introduced by *FA 2006*. Subject to certain exceptions, the changes have effect in determining whether an individual is regarding as having, on or after 6 April 2006, an interest in a settlement (whenever the settlement was created). However, they do not apply if the disposal giving rise to the gain to be held over is made on or before 6 April 2006:

(i)   The condition in (a) above is extended to include any property that '*is or may at any time be comprised in the settlement*' etc;

(ii)   An individual is now regarded as having an interest in a settlement if:

(a)   any property which is or may at any time be comprised in the settlement, or any derived property, is, or will or may become, payable to or applicable for the benefit of a child of the individual, at a time when that child is a dependent child of his, in any circumstances whatsoever; or

(b)   a dependent child of the individual enjoys a benefit deriving directly or indirectly from any property which is comprised in the settlement or any derived property.

(iii)   'Dependent child' means a child who is under the age of 18, is unmarried, and does not have a civil partner. 'Child' includes a stepchild (*FA 2006, Sch 12, para 4*).

Arrangement

13.32   An arrangement includes any scheme, agreement or understanding, whether or not legally enforceable (*TCGA 1992, s 169G*).

Derived property

13.33   Property is 'derived property', in relation to any other property if it is:

(a)   income from that other property;

(b)   property directly or indirectly representing either proceeds of that other property or proceeds of income from that other property; or

(c)   income from property that is derived property because it is within (b) above (*TCGA 1992, s 169F(6)*).

Claims

13.34   The relief must be claimed by both donor and donee. However, if the gift is made into a trust, the relief claim is made by the donor alone.

HMRC require claimants to use the form in their tax return helpsheet IR 295, or a copy of the form. Their guidance refers to 'serious problems' having arisen in some cases from a lack of information held by the donee at the time of the eventual disposal of the asset. A claim must be made by the taxpayer personally, or by his personal representatives (CG 66914).

The claim will usually be made when submitting the tax return, but otherwise it must be made within five years from 31 January following the end of the tax year in which the disposal was made (*TMA 1970, s 43*). This time limit may be effectively extended where an assessment is made to recover tax lost through fraudulent or negligent conduct (under *TMA 1970, s 36*).

HMRC will accept claims to hold-over relief under either *TCGA 1992, s 165* or *TCGA 1992, s 260*, in certain circumstances, without agreeing the market value of the asset transferred (see **13.46**).

Incorporation of a business

13.35   Hold-over relief under *TCGA 1992, s 165* may be available where a business carried on by an individual or a partnership is transferred to a company. Incorporation is examined further in **Chapter 15**.

Where the business together with all of its assets (or all of its assets other than cash) is transferred to the company as a going concern in exchange for shares in the company, roll-over relief under *TCGA 1992, s 162* (see **15.1**) may be available. That relief is given automatically – it does not need to be claimed – unless the taxpayer makes an election for the relief not to apply.

Where the taxpayer cannot meet the conditions of *TCGA 1992, s 162* (eg where he wishes to retain the business property or other assets outside the company) then hold-over relief under *TCGA 1992, s 165* may provide a useful alternative relief to defer gains on the assets actually transferred. The transfer to the company must, however, be a disposal made otherwise than by way of a bargain at arm's length. In most cases the transaction will be deemed to be made otherwise than by way of a bargain at arm's length because it will be made between connected persons (see **3.10**).

Where a claim to hold-over relief under *TCGA 1992, s 165* is made in relation to the incorporation of a business and there is actual consideration for the disposal, the held-over gain is reduced as explained at **13.7**. Care is needed where the consideration for goodwill, for example, takes the form of shares issued in exchange for assets because the amount of that consideration is determined by reference to the market value of the shares.

However, hold-over relief should be available without restriction on the transfer of goodwill if:

- the shares are subscribed for separately;

- goodwill is transferred to the company for a nominal cash sum;

- other assets are transferred at their book value; and

- the total consideration is credited to the transferor's loan account with the company.

HMRC guidance indicates that each asset will be considered separately providing there is no reason to suppose that the sale price of any of the assets is 'excessive'. HMRC may ask to see the sale agreement and compare it with the company's opening statement of affairs in order to determine precisely what consideration has been given for the various assets (CG 66978, CG 66979).

Example 13.8

Susan has carried on her antique dealing business for ten years. She let the shop premises for one year before she commenced trading. In October 2006, Susan transferred the business as a going concern to a limited company that she formed with share capital of £1,000 held wholly by her. The transfer consideration is £1.

The gain arising in respect of the freehold premises is £165,000 and on goodwill it is £45,000 (both after deducting indexation allowance to April 1998). Susan and the company must jointly elect to hold over the gain on the gift of business assets to the company.

	Freehold £	Goodwill £	Total £
Total gains	165,000	45,000	200,000
Reduction for non-trade use 1/11 yrs	(15,000)		(15,000)
Held-over gains	150,000	45,000	195,000

The remaining gains of £15,000 are chargeable, but are eligible for taper relief.

Interaction with other reliefs

13.36   Hold-over relief for gifts is given after indexation allowance and other reliefs (eg roll-over relief on the incorporation of a business under *TCGA 1992, s 162*), but before taper relief. Where hold-over relief is obtained without restriction, any taper relief relating to the transferor's period of ownership is lost. Taper relief is discussed in **Chapter 11** and the interaction of various reliefs is examined further in **Chapter 15**.

GIFTS ON WHICH INHERITANCE TAX IS CHARGEABLE, ETC

13.37   Hold-over relief is available for gifts on which inheritance tax is immediately chargeable (or would be chargeable but for an exemption or the availability of the inheritance tax nil rate band). Such gifts include transfers to and from discretionary trusts (*TCGA 1992, s 260*).

Where such a hold-over claim is made (or could have been made) a deduction is available, in computing the gain on the subsequent disposal, for any IHT charged on the gift (see **13.42**).

Conditions

13.38   Both the transferor and the transferee may be either an individual or trustees of a settlement. Where the conditions set out below are met, the relief remains subject to various restrictions including:

- the restrictions set out in **13.8** in relation to *TCGA 1992, s 165* relief; and

- the exclusion mentioned at **13.43** for gifts to non-residents (*TCGA 1992, s 260(1)*).

The relief applies to a disposal that is made otherwise than under a bargain at arm's length, where the disposal meets any of the following conditions:

(a)   it is a chargeable transfer for inheritance tax purposes (or would be a chargeable transfer but for the annual exemption for gifts) and is not a potentially exempt transfer (see *IHTA 1984, ss 2, 3A* and *19*);

(b)   it is an exempt transfer to a political party, or an exempt transfer to a maintenance fund for historic buildings, etc, or a conditionally exempt transfer of designated property (*IHTA 1984, ss 24, 27, 30*);

(c)   it is a disposition whereby property enters a maintenance fund meeting certain conditions and *IHTA 1984, s 57A* applies to the disposition;

(d)   it is a transfer made by the trustees of an accumulation and maintenance trust, and inheritance tax is not chargeable by virtue of *IHTA 1984, s 71(4)*;

(e)   it is a transfer made after 21 March 2006 by trustees of a trust for a bereaved minor, and inheritance tax is not chargeable by virtue of *IHTA 1984, s 71B(2)*;

(f)   it is a transfer made after 21 March 2006 by trustees of an age 18–25 trust, and inheritance tax is not chargeable by virtue of *IHTA 1984, s 71E(2)*;

(g)   it is a transfer of a work of art, etc qualifying for the conditional exemption in *IHTA 1984, s 78(1)*; or

(h)   it is a disposal of an asset comprised in a settlement and the provisions of *IHTA 1984, Sch 4, para 9, 16,* or *17* (dealing with transfers to maintenance funds for historic buildings, etc) apply to reduce or eliminate an inheritance tax charge where the asset becomes comprised in another settlement.

Conditions (e) and (f) were added with effect from 22 March 2006 (*TCGA 1992, s 260(2); FA 2006, Sch 20, para 32*).

Operation of TCGA 1992, s 260 relief

13.39   The effect of this relief, which must be claimed (see **13.45**), is that the 'held-over gain' (see below) is deducted from both:

- the chargeable gain (if any) that would otherwise accrue to the transferor; and

- the consideration which the transferee would otherwise be regarded as having given for the acquisition of the asset (*TCGA 1992, s 260(3)*).

The 'held-over gain' on a disposal, where this relief is not restricted by reference to actual consideration received for the disposal, is the chargeable gain that would have accrued in the absence of hold-over relief (*TCGA 1992, s 260(4)*).

The relief may be restricted where consideration is received (see **13.40**) or as described in **13.41**.

Consideration received

13.40   Where a claim to hold-over relief is made and there is actual consideration for the disposal, and that consideration exceeds the allowable expenditure deductible in computing the gain, the held-over gain is reduced by that excess. This restriction does not apply, however, to certain disposals deemed to occur in relation to accumulation and maintenance trusts, employee trusts or newspaper trusts (within *IHTA 1984, s 71(1)* or *s 72(1)*) (*TCGA 1992, s 260(5), (9)*).

Partial relief

13.41   If the disposal only partly meets the conditions in **13.38**, or the condition in **13.38**(h) is met and the inheritance tax charge is reduced but not eliminated, then hold-over relief applies only to an 'appropriate part' of the disposal (*TCGA 1992, s 260(10)*).

Relief for inheritance tax

13.42   Where there is a chargeable transfer for inheritance tax purposes as mentioned in **13.38**(a), CGT relief is available to the transferee as follows, whether or not hold-over relief is obtained under *TCGA 1992, s 260*.

The transferee is entitled to a deduction in computing for CGT purposes the chargeable gain accruing on his disposal of the asset. The deduction is equal to the inheritance tax attributable to the value of the asset, but it cannot exceed the amount of the chargeable gain before the deduction. The deduction is adjusted in the event that the inheritance tax is varied after it has been taken into account in this way (*TCGA 1992, s 260(7), (8)*).

Gifts to non-residents

13.43   Hold-over relief under *TCGA 1992, s 260* is denied where the transferee is:

(a)   neither resident nor ordinarily resident in the UK; or

(b)   an individual who is resident or ordinarily resident in the UK, where double taxation relief arrangements have the effect that he is regarded as resident in another territory and he would not be liable in the UK to tax on a gain arising on a disposal of the asset (*TCGA 1992, s 261*).

Emigration of transferee

13.44   Where hold-over relief has been given under either *TCGA 1992, s 165* or *TCGA 1992, s 260* on a disposal ('the relevant disposal') to an individual, and the transferee becomes neither resident nor ordinarily resident in the UK at a time when he has not disposed of the asset (see below), a chargeable gain equal to the held-over gain is deemed to accrue to the transferee immediately before that time. See **13.20**.

Claims

13.45   A claim for relief under *TCGA 1992, s 260* is made by the transferor and the transferee or, where the trustees of a settlement are the transferee, by the transferor alone. The standard hold-over relief claim form attached to HMRC helpsheet IR 295 must be used (see **13.34**).

The claim will usually be made when submitting the tax return, but must otherwise be made within five years from 31 January following the end of the tax year in which the disposal was made (*TCGA 1992, s 260(1)(c)*).

HMRC will accept claims to hold-over relief under either *TCGA 1992, s 165* or *TCGA 1992, s 260*, in certain circumstances, without agreeing the market value of the asset transferred (see **13.46**).

VALUATIONS

13.46   HMRC will accept claims to hold-over relief under either *TCGA 1992, s 165* or *TCGA 1992, s 260*, in certain circumstances, without formal agreement of the market value of the asset transferred. The conditions and procedures are set out in HMRC statement of practice SP 8/92 and summarised below.

The market value rule (see **13.1**) requires the transferor to establish the market value of the asset at the date of the transfer in order to compute the chargeable gain accruing and the held-over gain where a claim is made. However, where hold-over relief is available without restriction, agreement of the asset's market value at the date of transfer has no bearing on the transferor's CGT liability.

HMRC will admit a claim to hold-over relief without requiring a computation of the held-over gain where both the transferor and transferee complete the 'request for valuations to be deferred', found on page seven of HMRC's helpsheet IR 295 (and forming the second page of the hold-over relief claim). The form requires:

- a joint application by the transferor and the transferee;

- details of the asset, its history and an informal estimate of the asset's market value at the date of transfer – such an estimate is not binding on either the claimants or HMRC; and

- a statement that both parties are satisfied that the value of the asset at the date of transfer was such that there would be a chargeable gain but for the claim (helpsheet IR 295).

HMRC's guidance indicates that taxpayers will not be asked for a computation of the held-over gain so long as the asset is properly identified and the formalities of the hold-over relief claim are satisfied. The requirement for both parties to sign the application for deferral of the valuation applies where the transferee is a body of trustees, even though the trustees are not required to sign the actual hold-over claim. HMRC regards it as essential that anyone whose liability may be affected by the valuation has agreed to the postponement (CG 67131, CG 67132).

Once HMRC has accepted a hold-over relief claim made on this basis, the claim may not be withdrawn. The relevant statutory provisions will be applied, and assessments made as necessary, if it emerges that any information provided by either the transferor or transferee was incorrect or incomplete.

HMRC will not apply the statement of practice in a case where the held-over gain is restricted as shown in **13.8** (as provided in *TCGA 1992, Sch 7, paras 5, 6* and *7*) because the amount of chargeable gain accruing to the transferor depends in such a case on a valuation being made.

In some other cases it will be necessary to establish market value before a later disposal of the asset by the transferee. The statement of practice outlines some of those circumstances in relation to:

- assets held at 31 March 1982;
- retirement relief;

13.46   *Hold-over relief for gifts*

- relief in respect of deferred charges on gains before 31 March 1982; and
- time apportionment for assets held on 6 April 1965.

Chapter 14

Roll-over relief for business assets

INTRODUCTION

14.1　　The effect of roll-over relief is to defer a chargeable gain where the proceeds of disposal of business assets (the 'old assets') are used to invest in new business assets. The old and the new assets must be used in the business. The relief must be claimed. Spouses and civil partners are separate persons for roll-over relief. The rules specific to companies are examined in **Chapter 9**; this chapter is of general application except where stated otherwise.

Roll-over relief is applied by deducting the gain from the acquisition cost of the new assets. The claim does not affect the tax position of the other parties to the transactions. The gain deferred – or rolled over – in this way may give rise to a CGT liability on a disposal of the replacement assets, but roll-over relief may be claimed on that disposal if the conditions are met. A chargeable gain may arise on the disposal of the old assets if the relief claimed on that disposal is restricted (*TCGA 1992, s 152*).

A rolled over gain escapes CGT in the event of the taxpayer's death. In some cases, however, the gain on the old asset is 'postponed' instead of being 'rolled over' or deducted from the cost of the new asset.

There are separate time limits for reinvestment of the consideration for the disposal (see **14.35**) and claims (see **14.37**). Both the assets disposed of and the replacement assets must fall within one of the classes of asset listed in **14.15**, but the new assets need not fall within the same class as the old assets.

Where a provision of *TCGA 1992* fixes the consideration deemed to be given for the acquisition or disposal – for example, transactions between connected persons are treated as undertaken for a consideration equal to market value – the deemed consideration is treated as the actual consideration for the purpose of roll-over relief (*TCGA 1992, s 152(10)*).

CONDITIONS

General

14.2   Roll-over relief must be claimed. It is available if the taxpayer:

- carries on a trade;

- disposes of assets (or his interest in assets) used only for the purposes of that trade throughout the period of ownership (the 'old assets');

- applies the consideration obtained for the disposal in acquiring other assets (or an interest in other assets) (the 'old assets'); and

- uses the new assets solely for the purposes of the trade.

The effect of the relief is that:

(a)   the consideration for the disposal of the old assets is reduced to the amount that would give rise to neither a gain nor a loss accruing on the disposal; and

(b)   the amount (or value) of the consideration that the taxpayer gives for the acquisition of the new assets is reduced by the amount of the reduction in (a).

The CGT treatment of the other parties to the transactions is not affected. Both the old assets and new assets must be within the classes of assets listed in *TCGA 1992, s 155*, although they do not need to be in the same class as each other (see **14.15**) (*TCGA 1992, s 152(1)*).

'Trade' has the same meaning for roll-over relief as it has in the Income Tax Acts, and *ICTA 1988, s 832* provides that 'trade' includes every trade, manufacture, adventure or concern in the nature of trade. However, relief is extended to other activities (see **14.9**) (*TCGA 1992, s 158(2)*).

Tracing the disposal proceeds

14.3   It is not normally necessary to trace the actual proceeds and match them to the funds invested in the new assets. The new assets can, for example, be funded by borrowings. HMRC recognise that seeking to trace the disposal proceeds through to the acquisition of the new assets would result in relief being denied in most cases. Where the new asset is acquired before the old one is disposed of, the disposal consideration cannot be applied in this way. Where the disposal comes first, the consideration is likely to be put to some other purpose. Paying the proceeds into a bank account, for example, gives rise to the acquisition of a debt.

There is an exception, however, where the taxpayer is seeking an extension to the reinvestment time limits. In this case he may need to be able to demonstrate a continuing intention to reinvest the disposal consideration within the extended time limit (see **14.36**) (CG 60770, CG 60771).

Allocating the consideration

14.4   Where there is more than one acquisition HMRC will accept the taxpayer's allocation of the gain to be rolled over against the new assets. HMRC consider that there must be a specific allocation before the claim can be allowed (CG 60775, CG 60776).

Residence

14.5   HMRC accept that relief may be claimed even if the replacement assets are outside the UK, except in the case of furnished holiday accommodation which must be in the UK. Relief will not be denied where all the conditions are met but, at the time the new assets are acquired, the taxpayer has ceased to be resident or ordinarily resident in the UK (CG 60253).

However, there is a potential charge for 'temporary non-residents' (see **5.16**) where a gain has been the subject of a roll-over relief claim (either under the normal rules or under the special rules for new assets that are depreciating assets, see **14.31**) and there is a disposal of the new asset during a period of temporary non-residence. The gain may be treated as accruing to the temporary non-resident on his return to the UK (see **5.17**) (*TCGA 1992, s 10A(3), (4)* (CG 26230)).

Non-residents with UK branch, etc

14.6   However, if a gain arising on the old assets would be chargeable under *TCGA 1992, s 10(1)* (non-resident with a UK branch or agency) or *TCGA 1992, s 10B* (non-resident company with a UK permanent establishment) then roll-over relief is not available unless the new assets, immediately after they are acquired, would also fall within *s 10(1)* or *s 10B* on a disposal (*TCGA 1992, s 159(1)*).

This condition does not apply if:

(a)   the relevant acquisition takes place after the disposal and the taxpayer is resident or ordinarily resident in the UK immediately after the acquisition; or

(b)   immediately after the time the new assets are acquired:

- the taxpayer is a 'dual resident', ie a person who is both resident or ordinarily resident in the UK and regarded for double tax relief purposes as resident elsewhere, and

- the assets are 'prescribed assets', ie assets specified in a double tax agreement with the effect that the dual resident is regarded as not liable in the UK to tax on gains accruing to him on a disposal (*TCGA 1992, s 159(2), (3), (5)*).

Other conditions

14.7   There are conditions relating to qualifying activities (see **14.8**); assets (see **14.15**); and the time when the new assets must be taken into use (see **14.22**).

QUALIFYING ACTIVITIES

14.8   Roll-over relief is available where a person carrying on a trade reinvests the proceeds of disposal of assets used for the purposes of the trade in the acquisition of new assets to be used for the purposes of the same trade. See below regarding qualifying activities other than trades.

No relief is due if the new assets are acquired wholly or partly for the purpose of realising a gain from their disposal (*TCGA 1992, s 152(5)*).

HMRC accept that this rule is not intended to deny relief merely because it is expected the asset will be sold at a profit at some stage. HMRC guidance says:

'The point turns on the claimant's intentions at the time of acquisition. If the intention is to keep the asset and to use it for trade purposes, relief may be allowed. If the intention is to dispose of the asset and its trade use is merely a temporary convenience, relief should be denied. An example is where a farmer acquires more land than is required (perhaps because the vendor will not sell less than an entire estate) and intends to dispose of the surplus, often to finance the cost of the part retained' (CG 60406).

A person who carries on two or more trades, either at the same time or in succession, is regarded as carrying on a single trade (*TCGA 1992, s 152(8)*).

HMRC are prepared to regard trades as being carried on 'successively' if the interval does not exceed three years, but the time limits for reinvestment must still be met (see **14.35**). Relief will be available, but may be restricted by reference to non-trade use, if the old assets are disposed of during the interval. New assets acquired during the interval may qualify as replacement assets provided they are not used or leased for any purpose before the new trade begins, and are taken into use for the purpose of the trade on commencement (HMRC statement of practice SP 8/81; CG 60501).

Activities other than trades

14.9   The main roll-over relief provisions in *TCGA 1992, ss 152–157* refer only to trades. The relief is extended to replacement of assets used for the purpose of a profession, vocation, office or employment (*TCGA 1992, s 158*).

Where relief is claimed in respect of assets used for the purposes of the claimant's office or employment, it will not be denied because the asset is also used by the employer for the purposes of the employer's trade. HMRC regard the 'sole use' condition as satisfied unless the asset is used for some purpose 'alien to' the office or employment (CG 60540–60544).

So far as land and buildings are concerned, the employee must occupy the asset as owner and not merely as a licensee of the employer. HMRC guidance says:

> 'If land or buildings are owned by an employee etc, but made available to the employer for general use in his trade, the employee etc may nonetheless satisfy the occupation test of *TCGA 1992, s 155* provided the employer does not make any payment (or give other consideration) for his use of the property nor otherwise occupy it under a lease or tenancy. The qualifying use of assets by an employee etc for the purposes of *TCGA 1992, ss 152* and *153* will include any use or occupation of those assets by him, in the course of performing the duties of his employment or office, as directed by the employer' (HMRC statement of practice SP 5/86).

A taxpayer who meets the conditions of *TCGA 1992, s 152* by reference to his office or employment and at the same time meets the conditions of *TCGA 1992, s 157* (see **14.10**) may choose under which heading he wishes to claim relief (CG 60505).

The taxpayer may carry on two different activities, for example a trade and an employment, at the same time or successively. The fact that the two activities are different does not prevent relief applying so long as the various conditions including, where appropriate, the terms of HMRC statement of practice SP 8/81 (see above) are met.

'Trade', 'profession', 'vocation', 'office' and 'employment' have the same meaning for roll-over relief as they have in the Income Tax Acts, so that farming, and the commercial letting of furnished holiday accommodation in the UK that falls within *TCGA 1992, s 241*, may qualify (*TCGA 1992, ss 158(2), 241(3)*).

The relief also applies to the replacement of assets used for the purposes of the following activities, as it applies in relation to trades:

- the discharge of the functions of a public authority;

- the occupation of woodlands managed by the occupier on a commercial basis;

- the activities of a non-profit making body that are wholly or mainly directed to the protection or promotion of its members' trade or professional interests; and

- the activities of an unincorporated association or other body chargeable to corporation tax, but not established for profit, whose activities are wholly or mainly carried on otherwise than for profit, for example, trade unions, sports clubs and local constituency associations of political parties. The body must use the assets for the purpose of its activities, and in the case of land and buildings within Head A of Class 1 (see **14.15**) the body must both occupy and use them for those activities (rather than letting them). By concession (ESC D15), HMRC regard relief as being available where the assets are held by a company in which at least 90% of the shares are held by or on behalf of such a body or its members (*TCGA 1992, s 158(1)*).

Trade carried on by the taxpayer's personal company

14.10 The relief is extended to the situation where the owner of the asset is an individual but the trade is carried on by a company. The individual is deemed to be carrying on the trade(s), for the purpose of the conditions in *TCGA 1992, ss 152–156*, where:

(a) the person disposing of the old assets (or an interest in them) and acquiring the new assets (or an interest in them) is an individual; and

(b) the trade or trades in question are carried on by a company which is his 'personal company' (*TCGA 1992, s 157*).

The condition in (b) must be met both at the time of the disposal and at the time of the acquisition referred to in (a). A company is the taxpayer's 'personal company' if he can exercise at least 5% of the voting rights.

HMRC consider that both the old and new assets must be used for qualifying activities of the same personal company, on the basis that *TCGA 1992, s 157* directs that *TCGA 1992, s 52* should be read as if it said:

'If the consideration which an individual obtains for the disposal of ... the old assets used and used only for the purposes of the trade carried on by his ... personal company ... is applied by him in acquiring ... the new assets which on the acquisition are taken into use, and used only, for the purposes of the trade carried on by that ... personal company ... ' (CG 60504).

Trade carried on by a partnership

14.11   The CGT treatment of partnerships is examined in detail in **Chapter 6**. Roll-over relief extends to a business partner's interest in the chargeable assets of a partnership (*TCGA 1992, s 157*).

Where the partnership disposes of an asset qualifying for relief, or there is a reduction in the partner's share of the partnership's capital assets following a change in the asset-sharing ratio, the partner may obtain roll-over relief by means of either:

- the partnership's acquisition of qualifying assets in which the partner has an interest; or

- the partner's acquisition in qualifying assets, either used by the partnership (see below) or unrelated to the partnership's business.

Relief is also available for assets used in the partnership's trade but owned by an individual partner rather than the partnership. This applies even if the partner receives rent for the use of the asset (HMRC statement of practice D11).

Where land used for the purposes of a partnership's trade is 'partitioned' by the partners on a dissolution of the partnership, strictly speaking no roll-over relief is due because an exchange of interests in a single asset does not involve the acquisition of 'other assets'. By concession, HMRC will treat the land acquired as a new asset providing that:

- the partnership is dissolved immediately after the exchange; and

- the former partners retain an interest only in land used by them in a new trading enterprise and do not retain any interest in that part of the land no longer used by them for trade purposes (HMRC concession ESC D23).

Spouse and civil partners

14.12   In *Tod v Mudd* [1986] 60 TC 237, Ch D, it was established that spouses are separate persons for the purpose of roll-over relief so that the conditions for relief apply separately to each person's interest in an asset used by a husband and wife partnership. Mr Mudd and his wife acquired as tenants in common a new asset in the form of a property. They used it as to 75% as a guest house, and the remaining 25% as their residence.

A trust deed recorded that the property would be held by them upon trust as to 75% for Mr Mudd and as to 25% for his wife. Mr Mudd claimed that 75% of the cost of acquisition of the premises qualified for roll-over relief in relation to his earlier disposal of his accountancy practice.

It was held that he was entitled to relief only in respect of the proportion (75%) of his undivided share (75%) of the premises. The same principle would extend, with effect from 5 December 2005, to civil partners who are also partners in business.

Limited liability partnerships

14.13 A limited liability partnership (LLP) is treated for CGT purposes in the same way as any other partnership while it is trading, despite being a body corporate. The LLP itself is regarded as transparent for CGT purposes, with each member being charged to tax on his share of any gains accruing to the LLP (*TCGA 1992, s 59A*).

However, when an LLP ceases to trade, it loses its tax 'transparency' and reverts to its corporate status (unless there is merely a temporary break in trading where, for example, the LLP has ceased to carry on one trade and disposed of its assets in order to raise funds to start another trade) (*TCGA 1992, s 59A(2), (3)*).

Any gains rolled over or postponed by a member of the LLP might escape as a result of the reversion to corporate status but for a special rule that deems the member to have realised a chargeable gain immediately before the LLP ceased to be transparent. This rule operates as set out below:

- Where, immediately before 'the time of cessation of trade' (see below), an LLP member holds an asset (or an interest in an asset) that he acquired for a consideration treated as reduced by virtue of a roll-over relief claim under *s 152* or *s 153*, he is treated as if a chargeable gain equal to the amount of the reduction accrued to him immediately before that time.

- Where a gain postponed by virtue of a *s 154(2)* claim (see **14.13**) made by an LLP member has not accrued before the time of cessation of trade, he is treated as if that gain accrued immediately before that time.

- 'The time of cessation of trade', is the time when *s 59A(1)* ceases to apply to the LLP, ie when it loses its tax transparency (*TCGA 1992, s 156A*).

Groups of companies

14.14 The trades carried on by members of a group of companies (as defined) are treated as a single trade for roll-over relief purposes. The rules specific to companies are examined in **Chapter 9**.

ASSETS

14.15 Both the old assets and the new assets must fall within one of the nine classes listed in *TCGA 1992, s 155*, but they do not have to fall within the same class as each other. These classes are summarised in Table 14.1, and explained further in the following paragraphs.

Table 14.1

Class 1, Head A (see below)	1. Any building or part of a building, and any permanent or semi-permanent structure in the nature of a building, occupied (as well as used) only for the purposes of the trade. 2. Any land occupied (as well as used) only for the purposes of the trade.
Class 1, Head B	Fixed plant or machinery that does not form part of a building or of a permanent or semi-permanent structure in the nature of a building.
Class 2	Ships, aircraft and hovercraft
Class 3	Satellites, space stations and spacecraft (including launch vehicles)
Class 4	Goodwill
Class 5	Milk quotas and potato quotas
Class 6	Ewe and suckler cow premium quotas
Class 7	Fish quotas
Class 7A	Payment entitlements under the single payment scheme for farmers
Class 8	Certain rights and assets of Lloyd's underwriters

Land and buildings

14.16 Head A of Class 1 is excluded where the trade is a trade of dealing in or developing land. However, Head A can apply where a profit on the sale of any land held for the purposes of the trade would not form part of the trading profits.

Head A does not apply where the trade is a trade of providing services for the occupier of land in which the trader has an estate or interest. A lessor of tied premises is treated as both occupying and using the premises for the purposes of the trade (*TCGA 1992, s 156*).

Fixed plant or machinery

14.17 It was established in *Williams v Evans* [1982] 59 TC 509, Ch D that in Head B of Class 1, the word 'fixed' applies to both plant and machinery. Motor vehicles, for example, would normally be excluded. HMRC apply four tests in determining whether an item of plant or plant or machinery is fixed:

(a)   In the context of the particular trade, is the object plant or machinery as opposed to, for example, trading stock or part of a building?

(b)   Does the taxpayer intend to hold the object in a particular location indefinitely?

(c)   Is the location of the object in a particular site essential to its function in the trade?

(d)   What means of permanent fixing are available, or necessary, without rendering the object part of the land or buildings, and without damaging or destroying the object? (CG 60970–60975).

Ships, aircraft, etc

14.18   HMRC accept that 'ships' in Class 3 includes fishing boats, motorised cruisers and yachts, and that 'aircraft' includes aeroplanes, helicopters, airships and hot air balloons (CG 61060).

Goodwill

14.19   With regard to goodwill, in *Balloon Promotions Ltd v HMRC* [2006] SPC 524 a franchisee operating a restaurant business sold the business to the franchisor and allocated part of the consideration to goodwill not inherent in the property. HMRC contended that there was no saleable goodwill and that the consideration represented compensation for early termination of the franchise agreements. The Special Commissioner held that goodwill was attached to the franchisee's business, and that the consideration obtained for it qualified for roll-over relief. He also questioned the approach taken by HMRC in their capital gains tax manual, which categorises goodwill into three types.

Companies: intangible assets

14.20   Classes 4 to 7 in Table 14.1 do not apply to companies, except where transitional rules apply for acquisitions before 1 April 2002, because the assets listed are now included in the corporation tax regime for intangible assets introduced in the *Finance Act 2002*. See **Chapter 9**.

Acquisition of 'other assets'

14.21   The legislation refers to investment in 'other assets' but by concession, where a person disposes of a trade (or a trade asset) and repurchases the same asset later for purely commercial reasons, HMRC will regard that asset as a 'new asset' unless the disposal and reacquisition 'appears to have been carried out for avoidance purposes'. This concession may be applied to partnership changes resulting in reacquisition of fractional shares in partnership assets (HMRC concession ESC D16).

However, it was held in *Watton v Tippett* [1997] 69 TC 491, CA that a gain arising on a part disposal of land and buildings cannot be rolled over against the acquisition of the part retained after the part disposal.

By concession, capital expenditure to enhance the value of other assets is treated as incurred in acquiring other assets provided that:

- the other assets are used only for the purposes of the trade; or

- on completion of the work, the assets are immediately taken into use and used only for the purposes of the trade (HMRC concession ESC D22).

Another concession applies where a person carrying on a trade uses the proceeds from the disposal of an old asset to acquire a further interest in another asset that is already in use for the purposes of the trade. That further interest is treated as a new asset taken into use for the purposes of the trade (HMRC concession ESC D25).

A right to unascertainable future consideration may be received as part of the consideration for disposal of the old asset. Roll-over relief is not available on a later disposal of that right because the right is not among the classes of asset listed in **14.15** (CG 14970, CG 60430).

NEW ASSETS TO BE USED 'ON ACQUISITION'

14.22   A new asset must be taken into use for the purpose of the business 'on the acquisition' of the asset if it is to form part of a roll-over relief claim (*TCGA 1992, s 152(1)*).

HMRC interpret this as meaning that the asset must be taken into use at the time any contracts are completed – by conveyance or delivery – and possession has been obtained. See also **14.24** regarding the period of ownership, in relation to the restriction of relief where there is non-business use.

However, allowance is made for necessary alterations, adaptations or other steps required before the asset can be taken into use. HMRC guidance indicates that relief should not be denied solely on the grounds that the asset was not brought into use as soon as it was acquired, provided that it was brought into use as soon as practicable after the acquisition and without unnecessary delay. HMRC would expect the interval to be short in most cases (CG 60830–60832).

In *Milton v Chivers* [1996] STC (SCD) 36 the Special Commissioner held that the phrase 'on the acquisition' did not mean 'immediately on the acquisition' but it did mean that the taking into use and the acquisition must be 'reasonably proximate' to one another.

By concession, HMRC will allow relief where a new asset is not taken into use for the purposes of a trade immediately on acquisition but:

* the owner proposes to incur capital expenditure on enhancing its value;

* any work arising from such expenditure begins as soon as possible after acquisition and is completed within a reasonable time;

* the asset is taken into use – and in the case of land and buildings, occupied – for the purpose of the trade (and for no other purpose) on completion of the work; and

* the asset is neither let nor used for any non-trading purpose in the period between acquisition and the time it is taken into use for the purpose of the trade (HMRC concession ESC D24).

HMRC regard this approach as an interpretation of *TCGA 1992, s 152(1)* that gained judicial approval in *Steibelt (Inspector of Taxes) v Paling* [1999] 71 TC 376, Ch D, rather than as a concession, but have indicated that they will continue to draw on that interpretation where appropriate (CG 60850).

ASSETS USED ONLY PARTLY FOR BUSINESS PURPOSES

14.23 It is necessary, in the following situations, to calculate the acquisition or disposal consideration relating to a deemed 'separate asset' qualifying for roll-over relief:

* Where, during the period of ownership (or any substantial part of it), part of a building or structure is used for the purposes of a trade and part is not so used, then the part used for trade purposes – together with any land occupied for purposes ancillary to it – is treated as a separate asset. HMRC regard this rule, together with the reference in Head A of Class 1 of the list of qualifying assets to 'any building or part of a building', as applying to the new assets as well as the old assets. The rule applies only

to buildings, so that other assets must be used for the purpose of the business and no other purpose (*TCGA 1992, s 152(6)*; CG 60520).

• If the old asset was not used for the purposes of the trade throughout the period of ownership, then a part of the asset representing its use for the purposes of the trade is treated as a separate asset used wholly for the purposes of the trade. This part is to be calculated having regard to the time and extent to which it was, and was not, used for the purposes of the trade (*TCGA 1992, s 152(7)*).

Any period of ownership before 31 March 1982 is ignored for these purposes. Any apportionment of consideration for the above purposes is to be made in a just and reasonable manner and where appropriate HMRC will seek to ensure that all parties to a transaction are bound by the same apportionment of the total consideration (*TCGA 1992, s 152(11)*; CG 60303).

Example 14.1

Khaled bought a freehold property on 1 September 2003 and let it to a tenant for one year before occupying and using it for the purpose of his trade on 1 September 2004. He used the whole of the property for the purpose of the trade until he sold it on 1 September 2006 for £150,000.

A chargeable gain of £90,000 accrued. Two-thirds of the gain arising, ie £60,000, may be deferred if Khaled reinvests the proceeds of £150,000 in qualifying assets.

The period of ownership

14.24   HMRC consider that the period of ownership of an asset for roll-over relief purposes is the period of beneficial ownership and possession. This period may not be the same as the period from the time of the acquisition and the time of disposal, as defined for the general purposes of CGT. For example, *TCGA 1992, s 28* provides that where an asset is acquired under an unconditional contract the time at which the acquisition is made is the time the contract is made (and not, if different, the time at which the asset is conveyed or transferred). However, beneficial ownership may not be obtained until completion and the period of ownership for roll-over relief begins when beneficial ownership is obtained, but HMRC have indicated that they will not pursue 'trivial adjustments' (CG 60520–60528).

OPERATION OF THE RELIEF

Full relief

14.25   Roll-over relief is given without restriction if an amount equal to the net consideration for the disposal (after deducting allowable costs of disposal) of the old asset is reinvested in a new, qualifying asset. For this purpose the net consideration for the old asset is compared with the cost of acquisition, including allowable incidental costs, of the replacement asset (CG 60772).

First, the actual consideration for the disposal is reduced and treated as if it were of such an amount as would give rise to neither a gain nor a loss. Where indexation allowance is available on the disposal (see **3.59**) this means that the disposal proceeds are deemed to be equal to the sum of the original cost and the indexation allowance. Then the amount of this reduction is deducted from the amount (or value used for CGT purposes) of the consideration for the acquisition of the new asset.

Example 14.2

Arthur sold a business asset qualifying for roll-over relief on 1 October 2005. The consideration for the disposal was £90,000 and incidental costs of disposal were £5,000. He acquired a replacement asset on 1 January 2007 for £84,000 and incurred incidental costs of acquisition amounting to £4,000. The total cost of acquisition is £88,000 and full roll-over relief is due because this exceeds the net proceeds of £85,000.

The net consideration of £85,000 is reduced to the sum that gives rise to neither a gain nor a loss on the disposal, and that reduction is set against the acquisition cost of the new asset.

Taper relief

14.26   The gain to be rolled over is computed before any taper relief is given. This is because taper relief applies only to 'chargeable' gains, and the effect of roll-over relief is to reduce the amount of a chargeable gain. On a disposal of the new asset, any taper relief will be computed by reference to the period of ownership of the new asset only. This means that for taxpayers other than companies (which are not eligible for taper relief but continue to receive indexation allowance) the benefit of any roll-over relief claim must be weighed against the potential loss of taper relief (*TCGA 1992, ss 2A(1), 152(1)*).

Partial relief

14.27   Some relief may be available if only a part of the consideration for the disposal of the old assets is reinvested in new assets. The part not reinvested must be less than the amount of the gain if any relief is to be obtained. In this situation:

(a)   the chargeable gain is reduced to the amount not reinvested; and

(b)   the amount of this reduction is deducted from the consideration for the acquisition of the new asset.

The reduction in (a) and (b) does not affect the tax treatment of the other parties to the transactions (*TCGA 1992, s 153(1)*).

Example 14.3

Bernard sold a qualifying asset in October 2006 for £150,000, realising a chargeable gain of £50,000. He acquired a new qualifying asset in June 2009 for £120,000. Bernard is treated in effect as having reinvested the cost of the old asset, ie £100,000, first.

The remaining £20,000 invested is treated as derived from the gain, so that £30,000 of the gain was not reinvested. The chargeable gain accruing on disposal of the old asset is reduced by £20,000 to £30,000, and the acquisition cost of the new asset is also reduced by £20,000.

Assets held on 31 March 1982

14.28   CGT was 'rebased' in 1988 to eliminate gains arising before 31 March 1982. A special rule applies to the 'deferred charge' arising where roll-over relief was obtained on a disposal before 6 April 1988 of an asset held on 31 March 1982. If no adjustment were made on the occasion of a post-1988 disposal of the new asset, the pre-1982 element of the deferred gain would be taxed. In broad terms and subject to certain exceptions, where the deferred gain accrues after 5 April 1988, it is halved (see **3.75**) (*TCGA 1992, Sch 4*).

DEEMED CONSIDERATION AND DEEMED DISPOSALS

14.29   Any provision of *TCGA 1992* fixing the amount of consideration deemed to be given for the acquisition or disposal of an asset – for example, where a transaction between connected persons is treated as having a consideration equal to the market value of the asset – is applied before roll-over relief. This means that in some cases the amount that the taxpayer needs to 'reinvest' to secure full relief will be greater than the proceeds actually received (*TCGA 1992, s 152(10)*).

HMRC do not consider that relief is available where there is a deemed disposal and reacquisition of the same asset, because the deemed consideration for the deemed disposal is not available to be applied in acquiring 'other assets'.

However, relief may be available where a qualifying asset is deemed to be disposed of or deemed to be acquired. For example, gains arising when a capital sum is derived from an asset, or when an asset is appropriated to trading stock, may be the subject of a claim. A deemed acquisition of a qualifying asset, for example, acquisition of an asset as legatee, may also give rise to roll-over relief.

Expenditure reimbursed from public funds

14.30   *Wardhaugh v Penrith Rugby Union Football Club* [2002] 74 TC 499, Ch D established that for roll-over relief purposes the amount or value of the consideration taken to be applied in the acquisition of the new asset is the amount before any reduction under *TCGA 1992, s 50*. That section provides that a CGT computation excludes any expenditure met directly or indirectly by the Crown or by any government, public or local authority. HMRC argued that *TCGA 1992, s 152(10)* (see **14.29**) applied but the court disagreed on the basis that *TCGA 1992, s 50* related to the non-deductibility of acquisition expenditure. It was not a provision that fixed the amount of the consideration deemed to be given for the acquisition of an asset.

DEPRECIATING ASSETS

14.31   Special rules apply where the new assets are 'depreciating assets'. The provisions of *TCGA 1992, ss 152* and *153* (roll-over relief for business assets) and *TCGA 1992, s 229* (roll-over relief on disposals to employee share ownership trusts) are modified and the following definitions are applied for the purpose of the special rules described below:

- the 'held-over gain' is the amount by which, under the normal rules, the chargeable gain on one asset ('asset No 1') is reduced, with a corresponding reduction of the allowable expenditure on another asset ('asset No 2'); and

- where a gain of any amount is described as being 'carried forward to any asset', this refers to (i) a reduction of that amount in a chargeable gain, coupled with (ii) a reduction of the same amount in expenditure allowable in respect of the asset (*TCGA 1992, s 154(1)*).

An asset is a 'depreciating asset' at a particular time if it is a wasting asset (as defined in *TCGA 1992, s 44*) at that time, or will become a wasting asset within ten years. *TCGA 1992, s 44* provides that, subject to certain exceptions, an asset is a wasting asset if it has a predictable life not exceeding 50 years. An asset is a depreciating asset, therefore, if it has a predictable life of no more than 60 years (*TCGA 1992, s 154(7)*).

Postponing the held-over gain

14.32   Where asset No 2 is a depreciating asset, the gain accruing on asset No 1 is not carried forward as described above. Instead, the taxpayer is treated as if the held-over gain did not accrue until the first of the following events occurs:

- he disposes of asset No 2;

- he ceases to use asset No 2 for the purposes of a trade carried on by him; or

- the expiration of a period of ten years beginning with the acquisition of asset No 2 (*TCGA 1992, s 154(2)*).

By concession, no gain is deemed to accrue under this rule where the asset ceases to be used for the purpose of the trade because of the taxpayer's death (HMRC concession ESC D45).

Acquisition of a third asset

14.33   The taxpayer might acquire asset No 3, a non-depreciating asset, before the postponed gain is deemed to accrue as set out in **14.32**. In such a case he could make a claim to roll over the gain on the disposal of asset No 1 against the acquisition cost of asset No 3. The time limits for reinvestment (see **14.35**) would be regarded as met and the initial claim, relating to the acquisition of asset No 2, would be treated as withdrawn. The claim to roll-over relief against the cost of asset No 3 would be limited to the amount of the gain that was held over on the acquisition of asset No 2 (*TCGA 1992, s 154(4), (5)*).

The amount invested in asset No 3 may be less than the net proceeds of asset No 1. In that event the above rule might give rise to a CGT liability because only partial relief would be available. However, the taxpayer may ask for the postponed gain to be treated as derived from two separate assets. The effect would be to split the gain on disposal of asset No 1 into two parts:

- the first part being rolled over against the acquisition of asset No 3 (as in **14.25**); and

- the second part being postponed (as in **14.32**) (*TCGA 1992, s 154(4), (6)*).

Transfer to a European Company or Societas Europaea ('SE')

14.34   The treatment of the postponed gain is modified where the taxpayer transfers asset No 2, or shares in a company that holds asset No 2, to an 'SE' in circumstances in which *TCGA 1992, s 140E* (merger leaving assets within UK tax charge) applies. The postponed gain is not brought into charge. Instead, the SE is treated as though it claimed the roll-over relief (*TCGA 1992, s 154(2A)*; *F(No 2)A 2005, s 64(3)*).

REINVESTMENT: TIME LIMITS

14.35   The general rule is that the new asset must be acquired in the period beginning one year before, and ending three years after, the disposal of the old asset, but this period may be extended in some circumstances. Relief is available only if the acquisition of the new assets (or an interest in them) takes place in the period beginning 12 months before and ending 3 years after the disposal of the old assets (or an interest in them), or at such earlier or later time as HMRC may allow (see below) (*TCGA 1992, s 152(3)*).

An unconditional contract for the acquisition, made within the time limit, will be sufficient. The relief may be applied on a provisional basis where an unconditional contract for the acquisition is entered into, without waiting to see whether the contract is completed. Adjustments are to be made as necessary when the outcome is known. This rule is separate from the facility for the taxpayer to claim provisional relief before he has entered into any contract for acquisition of a replacement asset (see **14.41**) ((*TCGA 1992, s 152(4)*).

Where the replacement asset is newly constructed, or represented by improvement to an existing asset, HMRC consider that the date of acquisition may be taken as the date on which the asset or the works are completed and ready for use (CG 60623).

Extension of time limits for reinvestment

14.36   HMRC guidance indicates that extension of the time limits is permitted where the claimant can demonstrate that he:

● firmly intended to acquire replacement assets within the time limit;

● was prevented from doing so by some fact or circumstance beyond his control; and

● acted 'as soon as he reasonably could' after ceasing to be so prevented.

Each case is considered on its merits. Circumstances outside the claimant's control might include the death or serious illness of a vital party at a crucial time; unsettled disputes; difficulty in establishing good title or finding suitable replacement assets; or delay in receipt of disposal proceeds. They would not normally include a change of intention at a late stage, or a shortage of funds that arose because the taxpayer spent the proceeds on something other than new, qualifying assets (CG 60640).

The discretion available to the Board of HM Revenue and Customs has been delegated so that in the following circumstances the Area Director Compliance or the Band B Compliance Team Leader in an Area Office may allow an extension:

* in the case of land that has been disposed of under a compulsory purchase order, or is under the threat of such an order, so long as the conditions set out in Statement of practice SP D6 (see below) are satisfied; or

* where the new asset was acquired within three years before or six years after the disposal of the old asset and there are acceptable reasons for the delay (CG 60641).

If the acquisition of the new asset took place more than a year before the disposal of the old asset, relief might still be obtained if the delay between the acquisition and the subsequent disposal occurred because of:

* the threat of compulsory acquisition of the old asset;
* difficulty in disposing of the old asset;
* the acquisition of land with the intention of building on it; or
* the need to have new premises functioning before the old premises could be vacated (CG 60642).

Where land is acquired by a local authority under a compulsory purchase order and leased back to the taxpayer for a period before it is developed, HMRC are prepared to extend the reinvestment time limit as indicated in statement of practice SP D6, which reads:

'Where new town corporations and similar authorities acquire by compulsory purchase land for development and then immediately grant a previous owner a lease of the land until they are ready to commence building, [HMRC] will be prepared to extend the time limit for rollover relief under *TCGA 1992, ss 152 to 158* to 3 years after the land ceases to be used by the previous owner for his trade, provided that there is a clear continuing intention that the sale proceeds will be used to acquire qualifying assets; assurances will be given in appropriate cases subject to the need to raise a protective assessment if the lease extends beyond the statutory 6-year time limit for making assessments.'

In this situation HMRC will look for evidence of the taxpayer's continuing intention to reinvest the disposal proceeds within the extended time limit, including:

- an annual affirmation from the taxpayer or agent that such is the intention; and

- an assurance that the disposal proceeds remain available (though not necessarily in a completely liquid form) for the purchase. HMRC say that temporary investment of the funds even in equities or real property, 'should not of itself be taken as making the proceeds unavailable' (CG 60663).

HMRC also recognise that in many compulsory acquisition cases there can be a long delay between the disposal of the land and the agreement and receipt of compensation. They may extend the reinvestment time limit in such cases so that relief is available where the new assets are acquired within 12 months before and three years after the first receipt of compensation (CG 60666).

CLAIMS

Time limits

14.37   The time limits set out below begin with the end of the year of assessment or accounting period in which the disposal takes place, or the one in which the new assets are acquired, whichever is the later. See **14.41** below regarding provisional relief. The time limits may be extended in the event of an assessment being made to recover tax lost through fraud or neglect. A claim may be made after a CGT assessment has become final.

Individuals, trustees and personal representatives

14.38   No claim to roll-over relief may be made more than five years after 31 January following the tax year to which it relates. This is the general time limit for claims (*TMA 1970, s 43*).

Companies

14.39   A company may make a claim within six years from the end of the accounting period to which it relates. This is the general time limit for claims to relief from corporation tax (*FA 1998, Sch 18, para 55*).

How to claim

14.40   A claim must be in writing and must specify:

- the claimant;

- the assets disposed of;

- the date of disposal of each of those assets;

- the consideration received for the disposal of each of those assets;

- the assets acquired;

- the dates of acquisition of each of those assets (or the dates on which unconditional contracts for acquisition were entered into);

- the consideration given for each of those assets; and

- the amount of the consideration received for the disposal of each of the specified assets that has been applied in the acquisition of each replacement asset (CG 60606).

HMRC provide a claim form in their self-assessment helpsheet IR 290.

Provisional relief

14.41   In some cases the CGT payable on the gain arising on the disposal may become due before a claim to roll-over relief can be established. Provisional relief is available to ensure that the funds available for reinvestment are not depleted by a payment of tax that would be recovered later. The taxpayer is required to make a declaration, in his tax return for the year of assessment (or accounting period) in which the disposal took place, that:

(a)   the whole (or a specified part) of the consideration will be applied in the acquisition of, or of an interest in, other assets ('the new assets') which on the acquisition will be taken into use, and used only, for the purposes of the trade;

(b)   the acquisition will take place as mentioned within the time limits for reinvestment set out in *TCGA 1992, s 152(3)* (see **14.35**); and

(c)   the new assets will be within the classes listed in *TCGA 1992, s 155* (see **14.15**).

The declaration may be made on the form provided in HMRC's helpsheet IR 290. Until the declaration ceases to have effect (see below), relief will be available as if the taxpayer had acquired the new assets and made a claim for relief. The rules set out in *s 152* regarding partial business use, successive trades, deemed consideration and apportionments are applied accordingly (*TCGA 1992, s 153A*).

Declaration ceasing to have effect

14.42   The declaration ceases to have effect:

- if it is withdrawn before the 'relevant day', on the day on which it is withdrawn;

- if it is superseded by a valid claim to roll-over relief, on the day on which it is superseded;

- in other cases, on the 'relevant day' (*TCGA 1992, s 153A(3)*).

The 'relevant day' for CGT is the third anniversary of the 31st January following the year of assessment in which the disposal of the old assets took place. For corporation tax, it is the fourth anniversary of the last day of the accounting period in which the disposal took place (*TCGA 1992, s 153A(5)*).

Once a declaration has ceased to have effect all necessary adjustments are to be made, including the making or amending of assessments, irrespective of any time limits that would otherwise apply. If the taxpayer who has obtained provisional relief dies before the relevant day and before having made a valid claim to roll-over relief, HMRC will ask his personal representatives to withdraw the declaration (*TCGA 1992, s 153A(4)*; CG 60705).

Interest and penalties

14.43   Interest may be charged on any tax ultimately found to be payable in the event that the taxpayer does not proceed with reinvestment, or partial relief only is obtained. HMRC guidance says: 'The deterrent of frivolous declarations lies in the taxpayer's liability to pay interest from the time the tax should have been paid if the declared intention does not lead to an acquisition. Only if, exceptionally, the declaration is clearly found to have been made fraudulently or negligently should you consider the possibility of penalties' (CG 60704).

INTERACTION WITH OTHER RELIEFS

Taper relief

14.44   Where roll-over relief is claimed, the gain to be rolled over is computed before any taper relief is given, because taper relief applies only to 'chargeable' gains, and the effect of roll-over relief is to reduce the amount of a chargeable gain. This means that a roll-over relief claim can result in a significant loss of taper relief (see **11.43**).

Incorporation

14.45   Roll-over relief under *TCGA 1992, s 152* takes precedence over relief on the transfer of a business to a company under *TCGA 1992, s 162* (see **15.19**).

Roll-over relief on the transfer of a business to a company in exchange for shares is given automatically under *TCGA 1992 s 162*, although the taxpayer may elect to disapply the relief on such a transfer after 5 April 2002. If a *TCGA 1992, s 152* roll-over relief claim is made later, the computation of any *TCGA 1992, s 162* relief given may be reopened and revised.

However, HMRC consider that this is not possible once there has been a disposal of any of the shares and an assessment of a chargeable gain on that disposal has become final and conclusive (CG 61561).

Chapter 15

Incorporation of a business

15.1   There is a disposal of assets for CGT purposes, usually at market value, where a sole trader or partnership transfers a business to a company. Those assets may include goodwill, something that is easily overlooked if it does not appear on the balance sheet.

However, incorporation relief – a form of roll-over relief – may be available to defer the gain arising (*TCGA 1992, s 162*). Alternatively, hold-over relief (for gifts of business assets) may be available in some circumstances, as discussed in **15.20** and **Chapter 13** (*TCGA 1992, s 165*).

INCORPORATION RELIEF: CONDITIONS

15.2   A chargeable gain on the disposal of business assets may be rolled over where the disposal is the transfer of a business to a company. No claim is required. The key conditions are set out below:

- the transfer must be made by a person other than a company (see below);
- the business must be transferred as a going concern;
- the transfer must include the whole assets of the business, or the whole of those assets other than cash; and
- the transfer must be made wholly or partly in exchange for shares issued by the company to the transferor – these shares are known as the 'new assets' (*TCGA 1992, s 162(1)*).

Incorporation relief is available, therefore, for transfers by an individual, trustee or personal representative. 'Company' includes any unincorporated association (but not a partnership), so that the first condition above means that relief is not available where an unincorporated association transfers a business to a company (*TCGA 1992, s 288(1)*).

Effect of the relief

15.3   The effect of the relief is that the total of the chargeable gains less allowable losses accruing on the transfer of assets (the 'old assets') to the company is deducted from the acquisition cost of the shares received in exchange for those assets.

The gains are therefore deferred until a subsequent disposal of the shares. Where the shares are not all of the same class, the relief is apportioned by reference to the market value of the shares (*TCGA 1992, s 162(2), (3)*).

Full relief is available only where the business assets are exchanged wholly for shares in the company.

Partial relief

15.4　If the transfer is made partly for cash, the gains are apportioned by reference to the value of the shares and the other proceeds received. The amount of relief available is found by applying the fraction A/B to the gain on the old assets, where:

- A is the 'cost of the new assets', ie the shares; and
- B is the value of the whole of the consideration received in exchange for the business.

The cost of the shares (A) is found by adding together the items of expenditure that would be allowable as a deduction (under *TCGA 1992, s 38(1)(a)*) in the event of a chargeable gain arising on a disposal of the shares. This will normally be the market value of the assets transferred to the company (see **15.14**). The relief cannot exceed the cost of the shares. The gains attributed to the shares are rolled over, while the remaining gains are immediately chargeable to CGT (*TCGA 1992, s 162(4), (5)*).

See **15.14** regarding the consideration received for the transfer and how relief is restricted where part of the consideration is not in the form of shares.

Partnerships

15.5　Where the business transferred to the company was carried on in partnership, incorporation relief is computed separately for each individual based on the consideration he receives. Relief is not denied to the individuals where one of the partners is a company, so long as the whole of the business is transferred to a company, but as indicated above the corporate partner is not eligible for relief.

This means that it is possible to obtain incorporation relief for a partner who transfers his interest in the business in exchange for shares, while his fellow partner who receives only cash for his interest is unable to roll over any capital gain arising. This provides considerable flexibility when arranging the transfer of a business previously carried on by a partnership.

Transfer of all assets

15.6   The requirement that all assets (except cash) must be transferred to the company may be unattractive to the business proprietor. For example, transfers of land and buildings may result in substantial stamp duty land tax liabilities.

As an alternative to securing incorporation relief under *TCGA 1992, s 162* the proprietor may consider retaining assets outside the company and transferring the remaining chargeable assets to the company for a consideration less than market value. In those circumstances hold-over relief for gifts, under *TCGA 1992, s 165* (see **15.20**), may be available.

Election to forego incorporation relief

15.7   Incorporation relief under *TCGA 1992, s 162* does not have to be claimed. For transfers prior to 6 April 2002 the relief was mandatory if all the conditions were met. However, the taxpayer may elect to disapply the relief where the transfer takes place on or after that date.

This may be beneficial if, for example, the shares are sold shortly after the incorporation, because incorporation relief causes any accrued taper relief on the business assets transferred to the company to be lost. The election may result in a gain arising on incorporation, but business asset taper relief and the CGT annual exemption may reduce or eliminate the tax liability. Once an election is made, all necessary adjustments – eg by means of discharge or repayment of tax – are made to give effect to it (*TCGA 1992, s 162A(1), (6)*).

If two or more individuals owned the business transferred to the company – including ownership by a partnership of which they are partners – then each of them is entitled to make an election as he sees fit in relation to his own share of the gain accruing on the old assets and his share of the new assets (*TCGA 1992, s 162A(7), (8)*).

The election must be made by a notice given to HMRC no later than the relevant date, which is:

- the first anniversary of 31 January following the year of assessment in which the transfer took place, where the transferor has disposed of all the new assets by the end of the year of assessment following the one in which the transfer took place; or

- the second anniversary of 31 January following the year of assessment in which the transfer took place in any other case.

For the purpose of this time limit a disposal of new assets by the transferor is ignored if it is a disposal to a spouse or civil partner falling within the no gain/no loss provisions of *TCGA 1992, s 58* (see **3.67**). A later disposal by the transferee spouse or civil partner is treated as a disposal by the transferor unless it is a disposal to the transferor (*TCGA 1992, s 162A(2)–(5)*).

Example 15.1

James and Jill ran a computer software business in partnership for many years until they transferred the business to JJ Software Limited in June 2006 in exchange for shares in the company. The asset of goodwill was not shown in the partnership balance sheet. In October 2006 they sold their shares for £1m more than the net asset value of the partnership business prior to incorporation. This excess represented the goodwill that was owned by the partnership but had no acquisition cost for CGT.

In the absence of an election to forego incorporation relief, the gain of £1m would be rolled over against the cost of the shares and a gain of the same amount would arise on the sale of the shares. No taper relief would be due because the shares would have been held for less than 12 months.

If an election is made, incorporation relief does not apply and the gain of £1m on the goodwill is eligible for the maximum taper relief, reducing the amount chargeable to 25% of the gain, or £250,000. The gains accruing on other assets would also have to be considered. The election must be made by 31 January 2010 (the first anniversary of 31 January following the year of assessment in which the transfer took place) because the shares were sold by the end of the year of assessment following the one in which the incorporation took place.

Business

15.8   The relief applies to the transfer of a 'business', which is not defined in the legislation (*TCGA 1992, s 162(1)*). HMRC regard 'business' as taking its normal meaning, which is 'wider than trade' (and would probably include a profession or vocation). HMRC guidance recognises that it is not always easy to draw the line between a business and other activities, but a claim that the passive holding of investments or an investment property amounted to a business is likely to be resisted (CG 65713).

HMRC regard the Malaysian tax case *American Leaf Blending Co Sdn Bhd v Director-General of Inland Revenue* [1978] STC 561, heard by the Privy Council, as useful authority and an indication that property letting activities may constitute a business if carried on by a company but not where those activities are carried on by a private individual. Lord Diplock said:

'In the case of a private individual it may well be that the mere receipt of rents from property that he owns raises no presumption that he is carrying on a business. In contrast ... in the case of a company incorporated for the purpose of making profits for its shareholders any gainful use to which it puts any of its assets prima facie amounts to the carrying on of a business.'

While the carrying on of a business usually called for some activity, that activity may be 'intermittent with long intervals of quiescence in between,' Lord Diplock added. HMRC stress the importance of looking at the context in which the courts have considered the meaning of 'business', and add that the word may be interpreted differently when contrasting individuals and companies.

HMRC also cite *CIR v The Marine Steam Turbine Co Ltd* [1919] 12 TC 174, KB. The company received royalties and was held not to be carrying on a business for the purposes of excess profits duty. Rowlatt J said that if a 'private person' occupied the company's position it would be 'ludicrous to speak of him as carrying on a business'. He considered that 'business' meant an 'active occupation or profession continuously carried on' (CG 65713–65715).

Going concern

15.9   The business must be transferred as a 'going concern' together with all of the assets of the business (*TCGA 1992, s 162(1)*). HMRC take this to mean that the transfer must comprise 'something more than a collection of assets'.

HMRC guidance refers to an Australian case, *Reference under the Electricity Commission (Balmain Electric Light Co Purchase) Act 1950* [1957] 57 SR (NSW) 100, cited in *CIR v Gordon* (see below), where Sugerman J said:

'To describe an undertaking as a "going concern" imports no more than that, at the point of time to which the description applies, its doors are open for business; that it is then active and operating, and perhaps also that it has all the plant etc which is necessary to keep it in operation, as distinct from its being only an inert aggregation of plant.'

In *Gordon v CIR* [1991] 64 TC 173 CS Lord Hope said the Special Commissioner had considered the ability of the business to continue as a going concern for some time in the future after the transfer to the company, but the question whether the activities could be carried on without interruption should be directed to the date of the transfer, and not to some later date (CG 65716–65718). Lord Hope referred to *Kenmir Ltd v Frizzell* [1968] 1 WLR 329 in which Widgery J said that the vital consideration was 'whether the effect of the transaction was to put the transferee in possession of a going concern the activities of which he could carry on without interruption'.

Assets of the business

15.10 The transfer must include the whole assets of the business, or the whole of those assets other than cash. HMRC regard cash as including sums held in a bank deposit or current account (*TCGA 1992, s 162(1)*; CG 65719).

If an asset is a business asset it must be transferred to the company. Whether an asset is on the balance sheet is not conclusive, and an asset may remain a business asset after it has been taken off the balance sheet. See **15.11** regarding goodwill.

Goodwill

15.11 The goodwill of the business may not appear on the balance sheet, but the valuation of goodwill should not be overlooked on the transfer of the business to the company. It is important, however, not to overvalue goodwill. Note, however, that HMRC may consider that there is no saleable goodwill in some cases (see **14.19** regarding a recent case where a Special Commissioner questioned HMRC's published guidance).

Example 15.2

In November 2006, Henry transferred his sole trader business with all its assets and liabilities to IQ Limited in consideration for 100 shares in IQ Limited. He did not elect for incorporation relief not to apply. The only chargeable asset of the business is goodwill, which Henry created himself. The value of the business transferred is agreed as follows:

	Value £
Goodwill	250,000
Non-chargeable assets	100,000
Cash	25,000
	375,000
Creditors	(255,000)
Net value of the business	120,000

The gain arising on the transfer is £250,000. The consideration for the business is wholly in the form of shares, so the shares are worth £120,000. The amount of the gain to be rolled over cannot exceed the cost of the shares, which is £120,000.

Thus £120,000 of the gain is rolled over and the balance of £130,000 is chargeable to CGT in 2006/07 (subject to taper relief).

Liabilities

15.12 The company may well assume some or all of the liabilities of the business, although there is no requirement for liabilities as well as assets to be transferred to the company. The company's assumption of liabilities is additional consideration for the business, but by concession (ESC D32), HMRC do not take this point because they recognise that the transferor does not receive cash to meet the tax liability that would arise by reference to that consideration.

HMRC also recognise that the transfer of liabilities reduces the value of the shares issued to the transferor. Concession D32 reads:

> 'Where liabilities are taken over by a company on the transfer of a business to the company, HMRC are prepared for the purposes of the "rollover" provision in *TCGA 1992, s 162* not to treat such liabilities as consideration. If therefore the other conditions of *s 162* are satisfied, no capital gain arises on the transfer. Relief under *s 162* is not precluded by the fact that some or all of the liabilities of the business are not taken over by the company.'

Any personal liabilities of the transferor assumed by the company, including his capital account and any tax liability relating to the transfer of the business, are outside the terms of this concession and are treated as part of the consideration. The concession does not affect the calculation of the net cost of the shares (CG 65745–65749).

Where incorporation relief is obtained by concession, the taxpayer is required by statute to account for the deferred gain becoming chargeable (*TCGA 1992, ss 284A, 284B*).

Computing the relief

15.13 The chargeable gains and allowable losses accruing on the transfer of chargeable assets to the company are computed and the net gains are aggregated. The next step is to identify:

(a)   the consideration in shares; and

(b)   consideration other than shares.

See **15.14** regarding the task of identifying and quantifying the consideration for the transfer. The proportion of the aggregate net gains relating to (a) is deducted from the allowable expenditure on the acquisition of the shares. This reduction cannot exceed the allowable expenditure. The proportion relating to (b) is chargeable to tax but business asset taper relief and the annual CGT exemption may be available. HMRC will not accept that, for example, cash consideration is given for one asset and shares for another (CG 65744).

Example 15.3

Walter carries on an antiquarian bookselling business. He decides to form a company, W Limited, to carry on the business. In August 2006 he transfers the whole of the business undertaking, assets and liabilities to W Limited in exchange for shares and an amount left outstanding on interest-free loan. The business assets and liabilities transferred are valued as follows:

		Value	Chargeable gain
Assets	£	£	£
Freehold shop premises		80,000	52,000
Goodwill		36,000	26,000
Fixtures and fittings		4,000	0
Trading stock		52,000	0
Debtors		28,000	0
		200,000	
Liabilities			
Mortgage on shop	50,000		
Trade creditors	20,000	(70,000)	
		130,000	78,000

The company issues 100,000 £1 ordinary shares, valued at par, to Walter in August 2006. The amount left outstanding on the loan account is £30,000. In March 2007, Walter sells 20,000 of his shares for £45,000 to Dusty. Walter's remaining shareholding is then worth £155,000. Walter does not make an election for incorporation relief not to apply to the incorporation.

Incorporation

•   The amount of chargeable gain rolled over on transfer of the business is:
       £78,000 x (£100,000/£130,000) = £60,000

321

- The chargeable gain of £18,000 remaining (£78,000 – £60,000) is eligible for taper relief. The acquisition cost of Walter's shares is £40,000 (£100,000 – £60,000).

Sale of shares

- Walter realises a chargeable gain for 2006/07 on the sale of shares to Dusty:

	£
Disposal consideration	45,000
Allowable expenditure:	
£40,000 x [45,000/(45,000 + 155,000)]	(9,000)
Chargeable gain	36,000

Consideration for the transfer

15.14   The transfer must be made wholly or partly in exchange for shares actually issued by the company to the transferor – these shares are known as the 'new assets' (*TCGA 1992, s 162(1)*). It is important that the necessary documentation be prepared to demonstrate what has been transferred to the company and precisely what the company has given in return.

HMRC accept that there may sometimes be a delay in issuing the shares, where, for example, the authorised capital of the company has to be increased. Relief is not denied so long as the issue of shares takes place 'fairly promptly' after the reason for the delay has gone. The task should not be left until the company's first accounts are prepared.

Relief is not available if the shares are issued:

- in consideration for something other than the transfer of the business; or
- to settle a loan account representing cash consideration.

Consideration in the form of shares

15.15   The transferor does not have to acquire any specific level of shareholding in the company. The number of shares may be decided in advance of the transfer, leaving the share premium to be calculated later by reference to the value of the business assets transferred to the company. The transferor is not required to work for the company.

As indicated in **15.3**, where the shares are not all of the same class, the relief is apportioned by reference to their relative market values.

The shares issued do not have to be ordinary shares, but if, for example, redeemable preference shares are issued the relief may be denied by virtue of the anti-avoidance provisions in *ICTA 1988, s 703*. The taxpayer should consider requesting an advance clearance under *ICTA 1988, s 707*.

The cost of the shares

15.16   As indicated in **15.3**, the effect of the relief is that the net gains accruing on the transfer of assets (the 'old assets') to the company is reduced. That reduction is then apportioned among the new assets and goes to reduce the allowable expenditure otherwise deductible on a future disposal of each new asset (*TCGA 1992, s 162(2)*).

The reduction is found by applying the fraction A/B to the gain on the old assets, where:

- A is the 'cost of the new assets' (see below); and
- B is the value of the whole of the consideration received by the transferor.

The 'cost of the new assets' is found by adding together the items of expenditure that would be allowable as a deduction in computing the chargeable gain arising on a disposal of the new assets. The reduction is apportioned between shares of different classes on the basis of their relative market values. The date of disposal of the business is taken to be the date of acquisition of the shares.

The transferor and transferee company will normally be connected persons (see **3.16**), so that the chargeable assets will pass to the company at market value. The transferor's cost of acquiring the shares is, therefore, normally the market value of what he gives for those shares, ie the value of the business.

HMRC regard the value of the business as, broadly, the difference between its assets and liabilities – concession D32 relating to liabilities (see **15.12**) is not in point. This may mean that incorporation relief is restricted because the amount of the relief set against the cost of the shares cannot exceed that cost. That cost may be very small in the case where the business has significant liabilities.

Consideration other than shares

15.17   Where part of the consideration for the transfer is in a form other than shares, a proportion of the gains accruing on the transfer will be chargeable.

Such consideration would include a credit balance on the transferor's loan or current account with the company (except where the balance represents consideration which is to be satisfied in the form of shares and there is a delay in issuing the shares) (see **15.14**). HMRC do not accept that cash consideration or other consideration can be regarded as being given for one or more specified assets (CG 65744).

It may well be beneficial to arrange for part of the consideration to be in the form of a loan account balance, given that:

• any gain accruing on that part of the consideration may well be eligible for taper relief and/or the CGT annual exemption; and

• the transferor may not wish to 'lock in' all of the consideration in the form of shares in the company.

Taper relief

15.18 As explained in **11.44**, incorporation relief (under *TCGA 1992, 162*) is applied before taper relief. For taper relief purposes, the period of ownership of the old assets transferred to the business is ignored in calculating the qualifying holding period of the shares.

This means that where incorporation relief is obtained without restriction, taper relief that would otherwise be due in respect of the assets transferred is lost. However, as indicated in **15.7**, the taxpayer may elect under *s 162A* for the relief not to apply where the transfer takes place after 5 April 2002 (*TCGA 1992, s 162A*; CG 17912).

Example 15.4

On 1 November 2006 Jeremy transferred his business as a going concern to a company in return for shares in the company, and the conditions for relief under *TCGA 1992, s 162* were met. The business had commenced on 1 October 2003. A chargeable gain would accrue in 2006/07 on the transfer of goodwill to the company in the absence of incorporation relief, but the effect of *s 162* is that the gain is deducted instead from the acquisition value of Jeremy's shares in the new company.

Jeremy disposes of his shares on 1 December 2007. The qualifying holding period on that disposal runs from 1 November 2006 to 1 December 2007, giving one whole year, so that 50% of the gain on the disposal of shares in 2007/08 is chargeable.

An election to forego the incorporation relief (made within the time limits set out in *TCGA 1992, s 162A*) would give rise to a chargeable gain, accruing on 1 November 2006, on the disposal of goodwill to the company. However, the qualifying holding period in respect of that goodwill would be three whole years (1 October 2003 to 1 November 2006) so that only 25% of the 2006/07 gain would be chargeable.

Interaction with other reliefs

15.19   The interaction of the reliefs available on the disposal of business assets is summarised below.

- Roll-over relief for replacement of business assets (*TCGA 1992, s 152*) takes precedence over the other reliefs because it reduces the consideration to be taken into account in computing the gain on disposal.

- Incorporation relief on the transfer of a business to a company (*TCGA 1992, s 162*) follows, because it reduces the net chargeable gains accruing on the assets transferred to the company.

- Hold-over relief for gifts of business assets (*TCGA 1992, s 165*) also reduces the chargeable gains, but since incorporation relief under *TCGA 1992, s 162* is automatic (unless an election is made to forego it), it must take precedence over *TCGA 1992, s 165* relief.

Incorporation relief under *TCGA 1992, s 162* is applied before taper relief (see **15.18**).

Incorporation: using hold-over relief

15.20   A hold-over relief claim may be made on the transfer of a business to a company where *s 162* relief is either not available or is restricted. Hold-over relief may be useful if the sole trader or partners wish to retain assets outside the company, but the relief is restricted where there is actual consideration, either in the form of shares or a credit balance on a director's loan account with the company.

In order to qualify for hold-over relief the transfer to the company must be a disposal otherwise than by way of a bargain at arm's length, including a transaction deemed to be such because it is between connected persons.

Table 15.1 sets out some of the key features, to be considered by a taxpayer contemplating the incorporation of a business, of incorporation relief (*TCGA 1992, s 162*) and hold-over relief (*TCGA 1992, s 165*).

Table 15.1

Incorporation relief	**Hold-over relief for gifts of business assets**
Relief is automatic unless an election is made to disapply it	Relief must be claimed
Relief need not apply to all partners	Relief need not be claimed by all partners
Relief is given in full or in part on all chargeable assets transferred, depending on the extent of consideration other than shares	Relief may be claimed either on all assets or on certain assets only
Relief is available only if all the assets (or all the assets except cash) are transferred	Relief may be claimed even if some non-cash assets are not transferred
Gain is rolled over against the cost of the shares issued to the transferor(s) as consideration	Gain is held over against the cost of the chargeable asset(s) acquired by the company
Business must be transferred as a going concern	The transfer of one or more assets used for the purpose of the trade, etc will suffice
Loss of taper relief up to the date of incorporation	Loss of taper relief up to the date of the transfer

Chapter 16

Enterprise Investment Scheme

INTRODUCTION

16.1 The Enterprise Investment Scheme (EIS), designed to encourage investment in unquoted trading companies, replaced the Business Expansion Scheme in 1994.

Income tax relief at the rate of 20% of the amount subscribed for EIS shares is available, subject to various limits and conditions (see *Tottel's Income Tax 2006/07*). The CGT reliefs examined in this chapter provide for:

- gains to be free of CGT after, broadly, three years – see **16.2**; and

- deferral of a capital gain reinvested in EIS shares within, broadly, one year before and three years after the disposal giving rise to the gain – see **16.10**.

HMRC guidance is available at http://www.hmrc.gov.uk/eis/eis-index.htm. CGT reliefs for investments in venture capital trusts (VCTs) are examined in **17.2**.

CGT DISPOSAL RELIEF

16.2 A gain accruing on an individual's disposal of EIS shares is not a chargeable gain providing certain conditions are met. EIS shares are shares that have attracted income tax relief under the EIS scheme as set out in *ICTA 1988, Pt VII, Ch III*. There are detailed conditions in relation to the individual, company and its activities.

Disposal relief is not available to trustees. For HMRC guidance regarding this exemption, which HMRC call 'disposal relief', see HMRC's Capital Gains Manual at CG 62804 onwards and their self-assessment tax return helpsheet IR 297.

Conditions

16.3   A gain arising on a disposal of EIS shares is not a chargeable gain if:

(a)   the disposal is made after the end of the 'relevant period' (see below) referred to in *ICTA 1988, s 312(1A)(a)* – this is normally three years;

(b)   an amount of relief is attributable to the shares, ie the shares have qualified for EIS income tax relief;

(c)   that income tax relief has not been withdrawn; and

(d)   there would be a chargeable gain but for this relief (*TCGA 1992, s 150A*).

The income tax relief condition in (b) means that disposal relief is limited by reference to the maximum annual subscription for which income tax relief is available. This is £400,000 (£200,000 for 2005/06) in a year of assessment, regardless of when the shares are issued (*ICTA 1988, s 290(2)* as amended by *FA 2006, Sch 14, para 5*).

A gain accruing on a disposal within the relevant period is a chargeable gain, and any loss accruing is an allowable loss. However, a loss accruing on disposal after the relevant period is also allowable (see **16.4**).

A gain that does not qualify for disposal relief is a chargeable gain, but business asset taper relief should be available (see **Chapter 11**).

The 'relevant period' for shares issued after 5 April 2000 is the period ending immediately before the 'termination date' relating to those shares, and the termination date is the later of:

●   the third anniversary of the issue of the shares; and

●   the third anniversary of the commencement of the trade (*ICTA 1988, s 312(1), (1A)*).

For shares issued before 6 April 2000, the relevant period is normally the period of five years from the date of issue.

Losses

16.4   Disposal relief is excluded where a loss accrues on the disposal, with the result that a loss is an allowable loss. (If disposal relief was not excluded, a loss would not be an allowable loss because *TCGA 1992, s 16(2)* provides that a loss is not an allowable loss if a gain accruing on the same disposal would be a chargeable gain.)

The loss is an allowable loss whether or not EIS income tax relief is withdrawn. In calculating the loss, however, the taxpayer's allowable expenditure is reduced by the amount of the income tax relief obtained and not withdrawn. Relief for the loss may be claimed against income rather than set off against future capital losses, see **17.16** (*TCGA 1992, s 150A(1), (2), (2A)*; ICTA 1998, s 574).

Example 16.1

Christina subscribes £100,000 for new ordinary shares in an EIS company and obtains income tax relief of £20,000. She disposes of the shares after the termination date and the income tax relief is not withdrawn. Any gain accruing on disposal of the shares is not a chargeable gain, but any loss accruing is an allowable loss.

Example 16.2

Ralph subscribes £200,000 for EIS shares and obtains income tax relief of £40,000. He disposes of the shares within the relevant period for £150,000, and £30,000 of the income tax relief is withdrawn. His allowable loss is:

	£	£
Consideration		150,000
Allowable expenditure	200,000	
less income tax		
relief not withdrawn	(10,000)	
		(190,000)
Allowable loss		40,000

Restriction of disposal relief

16.5   Disposal relief is restricted where the taxpayer did not obtain income tax relief on the whole of the amount subscribed for the shares, unless that restriction was due solely to the fact that income tax relief is limited to the amount of the taxpayer's income tax liability.

This restriction applies to gains but not losses. It is normally a consequence of the subscription limit (see **16.3**) for income tax relief purposes. The fraction of the gain that is exempt in such a case is found by applying the fraction A/B to the gain, where:

- A is the amount of the income tax relief obtained; and

- B is an amount equal to tax at the lower rate (currently 20%) for that year on the amount subscribed for the shares (*TCGA 1992, s 150A(3); ICTA 1988, ss 832(1), 1A(1B)*).

Example 16.3

Richard subscribes £250,000 for shares in an EIS company in the tax year 2002/03, when the maximum amount on which income tax relief can be obtained is £150,000. He obtains income tax relief of £30,000 for that year. He sells the shares in 2006/07 for £400,000. His chargeable gain (before taper relief) is:

	£
Consideration	400,000
Allowable expenditure	(250,000)
Gain	150,000
Exemption:	
£150,000 x (30,000/50,000)	(90,000)
Chargeable gain	60,000

Identification rules

16.6   Where it is necessary to identify shares disposed of with acquisitions made at different times, or to establish whether the shares disposed of were shares that attracted income tax relief, the EIS identification rules in *ICTA 1988, s 299* are applied instead of the rules in *TCGA 1992*.

Broadly speaking, identification is made on a first in, first out basis. There are detailed rules for identification of shares acquired on the same day (*TCGA 1992, s 150A(4), (5)*).

Reorganisations, etc

16.7   The rules in *TCGA 1992, s 127* (equation of original shares and new holding) are to be applied, on a reorganisation of share capital within *TCGA 1992, s 126*, separately to each of the following kinds of shares. The effect of this rule is that shares of each kind are treated as a separate holding of original shares and identified with a separate new holding following the reorganisation:

- shares that have attracted income tax relief, where the investment has formed the basis of a deferral relief claim (see **16.10**) and there has been no chargeable event affecting the deferral relief;

- other shares that have attracted income tax relief; and

- shares that have not attracted income tax relief (*TCGA 1992, s 150A(6), (6A)*).

Where there is a rights issue in respect of an existing holding of ordinary shares, and either the existing shares or the new shares attract income tax relief, then the provisions of *TCGA 1992, ss 127* to *130* (which broadly treat the old and new shares as a single holding) do not apply to the existing holding (*TCGA 1992, s 150A(7)*).

Exchange of shares, etc

16.8   Where the rules in *TCGA 1992, ss 135* and *136* apply to exchanges of shares and securities in a company (A) for those in another company (B), their broad effect is that there is no disposal of the original holding in company A. Companies A and B are treated as if they were the same company and the exchange is treated as a reorganisation of its share capital.

These rules apply to EIS shares in company A only if the following conditions are met:

- company B has issued shares eligible for EIS income tax relief and has issued certificates to investors in respect of those shares (as required by *ICTA 1988, s 306(2)*);

- the shares in company B are new ordinary shares carrying no present or future preferential rights to dividends, or to assets in a winding up, and no present or future right to be redeemed; and

- the shares in company B are issued (i) on or after 29 November 1994, and (ii) outside the relevant period following company A's issue of EIS shares.

The rules in *TCGA 1992, ss 135* and *136* may also apply where a new company (C) meeting the conditions in *ICTA 1988, s 304A* acquires EIS shares in exchange for new shares in company C (*TCGA 1992, s 150A(8), (8A–8D)*).

The allowable expenditure deducted in computing the gain or loss on a disposal of EIS shares is adjusted in any case where the income tax relief was reduced following a reorganisation of share capital before 29 November 1994 (as provided by *ICTA 1988, s 305(2)* (*TCGA 1992, s 150A(9)*).

Reduction of income tax relief

16.9 Disposal relief is restricted if the EIS income tax relief was reduced because either or both of (a) or (b) below applied before the disposal (but after 28 November 1994):

(a) value is received from the company in circumstances where income tax relief is reduced under *ICTA 1988, s 300(1A)(a)*;

(b) there is a repayment, redemption, repurchase or payment in circumstances where income tax relief is reduced under *ICTA 1988, s 303(1A)(a)*.

In these circumstances the gain is computed in the normal way (applying any restriction required by *TCGA 1992, s 150A(3)* as mentioned in **16.5** above) and the exemption is then reduced by an amount found by applying the fraction A/B to the gain, where:

● A is the amount of the reduction in income tax relief; and

● B is the amount of income tax relief before the deduction.

Where the *TCGA 1992, s 150A(3)* restriction applies, the above fraction is applied to the exempt part of the gain and the deduction is made from that part (*TCGA 1992, s 150B*; CG 62812–62815).

CGT DEFERRAL RELIEF

16.10 Deferral of CGT is available where a chargeable gain accrues to an individual ('the investor') at any time after 28 November 1994 on the disposal of an asset and the investor makes a 'qualifying investment' (see **16.14**).

The relief is also available where the gain accrues on a deemed disposal under the rules for EIS deferral relief, VCT deferral relief (abolished for shares issued after 5 April 2004), or reinvestment relief under *TCGA 1992, s164A* (abolished for investments made after 5 April 1998). The time of the actual or deemed disposal giving rise to the gain is the 'accrual time'.

The asset disposed of – or deemed to be disposed of – may be any chargeable asset. The investment must be made, generally, within a period beginning one year before and ending three years after the accrual time (*TCGA 1992, s 150C, Sch 5B*).

There is no limit to the amount of the gain that can be deferred, but an individual cannot claim income tax relief for any amount subscribed for eligible shares that exceeds £400,000 (£200,000 for 2005/06) in a year of assessment (regardless of when the shares are issued) (*ICTA 1988, s 290*; *FA 2006, Sch 14, para 5*).

For HMRC guidance regarding CGT deferral relief, see their Venture Capital Schemes Manual at VCM 38000 onwards.

Residence condition

16.11   The investor must be resident or ordinarily resident in the UK:

- at the time when the gain accrues; and
- at the time when he makes the qualifying investment.

There are two further conditions to be satisfied in relation to residence status:

- the investor must not be regarded as resident in a territory outside the UK by virtue of any double taxation relief arrangements; and
- relief is not available if the effect of those arrangements is that he would not be liable to CGT in the UK on a disposal of the investment (disregarding for this purpose the exemption for a disposal of EIS shares in *TCGA 1992, s 150A*, see **16.2**) (*TCGA 1992, Sch 5B, para 1(1), (4)*).

Trustees

16.12   Trustees cannot claim EIS income tax relief or disposal relief. However, deferral relief is available to the trustees of a settlement where the asset on the disposal of which the chargeable gain accrued is settled property (a 'trust asset') (*TCGA 1992, Sch 5B, para 17(1)*).

Deferral relief applies to:

(a)   settled property in which there is no interest in possession (an interest in possession is, broadly, an immediate right to income of the settlement) so long as *all* the beneficiaries are individuals;

(b)   settled property in which the interests of the beneficiaries are interests in possession, if *any* of the beneficiaries are individuals (*TCGA 1992, Sch 5B, para 17(2)*).

Discretionary settlements and accumulation and maintenance settlements will fall within (a).

Where (b) applies but at the time of the disposal of the trust asset not all the beneficiaries are individuals, only a proportion of the gain that would accrue to the trustees on the disposal qualifies for deferral relief (*TCGA 1992, Sch 5B, para 17(3)*).

Deferral relief may be denied if the interests of the beneficiaries change between the time of the disposal and the time of the acquisition of the qualifying investment. Where either (a) or (b) above applies, relief is available only if it applies both (i) at the time of the disposal of the trust asset, and (ii) at the time of acquisition of the qualifying investment (*TCGA 1992, Sch 5B, para 17(4), (5)*).

There is a further condition where (b) applies. If not all the beneficiaries are individuals, the 'relevant proportion' (see below) at the time of acquisition of the qualifying investment must not be less than the relevant proportion at the time of the disposal of the trust asset (*TCGA 1992, Sch 5B, para 17(5)*).

If both individuals and others have interests in possession, 'the relevant proportion' is the proportion that A bears to B, where:

- A is the total amount of the income of the settled property representing interests held by beneficiaries who are individuals; and

- B is the total amount of all the income of the settled property (*TCGA 1992, Sch 5B, para 17(6)*).

There are complex anti-avoidance provisions relating to settled property (*TCGA 1992, Sch 5B, para 18*; see also VCM 41500–41650).

Postponing the gain

16.13   Deferral relief must be claimed (see **16.17**). The investor specifies the amount of the qualifying expenditure on the 'relevant shares' (ie the amount he has subscribed for the shares) that is to be set against a corresponding amount of the gain. The amount claimed cannot exceed the amount of gain before deduction of taper relief. See **16.25** regarding the interaction of deferral relief and taper relief.

The investor may well wish to limit the amount of his claim in order to utilise:

- any unused part of his CGT annual exemption;

- taper relief (which may result in only 25% of a gain accruing on disposal of business asset being chargeable – see **16.25**); or

- capital losses carried forward from earlier years of assessment.

Any part of the gain that has been matched with qualifying expenditure is treated as not having accrued at the accrual time (see **16.10**), but it is treated as accruing if there is a 'chargeable event' (see **16.19**) in relation to any of the shares (*TCGA 1992, Sch 5, para 2(2)*).

Any amount of the original gain that has not had expenditure set against it in this way is 'unmatched', and qualifying expenditure is 'unused' to the extent that it has not already been set against a chargeable gain (*TCGA 1992, Sch 5, para 2(1), (3), (4)*).

The 'relevant shares' are the shares acquired by the investor in making the qualifying investment (and still held by the investor at the time when the gain accrues, in a case where the investment is made before that time). This rule is modified to allow for bonus issues and reorganisations (*TCGA 1992, Sch 5, para 19(1A–1D)*).

The actual proceeds of the disposal on which the gain accrued do not have to be applied directly in subscribing for the new shares (VCM 38100).

Example 16.4

Kylie sold shares in June 2004 and a chargeable gain of £150,000 accrued to her. She subscribed £40,000 in November 2006, and a further £200,000 in May 2007, for eligible shares in an EIS company. She may claim deferral relief on up to £150,000 of chargeable gains but may wish to limit the claim to avoid wasting her 2004/05 annual exemption and any unused capital losses. She should also consider the impact of taper relief (see **16.25**).

Qualifying investment

16.14   The investor makes a qualifying investment if:

(a)   he subscribes for 'eligible shares' in a company and the shares are issued to him at a 'qualifying time'. If the accrual time (see **16.10**) is later than the qualifying time, the investor must still hold the shares at the accrual time;

(b)   he subscribes for the shares (other than any bonus shares) wholly in cash;

(c)   the company is a 'qualifying company' in relation to the shares – broadly, it must be an unquoted trading company but there are detailed conditions in *ICTA 1988, s 293*;

(d)   the shares (other than any bonus shares) are fully paid up when they are issued – shares are not fully paid up for this purpose if there is any undertaking to pay cash to any person in the future in relation to the acquisition;

(e)   the investor subscribes for the shares, and they are issued, for bona fide commercial purposes and not as part of arrangements the main purpose (or one of the main purposes) of which is the avoidance of tax (see below);

(f)   certain conditions in relation to who is carrying on the qualifying activities are satisfied in relation to the company – these are in *ICTA 1988, s 289(1A)*;

(g)   the shares (other than any bonus shares) are issued in order to raise money for the purpose of a qualifying business activity;

(h)   at least 80% of the money raised by the issue of the shares, together with the money raised by any other eligible shares of the same class issued by the company on the same day, is employed wholly for the purpose of that qualifying business activity no later than the time mentioned in *ICTA 1988, s 289(3)*, ie the end of the period of 12 months beginning with either the issue of the eligible shares or, if later, the commencement of the qualifying trade; and

(i)   all of the money so raised is employed wholly for that purpose not later than 12 months after the time mentioned in (h).

The conditions in (h) and (i) above are still satisfied if an amount of money is employed for another purpose, so long as that amount is not significant (*TCGA 1992, Sch 5B, para 1(2), (5)*).

HMRC consider that the condition in (e) above excludes a subscription that is motivated by benevolence. Their guidance says:

> 'This could be the case if, for example, the company were the proprietor of an unsuccessful professional football club and a supporter of the club paid a large premium for shares in the company; that may well not be a commercial subscription. Similarly, if the company is owned by a person whom the investor wishes to benefit and the investor pays a large premium for the shares with the object of increasing the value of the other person's shares, that too would not be a commercial subscription.'

HMRC also consider that deathbed investments are 'unlikely to be made for bona fide commercial purposes' (VCM 12140).

Eligible shares

16.15 'Eligible shares' take their meaning from the EIS income tax relief legislation, so that shares are eligible shares for deferral relief purposes if they are new ordinary shares which, throughout the following period, carry no present or future preferential right to dividends or to a company's assets on its winding up, and no present or future right to be redeemed. That period:

(a)   begins with the issue of the shares; and

(b)   ends immediately before the 'termination date' relating to those shares (*TCGA 1992, Sch 5B, para 19(1); ICTA 1988, s 289(7)*).

The termination date is the later of:

- the third anniversary of the issue of the shares; and

- the third anniversary of the commencement of the trade (*TCGA 1992, Sch 5B, para 19(1); ICTA 1988, s 312(1)*).

Example 16.5

Company A issued eligible shares on 1 January 2006 and used the funds for the purposes of a trade that commenced on 30 November 2005. The termination date is 1 January 2009.

Example 16.6

Company B issued eligible shares on 1 August 2006 and used the funds for the purposes of a trade that commenced on 1 September 2006. The termination date is 1 September 2009.

Time limits for reinvestment

16.16   The qualifying time in **16.14**(a) is any time in the period beginning one year before and ending three years after the accrual time, or any other such time as HMRC may allow (*TCGA 1992, Sch 5B, para 1(3)*).

HMRC guidance indicates that they will extend the standard time limits where the claimant can show that he:

- had a firm intention to comply with them, but

- was prevented from complying by some fact or circumstance beyond his control, and

- acted as soon as he reasonably could after ceasing to be so prevented.

Each case is considered on its own merits but examples of circumstances outside the claimant's control might include death or serious illness of a vital party at a crucial time, unsettled disputes or litigation or unexpected delay in receipt of disposal consideration.

HMRC say that a mere change of intention at a late stage, or a lack of funds due to the claimant having spent or invested the disposal consideration elsewhere, will not normally be regarded as circumstances beyond his control. If the claimant chooses to defer applying for shares until late in the standard reinvestment period, a subsequent issue of shares outside that period will not normally be regarded as a circumstance beyond his control (see VCM 38030 and VCM 68060, which refers to venture capital trust shares – VCT deferral relief was abolished in 2004 – but should be read for this purpose as referring to eligible shares in a qualifying EIS company).

Claims

16.17   The procedures and time limits for claims to deferral relief are set out by reference to the provisions for claims to income tax relief for an investment in EIS shares. *ICTA 1988, s 306* is applied with some modifications, so that:

(a)   a claim may not be made earlier than the time when the requirement in *ICTA 1988, s 289A(6)* is first satisfied – broadly, this requirement is that the trade (or research and development) concerned has been carried on for four months;

(b)   a claim may not be made later than five years after 31 January following the year of assessment in which the shares were issued; and

(c)   no claim may be made unless the claimant has received a certificate from the company, certifying that the conditions for relief (other than those relating to the investor) are satisfied in relation to the shares.

The company is required, before issuing the certificate mentioned in (c), to declare to HMRC that certain conditions have been, and remain, satisfied. Further details of the company's obligations in this regard, and penalties for non-compliance, are set out in *ICTA 1988, s 306 (TCGA 1992, Sch 5B, para 6)*.

There is no provisional relief. A claim may not be made before the shares are issued. The investor is required to submit to HMRC part 2 of the form EIS 3 completed by the company, which includes a claim form. The claim may be made either in the tax return or separately. The form EIS 3 should show:

- the amount paid on subscription for the shares;

- the company in which the investment has been made;

- the date the shares were issued;

- the office that deals with the company and the company's tax reference; and

- the chargeable gains against which deferral relief is claimed (VCM 38500).

Although there is no statutory clearance procedure, HMRC officers may give a provisional opinion on the basis of the information available to them, subject to review following receipt of a claim. Investors asking about the qualifying status of a company are referred to an officer of the EIS company. HMRC's small company enterprise centre will assist the company with regard to its qualifying status (VCM 38550).

Failure of conditions

16.18   The shares forming the investment are treated as never having been eligible for relief if the condition in **16.14**(g), relating to the purpose of the share issue, is not met (*TCGA 1992, Sch 5, para 1A(3)*).

The shares cease to be eligible shares on the date of an event occurring after they have been issued, if as a result of that event either of the following conditions is not satisfied:

- the qualifying company condition in **16.14**(c); or
- the condition in **16.14**(f) relating to who carries on the qualifying activities (*TCGA 1992, Sch 5, para 1A(1), (2)*).

If either of the conditions in **16.14**(h) and (i) above relating to the company's use of the money subscribed is not met, the shares are treated as:

- never having been eligible shares if the claim is made after the time limit mentioned in **16.14**(h) or (i) has expired; or
- ceasing to be eligible shares on the expiration of that time limit in any other case (*TCGA 1992, Sch 5, para 1A(4), (4A)*).

A notice, given by either the company or HMRC as appropriate, is required before any of these provisions can take effect (*TCGA 1992, Sch 5, para 1A(5), (6), (7)*).

Chargeable events

16.19   The effect of a chargeable event is explained at **16.21**. There is a chargeable event in relation to the shares if, after the qualifying investment has been made:

(a)   the investor disposes of the shares otherwise than by means of a 'disposal within marriage or civil partnership' (ie a no gain/no loss transfer between spouses or civil partners);

(b)   the shares are disposed of (but not to the investor) by a person who acquired them on a disposal that the investor made within marriage or civil partnership;

(c)   the investor becomes 'a non-resident' (ie a person who is neither resident nor ordinarily resident in the UK) while holding the shares and before the termination date – but see below regarding a temporary change of residence status;

(d)   a person who acquired the shares on a disposal within marriage or civil partnership becomes a non-resident while holding them and before the termination date; or

(e)   the shares cease (or are treated as ceasing) to be eligible shares, for example, where the company carries on non-qualifying activities (*TCGA 1992, Sch 5, para 3(1)*).

A temporary change of residence status does not give rise to a chargeable event as described in (c) or (d) above where the investor or the transferee, as the case may be:

● becomes a non-resident because he works in an employment or office and all the duties are performed outside the UK;

● becomes resident or ordinarily resident in the UK once again within three years from the time he became a non-resident; and

● has not disposed of any of the shares in the meantime – a person being taken to have disposed of any shares only if there has been such a disposal as would have been a chargeable event if he was UK resident (*TCGA 1992, Sch 5, para 3(3), (4)*).

The investor or the company is required to notify HMRC of the chargeable event within 60 days or, in specified cases, within 60 days of coming to know of the event. *TCGA 1992, Sch 5, para 16* sets out the detailed notification requirements and HMRC information powers.

Death of investor or transferee

16.20   An event within **16.19**(a) to (e) above is not a chargeable event, in relation to shares held by the deceased immediately before his death, if the event occurs at or after the time of the death of either (i) the investor, or (ii) a person who acquired any of the relevant shares on a disposal within marriage or civil partnership (*TCGA 1992, Sch 5, para 3(5)*).

Effect of chargeable event

16.21   Broadly, the 'deferred gain' (see below) becomes chargeable if a chargeable event (see **16.19**) occurs. A chargeable gain accrues on the occasion of a chargeable event in relation to any of the shares. The amount of the chargeable gain is equal to the part of the deferred gain that is attributable (see below) to the shares involved in the chargeable event (*TCGA 1992, Sch 5, para 4(1)*).

The 'deferred gain' is the amount of the original gain that has been matched against qualifying expenditure, less the amount of any gain treated as accruing as a result of an earlier chargeable event (*TCGA 1992, Sch 5, para 4(7)*).

The deferred gain attributable to any shares is found by attributing a proportionate part of the gain to each of the relevant shares held immediately before the chargeable event occurs (*TCGA 1992, Sch 5, para 4(6)*; VCM 38250).

Example 16.7

Monique subscribes £40,000 for eligible shares in 2004/05 and makes a claim to defer a chargeable gain of £20,000 accruing on the disposal of an investment property in 2003/04. She sells the shares in 2006/07. The whole of the deferred gain of £20,000 becomes chargeable for 2006/07.

Example 16.8

Finbar subscribes £70,000 for eligible shares in 2004/05 and makes a claim to defer a chargeable gain of £30,000 accruing on the disposal of land in 2003/04. He sells 50% of the shares in 2006/07. The same proportion of the deferred gain, ie £15,000, becomes chargeable for 2006/07.

See **16.25** below regarding the effect of taper relief.

Identification rules

16.22   It may be necessary for this purpose to determine whether deferral relief is attributable to the shares disposed of (including disposal by means of a no gain/no loss disposal within marriage or civil partnership).

Broadly speaking, identification is made on a first in, first out basis and the normal identification rules in *TCGA 1992, Pt IV, Ch I* are modified accordingly. There are detailed rules for identification of shares acquired on the same day and to cater for reorganisations (*TCGA 1992, Sch 5, para 4(2)–(5)*; VCM 38280).

Chargeable person

16.23   The chargeable gain accruing on the occurrence of a chargeable event is treated as accruing, as the case may be, to:

(a)   the person who makes the disposal;

(b)   the person who becomes a non-resident;

(c)   the person who holds the shares when they cease (or are treated as ceasing) to be eligible shares.

With regard to (c), if the investor has transferred some of his shares on a no gain/no loss disposal within marriage or civil partnership and the transferee retains those shares at the time of the chargeable event, then the gains accruing to the investor and the transferee are computed separately (*TCGA 1992, Sch 5, para 5*).

Reorganisations, etc

16.24   The rules in *TCGA 1992, s 127* (equation of original shares and new holding) are to be applied, on a reorganisation of share capital within *TCGA 1992, s 126*, separately to each of the following kinds of shares. The effect of this rule is that shares of each kind are treated as a separate holding of original shares and identified with a separate new holding following the reorganisation:

- shares to which both CGT deferral relief and income tax relief are attributable;

- shares to which CGT deferral relief only is attributable; and

- shares to which deferral relief is not attributable (*TCGA 1992, Sch 5, para 7(1)*).

Where there is a rights issue in respect of an existing holding of ordinary shares, and either the existing shares or the new shares are shares to which deferral relief is attributable, then the provisions of *TCGA 1992, ss 127* to *130* (broadly, treating the old and new shares as a single holding) do not apply to the existing holding (*TCGA 1992, Sch 5, para 7(2)*).

If a company (B) that has only subscriber shares acquires all the shares in an EIS company (A) in exchange for shares of a 'corresponding description' (see below) in company B, and the conditions in *TCGA 1992, s 135* are met so that *TCGA 1992, s 127* applies, the share exchange is not treated as involving a disposal of the shares in company A. The shares in company B attract deferral relief in place of the shares in company A and there are detailed rules setting out the effect of this treatment.

Shares in company B are of a 'corresponding description' where, if they were shares in company A, they would be of the same class and carry the same rights as the original shares. Shares are of the same class where they would be so treated if dealt with on the Stock Exchange (*TCGA 1992, Sch 5, para 8*).

Further detailed rules deal with reconstructions and amalgamations where CGT deferral relief, but not EIS income tax relief, is attributable to the shares (*TCGA 1992, Sch 5, para 9*).

EIS deferral relief: interaction with taper relief

16.25   The application of taper relief in relation to deferred or 'postponed' gains is examined in **11.39**. Broadly, when the postponed gain becomes chargeable, taper relief on the deferred gain is calculated by reference to the date of the original disposal. No further taper relief is available for the period from that date to the date of the chargeable event (but see **16.26** regarding serial EIS investments).

The Special Commissioner held in *Daniels v Revenue and Customs Commissioners* [2005] SpC 489 that deferral relief should be deducted from the chargeable gains accruing in the year of assessment before applying taper relief, because 'taper relief only applies to chargeable gains that the 1992 Act treats as accruing in the particular year of assessment'.

The taxpayer may restrict the amount of his deferral relief claim to take account of taper relief and any unused part of the annual exemption (*TCGA 1992, Sch A1, para 16(1)*).

Taper relief and serial EIS investments

16.26   The qualifying holding period for taper relief purposes (see **11.4**) may be extended in certain circumstances, increasing the taper relief that would otherwise be available, where gains that accrue on the disposal of EIS shares are themselves deferred by being matched with a second EIS investment and subsequently become chargeable (*TCGA 1992, s 150D, Sch 5BA*).

This special treatment applies where:

(a)   a chargeable gain ('the original gain') accrues on the disposal of shares ('the original shares') to which EIS deferral relief and/or income tax relief is attributable;

(b)   all or part of the original gain is deferred by being matched with a qualifying investment;

(c)   a chargeable gain ('the revived gain') is deemed to accrue on a later disposal ('the relevant disposal') of that investment; and

(d)   the original shares were issued after 5 April 1998 and disposed of after 5 April 1999 (*TCGA 1992, Sch 5BA, para 1(1), (2)*).

The qualifying holding period of the original shares in these circumstances is the period beginning with the date of issue of the original shares and ending with the date of the relevant disposal. Therefore, the holding periods of the two investments are taken together. However, a period when neither the original shares nor the reinvestment shares were held does not count for the purposes of taper relief (*TCGA 1992, Sch 5BA, para 1(3), (4)*).

The extent to which the business asset rate of taper relief is available is determined, broadly, on the assumption that the original shares and the reinvestment shares are the same asset (*TCGA 1992, Sch 5BA, para 1(3), (4)*; VCM 38250, VCM 43010).

Anti-avoidance rules

Reinvesting in the same company or a group company

16.27   The taxpayer does not make a qualifying investment – and is not, therefore, entitled to deferral relief – if the disposal giving rise to the gain that the taxpayer seeks to defer was the disposal of holding shares in a company (A) and:

- the qualifying company (see **16.14**) is company A itself; or
- the qualifying company is a company that either (i) was a member of the same group of companies (see below) as company A at the time of the above-mentioned disposal, or (ii) is a member of such a group when the eligible shares are issued (*TCGA 1992, Sch 5, para 10(1)*).

Eligible shares in a 'relevant company' (see below) are not regarded as a qualifying investment where the shares are issued after the taxpayer has already made a qualifying investment in a company (B) (the 'acquired holding') and obtained deferral relief on the disposal of either an asset (A) or shares in a company (A). A company is a 'relevant company' for this purpose if:

- where the taxpayer has disposed of any of the acquired holding in company B, it is either company B itself or a company that was a member of the same group of companies as company B at any time since the acquisition of the 'acquired holding' of shares in company B;
- it is company A, ie it is the company the disposal of whose shares gave rise to the deferral relief claim by virtue of the acquisition of the holding in company B; or
- it is a company which was a member of the same group of companies as company A at the time of the disposal of shares in company A or the time of the acquisition of the holding in company B (*TCGA 1992, Sch 5, para 10(2), (3)*).

A group of companies for this purpose comprises a company that has one or more 51% subsidiaries, together with those subsidiaries (*TCGA 1992, Sch 5, para 10(4)*).

Pre-arranged exits

16.28 Where an individual subscribes for eligible shares ('the shares') in a company, the shares are not eligible shares – so that no deferral relief is available – if there are 'relevant arrangements' (see below) that include any of the following:

(a) arrangements with a view to the repurchase, exchange or other disposal of the shares (or of other shares in or securities of the same company) – subject to an exception for certain exchanges of shares, etc;

(b) arrangements for the cessation of a trade carried on, or to be carried on, by the company or a person connected with it, except where the arrangements apply only on a winding up for bona fide commercial reasons that does not feature in the relevant arrangements;

(c) arrangements for the disposal of the company's assets (or of the assets of a person connected with the company), or of a substantial amount of those assets, subject to the exception mentioned in (b) for a winding up; and

(d) arrangements the main purpose of which (or one of the main purposes of which) is to provide protection for people investing in shares in the company against the risks attached to the investment, however that protection is provided, but excluding protection that a company would reasonably be expected to provide for itself (or, in the case of the parent company of a trading group, for its subsidiaries).

'Relevant arrangements' are the arrangements under which the shares are issued and any other arrangements, made before that share issue, in relation to it or in connection with it. 'Arrangements' include any scheme, agreement or understanding, whether or not legally enforceable (*TCGA 1992, Sch 5, paras 11, 19(1)*).

Put and call options

16.29 Special rules apply to put and call options. These do not affect the above rules relating to pre-arranged exits (*TCGA 1992, Sch 5, para 12(4)*).

Options granted after shares are issued

16.30 Shares issued to the investor cease to be eligible shares on the date of the grant, during the 'relevant period' (see **16.32**), of:

(a)   a put option granted to the investor, where the exercise of the option would bind the grantor to buy the shares from the investor; or

(b)   a call option granted by the investor, where the exercise of the option would bind the investor to sell the shares to the grantee.

The shares affected by this rule are those to which the option relates, ie the shares that would be treated as disposed of in pursuance of the option if (i) the option were exercised immediately after the grant, and (ii) there was an immediate disposal of the shares acquired on exercise of the option (*TCGA 1992, Sch 5, para 12*).

Options granted before shares are issued

16.31   If an option within (a) or (b) above is granted before the date on which the shares are issued, the shares are treated as never having been eligible shares (*TCGA 1992, Sch 5, para 12(2)(a)*).

Relevant period

16.32   The 'relevant period' for shares issued after 5 April 2000 is the period beginning with the incorporation of the company, or if the company was incorporated more than two years before the date on which the shares were issued, two years before that date. It ends immediately before the termination date (see **16.15**) (*TCGA 1992, Sch 5, para 19(1); ICTA 1998, s 312(1A)(a)*).

Value received by the investor

16.33   A chargeable event may arise if the investor receives value other than 'insignificant' value from the company at any time in the 'period of restriction'. The whole of the deferred gain becomes chargeable – there is no apportionment even if the value received represents only a part of the investment (*TCGA 1992, Sch 5B, para 13A*).

The 'period of restriction' is the period beginning one year before the shares are issued and ending immediately before the termination date (see **16.15**) relating to the shares (*TCGA 1992, Sch 5B, para 19(1)*).

An amount is of 'insignificant value' if (i) it is no more than £1,000, or (ii) it is greater than £1,000 but is insignificant in relation to the investment set against gains in a deferral relief claim.

HMRC guidance says that 'insignificant' should be given its dictionary meaning of 'trifling or completely unimportant'. HMRC also consider that if a receipt of value falls within periods of restriction relating to more than one share issue, there is no apportionment and the receipt must be taken into account in regard to each issue (VCM 40300, VCM 40350).

However, no amount of value received is treated as a receipt of insignificant value if arrangements existed, in the period of 12 months prior to the share issue, which provided for the investor (or an 'associate' of his) to receive value from the issuing company (or a person connected with it) in the period of restriction. 'Associate' takes its meaning from *ICTA 1988, s 417(3), (4)* except that brothers and sisters are excluded (*TCGA 1992, Sch 5, paras 13A(2)–(5), 19(1)*).

The shares are treated as never having been eligible shares if the investor receives value before the date of issue of the shares. If he receives value after that date, the shares cease to be eligible shares on the date when the value is received. There is no receipt of value by virtue of a disposal of shares that gives rise to a chargeable event (see **16.19**) (*TCGA 1992, Sch 5, para 13(1), (6)*).

Receipts of insignificant value during the period of restriction are aggregated for this purpose, and a chargeable event arises if the total value of the receipts is not an amount of insignificant value (*TCGA 1992, Sch 5, para 13(1B)*).

The investor receives value from the company if the company does anything that is mentioned in the first column of Table 16.1 below, and the value received by the investor in each case is as set out in the second column (*TCGA 1992, Sch 5, paras 13(2), (8), 13A(1)*).

Table 16.1

The company	The value received is
repays, redeems or repurchases any of its share capital or securities belonging to the investor or pays him to give up his right to any of the share capital or any security on its cancellation or extinguishment; repays, under arrangements connected with the acquisition of the shares, any debt owed to him other than a debt incurred by the company (i) on or after the date of issue of the shares, and (ii) otherwise than in consideration of extinguishment of a debt incurred before that date; or pays him to give up his right to any debt on its extinguishment	the amount received by the investor or, if greater, the market value of the share capital, securities or debt

347

The company	**The value received is**
releases or waives his liability to the company or discharges, or undertakes to discharge, his liability to someone else (a liability that is not discharged within 12 months of the time when it ought to have been discharged is treated as released or waived for this purpose)	the amount of the liability
makes a loan or advance to him that is not repaid in full before the shares are issued (see below)	the amount of the loan or advance less the amount of any repayment made before the issue of the shares
provides a benefit or facility for him	the cost to the company of providing the benefit or facility less any consideration given for it by the investor
disposes of an asset to him for no consideration, or for a consideration less than (or worth less than) the asset's market value; or acquires an asset from him for a consideration more than (or worth more than) the asset's market value	the difference between the market value of the asset and the consideration (if any) given for it
makes any payment to him other than a 'qualifying payment' (see below)	the amount of the payment

The investor also receives value from the company if a person connected with the company (as defined in *ICTA 1988, s 291*) either buys any of its share capital or securities belonging to the individual, or pays him for giving up a right in relation to any share capital or securities of the company. In this case the value received is the amount received by the investor or, if greater, the market value of the share capital or securities (*TCGA 1992, Sch 5, paras 13(5), 13A(1)*).

A loan is regarded as being made by the company to the investor where he incurs a debt to the company (other than an 'ordinary trade debt'), or a debt due from the investor to a third party is assigned to the company. An 'ordinary trade debt' is a debt for goods or services supplied in the ordinary course of a trade or business, so long as the credit period is no longer than six months and no longer than that normally given to customers of the business (*TCGA 1992, Sch 5, para 13(3), (11)*).

A debt or a liability is disregarded if a qualifying payment (see below) would discharge it, and a benefit or facility is disregarded if payment of equal value would be a qualifying payment (*TCGA 1992, Sch 5, para 13(9)*).

A 'qualifying payment' includes:

- a payment (by any company) of reasonable remuneration for service as an officer or employee, having regard to the duties of that position;

- a payment or reimbursement (by any company) of travelling or other expenses wholly, exclusively and necessarily incurred by the payee in the performance of duties as an officer or employee of that company;

- the payment (by any company) of any interest representing no more than a reasonable commercial return on money lent to that company;

- the payment (by any company) of a dividend or other distribution not exceeding a normal return on any investment in that company's shares or securities;

- a payment for the supply of goods that does not exceed their market value;

- a payment for the acquisition of an asset that does not exceed its market value;

- the payment (by any company), of a reasonable and commercial rent for property occupied by the company;

- reasonable and necessary remuneration paid (by any company) for services rendered to that company in the course of a UK trade or profession where the payment is included in the profits of that trade or profession for tax purposes; and

- a payment in discharge of an ordinary trade debt (*TCGA 1992, Sch 5, para 13(7)*).

The scope of these provisions is widened so that:

- a payment or disposal to the investor includes a payment or disposal made to him indirectly, or to his order, or for his benefit;

- anything received by an associate of the investor is treated as received by the investor; and

- a reference to a company includes a reference to a person who is connected with the company at any time in the 'relevant period' (see below) (*TCGA 1992, Sch 5, para 13(10)*).

The 'relevant period' for shares issued after 5 April 2000 is the period beginning with the incorporation of the company, or if the company was incorporated more than two years before the date on which the shares were issued, two years before that date. It ends immediately before the termination date (*TCGA 1992, Sch 5, para 19(1); ICTA 1998, s 312(1A)(a)*).

Value received by another person

16.34   Value received by persons other than the investor may give rise to a chargeable event. Detailed rules are set out in *TCGA 1992, Sch 5B, paras 14, 14AA* and *14A*.

Replacement value

16.35 Value received by the investor (the 'original value') may be disregarded where, broadly:

- the shares were issued after 6 March 2001 or the original value was received after that date;

- the original value was received in any of the circumstances set out in Table 16.1 (see **16.33**), except for value received in connection with the repayment of a debt;

- the person from whom the original value was received (the 'original supplier') receives replacement value in the form of a 'qualifying receipt', from the person who received the original value (the 'original recipient');

- the replacement value is not less than the original value; and

- the receipt of replacement value is not disregarded.

In broad terms, a 'qualifying receipt' may arise by means of a payment by the original recipient or the transfer of an asset between him and the original supplier for a consideration greater or less than market value. The detailed rules are set out in *TCGA 1992, Sch 5, paras 13B, 13C*.

Investment-linked loans

16.36 If an 'investment-linked loan' (see below) is made by any person, at any time in the relevant period, to an individual who subscribes for eligible shares (or to his associate), the shares are treated as:

- never having been eligible shares, if the loan is made on or before the date of the issue of the shares; and

- ceasing to be eligible shares when the loan is made, if it is made after that date.

A loan is 'investment-linked' if it would not have been made – or would not have been made on the same terms – if the individual had not subscribed for, or had not been proposing to subscribe for, the shares.

A loan is regarded as made by a person to an individual if the person gives him any credit, or a debt due from the individual to someone else is assigned to that person (*TCGA 1992, Sch 5B, para 16*).

HMRC have said that their primary concern is why the lender made the loan rather than why the borrower applied for it and relief is not necessarily denied just because a loan is used to finance the investment. HMRC said in statement of practice SP 6/98:

'The test is whether the lender makes the loan on terms which are influenced by the fact that the borrower, or an associate of the borrower, has acquired, or is proposing to acquire, the shares.

The rules would not have effect to deny or withdraw relief where a person proposing to acquire shares receives a loan from a bank, if the bank would have made a loan on the same terms to a similar borrower who was intending to use it for a different purpose. But if, for example, a loan is made on a specified security which consists of, or includes, the shares in question, it would be one which would not otherwise have been made on the same terms.

In such a case, the loan would be linked with the shares, and the investor would not qualify for relief in respect of them. This would apply only where the shares, or any rights associated with them, are specified as all or part of the security. It would not apply, for example, in any case where the lender had recourse against the borrower's assets generally.

In considering the terms of any particular loan, HMRC will have regard to such features as the qualifying conditions which must be satisfied by the borrower, the existence of incentives or benefits offered to the borrower, the time allowed for repayment, the amount of repayment'.

Chapter 17

Other reliefs

INTRODUCTION

17.1 Various exemptions for certain persons, assets or gains are examined in **Chapter 1**. Double taxation relief is examined in **Chapter 3**. The following provisions which reduce or defer liability to CGT or corporation tax on chargeable gains are discussed in **Chapter 2**:

- small part disposals – **2.5**;
- no gain, no loss disposals – **2.7**;
- assets lost, destroyed or becoming of negligible value – **2.10**;
- capital sums applied in restoring the asset – **2.17**.

The CGT reliefs that are most likely to be met in practice are discussed in the following chapters:

- taper relief – **Chapter 11**;
- private residence relief – **Chapter 12**;
- hold-over relief for gifts – **Chapter 13**;
- roll-over relief for replacement of business assets – **Chapter 14**;
- incorporation relief – **Chapter 15**; and
- enterprise investment scheme reliefs – **Chapter 16**.

This chapter examines the following reliefs:

- disposal relief and deferral relief for investments in venture capital trusts – **17.2**;
- relief for losses on loans to traders – **17.11**;
- relief against income for losses on shares in unlisted trading companies – **17.16**;

- retirement relief on disposal of business assets (now abolished) – **17.22**; and

- reinvestment relief (now abolished) – **17.23**.

VENTURE CAPITAL TRUSTS

17.2 Venture capital trusts (VCTs) are quoted companies, similar to investment trusts, that specialise in investing in small unquoted trading companies. An approved VCT is exempt from corporation tax on chargeable gains.

The main conditions for approval include the requirement that at least 70% of the company's investments are in qualifying unquoted trading companies (including companies listed on the alternative investment market or AIM), with at least 30% of investments being in ordinary shares and no single holding representing more than 15% of the investments. There are also limits on the value of the company's (or group's) gross assets.

The reliefs available for VCT investors are similar to those available for investments in enterprise investment scheme shares (see **Chapter 16**):

- income tax relief (including an exemption for dividends – see *Tottel's Income Tax 2006/07*);

- capital gains tax disposal relief; and

- capital gains tax deferral relief (for VCT shares issued before 6 April 2004).

Disposal relief

17.3 A gain is not a chargeable gain if it accrues to an individual on a 'qualifying disposal' (see below) of ordinary shares in a company which:

- was a VCT when he acquired the shares; and

- is still a VCT at the time of the disposal.

Any loss accruing where these conditions are met is not an allowable loss. Shares are ordinary shares if they form part of the company's ordinary share capital, ie the issued share capital of the company, other than capital that confers a right to a fixed-rate dividend but no other right to share in the profits of the company (*TCGA 1992, s 151A(1), (7); ICTA 1988, s 832*).

A 'qualifying disposal' is a disposal of shares, made by an individual, which meets the following conditions:

(a)   the individual has attained the age of 18 at the time of the disposal;

(b)   the shares were not acquired in excess of the 'permitted maximum' (see below) for any year of assessment; and

(c)   he acquired the shares for bona fide commercial purposes and not as part of a scheme or arrangement the main purpose of which, or one of the main purposes of which, is the avoidance of tax (*TCGA 1992, s 151A(2)*).

Disposal relief is available regardless of whether the taxpayer subscribed for the shares or acquired them from someone else. The 'permitted maximum' in (b) above requires, broadly speaking, that in any tax year the market value of all VCT shares acquired by an individual (or his nominees) must not exceed £200,000 at the time of acquisition. This limit was £100,000 per tax year for VCT shares acquired before 6 April 2004 (*TCGA 1992, s 151A(6)*; *ITTOIA 2005, ss 709, 710*).

HMRC guidance indicates that the restriction in (c) above is likely to apply only in 'exceptional' circumstances, where, for example, artificial arrangements are made to convert shares that do not qualify for disposal relief into qualifying shares (VCM 66050).

Identification rules

17.4   It may be necessary to identify shares disposed of with particular acquisitions of shares in order to establish whether a disposal relates to shares acquired in excess of the permitted maximum for a year of assessment. For this purpose, the following rules replace the normal rules for identification of share and securities (see **4.2**):

• disposals of shares acquired by the same person on the same day are identified first with any shares acquired in excess of the permitted maximum, and then with other shares;

• a first-in, first-out basis applies to disposals of shares acquired on different days – disposals are identified first with the earliest acquisitions, and then with later acquisitions (*TCGA 1992, ss 151A(4), 151B(1)*); and

• a person who disposed of VCT shares acquired at a time when the company was not a VCT is treated as having disposed of those shares before he disposed of any other shares in the same VCT (*TCGA 1992, s 151A(5)*).

Reorganisations, etc

17.5   The rules in *TCGA 1992, s 127* (equation of original shares and new holding) are to be applied, on a reorganisation of share capital within *TCGA*

1992, s 126, separately to each of the following kinds of shares. The effect of this rule is that shares of each kind are treated as a separate holding of original shares and identified with a separate new holding following the reorganisation:

(a)   VCT shares that are eligible for both CGT disposal relief and income tax relief;

(b)   VCT shares that are eligible for CGT disposal relief but not income tax relief;

(c)   VCT shares that are eligible for income tax relief but not CGT disposal relief; and

(d)   other VCT shares (*TCGA 1992, s 151B(2), (3)*).

Where there is a rights issue in respect of an existing holding of ordinary shares, and either the existing shares or the new shares fall within (a) to (c) above, then the provisions of *TCGA 1992, ss 127* to *130* (which broadly treat the old and new shares as a single holding) do not apply to the existing holding (*TCGA 1992, s 151B(4)*).

Exchange of shares, etc

17.6   Where the rules in *TCGA 1992, ss 135* and *136* apply to exchanges of shares and securities in a company (A) for those in another company (B), their broad effect is that there is no disposal of the original holding in company A. Companies A and B are treated as if they were the same company and the exchange is treated as a reorganisation of its share capital.

Those rules do not apply to an exchange of shares where:

• the shares in company A are shares falling within paragraph **17.5**(a) or (b) above; and

• the shares in company B are not ordinary shares in a VCT (*TCGA 1992, s 151B(5)*).

Withdrawal of company's approval as a VCT

17.7   A person holding shares eligible for disposal relief is deemed to dispose of and reacquire those shares at their market value if the company's approval as a VCT is withdrawn. He is deemed to dispose of the shares at the time the withdrawal takes effect (ie the date on which the notice of withdrawal is issued) and to reacquire them immediately for a consideration equal to their market value at that time. The effect of this rule is to preserve the benefit of disposal relief for the period for which approval applied.

17.8 *Other reliefs*

There are detailed rules relating to (i) identification of shares in these circumstances, and (ii) the effect of any reduction in income tax relief, any chargeable event under the deferral relief rules, and the death of the shareholder (*TCGA 1992, s 151B(6), (7), (8)*).

If a provisional VCT approval is withdrawn and the company does not meet the conditions for approval subsequently, disposal relief is not available.

If full approval is withdrawn – so that the investor's shares are deemed to be disposed of and reacquired as mentioned above – and the company subsequently regains its VCT status, HMRC consider that the shares do not become eligible again for disposal relief because the company will not have been a VCT at the time of the deemed reacquisition (VCM 66950).

Deferral relief

17.8 An individual could defer a chargeable gain on the disposal of any asset by subscribing for ordinary shares in a VCT before 6 April 2004. Relief was available for subscriptions of up to £100,000 per tax year. No deferral relief was available unless the taxpayer received income tax relief on the subscription. The relief was withdrawn with effect for VCT shares issued after 5 April 2004 (*TCGA 1992, s 151A(3)* and *Sch 5C*, repealed by *FA 2004*).

Although new investments in VCTs do not qualify for deferral relief, claims may still be made within the time limit (see **17.9**) and gains already deferred may be brought back into charge by reason of a chargeable event (see **17.10**), so a brief summary of this relief remains relevant.

The relief was available to individuals who were resident or ordinarily resident in the UK both at the time when the gain accrued and at the time of the qualifying investment. An individual was excluded from relief if he was regarded for the purposes of double taxation relief arrangements as resident in a territory outside the UK and the effect of those arrangements was that he would not be liable to UK tax on a gain arising on a disposal (ignoring for this purpose the disposal relief in **17.3**).

The shares had to be subscribed for within a period beginning one year before, and ending one year after, the disposal on which the gain accrued. It is possible, therefore, to use deferral relief to defer gains accruing up to 5 April 2005. HMRC have statutory powers to extend these time limits, but no extension can result in deferral relief being available for VCT shares issued after 5 April 2004 (*TCGA 1992, Sch 5C, para 1* repealed by *FA 2004*).

Deferral relief for investment in VCT shares operated in a broadly similar manner to deferral relief for investment in enterprise investment scheme shares (see **Chapter 16**).

Claims

17.9   Deferral relief must be claimed within five years after 31 January following the later of:

- the tax year in which the gain accrued; or
- the tax year in which the VCT shares were issued.

Chargeable events

17.10   The deferred gain becomes chargeable if, broadly speaking:

- there is a disposal of the VCT shares (other than a no gain/no loss disposal to a spouse or civil partner);

- the investor's spouse or civil partner disposes (to someone other than the investor) of VCT shares originally acquired from the investor under a no gain/no loss disposal;

- VCT shares are exchanged for non-VCT shares;

- the investor, or a spouse or civil partner who has received the shares on a no gain/no loss transfer, becomes non-resident within a three-year qualifying period (five years for shares issued before 6 April 2000);

- HMRC withdraws the company's approval as a VCT; or

- income tax relief for the VCT investment is withdrawn or reduced in circumstances other than those outlined above.

The deferred gain is not clawed back on the death of the investor or on the death of a spouse or civil partner who acquired the shares on a no gain/no loss disposal (*TCGA 1992, Sch 5C, paras 3–6*, repealed by *FA 2004* with effect for shares issued after 5 April 2004).

LOANS TO TRADERS

17.11   Where a person (A) incurs a debt to another person (B), no chargeable gain accrues to the original creditor (B) on his disposal of the debt, except in the case of (i) a debt on a security, and (ii) money held in a foreign currency bank account that does not represent currency acquired for personal expenditure outside the UK (*TCGA 1992, ss 251, 252*).

For individuals, trustees and personal representatives, a debt is, therefore, not normally subject to CGT unless it is a 'debt on a security' (meaning, broadly, marketable loan stock).

Most loan stock is a type of 'qualifying corporate bond', which is an exempt asset (*TCGA 1992, s 115*). Therefore, as a general rule, gains on simple debts are exempt from CGT and no relief is available for losses.

However, the special rules summarised below make provision for allowable losses incurred on loans made after 11 April 1978 to UK traders. Relief is not available for amounts taken into account in computing income for tax purposes (*TCGA 1992, s 253*).

For companies, profits (and losses) on loans are generally treated as income (and deductions in computing income) under the 'loan relationship' rules. Such profits and losses are outside the scope of corporation tax on chargeable gains, therefore, regardless of whether the company is a borrower or a lender. Where part of a loan becomes irrecoverable on or after 1 April 1996, relief under *TCGA 1992, s 253* is available only to a company if the loan relationship rules do not apply to the loss.

Conditions

17.12   Relief is available for a 'qualifying loan', ie a loan in relation to which:

(a)   the borrower uses the money wholly for the purposes of a trade, profession or vocation, other than a trade, etc involving the lending of money, which he carries on;

(b)   the borrower is UK resident;

(c)   the borrower's debt is not a debt on a 'security' (as defined in *TCGA 1992, s 132*, ie any secured or unsecured loan stock or similar security of (i) any government, or (ii) any public or local authority, or (iii) any company) (*TCGA 1992, s 253(1), (2)*).

Where the money is lent to company A and that company lends it on to company B, and company B is a trading company in the same group, relief is available for the loan to company A as if company A had used the money for the purpose for which company B used it while a member of the group (*TCGA 1992, s 253(2)*).

HMRC accept that bank overdrafts and credit balances on directors' loan accounts, but not ordinary trade debts, are capable of being qualifying loans. HMRC consider that a loan used for 'mixed purposes' would not qualify. However, a proportion of a loan used partly for trade purposes and partly for non-trade purposes would qualify – for example, a loan for the construction of premises part of which are used for trade purposes (CG 65932, CG 65933).

Relief for irrecoverable loans

17.13   An allowable loss is treated as accruing to a taxpayer who has made a qualifying loan, and has made a claim to relief, if at the time he made the claim (or at an earlier time, see below):

- any amount of the outstanding principal has become irrecoverable;
- the claimant has not assigned his right to recover the amount; and
- the claimant and the borrower were not each other's spouses, civil partners, or companies in the same group, either at the time the loan was made or at any later time.

The amount of the allowable loss is the amount of the outstanding principal that has become irrecoverable. It is specifically provided that no relief is due if that amount is treated as a debit on a loan relationship (as discussed in **17.11**) (*TCGA 1992, s 253(3)*).

The taxpayer may specify an earlier time than the date of the claim (and possibly obtain the benefit of the allowable loss in an earlier tax year) if the outstanding amount was irrecoverable at that earlier time. However, the earlier time must be:

- for CGT purposes, not more than two years before the beginning of the year of assessment in which the claim is made; or
- for corporation tax purposes, not before the first day of the earliest accounting period ending not more than two years before the time of the claim (*TCGA 1992, s 253(3A)*).

HMRC accept that a loan has become irrecoverable where they come to the view that there was in fact 'no reasonable prospect' of recovery of the loan at the date of the claim (or at the earlier time mentioned above). They take account of funds potentially available as well as those currently available, and take the view that the initial presumption should be that the loan remains recoverable if the borrower continues to trade, even at a loss (CG 65950).

If there is a short period between the loan being granted and the date on which it is claimed to have become irrecoverable, HMRC may wish to establish what happened to the business in that period, and may examine in particular:

- what happened to make the loan irrecoverable so soon after it was made; and
- whether there was a reasonable prospect of recovery at the time the loan was made (CG 65951).

A loan is not treated as becoming irrecoverable if it has become so in consequence of the terms of the loan, any arrangements surrounding the loan, or any act or omission by the lender. HMRC guidance regards these conditions as anti-avoidance measures to exclude arrangements ranging from a gift presented as a loan to sophisticated schemes 'such as the siphoning of resources out of a company which then becomes unable to repay its loan' (*TCGA 1992, s 253(12)*; CG 65958).

Relief for payments made by a guarantor

17.14   Relief may be available to a taxpayer who has guaranteed the repayment of a qualifying loan (or a loan that would be a qualifying loan but for the condition in **17.12**(c)). An allowable loss is treated as accruing to such a taxpayer who has made a claim to relief, if at the time he made the claim:

- any amount of the outstanding principal or interest has become irrecoverable from the borrower;
- the taxpayer has made a payment under the guarantee, either to the lender or to a co-guarantor, relating to that amount;
- the taxpayer has not assigned any right, accruing to him in return for making the payment, to recover that amount;
- the lender and the borrower were not each other's spouses or civil partners, or companies in the same group, either at the time the loan was made or at any later time; and
- the taxpayer and the lender were not each other's spouses or civil partners, or companies in the same group, either at the time the guarantee was given or at any later time.

The amount of the allowable loss is:

- the amount of the payment made by the taxpayer in respect of the outstanding principal or interest that has become irrecoverable from the borrower, *less*

- any contribution payable to him by any co-guarantor (*TCGA 1992, s 253(4)*).

A loan is not treated as becoming irrecoverable if it has become so in consequence of the terms of the loan; any arrangements surrounding the loan; or any act or omission by the lender or guarantor (*TCGA 1992, s 253(12)*).

A claim in respect of a payment made under a guarantee must be made:

- for CGT purposes, within five years after 31 January following the year of assessment in which the payment was made; or
- for corporation tax purposes, within six years after the end of the accounting period in which the payment was made (*TCGA 1992, s 253(4A)*).

Recovery of loan or payment made under guarantee

17.15   If the taxpayer recovers any part of a loan or guarantee payment that has given rise to an allowable loss, the amount recovered is treated as a chargeable gain accruing at the time of recovery. The amount of the gain is so much of the loss as corresponds to the amount recovered. There are corresponding provisions for companies (*TCGA 1992, s 253(5)–(8)*).

The taxpayer is treated as recovering an amount if he receives – or directs someone else to receive – money or money's worth either in satisfaction of his right of recovery or in return for assigning that right. If he assigns the right under a bargain made otherwise than at arm's length (see **3.5**) he is treated as receiving money or money's worth equal to the market value of the right (*TCGA 1992, s 253(9)*).

Example 17.1

Patricia lent £10,000 to her sister Judy in June 2001 to help her continue in business. In May 2006, Judy's business collapsed and it was clear that she would not be able to repay the loan.

Patricia made a claim in her 2006/07 tax return that the loan had become irrecoverable at 5 April 2007. She may set off the resulting loss of £10,000 against any chargeable gains accruing in 2006/07, and carry any unused allowable loss forward indefinitely. Any part of the sum of £10,000 that is repaid at a later date will give rise to a chargeable gain equal to the amount repaid.

LOSSES ON SHARES IN UNLISTED TRADING COMPANIES

17.16   Relief against income chargeable to income tax or corporation tax (as opposed to relief against chargeable gains) may be claimed for a capital loss where the following conditions are satisfied. This relief is available only to individuals and investment companies. HMRC guidance says it is intended 'to provide investors in unlisted trading companies with some degree of financial insurance against failure' (*ICTA 1988, s 574(1)*; VCM 45010).

Relief for individuals

17.17   An individual who has subscribed for shares in a 'qualifying trading company' (see **17.19**), and incurs an allowable loss for CGT purposes on the disposal of the shares in a year of assessment, may claim relief from income tax on:

(a)   an amount of his income for that year equal to the amount of the loss; or

(b)   the whole of his income, where his income is less than the amount of the loss.

Alternatively, he may claim relief for the amount in (a) or (b) for the preceding year of assessment. No part of any loss may be relieved more than once. Once a loss has been relieved against income, it is no longer an allowable loss for CGT purposes. This relief must be claimed no later than 12 months after 31 January following the year of assessment in which the loss was incurred (*ICTA1988, s 574(1)*).

For this purpose an individual 'subscribes' for shares if:

- the company issues the shares to him in return for money or money's worth; or
- he acquires them from his spouse or civil partner by means of a lifetime transfer and the spouse or civil partner acquired them by subscription (*ICTA1988, s 574(3)*).

The disposal giving rise to the loss must be:

- a disposal by way of a bargain made at arm's length for full consideration;
- a disposal by way of a distribution in a dissolution or winding up of the company;
- a disposal involving the entire loss, destruction, dissipation or extinction of the asset (see *TCGA 1992, s 24(1)*); or
- a deemed disposal arising on a claim that the value of the asset has become negligible (under *TCGA 1992, s 24(2)*) (*ICTA1988, s 575(1)*).

There are detailed rules concerning company reorganisations and exchanges of shares; identification of shares disposed of with acquisitions; and value shifting (*ICTA 1988, s 576(1), (1A), (1B), (1C), (2)*).

Order of reliefs

17.18   Income tax relief claimed under *ICTA 1988, s 574* for the year of assessment in which the loss accrued takes priority over income tax relief claimed for the preceding year, for the purpose of establishing what losses remain and what income remains chargeable.

Income tax relief claimed under *ICTA 1988, s 574* for either the year of the loss or the preceding year takes priority over trading losses for which a claim has been made under either *ICTA 1988, s 380* (set-off against general income) or *ICTA 1988, s 381* (losses in early years of a trade available for set-off against general income of preceding years) (*ICTA 1988, s 574(2)*).

Qualifying trading company

17.19 A 'qualifying trading company' (see **17.17**) is a company that meets the conditions in (a) and (b) below:

(a) the company (i) is an 'eligible trading company' (see below) on the date of the disposal, or (ii) ceased to be an eligible trading company at a time within three years before that date and since that time it has not been:

- an excluded company,

- an investment company, or

- a trading company that is not an eligible trading company;

(b) the company:

- has been an eligible trading company for a continuous period of six years ending on the date in (a) (or at the time in (a)); or

- has been an eligible trading company for a shorter continuous period ending on that date (or at that time) and has not before the beginning of that period been an excluded company, an investment company or a trading company that is not an eligible trading company; and

- has carried on business wholly or mainly in the UK throughout the 'relevant period' (*ICTA 1988, s 576(4)*).

Several detailed definitions are provided, including:

- 'eligible trading company' is defined by reference to the 'qualifying companies' rules for the purpose of the enterprise investment scheme (*ICTA 1988, s 576(4A), (4B)*);

- 'trading company' means a company, other than an 'excluded company', which is either (i) a company whose business consists wholly or mainly of the carrying on of a trade or trades, or (ii) the holding company of a trading group;

- 'excluded company' means, broadly, a company (i) whose trade consists wholly or mainly of dealing in land, commodities or futures, or in shares, securities or other financial instruments, or is not carried on a commercial basis, or (ii) which is the holding company of a group other than a trading group, or (iii) which is a building society or a registered industrial and provident society; and

- 'relevant period' means the period ending with the date of disposal of the shares and beginning with company's incorporation (or, if later, one year before the date of issue of the shares (*ICTA 1988, s 576(5)*).

Various definitions and conditions are modified where the shares were issued before 6 April 1998.

Relief for companies

17.20   A similar relief to that described in **17.17** is available to an investment company incurring an allowable loss for corporation tax purposes on the disposal of shares, for which it subscribed, in a qualifying trading company. The company disposing of the shares must meet both of the following conditions:

(a)   it is an investment company on the date of disposal and (i) has been an investment company for a continuous period of six years ending on that date, or (ii) has been an investment company for a shorter continuous period ending on that date and was not a trading company or an excluded company before the beginning of that period; and

(b)   it was not, at any time when it held the shares, associated with (or a member of the same group as) the qualifying trading company (*ICTA 1988, s 573(1)*).

The company may make a claim, within two years after the end of the accounting period in which the loss was incurred, for the allowable loss to be set against income for corporation tax purposes as follows:

*   income of that accounting period; and
*   income of preceding accounting periods ending within a specified period (see below) if the company was then an investment company.

The specified period is the period of 12 months ending immediately before the accounting period in which the loss is incurred, and an apportionment may be required if that period was longer than 12 months. The loss is relieved against income of later periods before income of earlier periods (*ICTA 1988, s 573(2), (3)*).

There are detailed rules setting out the interaction between losses, charges and management expenses; specifying the order of reliefs; and providing various definitions (*ICTA 1988, s 573(4)–(6)*).

COMPULSORY PURCHASE ROLL-OVER RELIEF

17.21   If the proceeds from the compulsory disposal of land by an authority are reinvested in acquiring new land, a form of CGT roll-over relief may be available. The taxpayer – who may be an individual, trustee or company – may claim to defer the gain by setting it against allowable expenditure on replacement land (to be used for any purpose except as a dwelling house, see below) acquired within one year before and three years after the disposal.

This relief operates in a broadly similar manner to roll-over relief for replacement of business assets (see **Chapter 14**). However, it is:

- not available if the landowner advertised the land for sale, or otherwise indicated a willingness to sell;

- not available if the replacement property attracts principal private residence relief (see **Chapter 12**) within six years following its acquisition;

- restricted where the original proceeds are only partly reinvested (*TCGA 1992, ss 247* and *248*).

Example 17.2

David owns freehold land with an agreed 31 March 1982 value of £98,000. Part of the land is made the subject of a compulsory purchase order and compensation of £70,000 is agreed on 10 August 2006. The market value of the remaining land is £175,000. The indexation factor for the period March 1982 to April 1998 is 1.047. The chargeable gain accruing on the disposal is £12,684, computed as shown below. David acquires new land for £80,000 in December 2006, and claims roll-over relief:

	£	£
Disposal consideration Aug 2006		70,000
Market value in March 1982:		
£98,000 x [70,000 / (70,000+ 175,000)]		(28,000)
Unindexed gain		42,000
Indexation allowance £28,000 x 1.047		(29,316)
Chargeable gain (subject to taper relief)		12,684
Consideration for disposal		70,000
Allowable cost of land compulsorily purchased	28,000	
Add: indexation allowance	29,316	
Deemed consideration for disposal		(57,316)
Roll-over relief		12,684
Allowable cost of replacement land £80,000 – £12,684		67,316

RETIREMENT RELIEF

17.22   Retirement relief was abolished for disposals made after 5 April 2003. The effect of the relief was to reduce the amount of chargeable gains accruing on disposals of business assets (including, for this purpose, certain shares or securities of a company) made at a time when the taxpayer had either (i) attained the age of 50, or (ii) retired on ill-health grounds below that age (*TCGA 1992, ss 163, 164, Sch 6* before repeal by *FA 1998*).

The relief operated by reducing the amount of chargeable gains on certain disposals of business assets. It was phased out between 6 April 1999 and 5 April 2003 by means of a gradual reduction in the thresholds shown in Table 17.1 below.

Table 17.1

Tax year	100% relief on gains up to	50% relief on gains between
1998/99	£250,000	£250,001 – £1m
1999/2000	£200,000	£200,001 – £800,000
2000/01	£150,000	£150,000 – £600,000
2001/02	£100,000	£100,001 – £400,000
2002/03	£50,000	£50,001 – £200,000

Retirement relief was automatic in most cases – it did not require a formal claim by individuals aged 50 or over. However, individuals retiring on ill-health grounds were required to make a claim, supported by medical evidence, within one year after 31 January following the end of the tax year in which the qualifying disposal took place.

The amount of relief varied according to the length of time for which the conditions were met (the 'qualifying period') in relation to the disposal of certain assets. The rate of relief increased from 10% where the period was precisely one year, to 100% after ten years, with time apportionment for part of a year. Where the final qualifying period was less than ten years, separate periods of business activity could be aggregated if the gap between them was not more than two years. The relief was given after indexation allowance, but took precedence over incorporation relief, hold-over relief for gifts and taper relief.

Retirement relief applied only to chargeable business assets, such as land and buildings and goodwill. On the disposal of shares in a personal company, only a proportion of gains would qualify for retirement relief if the company had chargeable assets that were not business assets. The detailed rules were set out in *TCGA 1992, ss 163, 164, Sch 6* before their repeal by *FA 1998*, subject to transitional provisions.

REINVESTMENT RELIEF

17.23   Reinvestment relief (also known as roll-over relief on reinvestment) was abolished with effect for qualifying investments made after 5 April 1998. The effect of the relief was to defer the CGT liability arising on the disposal of any asset where the taxpayer acquired a qualifying investment (broadly limited to shares in unquoted trading companies) within a certain period (*TCGA 1992, ss 164A* to *164N* before repeal by *FA 1998*).

This relief was replaced by the deferral reliefs for investment in enterprise investment scheme shares (see **Chapter 16**) and venture capital trust shares (see **17.8**).

REINVESTMENT RELIEF

Index

[all references are to paragraph number]

A

Absolute entitlement
settlements, and   8.3
Accumulation and maintenance trusts
hold-over relief, and   8.24
Acquisition costs
assignment of lease, and   4.12
generally   3.38
incidental costs   3.39
wasting assets, and   4.26
Acquisition of assets on no gain, no loss transfer
assets held on 31 March 1982, and   3.73
indexation allowance   3.64–3.65
Administration of an estate
deeds of appointment   7.14
deeds of variation
  effect   7.17
  election   7.18
  generally   7.16
  introduction   7.14
disclaimers
  effect   7.17
  election   7.18
  generally   7.15
  introduction   7.14
general provisions   7.4
introduction   7.1
period prior to date of death, and
  general provisions   7.2
  losses of deceased   7.3
personal representatives   7.5
principal private residence relief, and   12.27–12.31

Administration of an estate – *contd*
transactions during administration
  allowable expenses   7.8
  annual exemption   7.10
  indexation   7.9
  introduction   7.7
  taper relief   7.9
  transfers to legatees   7.11–7.13
  valuation of assets   7.6
Aggregate market value
disposal in series of transactions, and   3.14
Agricultural grants
exempt assets, and   1.8
Aircraft
roll-over relief, and   14.18
Annual exemption
generally   1.16
indexation   1.17
losses, and   1.19
personal representatives, and   1.20
settlements, and   8.21–8.22
taxable amount   1.18
transactions during administration of estates, and   7.10
trustees, and   1.21
Annuities
exempt assets, and   1.8
retiring partners, and   6.14–6.16
Anti-avoidance
disclosure of schemes   10.3
Enterprise Investment Scheme, and
  pre-arranged exits   16.28
  put and call options   16.29–16.32

369

Anti-avoidance – *contd*
Enterprise Investment Scheme, and
– *contd*
  reinvestment in same
    company or group
    company   16.27
  replacement value   16.35
  value received by investor   16.33
  value received by other
    person   16.34
  fluctuations in value   11.29
  pre-arranged exits   16.28
  put and call options
    generally   16.29
    granted after shares issued   16.30
    granted before shares
     issued   16.31
    relevant period   16.32
  principal private residence
    relief , and
    Finance Act 2006, and   12.35
    'washing' gain   12.32–12.34
  Ramsay decision   10.4
  recent developments   10.2
  reinvestment in same
    company or group
    company   16.27
  replacement value   16.35
  taper relief, and
    fluctuations in value   11.29
    groups of companies   11.33
    inactive companies   11.30–11.33
    liquidation   11.32
    non-resident companies   11.35
    value shifting   11.34
  value received by investor   16.33
  value received by other
    person   16.34
  value shifting   11.34

Apportionment
  non-resident company's gains
    calculation of tax charge   5.28
    corporate participators   5.31
    disposal of interest in
     company   5.27
    exceptions   5.25
    introduction   5.23

Apportionment – *contd*
non-resident company's gains –
  contd
    losses   5.29
    participators   5.30
    set-off on distribution of
     gain   5.26
    trustees   5.32
    UK-resident participator, to   5.24
Appropriate proportion
  disposal in series of
    transactions, and   3.13
Art works
  exempt assets, and   1.8
Asset
  disposals, and   2.2
Assets derived from other
  assets
  consideration for disposal,
    and   3.47
  taper relief, and   11.37
Assets held on 6 April 1965
  generally   3.76
  land reflecting development
    value   3.78
  other assets   3.79
  quoted shares and securities   3.77
Assets held on 6 April 1965
  and 31 March 1982
  generally   3.74
  shares and securities   4.6
Assets held on 31 March 1982
  acquisition on no gain, no
    loss transfer   3.73
  deferred charges on gains   3.75
  election   3.70
  exceptions to rule   3.70
  excluded disposals   3.72
  general rule   3.69
  indexation allowance, and   3.63
  introduction   3.68
  roll-over relief, and   14.28
  shares and securities   4.6
Asset surplus sharing ratio
  partnerships, and   6.10
Assignment of lease
  acquisition costs   4.12

Assignment of lease – *contd*
enhancement costs 4.13
generally 4.11

B
Bare trustees
exempt persons, and 1.10
settlements, and 8.3
'Bed and breakfasting'
shares and securities, and 4.2
tax planning, and 10.17
Beneficial ownership
chargeable persons, and 1.5
Betting winnings
exempt assets, and 1.8
**Business Expansion Scheme
shares**
exempt assets, and 1.8
Buy to let properties
principal private residence
relief, and 12.17

C
Calculation of CGT
annual exemption
generally 1.16
indexation 1.17
losses, and 1.19
personal representatives,
and 1.20
taxable amount 1.18
trustees, and 1.21
chargeable amount 1.13
gains accruing to others 1.14
indexation allowance 1.12
introduction 1.11
rates of tax
companies 1.24
individuals 1.22
personal representatives 1.23
trustees 1.23
rebasing 1.12
taper relief 1.15
taxable amount 1.18
Capital allowances
computation of losses, and 3.55
wasting assets, and 4.24

Capital gains tax (CGT)
*and see under individual
headings*
basis of charge 1.1
calculation 1.11–1.24
chargeable persons 1.3–1.5
exemptions 1.6–1.10
historical background 1.2
introduction 1.1
legislative framework 1.2
self-assessment 1.25–1.37
Capital losses
companies, and 9.17
**Capital sums derived from
assets**
applied in restoring asset 2.17
capital/revenue issue 2.13
contractual rights 2.15
generally 2.12
introduction 2.6
money's worth 2.14
statutory rights 2.15
time of disposal 2.16
Cashback
exempt assets, and 1.9
Charge to tax
introduction 1.1
residence, and 5.1
Chargeable amount
calculation of CGT, and 1.13
Chargeable gains
companies, and 9.1
computation of gains and
losses, and 3.1
disposals, and 2.1
generally 1.1
Chargeable persons
beneficial ownership 1.5
exempt persons 1.10
generally 1.3
territorial limits 1.4
Charges
disposals, and 2.18
Charities
exempt persons, and 1.10
Chattels
exempt assets, and 1.8

Index

Chattels – *contd*
introduction 4.20
parts of a set 4.21
Child Trust Funds
exempt assets, and 1.9
Civil partners
computation of gains and
losses, and 3.67
hold-over relief, and 13.1
principal private residence
relief, and 12.23
roll-over relief, and 14.12
taper relief, and 11.5
tax planning, and 10.13
Clearance
corporate venturing scheme,
and 9.29
'Clogged shares'
shares and securities, and 4.1
**Community amateur sports
clubs (CASCs)**
exempt persons, and 1.10
Companies
basis of charge 9.1
capital losses 9.17
chargeable gains 9.1
computation 9.2
consideration for disposal to
connected persons, and 3.20
corporate venturing scheme
clearance 9.29
deferral relief 9.32
introduction 9.24
investing company 9.26
investment relief 9.30–9.31
issuing company 9.27
nature of investment 9.28
loss relief 9.33
types of available relief 9.25
groups of companies
definitions 9.4–9.5
depreciatory transaction
losses 9.14
dividend stripping 9.15
intra-group transfers 9.6–9.9
pre-entry losses and gains 9.16
roll-over relief 9.13

Companies – *contd*
groups of companies – *contd*
transfer of assets from
trading stock 9.12
transfer of assets to trading
stock 9.10–9.11
intra-group transfers
company leaving group 9.8–9.9
election to treat disposal as
if made by another
group member 9.7
generally 9.6
introduction 9.1
rates of tax, and 1.24
relief on disposal of shares
corporate venturing scheme 9.24–9.33
introduction 9.18
losses on shares in unlisted
trading companies 9.19
substantial shareholdings
exemption 9.20–9.23
replacement of business assets
relief 9.3
roll-over relief 9.3
substantial shareholdings
exemption
conditions affecting
investee company 9.22
conditions affecting
investing company 9.21
introduction 9.20
trading company 9.23
Compensation
exempt assets, and 1.8
**Compulsory purchase
roll-over relief**
generally 17.21
**Computation of gains and
losses**
acquisition costs
generally 3.38
incidental costs 3.39
acquisition of assets on no
gain, no loss transfer
assets held on 31 March
1982, and 3.73

Computation of gains and losses –
contd
  acquisition of assets on no gain, no
    loss transfer – *contd*
    indexation allowance   3.64–3.65
    assets derived from other
      assets   3.47
    assets held on 6 April 1965,
      and
      generally   3.76
      land reflecting development
        value   3.78
      other assets   3.79
      quoted shares and
        securities   3.77
    assets held on 6 April 1965
      and 31 March 1982, and   3.74
    assets held on 31 March
      1982, and
      acquisition on no gain, no
        loss transfer   3.73
      deferred charges on gains   3.75
      election   3.70
      exceptions to rule   3.70
      excluded disposals   3.72
      general rule   3.69
      indexation allowance   3.63
      introduction   3.68
  chargeable gains, and   3.1
  civil partners   3.67
  connected persons, disposal to
    'connected persons'   3.16–3.20
    generally   3.10
    losses, and   3.21
    series of transactions, in   3.11–
        3.15
  consideration for disposal
    assets derived from other
      assets   3.47
    connected persons, to   3.10–3.21
    contingent consideration   3.27–
        3.34
    deferred consideration   3.27–3.34
    delayed consideration   3.22–3.26
    introduction   3.3
    irrecoverable consideration   3.22–
        3.26

Computation of gains and losses –
contd
  consideration for disposal – *contd*
    market value rule   3.5–3.6, 3.44–
        3.45
    part disposals   3.46
    quoted shares and
      securities   3.7
    series of transactions   3.11–3.15
    sums chargeable as income   3.4
    unit trust holdings   3.8
    unquoted shares and
      securities   3.9
  contingent consideration
    ascertainable   3.28
    election to carry back loss
      on disposal of right   3.30–
        3.34
    generally   3.27
    unascertainable   3.29
  contingent liabilities   3.24
  deductible expenditure
    acquisition costs   3.38–3.39
    enhancement costs   3.40
    incidental costs   3.41
    introduction   3.37
    reimbursements from
      public funds, and   3.42
    trading income expenses,
      and   3.42
  deferred consideration
    ascertainable   3.28
    election to carry back loss
      on disposal of right   3.30–
        3.34
    generally   3.27
    unascertainable   3.29
  delayed consideration
    contingent liabilities   3.24
    disposals outside terms of
      TCGA 1992, s 49   3.25
    generally   3.22
    loan relationships, and   3.23
    purchaser's position   3.26
  disposal of assets on no gain,
    no loss transfer   3.66
  double tax relief
    deduction, by   3.85

Computation of gains and losses –
  contd
  double tax relief – *contd*
    double tax agreements 3.81
    introduction 3.80
    special withholding tax 3.84
    unilateral tax credit relief 3.82–
     3.83
  enhancement costs 3.40
  incidental costs
    acquisition, of 3.39
    disposal, of 3.41
  indexation allowance
    acquisition of assets on no
      gain, no loss transfer 3.64–
       3.65
    assets held on 31 March
      1982 3.63
    calculation 3.60
    disposal of assets on no
      gain, no loss transfer 3.66
    generally 3.59
    part disposals 3.62
    relevant allowable
      expenditure 3.61
  instalment payments of CGT,
    and
    due dates 3.36
    generally 3.35
  introduction 3.1
  irrecoverable consideration
    contingent liabilities 3.24
    disposals outside terms of
      TCGA 1992, s 49 3.25
    generally 3.22
    loan relationships, and 3.23
    purchaser's position 3.26
  loan relationships, and 3.23
  losses
    accruing on disposal to
      connected person 3.51
    capital allowances 3.55
    claims 3.49
    employment-related
      liabilities 3.54
    introduction 3.48
    loans to traders 3.56

Computation of gains and losses –
  contd
  losses – *contd*
    non-residents 3.50
    shares in trading
      companies, on 3.57
    trading losses 3.52
  market value rule for
    acquisitions
    connected persons, from 3.45
    generally 3.44
  market value rule for
    disposals
    ascertaining market value 3.6
    generally 3.5
    part disposals 3.46
    quoted shares and securities 3.7
  post-cessation expenditure 3.53
  rebasing
    acquisition on no gain, no
      loss transfer 3.73
    deferred charges on gains 3.75
    election 3.70
    exceptions to rule 3.70
    excluded disposals 3.72
    general rule 3.69
    introduction 3.68
    indexation allowance 3.63
  reimbursements from public
    funds, and 3.42
  series of transactions, in
    aggregate market value 3.14
    appropriate proportion 3.13
    generally 3.11
    groups of companies 3.15
    original market value 3.12
  spouses 3.67
  sums chargeable as income 3.4
  taper relief 3.58
  tax planning, and 10.8
  trading income expenses, and 3.42
  unit trust holdings 3.8
  unquoted shares and
    securities 3.9
  VAT, and 3.2
Connected persons
  business partners 3.19

Connected persons – *contd*
companies   3.20
consideration for disposal,
   and
    'connected persons'   3.16–3.20
    generally   3.10
    losses, and   3.21
    series of transactions, in   3.11–
       3.15
generally   3.16
individuals   3.17
market value rule for
   acquisitions, and   3.45
settlements, and   8.6
tax planning, and   10.15
trustees   3.18
Consideration for disposal
assets derived from other
   assets   3.47
'connected persons'
   business partners   3.19
   companies   3.20
   generally   3.16
   individuals   3.17
   trustees   3.18
connected persons, to
   'connected persons'   3.16–3.20
   generally   3.10
   losses, and   3.21
   series of transactions, in   3.11–
       3.15
contingent consideration
   ascertainable   3.28
   election to carry back loss
     on disposal of right   3.30–
       3.34
   generally   3.27
   unascertainable   3.29
contingent liabilities   3.24
deferred consideration
   ascertainable   3.28
   election to carry back loss
     on disposal of right   3.30–
       3.34
   generally   3.27
   unascertainable   3.29
delayed consideration
   contingent liabilities   3.24

Consideration for disposal – *contd*
delayed consideration – *contd*
   disposals outside terms of
     TCGA 1992, s 49   3.25
   generally   3.22
   loan relationships, and   3.23
   purchaser's position   3.26
introduction   3.3
irrecoverable consideration
   contingent liabilities   3.24
   disposals outside terms of
     TCGA 1992, s 49   3.25
   generally   3.22
   loan relationships, and   3.23
   purchaser's position   3.26
loan relationships, and   3.23
market value rule for
   acquisitions
    connected persons, from   3.45
    generally   3.44
market value rule for
   disposals
    ascertaining market value   3.6
    generally   3.5
part disposals   3.46
partnerships, and
   outside the accounts   6.12
   within the accounts   6.11
quoted shares and securities   3.7
series of transactions, in
   aggregate market value   3.14
   appropriate proportion   3.13
   generally   3.11
   groups of companies   3.15
   original market value   3.12
sums chargeable as income   3.4
unit trust holdings   3.8
unquoted shares and
   securities   3.9

Contingent consideration
ascertainable   3.28
election to carry back loss on
   disposal of right   3.30–3.34
generally   3.27
unascertainable   3.29

Contingent liabilities
consideration for disposal to
    connected persons, and   3.24
Corporate venturing scheme
clearance   9.29
deferral relief   9.32
introduction   9.24
investing company   9.26
investment relief   9.30–9.31
issuing company   9.27
nature of investment   9.28
loss relief   9.33
types of available relief   9.25
Costs of acquisition
assignment of lease, and   4.12
generally   3.38
incidental costs   3.39
wasting assets, and   4.26
Costs of enhancement
assignment of lease, and   4.13
generally   3.40
wasting assets, and   4.27

D

Death
disposals, and   2.9
exempt assets, and   1.8
Debts
exempt assets, and   1.8
generally   4.30
**Decorations for valour or
gallant conduct**
exempt assets, and   1.8
Deductible expenditure
acquisition costs
    generally   3.38
    incidental costs   3.39
assets derived from other
    assets   3.47
enhancement costs   3.40
incidental costs
    acquisition, of   3.39
    disposal, of   3.41
introduction   3.37
market value rule for
    acquisitions
    connected persons, from   3.45

Deductible expenditure – *contd*
market value rule for acquisitions –
    contd
    generally   3.44
    part disposals   3.46
    reimbursements from public
        funds, and   3.42
    settlements, and   8.20
    trading income expenses, and   3.42
    transactions during
        administration of estates,
        and   7.8
wasting assets, and
    acquisition costs   4.26
    enhancement costs   4.27
    introduction   4.25
    residual value   4.28
    scrap value   4.28
Deeds of appointment
generally   7.14
Deeds of variation
effect   7.17
election   7.18
generally   7.16
introduction   7.14
Deemed consideration
roll-over relief, and   14.29–14.30
Deemed disposals
generally   2.6
non-residents, by   2.21
roll-over relief, and   14.29–14.30
Deferral relief
corporate venturing scheme,
    and   9.32
Enterprise Investment
    Scheme, and
    anti-avoidance rules   16.27–16.36
    chargeable events   16.19–16.23
    chargeable person   16.23
    claims   16.17
    condition   16.11
    death of investor or
        transferee   16.20
    eligible shares   16.15
    failure of conditions   16.18
    identification rules   16.22
    introduction   16.10

Deferral relief – *contd*
Enterprise Investment Scheme, and
 – *contd*
 postponing the gain 16.13
 qualifying investment 16.14
 reinvestment time limits 16.16
 reorganisations 16.24
 residence 16.11
 taper relief, and 16.25–16.26
 trustees 16.12
 tax planning, and 10.10
 Venture capital trusts, and
 chargeable events 17.10
 claims 17.9
 generally 17.8
Deferred annuities
 exempt assets, and 1.8
Deferred charges on gains
 assets held on 31 March
 1982, and 3.75
Deferred consideration
 ascertainable 3.28
 election to carry back loss on
 disposal of right 3.30–3.34
 generally 3.27
 unascertainable 3.29
Delayed consideration
 contingent liabilities 3.24
 disposals outside terms of
 TCGA 1992, s 49 3.25
 generally 3.22
 loan relationships, and 3.23
 purchaser's position 3.26
Dependent relative relief
 principal private residence
 relief, and 12.36
Deposits
 disposals, and 2.22
Depreciating assets
 roll-over relief, and
 acquisition of third asset 14.33
 generally 14.31
 postponing held-over gain 14.32
 transfer to SE 14.34
**Depreciatory transaction
 losses**
 groups of companies, and 9.14

Destroyed assets
 generally 2.10
 replacement asset acquired 2.11
Diplomatic staff
 residence, and 5.6
Disclaimers
 effect 7.17
 election 7.18
 generally 7.15
 introduction 7.14
**Disclosure of tax avoidance
 schemes**
 tax planning, and 10.3
Discretionary trusts
 hold-over relief, and 8.24
 principal private residence
 relief, and 12.25
**Disposal of assets on no gain,
 no loss transfer**
 computation of gains and
 losses, and 3.66
Disposal relief
 Enterprise Investment
 Scheme, and
 conditions 16.3
 exchange of shares 16.8
 identification rules 16.6
 introduction 16.2
 losses 16.4
 reduction of income tax
 relief 16.9
 reorganisations 16.7
 restriction 16.5
 Venture capital trusts, and
 exchange of shares 17.6
 generally 17.3
 identification rules 17.4
 reorganisations 17.5
 withdrawal of company's
 approval 17.7
Disposals
 'asset' 2.2
 assets on no gain, no loss
 transfer, of 3.66
 beneficial interests, of
 general considerations 8.14

Index

Disposals – *contd*
  beneficial interests, of – *contd*
    purchase by one
      beneficiary of other
      interest 8.15
    purchase of life interest and
      reversion 8.16
  capital sums derived from
    assets
    applied in restoring asset 2.17
    capital/revenue issue 2.13
    contractual rights 2.15
    generally 2.12
    introduction 2.6
    money's worth 2.14
    statutory rights 2.15
    time of disposal 2.16
  chargeable gains, and 2.1
  charges, and 2.18
  death, and 2.9
  deemed disposals
    generally 2.6
    non-residents, by 2.21
  deposits, and 2.22
  destroyed assets
    generally 2.10
    replacement asset acquired 2.11
  'disposal' 2.3
  donatio mortis causa, and 2.9
  forfeited deposits 2.25
  hire-purchase transactions,
    and 2.19
  introduction 2.1
  lifetime gifts, and 2.9
  lost assets
    generally 2.10
    replacement asset acquired 2.11
  mortgages, and 2.18
  negligible value assets
    generally 2.10
    introduction 2.6
  no gain, no loss disposals 2.7
  non-residents, and 2.21
  options, and
    abandonment 2.24
    exercise 2.23
    generally 2.22

Disposals – *contd*
  'part disposal' 2.4
  partnerships, and
    distribution in kind 6.8
    generally 6.6
    part disposals 6.7
  settlements, and 2.20
  'small disposal' 2.5
  timing 2.8
  trustees, by
    general considerations 8.7
    overview 2.20
    person becoming absolutely
      entitled 8.8–8.11
    rates of tax 8.19
    termination of life interest
      on death of person
      entitled 8.12–8.13
  trusts, and 2.6
Distribution in kind
  partnerships, and 6.8
Dividend stripping
  groups of companies, and 9.15
Domicile
  see also Residence
  tax planning, and 10.6
Donatio mortis causa
  disposals, and 2.9
Double tax relief
  deduction, by 3.85
  double tax agreements 3.81
  introduction 3.80
  residence, and 5.33
  special withholding tax 3.84
  unilateral tax credit relief 3.82–3.83

E

Election
  rebasing, and 3.75
Employment-related liabilities
  computation of losses, and 3.54
Enhancement costs
  assignment of lease, and 4.13
  generally 3.40
  wasting assets, and 4.27

Enterprise Investment Scheme
anti-avoidance
    pre-arranged exits   16.28
    put and call options   16.29–16.32
    reinvestment in same
      company or group
      company   16.27
    replacement value   16.35
    value received by investor   16.33
    value received by other
      person   16.34
CGT deferral relief
    anti-avoidance rules   16.27–16.36
    chargeable events   16.19–16.23
    chargeable person   16.23
    claims   16.17
    condition   16.11
    death of investor or
      transferee   16.20
    eligible shares   16.15
    failure of conditions   16.18
    identification rules   16.22
    introduction   16.10
    postponing the gain   16.13
    qualifying investment   16.14
    reinvestment time limits   16.16
    reorganisations   16.24
    residence   16.11
    taper relief, and   16.25–16.26
    trustees   16.12
CGT disposal relief
    conditions   16.3
    exchange of shares   16.8
    identification rules   16.6
    introduction   16.2
    losses   16.4
    reduction of income tax
      relief   16.9
    reorganisations   16.7
    restriction   16.5
exempt assets, and   1.8
introduction   16.1
investment-linked loans   16.37
pre-arranged exits   16.28
put and call options
    generally   16.29
    granted after shares issued   16.30

Enterprise Investment Scheme – *contd*
  put and call options – *contd*
    granted before shares
      issued   16.31
    relevant period   16.32
  reinvestment in same
    company or group
    company   16.27
  replacement value   16.35
  value received by investor   16.33
  value received by other
    person   16.34
Estates in administration
deeds of appointment   7.14
deeds of variation
    effect   7.17
    election   7.18
    generally   7.16
    introduction   7.14
disclaimers
    effect   7.17
    election   7.18
    generally   7.15
    introduction   7.14
general provisions   7.4
introduction   7.1
period prior to date of death,
  and
    general provisions   7.2
    losses of deceased   7.3
personal representatives   7.5
principal private residence
  relief, and   12.27–12.31
transactions during
  administration
    allowable expenses   7.8
    annual exemption   7.10
    indexation   7.9
    introduction   7.7
    taper relief   7.9
    transfers to legatees   7.11–7.13
  valuation of assets   7.6
Estimated figures
tax returns, and   1.33
EU Savings Directive
withholding tax, and   3.84

Ewe premium quotas
roll-over relief, and   14.15
Exchange of joint interests
generally   4.18
Exchange of shares
Enterprise Investment
Scheme, and   16.8
Venture capital trusts, and   17.6
Exclusive right
settlements, and   8.4
Exemptions
exempt assets   1.7–1.9
exempt persons   1.10
introduction   1.6
tax planning, and   10.7

F

Filing date
tax returns, and   1.36
Fish quotas
roll-over relief, and   14.15
Fixed plant and machinery
roll-over relief, and   14.17
Foreign assets
exempt assets, and   1.8
non-UK domiciled taxpayers,
of
computation of gains   5.22
introduction   5.20
remittances   5.21
Foreign currency
exempt assets, and   1.8
Forfeited deposits
disposals, and   2.25
Furnished holiday lettings
generally   4.19

G

**Gains and losses, computation
of**
acquisition of assets on no
gain, no loss transfer
assets held on 31 March
1982, and   3.73
indexation allowance   3.64–3.65

Gains and losses, computation of –
contd
assets held on 6 April 1965,
and
generally   3.76
land reflecting development
value   3.78
other assets   3.79
quoted shares and
securities   3.77
assets held on 6 April 1965
and 31 March 1982, and   3.74
assets held on 31 March
1982, and
acquisition on no gain, no
loss transfer   3.73
deferred charges on gains   3.75
election   3.70
exceptions to rule   3.70
excluded disposals   3.72
general rule   3.69
introduction   3.68
indexation allowance   3.63
chargeable gains, and   3.1
civil partners   3,67
consideration for disposal
assets derived from other
assets   3.47
connected persons, to   3.10–3.21
contingent consideration   3.27–3.34
deferred consideration   3.27–3.34
delayed consideration   3.22–3.26
introduction   3.3
irrecoverable consideration   3.22–3.26
market value rule   3.5–3.6, 3.44–3.45
part disposals   3.46
quoted shares and
securities   3.7
series of transactions   3.11–3.15
sums chargeable as income   3.4
unit trust holdings   3.8
unquoted shares and
securities   3.9
deductible expenditure
acquisition costs   3.38–2.39

Gains and losses, computation of – *contd*

deductible expenditure – *contd*

enhancement costs	3.40
incidental costs	3.41
introduction	3.37
reimbursements from public funds, and	3.42
trading income expenses, and	3.42

disposal of assets on no gain, no loss transfer ... 3.66

double tax relief

deduction, by	3.85
double tax agreements	3.81
introduction	3.80
special withholding tax	3.84
unilateral tax credit relief	3.82–3.83

indexation allowance

acquisition of assets on no gain, no loss transfer	3.64–3.65
assets held on 31 March 1982	3.63
calculation	3.60
disposal of assets on no gain, no loss transfer	3.66
generally	3.59
part disposals	3.62
relevant allowable expenditure	3.61

instalment payments of CGT, and

due dates	3.36
generally	3.35

introduction ... 3.1

losses

accruing on disposal to connected person	3.51
capital allowances	3.55
claims	3.49
employment-related liabilities	3.54
introduction	3.48
loans to traders	3.56
non-residents	3.50

Gains and losses, computation of – *contd*

losses – *contd*

shares in trading companies, on	3.57
trading losses	3.52

market value rule

acquisitions form connected persons	3.45
ascertaining market value	3.6
generally	3.44
introduction	3.5
post-cessation expenditure	3.53
rebasing	3.68–3.75
spouses	3.67
taper relief	3.58
VAT, and	3.2

Gaming winnings

exempt assets, and	1.8

Gifts

hold-over relief, and

business assets, of	13.2–13.36
inheritance tax is chargeable, on which	13.37–13.45
introduction	13.1
overview	8.23–8.26
partnerships, and	6.1
valuations	13.46

Gifts of business assets

agricultural property	13.25
claims	13.34
conditions	13.3
consideration received	13.7
definitions	13.13–13.16
dissolution of civil partnership	13.18
divorce	13.18
dual-resident trusts, to	13.24
emigration of transferee	13.20–13.22
exceptions	13.4
foreign-controlled companies, to	13.23
generally	13.2
incorporation of business, on	13.35
inheritance tax, and	13.17

Gifts of business assets – *contd*
non-residents, to 13.19
operation 13.6
other reliefs, and 13.36
overview 8.25
partial claims 13.12
partial relief 13.8–13.11
qualifying assets 13.5
separation 13.18
settlor-interested settlements,
    to 13.27–13.33
trustees, and 13.26
valuations 13.46
Gilt-edged securities
exempt assets, and 1.8
Going concern
incorporation relief, and 15.9
Goodwill
incorporation relief, and 15.11
roll-over relief, and 14.19
Government securities
exempt assets, and 1.8
Grant of lease
generally 4.14
long lease 4.15
short lease 4.16
short sublease 4.17
Groups of companies
definitions 9.4–9.5
depreciatory transaction
    losses 9.14
disposal in series of
    transactions, and 3.15
dividend stripping 9.15
intra-group transfers
    company leaving group 9.8–9.9
    election to treat disposal as
      if made by another
      group member 9.7
    generally 9.6
pre-entry losses and gains 9.16
roll-over relief
    generally 14.14
    introduction 9.13
taper relief, and 11.33
transfer of assets from trading
    stock 9.12

Groups of companies – *contd*
transfer of assets to trading
    stock 9.10–9.11

H
Hire-purchase transactions
disposals, and 2.19
HMRC Statement of Practice
partnerships, and 6.21
Hold-over relief
accumulation and
    maintenance trusts, and 8.24
anti-avoidance 8.26
civil partnerships, and 13.1
discretionary trusts, and 8.24
gifts, for
    business assets, of 13.2–13.36
    inheritance tax is
      chargeable, on which 13.37–
        13.45
introduction 13.1
overview 8.23–8.26
partnerships, and 6.1
valuations 13.46
gifts of business assets, for
    agricultural property 13.25
    claims 13.34
    conditions 13.3
    consideration received 13.7
    definitions 13.13–13.16
    dissolution of civil
      partnership 13.18
    divorce 13.18
    dual-resident trusts, to 13.24
    emigration of transferee 13.20–
      13.22
    exceptions 13.4
    foreign-controlled
      companies, to 13.23
    generally 13.2
    incorporation of business,
      on 13.35
    inheritance tax, and 13.17
    non-residents, to 13.19
    operation 13.6
    other reliefs, and 13.36
    overview 8.25

Hold-over relief – *contd*
  gifts of business assets, for – *contd*
    partial claims   13.12
    partial relief   13.8–13.11
    qualifying assets   13.5
    separation   13.18
    settlor-interested
      settlements, to   13.27–13.33
    trustees, and   13.26
  incorporation relief, and
    generally   15.19
    use   15.20
  inheritance tax is chargeable,
    on which
    claims   13.45
    conditions   13.38
    consideration received   13.40
    emigration of transferee   13.44
    inheritance tax, and   13.42
    introduction   13.37
    non-residents, to   13.43
    operation   13.39
    overview   8.23–8.24
    partial relief   13.41
  interest in possession trusts,
    and   8.24
  market value rule, and   13.1
  partnerships, and   6.1
  principal private residence
    relief, and   8.26
  settlements, and
    anti-avoidance   8.26
    introduction   8.23
    s 165, under   8.25
    s 260, under   8.24
  settlor-interested settlements,
    and   8.26
  spouses, and 13.1
  tax planning, and   10.10
  transfer of assets into a trust,
    on
    claims   13.45
    conditions   13.38
    consideration received   13.40
    emigration of transferee   13.44
    inheritance tax, and   13.42
    introduction   13.37

Hold-over relief – *contd*
  transfer of assets into a trust, on –
    contd
    non-residents, to   13.43
    operation   13.39
    overview   8.23–8.24
    partial relief   13.41
    valuations   13.46
Homeworkers
  principal private residence
    relief, and   12.4

I
Identification rules
  Enterprise Investment
    Scheme, and
    deferral relief   16.22
    disposal relief   16.6
  shares and securities, and   4.2–4.7
  Venture capital trusts, and   17.4
Incidental costs
  acquisition, of   3.39
  disposal, of   3.41
Incorporation relief
  assets of business   15.10
  'business'   15.8
  computation
    consideration   15.14
    consideration in form of
      shares   15.15–15.16
    consideration other than
      shares   15.17
    cost of shares   15.16
    generally   15.13
  conditions   15.2
  effect   15.3
  election to forego   15.7
  'going concern'   15.9
  goodwill   15.11
  hold over relief, and
    generally   15.19
    use   15.20
  introduction   15.1
  liabilities   15.12
  partial relief   15.4
  partnerships, and   15.5

Incorporation relief – *contd*
roll-over relief, and
 generally   14.45
 introduction   15.19
taper relief, and   15.18
tax planning, and   10.10
transfer of all assets   15.6

Indexation
annual exemption, and 1.17

Indexation allowance
acquisition of assets on no
 gain, no loss transfer 3.64–
            3.65
assets held on 31 March 1982 3.63
calculation   3.60
disposal of assets on no gain,
 no loss transfer   3.66
generally   3.59
overview   1.12
part disposals   3.62
relevant allowable expenditure 3.61
taper relief, and   11.42
tax planning, and   10.9
transactions during
 administration of estates,
 and   7.9

Individual Savings Accounts
exempt assets, and   1.8

**Inheritance tax is chargeable,
gifts on which**
claims   13.45
conditions   13.38
consideration received 13.40
emigration of transferee 13.44
inheritance tax, and   13.42
introduction   13.37
non-residents, to   13.43
operation   13.39
overview   8.23–8.24
partial relief   13.41
valuations   13.46

Instalment payments
due dates   3.36
generally   3.35

Intangible assets
roll-over relief, and   14.20

Interest
roll-over relief, and   14.43
Interest in possession trusts
hold-over relief, and   8.24
Interests in settled property
exempt assets, and   1.8
Intra-group transfers
company leaving group 9.8–9.9
election to treat disposal as if
 made by another group
 member   9.7
generally   9.6
Investment-linked loans
Enterprise Investment
 Scheme, and   16.37
Investment relief
corporate venturing scheme,
 and   9.30–9.31
Irrecoverable consideration
contingent liabilities   3.24
disposals outside terms of
 TCGA 1992, s 49   3.25
generally   3.22
loan relationships, and 3.23
purchaser's position   3.26

J
Job-related accommodation
principal private residence
 relief, and   12.14–12.15

L
Land
assignment of lease
 acquisition costs   4.12
 enhancement costs   4.13
 generally   4.11
exchange of joint interests 4.18
furnished holiday lettings 4.19
grant of lease
 generally   4.14
 long lease   4.15
 short lease   4.16
 short sublease   4.17
introduction   4.8
leases
 assignment   4.11–4.13

Land – *contd*
  leases – *contd*
    generally   4.10
    grant   4.14–4.17
    part disposals   4.9
    roll-over relief, and   14.16
Leases
  assignment
    acquisition costs   4.12
    enhancement costs   4.13
    generally   4.11
  grant
    generally   4.14
    long lease   4.15
    short lease   4.16
    short sublease   4.17
  introduction   4.10
Legatees
  taper relief, and   11.2
  transactions during
    administration of estates,
    and   7.11–7.13
Life insurance
  exempt assets, and   1.8
Life interests
  settlements, and   8.10
Lifetime gifts
  disposals, and   2.9
Limited liability partnerships
  and see Partnerships
  generally   6.19
  roll-over relief, and   14.13
Lloyds' underwriters
  exempt assets, and   1.9
  roll-over relief, and   14.15
Loan relationships
  consideration for disposal to
    connected persons, and   3.23
Loans to traders
  computation of losses, and   3.56
  conditions   17.12
  generally   17.11
  recovery of loan or payment
    made under guarantee   17.15
  relief for irrecoverable loans   17.13
  relief for payments made by
    guarantor   17.14

Losses
  annual exemption, and   1.19
  computation
    accruing on disposal to
      connected person   3.51
    capital allowances   3.55
    claims   3.49
    employment-related
      liabilities   3.54
    introduction   3.48
    loans to traders   3.56
    non-residents   3.50
    shares in trading
      companies, on   3.57
    trading losses   3.52
  consideration for disposal to
    connected persons, and   3.21
  corporate venturing scheme,
    and   9.33
  Enterprise Investment
    Scheme, and   16.4
  generally   1.6
  shares in unlisted trading
    companies, on
    generally   17.16
    order of reliefs   17.18
    qualifying trading company   17.19
    relief for companies   17.20
    relief for individuals   17.17–17.19
  taper relief, and   11.41
  tax planning, and   10.12
Lost assets
  generally   2.10
  replacement asset acquired   2.11

M
Main residence relief
  anti-avoidance
    Finance Act 2006, and   12.35
    'washing' gain   12.32–12.34
  buy to let properties   12.17
  civil partnership, and   12.23
  'curtilage'
    generally   12.5
    other forms of
      accommodation   12.9
    permitted area   12.6

385

Main residence relief – *contd*
  'curtilage' – *contd*
    residual building plot   12.8
    surplus area   12.7
  delay in taking up occupation   12.11
  dependent relative relief   12.36
  discretionary trusts   12.25
  estates in administration   12.27–12.31
  Finance Act 2006, and   12.35
  hold-over relief, and   8.26
  homeworkers   12.4
  job-related accommodation   12.14–12.15
  nil rate band discretionary
    will trusts   12.26
  nomination of main residence
    civil partnership, and   12.23
    introduction   12.19
    marriage, and   12.23
    special considerations   12.22
    variation   12.20–12.21
  'overlap' relief   12.12
  periods of residence
    delay in taking up
      occupation   12.11
    job-related
      accommodation   12.14–12.15
    'overlap' relief   12.12
    introduction   12.10
    'sandwich' reliefs   12.13
    trusts, and   12.16
  personal representatives
    discretionary trusts   12.25
    estates in administration   12.27–12.31
    generally   12.24
    nil rate band discretionary
      will trusts   12.26
  quality of occupation   12.1–12.3
  residence
    extent of 'curtilage'   12.5–12.9
    homeworkers   12.4
    quality of occupation   12.1–12.3
    use partly for business
      purposes   12.4
  residual building plot   12.8

Main residence relief – *contd*
  'sandwich' reliefs   12.13
  settlements, and   8.34
  tax planning, and   10.14
  trustees
    discretionary trusts   12.25
    estates in administration   12.27–12.31
    generally   12.24
    nil rate band discretionary
      will trusts   12.26
  trusts, and   12.16
  two or more residences
    civil partnership, and   12.23
    introduction   12.18
    marriage, and   12.23
    nomination of main
      residence   12.19
    special considerations   12.22
    variation of nomination   12.20–12.21
  use partly for business
    purposes   12.4
  'washing' gain   12.32–12.34
Market value
  acquisitions, for
    connected persons, from   3.45
    generally   3.44
  disposals, for
    ascertaining market value   3.6
    generally   3.5
  disposals in series of
    transactions, and   3.12
  hold-over relief, and   13.1
  partnerships, and   6.18
Medals for valour or gallantry
  exempt assets, and   1.8
Milk quotas
  roll-over relief, and   14.15
Mortgages
  disposals, and   2.18
Motor cars
  exempt assets, and   1.8

N
Negligible value, assets with
  generally   2.10

Negligible value, assets with – *contd*
introduction 2.6
**Nil rate band discretionary
will trusts**
principal private residence
relief, and 12.26
No gain, no loss disposals
disposals, and 2.7
Nominees
exempt persons, and 1.10
Non-residents
business in UK, with
companies 5.15
individuals 5.12–5.14
introduction 5.11
computation of losses, and 3.50
disposals, and 2.21
roll-over relief, and 14.6
Notice to deliver
tax returns, and 1.27

O
Offshore settlements
charge to tax on emigration 8.41
general considerations 8.39
residence 8.40
Options
abandonment 2.24
exercise 2.23
generally 2.22
taper relief, and 11.36
Overlap relief
principal private residence
relief, and 12.12

P
Part disposal
consideration for disposal to
connected persons, and 3.46
generally 2.4
leases, and 4.9
partnerships, and 6.7
Partial relief
hold-over relief, and
gifts of business assets, for 13.8–
13.11
inheritance tax is
chargeable, on which 13.41

Partial relief – *contd*
incorporation relief, and 15.4
roll-over relief, and 14.27
Partnerships
annuities to retiring partners 6.14–
6.16
asset surplus sharing ratio 6.10
consideration for disposal
outside the accounts 6.12
within the accounts 6.11
disposal of assets
distribution in kind 6.8
generally 6.6
part disposals 6.7
dissolution, and 6.8
distribution in kind 6.8
fractional shares
change in 6.9–6.17
deductible expenditure 6.4
generally 6.3
goodwill 6.5
HMRC Statement of Practice 6.21
hold-over relief 6.1
incorporation relief, and 15.5
introduction 6.1
joining partners 6.13
leaving partners 6.13–6.14
market value rule 6.18
'other assets' 6.2
part disposals 6.7
'partnership asset' 6.2
residence 6.29
retirement relief 6.1
roll-over relief, and
generally 14.11–14.12
introduction 6.1
Payment of tax
generally 1.37
instalments, by
due dates 3.36
generally 3.35
Penalties
roll-over relief, and 14.43
'Person'
definition 1.1
Personal company
roll-over relief, and 14.10

Personal Equity Plans
exempt assets, and   1.8
Personal representatives
administration of estates, and   7.5
annual exemption, and   1.20
principal private residence
relief, and
discretionary trusts   12.25
estates in administration   12.27–
12.31
generally   12.24
nil rate band discretionary
will trusts   12.26
rates of tax, and   1.23
reporting limits, and   1.31
self-assessment, and   1.25
taper relief, and   11.2
Planning
avoidance, and
disclosure of schemes   10.3
Ramsay decision   10.4
recent developments   10.2
'bed and breakfasting'   10.17
business asset status   10.11
civil partners   10.13
computation of gains, and   10.8
connected persons   10.15
deferral relief, and   10.10
disclosure of tax avoidance
schemes   10.3
domicile   10.6
exemptions, and   10.7
generally   10.5
hold-over relief, and   10.10
incorporation relief, and   10.10
indexation allowance, and   10.9
introduction   10.1
losses   10.12
ownership of assets   10.16
principal private residence
relief   10.14
Ramsay decision   10.4
recent developments   10.2
residence   10.6
roll-over relief, and   10.10
spouses   10.13
taper relief, and   10.9

Pooling
shares and securities, and   4.1
Post-cessation expenditure
computation of gains and
losses, and   3.53
Postponed gains
taper relief, and   11.39
Potato quotas
roll-over relief, and   14.15
Pre-arranged exits
Enterprise Investment
Scheme, and   16.28
Pre-entry losses and gains
groups of companies, and   9.16
**Principal private residence
relief**
anti-avoidance
Finance Act 2006, and   12.35
'washing' gain   12.32–12.34
buy to let properties   12.17
civil partnership, and   12.23
'curtilage'
generally   12.5
other forms of
accommodation   12.9
permitted area   12.6
residual building plot   12.8
surplus area   12.7
delay in taking up occupation   12.11
dependent relative relief   12.36
discretionary trusts   12.25
estates in administration   12.27–
12.31
Finance Act 2006, and   12.35
hold-over relief, and   8.26
homeworkers   12.4
job-related accommodation   12.14–
12.15
nil rate band discretionary
will trusts   12.26
nomination of main residence
civil partnership, and   12.23
introduction   12.19
marriage, and   12.23
special considerations   12.22
variation   12.20–12.21
'overlap' relief   12.12

Principal private residence relief –
contd
periods of residence
  delay in taking up
    occupation 12.11
  job-related
    accommodation 12.14–
                 12.15
  'overlap' relief 12.12
  introduction 12.10
  'sandwich' reliefs 12.13
  trusts, and 12.16
personal representatives
  discretionary trusts 12.25
  estates in administration 12.27–
                 12.31
  generally 12.24
  nil rate band discretionary
    will trusts 12.26
quality of occupation 12.1–12.3
residence
  extent of 'curtilage' 12.5–12.9
  homeworkers 12.4
  quality of occupation 12.1–12.3
  use partly for business
    purposes 12.4
residual building plot 12.8
'sandwich' reliefs 12.13
settlements, and 8.34
tax planning, and 10.14
trustees
  discretionary trusts 12.25
  estates in administration 12.27–
                 12.31
  generally 12.24
  nil rate band discretionary
    will trusts 12.26
trusts, and 12.16
two or more residences
  civil partnership, and 12.23
  introduction 12.18
  marriage, and 12.23
  nomination of main
    residence 12.19
  special considerations 12.22
  variation of nomination 12.20–
                 12.21

Principal private residence relief –
contd
use partly for business
  purposes 12.4
'washing' gain 12.32–12.34
Private residences
and see Principal private
  residence relief
exempt assets, and 1.8
settlements, and 8.34
tax planning, and 10.14
Provisional figures
tax returns, and 1.35
Provisional relief
roll-over relief, and
  declaration ceasing to have
    effect 14.42
  generally 14.41
  interest and penalties 14.43
Public funds
deductible expenditure, and 3.42
roll-over relief, and 14.30
Put and call options
generally 16.29
granted after shares issued 16.30
granted before shares issued 16.31
relevant period 16.32

Q
Qualifying corporate bonds
exempt assets, and 1.8
Quotas
roll-over relief, and 14.15
Quoted shares and securities
assets held on 6 April 1965,
  and 3.77
consideration for disposal to
  connected persons, and 3.7

R
***Ramsay* decision**
tax planning, and 10.4
Rates of tax
companies 1.24
individuals 1.22
personal representatives 1.23
settlements, and
  actual disposals and losses 8.19

Rates of tax – *contd*
settlements, and – *contd*
   allowable expenditure 8.20
   general considerations 8.18
   taper relief, and
     business asset status for
       part of relevant period 11.26
     generally 11.25
     mixed use 11.27
     transfers between spouses 11.28
   trustees 1.23

Rebasing
acquisition on no gain, no
   loss transfer 3.73
deferred charges on gains 3.75
election 3.70
exceptions to rule 3.70
excluded disposals 3.72
general rule 3.69
introduction 3.68
overview 1.12

Reimbursements from public funds
deductible expenditure, and 3.42

Reinvestment
Enterprise Investment
   Scheme, and
     anti-avoidance rules 16.27
     deferral relief 16.16
roll-over relief, and 14.35–14.36

Reinvestment relief
see also Deferral relief
generally 17.23

Reorganisations
Enterprise Investment
   Scheme, and
     deferral relief 16.24
     disposal relief 16.7
shares and securities, and 4.4
shares held at 31 March 1982,
   and 4.6
Venture capital trusts, and 17.5

Replacement of business assets relief
companies, and 9.3

Replacement value
Enterprise Investment
   Scheme, and 16.35

Reporting limits
tax returns, and 1.29–1.32

Residence
apportionment of non-resident
   company's gains
     calculation of tax charge 5.28
     corporate participators 5.31
     disposal of interest in
       company 5.27
     exceptions 5.25
     introduction 5.23
     losses 5.29
     participators 5.30
     set-off on distribution of
       gain 5.26
     trustees 5.32
     UK-resident participator, to 5.24
arriving in the UK 5.8
charge to tax, and 5.1
diplomatic staff 5.6
disputes as to status 5.7
double tax relief 5.33
Enterprise Investment
   Scheme, and 16.11
foreign assets of non-UK
   domiciled taxpayers
     computation of gains 5.22
     introduction 5.20
     remittances 5.21
introduction 5.1
leaving the UK 5.9–5.10
location of assets 5.34
meaning 5.2
non-residents doing business
   in UK
     companies 5.15
     individuals 5.12–5.14
     introduction 5.11
partnerships, and 6.29
roll-over relief, and
   general 14.5
   non-residents with UK
     branch, etc 14.6
summary table 5.35

Residence – *contd*
tax planning, and   10.6
temporary non-residence
  assets acquired after
     departure from UK   5.19
  gains accruing in year of
     return   5.18
  generally   5.16–5.17
temporary presence   5.4
territorial limits, and   5.3
visiting armed forces   5.5

Residual building plot
principal private residence
  relief, and   12.8

Residual value
wasting assets, and   4.28

Retirement relief
generally   17.22
partnerships, and   6.1

Returns
estimated figures   1.33
filing date   1.36
introduction   1.26
notice to deliver   1.27
provisional figures   1.35
reporting limits   1.29–1.32
supporting information   1.28
valuations   1.34

Roll-over relief
aircraft   14.18
allocating jurisdiction   14.4
assets
  aircraft   14.18
  fixed plant and machinery   14.17
  generally   14.15
  goodwill   14.19
  intangible assets   14.20
  land and buildings   14.16
  other   14.21
  ships   14.18
assets held on 31 March 1982   14.28
civil partners, and   14.12
claims
  method   14.40
  provisional relief   14.41–14.43
  time limits   14.37–14.39

Roll-over relief – *contd*
claims time limits
  companies   14.39
  generally   14.37
  individuals   14.38
  personal representatives   14.38
  trustees   14.38
companies, and   9.3
compulsory purchase, and   17.21
conditions
  allocating jurisdiction   14.4
  general   14.2
  other   14.7
  residence   14.5–14.6
  tracing disposal proceeds   14.3
deemed consideration   14.29–14.30
depreciating assets
  acquisition of third asset   14.33
  generally   14.31
  postponing held-over gain   14.32
  transfer to SE   14.34
ewe premium quotas   14.15
fish quotas   14.15
fixed plant and machinery   14.17
goodwill   14.19
groups of companies
  generally   14.14
  introduction   9.13
incorporation relief, and
  generally   14.45
  introduction   15.19
intangible assets   14.20
interest   14.43
introduction   14.1
land and buildings   14.16
limited liability partnerships   14.13
Lloyd's underwriters   14.15
milk quotas   14.15
new assets to be used 'on
  acquisition'   14.22
non-residents with UK
  branch, etc   14.6
non-trades activities   14.9
operation of
  assets held on 31 March
    1982   14.28
  full relief   14.25–14.26

Roll-over relief – *contd*
  operation of – *contd*
    partial relief | 14.27
  other assets | 14.21
  partly for business purposes | 14.23
  partnerships, and
    generally | 14.11–14.12
    introduction | 6.1
  penalties | 14.43
  period of ownership | 14.24
  personal company | 14.10
  potato quotas | 14.15
  provisional relief
    declaration ceasing to have
      effect | 14.42
    generally | 14.41
    interest and penalties | 14.43
  public funds, expenditure
    from | 14.30
  qualifying activities
    generally | 14.8
    groups of companies | 14.14
    limited liability
      partnerships | 14.13
    non-trades activities | 14.9
    trade carried on by
      partnership | 14.11–14.12
    trade carried on by
      personal company | 14.10
  quotas | 14.15
  reinvestment | 14.35–14.36
  residence
    general | 14.5
    non-residents with UK
      branch, etc | 14.6
  satellites and space stations | 14.15
  settlements, and | 8.33
  ships | 14.18
  single payment scheme for
    farmers | 14.15
  Societas Europaea (SE), and | 14.34
  spouses, and | 14.12
  suckler cow premium quotas | 14.15
  taper relief, and
    generally | 14.26
    introduction | 14.44
    overview | 11.43

Roll-over relief – *contd*
  tax planning, and | 10.10
  time limits
    claims | 14.37–14.39
    reinvestment | 14.35–14.36
  tracing disposal proceeds | 14.3

S

'Sandwich' reliefs
  principal private residence
    relief, and | 12.13
Satellites and space stations
  roll-over relief, and | 14.15
SAYE savings schemes
  exempt assets, and | 1.8
Scrap value
  wasting assets, and | 4.28
Securities
  and see Shares and securities
  exempt assets, and | 1.8
Self-assessment
  introduction | 1.25
  payment of tax | 1.37
  returns
    estimated figures | 1.33
    filing date | 1.36
    introduction | 1.26
    notice to deliver | 1.27
    provisional figures | 1.35
    reporting limits | 1.29–1.32
    supporting information | 1.28
    valuations | 1.34
**Series of transactions, disposal
  in**
  aggregate market value | 3.14
  appropriate proportion | 3.13
  generally | 3.11
  groups of companies | 3.15
  original market value | 3.12
Settlements
  'absolute entitlement' | 8.3
  allowable expenditure | 8.20
  annual exemption | 8.21–8.22
  'bare trusts' | 8.3
  'connected persons' rule | 8.6
  creation
    'connected persons' rule | 8.6

Settlements – *contd*
creation – *contd*

    general provisions   8.5
   definition
      'absolute entitlement'   8.3
      'bare trusts'   8.3
      'exclusive right'   8.4
      general considerations   8.2
   disposal of beneficial interests
      general considerations   8.14
      purchase by one
        beneficiary of other
        interest   8.15
      purchase of life interest and
        reversion   8.16
   disposals by trustees
      general considerations   8.7
      overview   2.20
      person becoming absolutely
        entitled   8.8–8.11
      rates of tax   8.19
      termination of life interest
        on death of person
        entitled   8.12–8.13
   'exclusive right'   8.4
   hold-over relief
      anti-avoidance   8.26
      generally   8.23
      s 165, under   8.25
      s 260, under   8.24
   introduction   8.1
   life interest released in favour
      of remaindermen   8.10
   offshore settlements
      charge to tax on emigration   8.41
      general considerations   8.39
      residence   8.40
   person becoming absolutely
      entitled
      introduction   8.8
      life interest released in
        favour of
        remaindermen   8.10
      power to advance or
        appoint capital   8.11

Settlements – *contd*
person becoming absolutely entitled
  – *contd*

   termination of trust after
      term of years and/or
      contingency   8.9
   principal private residence
      relief   8.34
   purchase by one beneficiary
      of other interest   8.15
   purchase of life interest and
      reversion   8.16
   rates of tax
      actual disposals and losses   8.19
      allowable expenditure   8.20
      general considerations   8.18
   roll-over relief   8.33
   settlor-interested settlements
      computation of gains   8.38
      general considerations   8.36–8.37
   small disposal rule   8.35
   sub-fund elections   8.17
   taper relief
      disposal of other assets   8.30–8.31
      disposal of shares after
        4 April 2000   8.29
      disposal of shares before
        5 April 2000   8.28
      introduction   8.27
      property settled by a
        company   8.32
   termination of life interest on
      death of person entitled
      generally   8.12
      settlement continues, where   8.13
   termination of trust after term
      of years and/or
      contingency   8.9
   vulnerable beneficiary trusts
      'disabled person'   8.43
      general considerations   8.42
      'relevant minor'   8.44
      tax treatment   8.45

Settlor-interested settlements
   computation of gains   8.38
   general considerations   8.36–8.37

Settlor-interested settlements – *contd*
hold-over relief, and   8.26
Share reorganisations
taper relief, and   11.38
Shares and securities
'bed and breakfasting'   4.2
'clogged shares'   4.1
identification   4.2–4.7
introduction   4.1
pooling, and   4.1
reorganisations, and   4.4
'securities'   4.1
'shares'   4.2–4.4
shares held at 31 March 1982,
and   4.6
shares held at 5 April 1998,
and   4.5
stock dividends, and   4.4
taper relief
generally   11.7
holding companies   11.13–11.14
introduction   4.2
joint venture companies   11.18
material interest   11.17
post-5 April 2000
ownership   11.8–11.18
pre-6 April 2000
ownership   11.19–11.20
qualifying company   11.9
trade   11.12
trading company   11.10–11.11
trading group   11.15–11.16
trading companies, in   3.57
Shares in trading companies,
losses on
computation of losses, and   3.57
generally   17.16
order of reliefs   17.18
qualifying trading company 17.19
relief for companies   17.20
relief for individuals   17.17–17.1
Ships
roll-over relief, and   14.18
Single payment scheme for
farmers
roll-over relief, and   14.15

Small disposal
generally   2.5
settlements, and   8.35
Societas Europaea (SE)
roll-over relief, and   14.34
Spouses
computation of gains and
losses, and   3.67
hold-over relief, and   13.1
roll-over relief, and   14.12
taper relief, and   11.5
tax planning, and   10.13
Sterling
exempt assets, and   1.8
Stock
election   4.32–4.33
generally   4.31
Stock dividends
shares and securities, and   4.4
Sub-funds election
settlements, and   8.17
Sublease
generally   4.17
Substantial shareholdings in
trading companies
conditions affecting investee
company   9.22
conditions affecting investing
company   9.21
exempt assets, and   1.8
introduction   9.20
trading company   9.23
Suckler cow premium quotas
roll-over relief, and   14.15
Sums chargeable as income
consideration for disposal to
connected persons, and   3.4

T
Taper relief
anti-avoidance
fluctuations in value   11.29
groups of companies   11.33
inactive companies   11.30–11.33
liquidation   11.32
non-resident companies   11.35
value shifting   11.34

Taper relief *– contd*
assets derived from other
    assets 11.37
business assets
    introduction 11.6
    other assets 11.21–11.24
    shares and securities 11.7–11.20
calculation of CGT, and 1.15
computation of gains and
    losses, and 3.58
Enterprise Investment
    Scheme, and 16.25–16.26
groups of companies 11.33
inactive companies 11.30–11.33
incorporation relief, and 15.18
indexation allowance 11.42
introduction 11.1
legatees 11.2
losses 11.41
non-shares assets
    introduction 11.21
    post-5 April 1998
        ownership 11.24
    post-5 April 2000
        ownership 11.23
    post-5 April 2004
        ownership 11.22
non-UK domiciled taxpayer
    disposing of foreign
    assets 11.40
operation of
    introduction 11.3
    qualifying holding period 11.4
    transfers between spouses 11.5
options 11.36
personal representatives 11.2
postponed gains 11.39
qualifying holding period 11.4
rate
    business asset status for
        part of relevant period 11.26
    generally 11.25
    mixed use 11.27
    transfers between spouses 11.28
roll-over relief, and
    generally 14.26
    introduction 14.44

Taper relief *– contd*
roll-over relief, and *– contd*
    overview 11.43
settlements, and
    disposal of other assets 8.30–8.31
    disposal of shares after
        4 April 2000 8.29
    disposal of shares before
        5 April 2000 8.28
    introduction 8.27
    property settled by a
        company 8.32
share reorganisations 11.38
shares and securities, and
    generally 11.7
    holding companies 11.13–11.14
    introduction 4.2
    joint venture companies 11.18
    material interest 11.17
    post-5 April 2000
        ownership 11.8–11.18
    pre-6 April 2000
        ownership 11.19–11.20
    qualifying company 11.9
    trade 11.12
    trading company 11.10–11.11
    trading group 11.15–11.16
tax planning, and 10.9
transactions during
    administration of estates,
    and 7.9
transfer of business to
    company 11.44
transfers between spouses 11.5
trustees 11.2
value shifting 11.34

Tax planning
avoidance, and
    disclosure of schemes 10.3
    Ramsay decision 10.4
    recent developments 10.2
'bed and breakfasting' 10.17
business asset status 10.11
civil partners 10.13
computation of gains, and 10.8
connected persons 10.15

Tax planning – *contd*
deferral relief, and   10.10
disclosure of tax avoidance
    schemes   10.3
domicile   10.6
exemptions, and   10.7
generally   10.5
hold-over relief, and   10.10
incorporation relief, and   10.10
indexation allowance, and   10.9
introduction   10.1
losses   10.12
ownership of assets   10.16
principal private residence
    relief   10.14
Ramsay decision   10.4
recent developments   10.2
residence   10.6
roll-over relief, and   10.10
spouses   10.13
taper relief, and   10.9
Tax returns
estimated figures   1.33
filing date   1.36
introduction   1.26
notice to deliver   1.27
provisional figures   1.35
reporting limits   1.29–1.32
supporting information   1.28
valuations   1.34
Taxable amount
calculation of CGT, and   1.18
Temporary non-residence
assets acquired after departure
    from UK   5.19
gains accruing in year of
    return   5.18
generally   5.16–5.17
Temporary residence
generally   5.4
Territorial limits
generally   1.4
residence, and   5.3
Trading expenses
deductible expenditure, and   3.42
Trading losses
computation of losses, and   3.52

Trading stock
election   4.32–4.33
generally   4.31
transfer of assets by
    companies   9.10–9.12
Transfer of assets into a trust
claims   13.45
conditions   13.38
consideration received   13.40
emigration of transferee   13.44
inheritance tax, and   13.42
introduction   13.37
non-residents, to   13.43
operation   13.39
overview   8.23–8.24
partial relief   13.41
valuations   13.46
**Transfer of business to
company**
taper relief, and   11.44
Trustees
annual exemption, and   1.21
consideration for disposal to
    connected persons, and   3.18
Enterprise Investment
    Scheme, and   16.12
principal private residence
    relief, and
    discretionary trusts   12.25
    estates in administration   12.27–
                                12.31
    generally   12.24
nil rate band discretionary
    will trusts   12.26
rates of tax, and   1.23
reporting limits, and   1.32
self-assessment, and   1.25
taper relief, and   11.2
Trusts
'absolute entitlement'   8.3
allowable expenditure   8.20
annual exemption   8.21–8.22
'bare trusts'   8.3
'connected persons' rule   8.6
creation
    'connected persons' rule   8.6
    general provisions   8.5

Trusts – *contd*
deemed disposals, and   2.6
definition
  'absolute entitlement'   8.3
  'bare trusts'   8.3
  'exclusive right'   8.4
  general considerations   8.2
disposal of beneficial interests
  general considerations   8.14
  purchase by one
    beneficiary of other
    interest   8.15
  purchase of life interest and
    reversion   8.16
disposals by trustees
  general considerations   8.7
  introduction   2.6
  overview   2.20
  person becoming absolutely
    entitled   8.8–8.11
  rates of tax   8.19
  termination of life interest
    on death of person
    entitled   8.12–8.13
'exclusive right'   8.4
hold-over relief
  anti-avoidance   8.26
  generally   8.23
  s 165, under   8.25
  s 260, under   8.24
introduction   8.1
life interest released in favour
  of remaindermen   8.10
offshore settlements
  charge to tax on emigration 8.41
  general considerations   8.39
  residence   8.40
person becoming absolutely
  entitled
  introduction   8.8
  life interest released in
    favour of
    remaindermen   8.10
  power to advance or
    appoint capital   8.11

Trusts – *contd*
person becoming absolutely entitled
  – *contd*
  termination of trust after
    term of years and/or
    contingency   8.9
principal private residence
  relief, and
  generally   12.16
  introduction   8.34
purchase by one beneficiary
  of other interest   8.15
purchase of life interest and
  reversion   8.16
rates of tax
  actual disposals and losses 8.19
  allowable expenditure   8.20
  general considerations   8.18
roll-over relief   8.33
settlor-interested settlements
  computation of gains   8.38
  general considerations   8.36–8.37
small disposal rule   8.35
taper relief
  disposal of other assets   8.30–
                         8.31
  disposal of shares after
    4 April 2000   8.29
  disposal of shares before
    5 April 2000   8.28
  introduction   8.27
  property settled by a
    company   8.32
termination of life interest on
  death of person entitled
  generally   8.12
  settlement continues, where 8.13
termination of trust after term
  of years and/or
  contingency   8.9
vulnerable beneficiary trusts
  'disabled person'   8.43
  general considerations   8.42
  'relevant minor'   8.44
  tax treatment   8.45

U

Unilateral tax credit relief
double tax relief, and   3.82–3.83
Unit trust holdings
consideration for disposal to
  connected persons, and   3.8
**Unquoted shares and
  securities**
consideration for disposal to
  connected persons, and   3.9

V

Valuations
administration of estates, and   7.6
hold-over relief, and   13.46
tax returns, and   1.34
Value shifting
taper relief, and   11.34
Variation deeds
effect   7.17
election   7.18
generally   7.16
introduction   7.14
VAT
computation of gains and
  losses, and   3.2
Venture capital trusts
deferral relief
  chargeable events   17.10
  claims   17.9
  generally   17.8
disposal relief
  exchange of shares   17.6
  generally   17.3
  identification rules   17.4
  reorganisations   17.5

Venture capital trusts – *contd*
  disposal relief – *contd*
    withdrawal of company's
      approval   17.7
  exempt assets, and   1.8
  generally   17.2
Visiting armed forces
residence, and   5.5
Vulnerable beneficiary trusts
'disabled person'   8.43
general considerations   8.42
'relevant minor'   8.44
tax treatment   8.45

W

'Washing' gain
principal private residence
  relief, and   12.32–12.34
Wasting assets
capital allowances, and   4.24
deductible expenditure
  acquisition costs   4.26
  enhancement costs   4.27
  introduction   4.25
  residual value   4.28
  scrap value   4.28
definition   4.23
exempt assets, and   1.8
introduction   4.22
Winnings
exempt assets, and   1.8
Withholding tax
double tax relief, and   3.84
Woodlands
exempt assets, and   1.8
Works of art
exempt assets, and   1.8